ANCIENT EGYPT
THE GREAT DISCOVERIES

ANCIENT EGYPT
THE GREAT DISCOVERIES

A Year-by-Year Chronicle

NICHOLAS REEVES

With 598 illustrations, 234 in color

Thames & Hudson

CONTENTS

Preface 6

Chronology 7

Map 8

Introduction 10

1798–1850
I THE BIRTH OF INTEREST 12

1799   The Rosetta Stone: Cracking
          the Hieroglyphic Code 14

1816–18   The Adventure Begins:
          The Great Belzoni 18

1820   Captain Caviglia and
          the Colossus of Ramesses II 26

1822–25   Passalacqua and
          the Tombs of Two Mentuhoteps 27

1824   The Tomb of an Egyptian Hero:
          General Djehuty 30

1827   The First Intact Burial of an Egyptian
          King: Nubkheperre Intef 32

1834   The Gold of Meroe: Ferlini's Treasure 35

1850–1881
II THE FIRST ARCHAEOLOGISTS 38

1851   The Burial Place of the Apis Bulls:
          Mariette and the Serapeum 40

1855   The Harris Papyri: The Greatest
          Collection Ever Found 45

1857   Prince Plonplon and the
          Burial of Kamose 47

1859   An Egyptian Queen:
          The Coffin and Jewels of Ahhotep 50

1860   Finding the Tomb of Hesyre,
          Chief Royal Scribe 55

1881   The Pyramid Texts: The World's
          Oldest Religious Literature 60

1881–1914
III THE GLORY YEARS 62

1881   Royal Mummies: The Deir
          el-Bahri Cache 64

1883   Greeks in Egypt: Naukratis 67

1886   The Tomb of Sennudjem, Servant
          in the Place of Truth 69

1887   Pharaoh's Diplomatic Archive:
          The Amarna Letters 72

1888   Faces from the Past:
          The Faiyum Portraits 76

1891   Mummies of the Priests
          of Amun: Bab el-Gasus 81

1891–92   Paintings from Akhenaten's
          Palace at el-Amarna 83

1894–95   Jewels of Egyptian Princesses:
          De Morgan at Dahshur 88

1895   The Finest Faience:
          The Tuna el-Gebel Find 92

1895   Predynastic Graves
          at Naqada 94

1897–99   Hierakonpolis:
          City of the Falcon-God 97

1898–99   Loret in the Valley of the Kings 101

1896   The Oxyrhynchus Papyri:
–1906   In Search of the Classics 107

1899   Tombs of Egypt's
          Earliest Kings at Abydos 109

1902–14   Theodore Davis in the Valley of the Kings:
          'A New Tomb Every Season' 113

1903   The Karnak Cachette: The Largest
          Find of Statues Ever Made 118

1904   In 'the Place of Beauties':
          Nefertari and her Tomb 121

1906   The Tomb of Kha,
          Architect of Pharaoh 126

1906   Two Treasures from Tell Basta 129

1908–10   Statues of Menkaure:
          Reisner at Giza 132

1912   Nefertiti, Icon of Ancient Egypt:
          The Workshop of the
          Sculptor Thutmose 134

1914   The Hidden Treasure
          of Sithathoriunet 138

1914–1945
IV PHARAOHS AND MORTALS 142

1915 The Tomb of Djehutynakht at
Deir el-Bersha 144

1915 The Jewels of Tell el-Muqdam 146

1916–20 Nubian Tombs of the 25th
Dynasty: Nuri and el-Kurru 147

1916 'The Treasure of Three
Egyptian Princesses' 150

1920 The Burials of Ashayet and 'Little Mayet' 153

1920 Letters from a Hectoring Father:
The Heqanakht Papers 154

1920 The Models of Meketre:
Ancient Egypt in Miniature 156

1920 Unwrapping the Mummy of Wah 158

1922 The Tomb of Tutankhamun 160

1923 The Slain Soldiers of an Egyptian King 167

1925 The Mystery Tomb of Hetepheres 168

1925 An Amarna King and his Queen:
The Karnak Colossi 172

1928 The Library of Kenherkhepshef,
Scribe and Scholar 174

1929 The Tomb of Queen Meryetamun 176

1931–34 Emery at Ballana and Qustul:
The Tombs of the X-Group 179

1935–39 Great Tombs of Early Egypt:
Emery at Saqqara 182

1936 The Tomb of the Parents of Senenmut,
Hatshepsut's Favourite 184

1936 The Tod Treasure:
Tribute from East and West 186

1939–46 Royal Tombs at Tanis: Treasures
of the Third Intermediate Period 189

1939 Amarna Reliefs
from Hermopolis 194

AFTER 1945
V DIGGING FOR ANSWERS 196

1947 The Tell el-Maskhuta Treasure 198

1952 The Lost Pyramid of Sekhemkhet 200

1954 Khufu's Boats at the
Great Pyramid 203

1964–71 The Sacred Animal Necropolis,
Saqqara 206

1965 The Akhenaten Temple Project:
Rebuilding by Computer 209

1974 The Unfinished Pyramid:
Secrets of Raneferef 212

1975 New Kingdom Tombs at Saqqara 215

1987 A Tomb for the Sons of Ramesses II 220

1987–97 Akhenaten's Prime Minister, Aperel 222

1987 Avaris and the Aegean:
Minoan Frescoes in Egypt 224

1989 The Luxor Statue Cache 226

1990 The Tombs of the Pyramid
Builders at Giza 229

1994 Egyptology Underwater:
Alexandria ad Aegyptum 232

1999 Valley of the Golden Mummies:
The Necropolis in the Oasis 237

2000 Epilogue 240

Glossary 242

Further Reading 242

Sources of Quotations 247

Illustration Credits 250

Index 251

PREFACE

PREFACE

In recent surveys by a well-known American television company, ancient Egypt topped the poll as the single most popular subject in a long list of topics relating to exploration. What is it about Egypt's ancient civilization that continues to captivate a popular audience? One answer, clearly, is the excitement surrounding the act of discovery, physical and intellectual, upon which Egyptology as a subject feeds, and as a result of which has been able so dramatically to grow. This book attempts to document and illustrate this development, and chart, by its triumphs, the discipline's rise and progress, seeking to convey at the same time something of the senses of wonder and curiosity which lie at its heart.

A single volume is able to offer but a selective taste of the many discoveries which have driven Egyptological progress; no one, indeed, is more aware than I how much more could and perhaps should have been included, well-known and not so, particularly at either end of the chronological spectrum. The final choice has inevitably been a personal one, and reflects those areas of the subject which attract me as an archaeologist, or which possess some other, perhaps less elevated, appeal.

This is a book for the incurable romantic rather than for the jaded professional. It makes little claim to originality, but if its text is able to entertain, inform and perhaps enthuse the popular audience at which it is aimed, then it will have served its purpose; if, as a handy summation of the work of others, it occasionally proves useful to my academic colleagues, then so much the better.

NICHOLAS REEVES, LONDON

The great Flinders Petrie directs excavations at the Ramesseum, Thebes in December 1895 (• p. 95) – a painting by Henry Wallis.

CHRONOLOGY

The precise dates of the Egyptian dynasties and of individual reigns are still the subject of much scholarly debate. The chronology employed here is based upon the useful listing provided by John Baines and Jaromír Málek in their *Atlas of Ancient Egypt* (Oxford, 1980), pp. 36–37.

PREHISTORIC PERIOD	**before c. 4000 BC**
Faiyum A Neolithic/el-Tarif	
Merimde Neolithic/Badari	
PREDYNASTIC PERIOD	**before c. 3000 BC**
[Omari A]/Naqada I	
Maadi/Naqada II–III	
EARLY DYNASTIC PERIOD	**c. 3000–2575**
'0'/1st Dynasties	c. 3000–2770
2nd Dynasty	2770–2649
3rd Dynasty	2649–2575
OLD KINGDOM	**2575–2134**
4th Dynasty	2575–2465
5th Dynasty	2465–2323
6th Dynasty	2323–2150
7th/8th Dynasties	2150–2134
FIRST INTERMEDIATE PERIOD	**2134–2040**
9th/10th Dynasties (Herakleopolitan)	2134–2040
11th Dynasty (Theban)	2134–2040
MIDDLE KINGDOM	**2040–1640**
11th Dynasty (all Egypt)	2040–1991
12th Dynasty	1991–1783
13th Dynasty	1783–after 1640
14th Dynasty	Minor kings contemporary with the 13th and 15th Dynasties

SECOND INTERMEDIATE PERIOD	**1640–1532**
15th Dynasty (Hyksos)	1640–1532
16th Dynasty (minor Hyksos)	Contemporary with the 15th Dynasty
17th Dynasty (Theban)	1640–1550
NEW KINGDOM	**1550–1070**
18th Dynasty	1550–1307
19th Dynasty	1307–1196
20th Dynasty	1196–1070
THIRD INTERMEDIATE PERIOD	**1070–712**
21st Dynasty	1070–945
22nd Dynasty	945–712
23rd Dynasty	c. 828–712
24th Dynasty (Sais)	724–712
25th Dynasty (Nubia and Thebes)	770–712
LATE PERIOD	**712–332**
25th Dynasty (Nubia and all Egypt)	712–657
26th Dynasty	664–525
27th Dynasty (Persian)	525–404
28th Dynasty	404–399
29th Dynasty	399–380
30th Dynasty	380–343
Second Persian Period	343–332
GRECO-ROMAN PERIOD	**332 BC–AD 395**
Macedonian Dynasty	332–304
Ptolemaic Dynasty	304–30
Roman Emperors	30 BC–AD 395

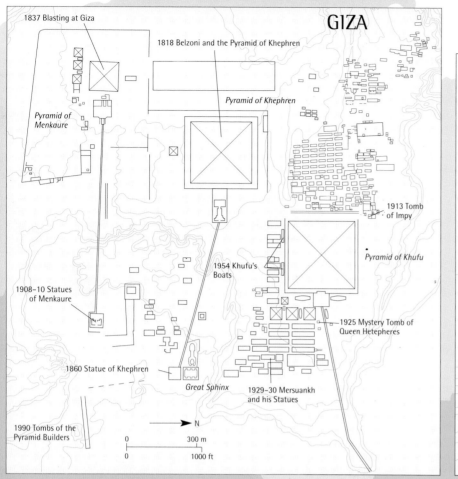

GIZA

1837 Blasting at Giza
1818 Belzoni and the Pyramid of Khephren
Pyramid of Khephren
Pyramid of Menkaure
1913 Tomb of Impy
Pyramid of Khufu
1954 Khufu's Boats
1908–10 Statues of Menkaure
1925 Mystery Tomb of Queen Hetepheres
1860 Statue of Khephren
Great Sphinx
1929–30 Mersuankh and his Statues
1990 Tombs of the Pyramid Builders

0   300 m
0   1000 ft
N

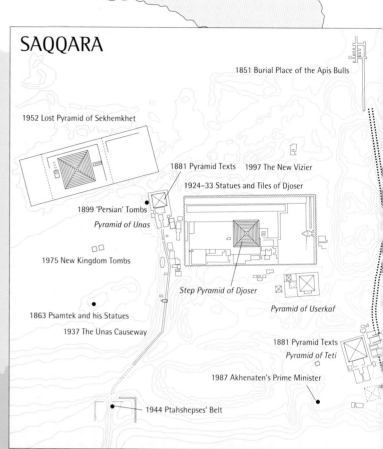

SAQQARA

1851 Burial Place of the Apis Bulls
1952 Lost Pyramid of Sekhemkhet
1881 Pyramid Texts   1997 The New Vizier
1924–33 Statues and Tiles of Djoser
1899 'Persian' Tombs
Pyramid of Unas
1975 New Kingdom Tombs
Step Pyramid of Djoser
1863 Psamtek and his Statues
1937 The Unas Causeway
Pyramid of Userkaf
1881 Pyramid Texts
Pyramid of Teti
1987 Akhenaten's Prime Minister
1944 Ptahshepses' Belt

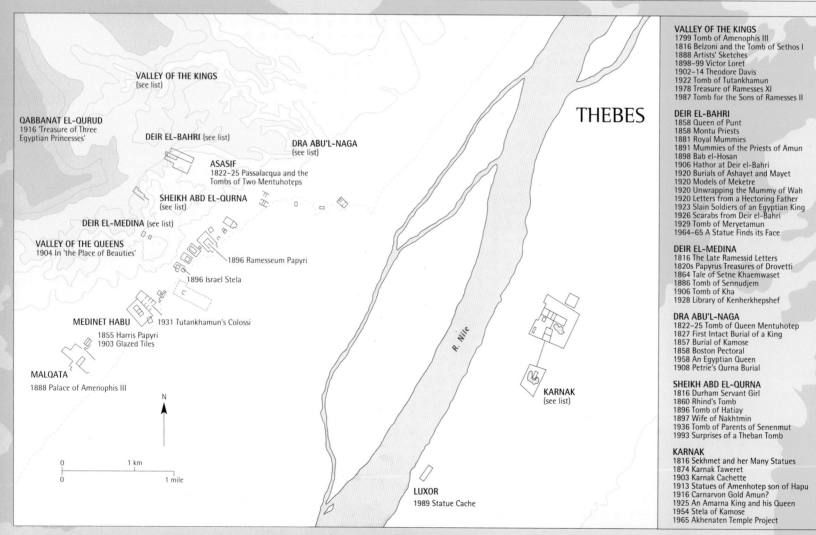

THEBES

VALLEY OF THE KINGS
(see list)

QABBANAT EL-QURUD
1916 'Treasure of Three Egyptian Princesses'

DEIR EL-BAHRI (see list)

DRA ABU'L-NAGA (see list)

ASASIF
1822–25 Passalacqua and the Tombs of Two Mentuhoteps

SHEIKH ABD EL-QURNA (see list)

DEIR EL-MEDINA (see list)

VALLEY OF THE QUEENS
1904 In 'the Place of Beauties'

1896 Ramesseum Papyri

1896 Israel Stela

MEDINET HABU
1931 Tutankhamun's Colossi
1855 Harris Papyri
1903 Glazed Tiles

MALQATA
1888 Palace of Amenophis III

R. Nile

KARNAK
(see list)

LUXOR
1989 Statue Cache

0   1 km
0   1 mile
N

VALLEY OF THE KINGS
1799 Tomb of Amenophis III
1816 Belzoni and the Tomb of Sethos I
1888 Artists' Sketches
1898–99 Victor Loret
1902–14 Theodore Davis
1922 Tomb of Tutankhamun
1978 Treasure of Ramesses XI
1987 Tomb for the Sons of Ramesses II

DEIR EL-BAHRI
1858 Queen of Punt
1858 Montu Priests
1881 Royal Mummies
1891 Mummies of the Priests of Amun
1898 Bab el-Hosan
1906 Hathor at Deir el-Bahri
1920 Burials of Ashayet and Mayet
1920 Models of Meketre
1920 Unwrapping the Mummy of Wah
1920 Letters from a Hectoring Father
1923 Slain Soldiers of an Egyptian King
1926 Scarabs from Deir el-Bahri
1929 Tomb of Meryetamun
1964–65 A Statue Finds its Face

DEIR EL-MEDINA
1816 The Late Ramessid Letters
1820s Papyrus Treasures of Drovetti
1864 Tale of Setne Khaemwaset
1886 Tomb of Sennudjem
1906 Tomb of Kha
1928 Library of Kenherkhepshef

DRA ABU'L-NAGA
1822–25 Tomb of Queen Mentuhotep
1827 First Intact Burial of a King
1857 Burial of Kamose
1858 Boston Pectoral
1958 An Egyptian Queen
1908 Petrie's Qurna Burial

SHEIKH ABD EL-QURNA
1816 Durham Servant Girl
1860 Rhind's Tomb
1896 Tomb of Hatiay
1897 Wife of Nakhtmin
1936 Tomb of Parents of Senenmut
1993 Surprises of a Theban Tomb

KARNAK
1816 Sekhmet and her Many Statues
1874 Karnak Taweret
1903 Karnak Cachette
1913 Statues of Amenhotep son of Hapu
1916 Carnarvon Gold Amun?
1925 An Amarna King and his Queen
1954 Stela of Kamose
1965 Akhenaten Temple Project

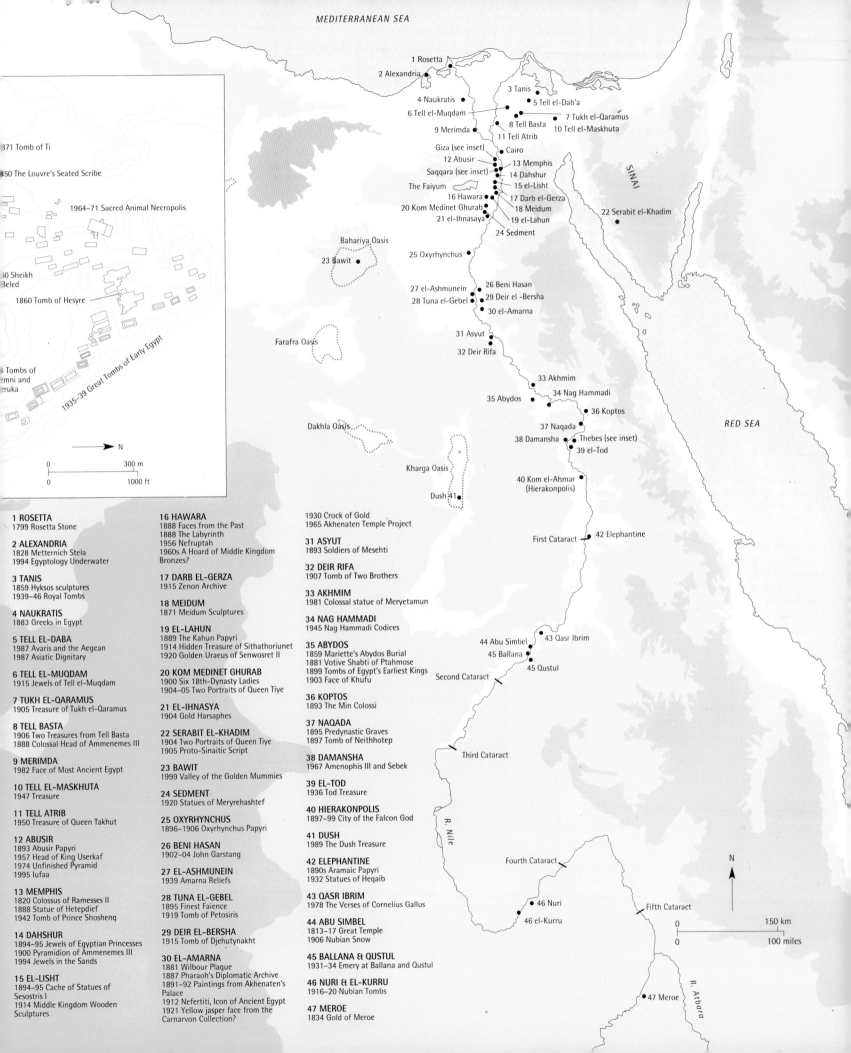

MEDITERRANEAN SEA

RED SEA

SINAI

R. Nile

R. Atbara

Map labels (numbered sites):

1 Rosetta
2 Alexandria
3 Tanis
4 Naukratis
5 Tell el-Dab'a
6 Tell el-Muqdam
7 Tukh el-Qaramus
8 Tell Basta
9 Merimda
10 Tell el-Maskhuta
11 Tell Atrib
Giza (see inset)
Cairo
12 Abusir
13 Memphis
Saqqara (see inset)
14 Dahshur
The Faiyum
15 el-Lisht
16 Hawara
17 Darb el-Gerza
20 Kom Medinet Ghurab
18 Meidum
21 el-Ihnasaya
19 el-Lahun
24 Sedment
22 Serabit el-Khadim
25 Oxyrhynchus
Bahariya Oasis
23 Bawit
26 Beni Hasan
27 el-Ashmunein
29 Deir el-Bersha
28 Tuna el-Gebel
30 el-Amarna
Farafra Oasis
31 Asyut
32 Deir Rifa
33 Akhmim
34 Nag Hammadi
35 Abydos
36 Koptos
Dakhla Oasis
37 Naqada
Thebes (see inset)
38 Damansha
39 el-Tod
Kharga Oasis
40 Kom el-Ahmar (Hierakonpolis)
Dush 41
First Cataract
42 Elephantine
44 Abu Simbel
43 Qasr Ibrim
45 Ballana
45 Qustul
Second Cataract
Third Cataract
Fourth Cataract
46 Nuri
46 el-Kurru
Fifth Cataract
47 Meroe

Inset (upper left):

371 Tomb of Ti
1850 The Louvre's Seated Scribe
1964–71 Sacred Animal Necropolis
1860 Sheikh el Beled
1860 Tomb of Hesyre
Tombs of Mereruka and Kagemni
1935–39 Great Tombs of Early Egypt
N
0 — 300 m
0 — 1000 ft

---

1 ROSETTA
1799 Rosetta Stone

2 ALEXANDRIA
1828 Metternich Stela
1994 Egyptology Underwater

3 TANIS
1859 Hyksos sculptures
1939–46 Royal Tombs

4 NAUKRATIS
1883 Greeks in Egypt

5 TELL EL-DABA
1987 Avaris and the Aegean
1987 Asiatic Dignitary

6 TELL EL-MUQDAM
1915 Jewels of Tell el-Muqdam

7 TUKH EL-QARAMUS
1905 Treasure of Tukh el-Qaramus

8 TELL BASTA
1906 Two Treasures from Tell Basta
1888 Colossal Head of Ammenemes III

9 MERIMDA
1982 Face of Most Ancient Egypt

10 TELL EL-MASKHUTA
1947 Treasure

11 TELL ATRIB
1950 Treasure of Queen Takhut

12 ABUSIR
1893 Abusir Papyri
1957 Head of King Userkaf
1974 Unfinished Pyramid
1995 Iufaa

13 MEMPHIS
1820 Colossus of Ramesses II
1888 Statue of Hetepdief
1942 Tomb of Prince Shoshenq

14 DAHSHUR
1894–95 Jewels of Egyptian Princesses
1900 Pyramidion of Ammenemes III
1994 Jewels in the Sands

15 EL-LISHT
1894–95 Cache of Statues of Sesostris I
1914 Middle Kingdom Wooden Sculptures

16 HAWARA
1888 Faces from the Past
1888 The Labyrinth
1956 Nefruptah
1960s A Hoard of Middle Kingdom Bronzes?

17 DARB EL-GERZA
1915 Zenon Archive

18 MEIDUM
1871 Meidum Sculptures

19 EL-LAHUN
1889 The Kahun Papyri
1914 Hidden Treasure of Sithathoriunet
1920 Golden Uraeus of Senwosret II

20 KOM MEDINET GHURAB
1900 Six 18th-Dynasty Ladies
1904–05 Two Portraits of Queen Tiye

21 EL-IHNASYA
1904 Gold Harsaphes

22 SERABIT EL-KHADIM
1904 Two Portraits of Queen Tiye
1905 Proto-Sinaitic Script

23 BAWIT
1999 Valley of the Golden Mummies

24 SEDMENT
1920 Statues of Meryrehashtef

25 OXYRHYNCHUS
1896–1906 Oxyrhynchus Papyri

26 BENI HASAN
1902–04 John Garstang

27 EL-ASHMUNEIN
1939 Amarna Reliefs

28 TUNA EL-GEBEL
1895 Finest Faience
1919 Tomb of Petosiris

29 DEIR EL-BERSHA
1915 Tomb of Djehutynakht

30 EL-AMARNA
1881 Wilbour Plaque
1887 Pharaoh's Diplomatic Archive
1891–92 Paintings from Akhenaten's Palace
1912 Nefertiti, Icon of Ancient Egypt
1921 Yellow jasper face from the Carnarvon Collection?

1930 Crock of Gold
1965 Akhenaten Temple Project

31 ASYUT
1893 Soldiers of Mesehti

32 DEIR RIFA
1907 Tomb of Two Brothers

33 AKHMIM
1981 Colossal statue of Meryetamun

34 NAG HAMMADI
1945 Nag Hammadi Codices

35 ABYDOS
1859 Mariette's Abydos Burial
1881 Votive Shabti of Ptahmose
1899 Tombs of Egypt's Earliest Kings
1903 Face of Khufu

36 KOPTOS
1893 The Min Colossi

37 NAQADA
1895 Predynastic Graves
1897 Tomb of Neithhotep

38 DAMANSHA
1967 Amenophis III and Sebek

39 EL-TOD
1936 Tod Treasure

40 HIERAKONPOLIS
1897–99 City of the Falcon God

41 DUSH
1989 The Dush Treasure

42 ELEPHANTINE
1890s Aramaic Papyri
1932 Statues of Heqaib

43 QASR IBRIM
1978 The Verses of Cornelius Gallus

44 ABU SIMBEL
1813–17 Great Temple
1906 Nubian Snow

45 BALLANA & QUSTUL
1931–34 Emery at Ballana and Qustul

46 NURI & EL-KURRU
1916–20 Nubian Tombs

47 MEROE
1834 Gold of Meroe

N
0 — 150 km
0 — 100 miles

INTRODUCTION

INTRODUCTION

'[Abou Abd Allah Mohammed Ben Abdurakim Alkaisi] was informed that those who [broke into the Great Pyramid] in the time of Al Mamoon, came to a small passage, containing the image of a man in green stone ... and that when it was opened a human body was discovered in golden armour, decorated with precious stones, in his hand was a sword of inestimable value, and above his head a ruby of the size of an egg, which shone like fire, and of which Al Mamoon took possession. The author ... states, that he himself saw the case, from which the body had been taken, and that it stood at the door of the king's palace at Cairo, in the year [AH] 511'
HOWARD VYSE

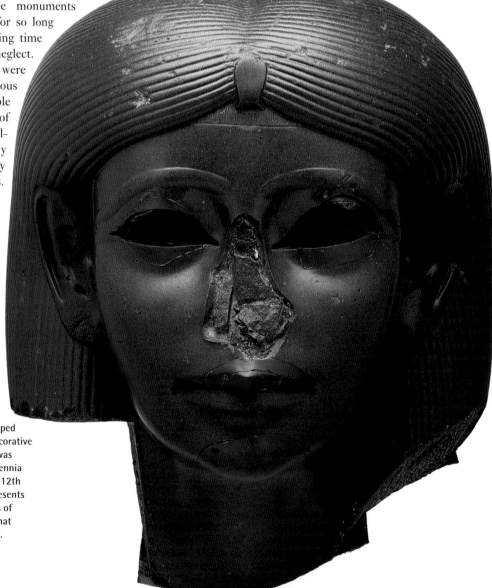

With the advent of Christianity, followed by the Arab conquest of AD 641, Egypt's pharaonic past fell into eclipse for over a thousand years. The 'secrets' of the hieroglyphic writing died with those last few scholarly priests who could still read and write it, and the monuments which had stood for so long unscathed by passing time fell into ruinous neglect. 'Idolatrous' images were smashed, and precious libraries and temple archives, the fruits of more than three millennia of scholarly endeavour, callously thrown to the flames.

(above) The medieval mystery of the Pyramids, aptly conjured up in an illustration (by William Harvey) from Edward William Lane's *The Thousand and One Nights.*

(right) Now in Brooklyn, this wonderful head in hard green stone, broken from a queenly sphinx, was acquired by the Scottish painter Gavin Hamilton in Rome in 1771. The likelihood is that it had been found at Tivoli, in the ruins of the villa of the emperor Hadrian (AD 117–38), who had shipped it from Egypt for its decorative value. Hadrian's taste was good – carved two millennia previously, early in the 12th Dynasty, the head represents one of the finest pieces of statuary known from that sculpturally rich period.

10

The Egypt of the ancients was gone; yet, in the centuries which followed, the pharaonic past would never wholly pass from view. The pyramids continued to dominate the Giza skyline, imposing still despite their brutal defacement by the architects of medieval Cairo; while the desert sands continued to yield up, with awesome regularity, their mysterious tribute of mummies and buried treasure. The reminders of Egypt's dynastic civilization were everywhere, and in abundance. What had gone was any understanding of the manner of men which had produced them – what these antiquities stood for, or sought to convey.

In Egypt itself, few at that time cared about the works of the pharaonic infidels beyond the financial benefits their heritage might, *insh'Allah* ('God willing'), provide. What local digging went on was for bullion alone; and bullion was not infrequently found.

In such pre-archaeological quests, one participant – el-Mamun, son of the 8th-century AD Caliph Harun el-Rashid – was particularly fortunate: as Arab lore suggests, he may well have stumbled upon the richly equipped mummy of Khufu himself, builder of the Great Pyramid, refitted and reburied, most probably, during the 7th century BC. But it was a treasure doubtless melted down as scrap, to produce more fitting ornamentation for one or other of the finder's fortunate wives.

Appalling though the prospect of such irreplaceable loss may be to the modern archaeologist, this greed for gold would, in time, develop into a different kind of hunger – for knowledge. This more intelligent curiosity in Egypt's ancient past first manifested itself not in the Nile valley but in Renaissance Europe, which had been gripped by a desire to understand the hieroglyphs and gain access to the 'hidden' learning of the ancients. But based, as these first attempts at interpretation inevitably were, on the garbled accounts of the Classical authors, even the most scholarly attempts at interpretation were doomed to fail.

For all the period's failings, the seed of a wider western interest had nevertheless been sown, and, as the 16th, 17th and 18th centuries progressed, an increasing number of intrepid explorers pushed on beyond Cairo to explore at first hand the ancient sites of Giza and Saqqara and the monuments of the upper Nile valley. Few of these travellers were by calling scholars, but rather they were merchants and adventurers, poorly equipped to interpret the marvels they encountered; yet they at least possessed the common sense to question and dismiss much of what had previously been reported as 'fable ... devised only to beget wonder'.

This realization was a turning point, and provided at last a foundation upon which modern scholarship could begin to build. With the expedition despatched by Napoleon Bonaparte in 1798, first-hand access to ancient Egypt mushroomed: visitors increased, accurate copies of the standing monuments and their inscriptions would be produced for the first time, and original antiquities made available in quantity for more leisurely examination in Europe. With Bonaparte's opening-up of pharaoh's long-closed land, the systematic study of its remains could be set in train, and the path to a new awareness of this strange, mysterious civilization at last entered upon.

(above) Frontispiece to *La Description de l'Égypte*: a conspectus of the wonders encountered by Napoleon Bonaparte's questing army.

(below) The bronze table 'Mensa Isiaca', a Roman or Alexandrian work of the 1st century AD in Egyptianizing style with divine images and pseudo-hieroglyphs. Rediscovered (in Rome?) at the start of the 16th century, it would for years prove a red herring to those seeking to establish the lost meaning of the mysterious and supposedly allegorical hieroglyphic script – including the 17th-century Jesuit orientalist and Copticist Athanasius Kircher, an otherwise sane and learned man whose 'theories ... exceed all bounds in their imaginative folly'.

1798–1850
SECTION 1
THE BIRTH OF INTEREST

'Soldiers, forty centuries look down upon you.'
NAPOLEON BONAPARTE

In 1798 Napoleon Bonaparte, then a 29-year-old general of the French Revolution, led a military force to Egypt, its ultimate, strategic aim to secure an alternative route to the riches of India which were at that time under British control. It was an ambition destined to fail. Following the British naval victory at Abuqir Bay only a month after the force's arrival, the 4,000-strong French army was cut off from home in a 3-year exile.

Unlike the usual military adventure, however, Napoleon's army was accompanied by a Commission of scientists and artists, and they made the best of the situation. Commission members set out to explore, measure, draw and describe everything in their path. As they progressed upstream, fighting disease and an often hostile populace, one wonderful discovery followed another in an overwhelming succession of monuments, statues – and mystery: for little of what they saw, in the days before Champollion's decipherment of hieroglyphs, could the voyagers either interpret or understand.

The final surrender of the French came in 1801, and the scholars could at last return home. Twenty-seven years later, following the meteoric rise and ultimate fall of Bonaparte, the last pages of their monumental report finally rolled off the presses. *La Description de l'Égypte* represented the culmination of 30 years of dedicated effort and eager anticipation: plate after plate of accurate drawings, detailed plans and extensive commentary illustrating those wonders of the ancient Nile which had for so long been trumpeted abroad by those who had taken part in the Corsican's Egyptian adventure.

With Napoleon's Expedition, the spark of Renaissance curiosity was well and truly kindled; the appearance of *La Description* would fan the flames. Within a decade, these would blaze wildly out of control as the *savants* were succeeded by the adventurers, and reverential study by an orgy of plunder, pillage and irreparable loss.

The alabaster sarcophagus of Sethos I from Belzoni's excavations in the Valley of the Kings (●p. 20), on display in Sir John Soane's house of architectural curiosities in London.

THE ROSETTA STONE:
CRACKING THE HIEROGLYPHIC CODE

1799 The Tomb of Amenophis III
1799 Denon's Papyrus

Discovery/excavation
1799
by
Pierre F. X. Bouchard

Site
el-Rashid (Rosetta)

Period
Ptolemaic Period, reign of
Ptolemy V, 196 BC

'They shall write the decree on a stela of hard stone in the script of the words of god [hieroglyphs], the script of documents [demotic] and the script of the Ionians [Greek] and set it up in the first-rank temples, the second-rank temples and the third-rank temples, in the vicinity of the divine image of pharaoh living forever.'

ROSETTA STONE (DEMOTIC VERSION)

Napoleon Bonaparte's Egyptian Expedition would reveal many wonders, but without any doubt the most important discovery made by the French scholars was the Rosetta Stone. This fragment from a large stela proved to be a bilingual decree – written in Egyptian (in both hieroglyphic and demotic scripts) and Greek – issued at Memphis on 27 March 196 BC by the Egyptian priesthood in honour of Ptolemy V on the anniversary of his succession. As the more fully preserved sections of the inscription state, it was but one of several stelae with the text of this decree erected throughout the land – though that found at Rosetta is the only one so far to have come to light.

The stela itself (which had perhaps originally been set up at the Delta site of Sais) was discovered just to the north of Rosetta (el-Rashid) in the middle of July 1799, during the coastal-defence works (to protect against British attack) then being carried out under the direction of one Lieutenant Pierre François Xavier Bouchard, an engineer of the revolutionary army; the site was an old fortress known to the French as 'Fort Julien'. The block had doubtless found its way to Rosetta as ballast in one of the many boats which plied the once-busy port in medieval times.

Bouchard was immediately struck by the three different scripts the stela bore, and alerted General Menou, his commanding officer. The discovery was at once announced to the scholars of the Institut d'Égypte – the possibility that the inscribed stela might provide the key to the ancient Egyptian scripts having been recognized. This hope would ultimately – and appropriately – be realized by a Frenchman, Jean François Champollion, a few years later. The satisfaction of possession, however, was to be denied the discoverers: the stone was ceded to the British, along with the Expedition's larger archaeological finds, by the terms of the Treaty of Alexandria in 1801, and eventually found its way to the British Museum in London, where, newly cleaned, it graces the galleries of the Department of Egyptian Antiquities (EA 24).

JEAN FRANÇOIS CHAMPOLLION, 'LE JEUNE' (1790–1832)

- Born Figeac, Lot, 23 December 1790
- Educated at the Lyceum, Grenoble, 1801–07 – observes the link between ancient Egyptian language and Coptic; Paris, 1807–09, studies under Sylvestre de Sacy
- Appointed lecturer in history and politics, Grenoble, 1809–16; doctorate, 1810
- Professor of history and geography, Royal College, Grenoble, 1818–21
- *Lettre à M. Dacier, relative à l'alphabet des hiéroglyphes phonétiques, employés par les Égyptiens …*, 1822
- Visits Egyptian collections in Turin, Leghorn, Rome, Naples, Florence, 1824
- *Précis du système hiéroglyphique des anciens Égyptiens …*, 1824
- Conservator of Egyptian collections, Louvre, 1826
- Franco-Tuscan expedition to Egypt with Ippolito Rosellini, 1828–29
- First professor of Egyptian history and archaeology, Collège de France, 1831
- Dies in Paris, 4 March 1832, aged just 42

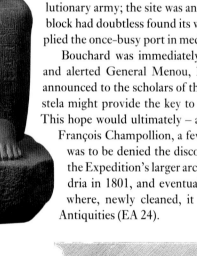

(right) So much of what the French encountered was new to Western eyes that they made the most magnificent discoveries at every turn. The pages of the *Description de l'Égypte* document their finds in exhaustive detail – here a shrine of Amenophis III (since destroyed) on Elephantine Island.

(left) The Rosetta Stone provided the key to the translation of the ancient Egyptian scripts. Recent cleaning has revealed the monument's original colour and material – a grey granitic rock, with pink veining; its former, basalt-like appearance was the result of artificial darkening carried out (reputedly with boot polish) at the beginning of the 19th century to offer a suitable contrast to the newly whitened texts.

(opposite) Brown quartzite block statue of the 12th-Dynasty official Senwosret-senebefni – one of seven Egyptian sculptures brought back from Egypt by Napoleon in 1799 to embellish Josephine's château at Malmaison. It subsequently passed via the collectors Lord Amherst of Hackney and William Randolph Hearst to the Brooklyn Museum.

The Genius of Champollion

'... however Mr. Champollion may have arrived at his conclusions, I admit them, with the greatest pleasure and gratitude, not by any means as superseding my system, but as fully confirming and extending it.'
THOMAS YOUNG

Before the French handed over the Rosetta Stone, several copies of the inscriptions were taken and made available to scholars for study. The first to grapple with the texts was the French orientalist Baron Antoine Isaac Sylvestre de Sacy, Champollion's future teacher; it was not long, however, before he had thrown up his hands in despair and passed on his copy to a Swedish colleague, Johan David Åkerblad. With the demotic Åkerblad was able to make some considerable headway, identifying the principal names as well as several other words. From these correlations, however, he jumped to the mistaken conclusion that the demotic script was essentially alphabetic in character – and on this misconception his research necessarily foundered.

Further crucial advances were made over a decade later, in 1814, by Thomas Young, the English physicist and polymath. Young was able to show that demotic was *not* alphabetic, and further that the cartouches (oval outlines encircling certain of the signs) in the incompletely preserved hieroglyphic version of the Rosetta text contained royal names. Among these he was able to recognize that of 'Ptolemy'; while another Englishman, W. J. Bankes, hazarded the reading 'Cleopatra' on an obelisk brought back from Philae by Giovanni Battista Belzoni (•p. 18) for Bankes's house at Kingston Lacy in Dorset. These were fundamental advances upon which Champollion was able brilliantly to build.

Champollion's interest in ancient Egypt went back to his childhood, and his determination to decipher the ancient script was of long standing and well founded. A linguistic genius, by the age of 12 he had absorbed the basics of Hebrew and Arabic, and in the years after began the study of Syriac, Chaldean, Chinese, Ethiopic, Sanskrit, Zend, Pahlavi, Parsee, Persian and other languages.

(above) The English scientist Thomas Young, whose linguistic interests drew him to attempt a decipherment of the newly discovered Rosetta Stone. The progress he made was limited, but contributed to Champollion's eventual success.

15

(above) The obelisk of Ptolemy VIII Euergetes II at Kingston Lacy, Dorset. The text on the base includes two cartouches: the first enclosing the name 'Ptolemy', previously identified on the Rosetta Stone by Thomas Young; and the second, as Bankes was able to show, that of Ptolemy VIII's wife, Cleopatra (III).

(right) A manuscript page from Champollion's ground-breaking *Grammaire égyptien*. The work did not appear until after his death at the early age of 42, and was seen through the press by his devoted brother, Jacques Joseph Champollion-Figeac.

By the time he was 16, the precocious youth had put forward (in a lecture in Grenoble) the view that Coptic, in which he had now begun to specialize, was the latest form of the ancient language of the hieroglyphs. This idea was not new – it had first been proposed by Athanasius Kircher in 1636 – but, thanks to the Rosetta Stone, Champollion was able to develop it further: by 1808 he had correctly identified 15 of the Rosetta decree's demotic signs with their Coptic equivalents.

Progress on the hieroglyphic section of the Rosetta decree was slow, but, by the time of Champollion's appointment in 1818 as Professor of History and Geography at the Royal College, Grenoble, inevitable. Within four years he would publish his first, revolutionary attempt at interpretation in the *Lettre à M. Dacier*, read before the Académie des Inscriptions et Belles-lettres in Paris – not to universal approbation – on 29 September 1822. His ideas were further developed in 1824 following a fruitful period of study in Turin, then the only European city with a truly representative Egyptian collection, in the *Précis du système hiéroglyphique*; and they would be presented in their fullest form after his death, in the posthumous *Grammaire* and *Dictionnaire* of 1836–41 and 1841–44. Much remained to be done – for the Egyptian writing system had evolved over a period of more than 3,000 years, and both the script itself and the language it was used to write had changed dramatically in that time; but the door to the ancient Egyptian mind now stood ajar. Further progress would be but a matter of time.

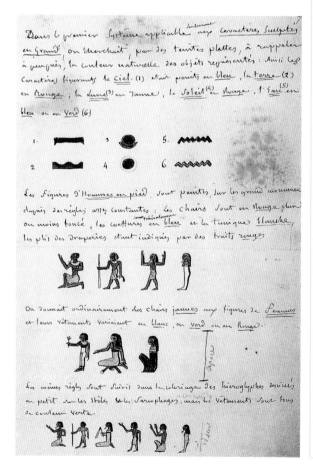

1799
The Tomb of Amenophis III

In 1799 Prosper Jollois and Édouard de Villiers du Terrage, two young engineers of Napoleon's Expedition, were detailed to explore the Valley of the Kings to the west of modern Luxor. During their survey they discovered the tomb of Amenophis III (WV22), grandfather of the 18th-Dynasty boy-king Tutankhamun (•p. 160). Only fragments of the pharaoh's burial equipment were recovered by the French – the tomb had been stripped in antiquity – and, since the hieroglyphs had not yet been deciphered, the name of its owner was still a mystery. But the burial had clearly been one of the most magnificent ever prepared in ancient times – as the shattered finds from Howard Carter's more careful clearance in 1915 and the recent excavations of Waseda University, Tokyo, have since underlined.

1799
Denon's Papyrus

'When [the corpse] was brought to me, I felt that I turned pale with anxiety; I was going to express my indignation at those who had violated the integrity of this mummy, when I perceived in its right hand ... a roll of papyrus .... I then blessed the avarice of the Arabs, and my good fortune, which had put me in possession of such a treasure, which I hardly dared to touch for fear of injuring this ... the oldest of all the books in the known world.'

The text in question, described and drawn by Vivant Denon, the well-known artist and co-ordinator of the French Commission, had been prepared for a relatively lowly priest named Djedhor, and contained a collection of spells from the Book of the Dead (a funerary compilation), dating from the period of Ptolemaic rule. Though of little independent textual interest today, it was, none the less, the first papyrus to have been found in place by a Western observer. Sadly, its present whereabouts are unknown.

(right) The spoils of war: a fragmentary obelisk of Nectanebo II of the 30th Dynasty, one of a pair surrendered to the British by Napoleon's defeated army. The two monuments, beautifully carved in the finest basalt, had been found reused in Cairo in a structure of the Islamic period.

(below) The monolithic sarcophagus of Nectanebo II, another trophy given up by the French. Removed from the king's now-lost tomb in Ptolemaic times, it had found later employment in the mosque of St Athanasius in Cairo.

THE FRENCH SURRENDER LIST:
objects now in the British Museum

The portable antiquities gathered by the French scholars (and indeed the objects chosen by their artists for the plates of the *Description de l'Égypte*) were, by today's standards, an odd and undiscerning assemblage, reflecting the limitations of antiquarian knowledge at that time. On the surrender of the French forces in 1801, the larger pieces passed to the government of King George III and thence to the British Museum; the smaller went home to France in the scholars' personal baggage. The surrender list included the famous Rosetta Stone: 'You want it…?', declared Menou, commander in charge of the French forces. 'You may pick it up whenever you please'. The Commission's natural history specimens were destined to go the same way, and with as little good grace. As Menou acidly declared:

> *'I have just been informed that several among our collection-makers wish to follow their seeds, minerals, birds, butterflies or reptiles wherever you [the British] choose to ship their crates. I do not know if they wish to have themselves stuffed for the purpose, but I can assure you that if the idea should appeal … I shall not prevent them.'*

BM NO.	DESCRIPTION
EA 24	Rosetta Stone
EA 523	obelisk of Nectanebo II
EA 524	obelisk of Nectanebo II
EA 10	sarcophagus of Nectanebo II
EA 23	sarcophagus of Hapimen
EA 86	sarcophagus of Khnumibremen
EA 66	fragmentary sarcophagus of Pepir…(?)
EA 9	colossal fist
EA 25	fragmentary kneeling statue of a man
EA 81	statue of the high priest Roy
EA 137	statue of Amenmose
EA 88	Sekhmet statue
no. uncertain	Sekhmet statue
no. uncertain	Sekhmet statue
no. uncertain	Sekhmet statue
no. uncertain	Sekhmet statue
no. uncertain	Sekhmet statue
EA 7	head of a ram
no. uncertain	fragmentary lion head
no. uncertain	fragmentary lion head
GRA Sculpture 1906	statue of Marcus Aurelius
GRA Sculpture 1944	statue of Septimius Severus
GRA Sculpture 2626	column

THE ADVENTURE BEGINS:
THE GREAT BELZONI

After 1816 The Durham Servant Girl • 1813–17 Abu Simbel
After 1819 An Early Glimpse of Amarna Art • After 1816 The Late Ramessid Letters
Before and after 1816 Sekhmet and her Many Statues

**Discovery/excavation
1816–18
by
Giovanni Battista Belzoni**

Sites
Thebes (Valley of the Kings,
tombs KV16, KV 17, KV19,
WV 23, and others);
Giza (Second Pyramid)

Periods
New Kingdom, 18th–20th
Dynasties, 1550–1070 BC;
Old Kingdom, 4th Dynasty,
2520–2494 BC

*'… we embarked for Egypt, where we remained from 1815 to 1819. Here I had the good
fortune to be the discoverer of many remains of antiquity of that primitive nation.'*
GIOVANNI BATTISTA BELZONI

The power vacuum left by the capitulation and expulsion of the French forces in Egypt
in September 1801 was filled by a former Macedonian mercenary, Muhammad Ali, who
had first come to Egypt to fight against the Napoleonic forces in 1799. In 1806, the Macedonian was confirmed in his position as Governor General of Egypt by the Sublime
Porte, and in 1811, after years of civil war, was able finally to annihilate the Mameluke
opposition and pacify the country. Unlike his predecessors, the new, 42-year-old Pasha
was a modernizer, eager for Western knowledge to develop his domain. From this time
on, foreign visitors to Egypt would generally be welcomed – and the rediscovery of the
monuments continued apace.

Although a failure in military terms, Napoleon's Expedition had opened the eyes of
an eager world to Egypt's immense antiquarian riches. The legacy of the land of the
pharaohs soon took Europe by storm – in art and architecture with the emergence of a
popular 'Egyptianizing' style, and in more academic circles with the intellectual challenge of Egypt's mysterious pictorial script, attempts at the decipherment of which had
been given a new edge by the discovery of the Rosetta Stone (•p. 14). Everything conspired to heighten demand – from the public for ever more information, and, in an
attempt to service this need, from the great European museums for antiquities to line
their sculpture galleries and fill their cabinets of curiosities.

It was to prove a dangerous time for Egypt's ancient past, which had been safely
ignored for millennia – especially since the new mania for all things pharaonic would

GIOVANNI BATTISTA
BELZONI (1778–1823)

- Born Padua, 5 November 1778
- Studies hydraulics in Rome,
  1794–98; prepares to enter
  Capuchin order of monks – an
  idea abandoned following the
  French occupation
- Travels Europe and visits
  England; employed as a
  strongman – 'The Patagonian
  Samson' – in the circus of
  Charles Dibdin Junior at
  Sadlers Wells Theatre
- Travels in Portugal and Spain,
  1812–13; Malta, 1814; Egypt,
  1815, where he attempts to sell
  a water-lifting device to
  Muhammad Ali
- Meets Henry Salt, 1816, who
  employs him to collect
  antiquities; digs in the Valley
  of the Kings, 1816–17; opens
  the great temple at Abu
  Simbel, 1817; exploration
  of the Second Pyramid,
  Giza, 1818
- Returns to England, 1819;
  publishes his *Narrative of
  the Operations and Recent
  Discoveries*, 1820; Egyptian
  Hall exhibition, 1821
- Dies 3 December 1823,
  Gwato, Benin, in search of
  the source of the Niger river

(above) The wily modernizer of
Egypt, Muhammad Ali, who
threw open Egypt's doors to the
investment – and curiosity – of
the West.

(right) Magnificent, purpose-
built case for the volumes of
the *Description de l'Égypte*
designed by Abbot Albert IV for
St Peter's Abbey, Salzburg. Its
Egyptianizing style is a
reflection of the 'French
madness' which swept Europe
during the first decades of the
19th century.

HENRY SALT
(1780–1827)

- Born Lichfield, 14 June 1780
- Trains as a portrait painter, 1797–1802; secretary to Viscount Valentia on his tour of the east, 1802–06; leads British government mission to Abyssinia, 1809–11
- British Consul-General, Egypt, 1815–27; undertakes extensive antiquarian researches through Belzoni, Caviglia (•p. 26), d'Athanasi (•p. 32); sells first collection to British Museum, 1823 (price £2,000), second collection to King of France, 1826 (price £10,000), third collection through Sotheby's, London, 1835 (realizing £7,168)
- Dies at Desukh, near Alexandria, 30 October 1827

coincide with the Pasha's wish and intention to industrialize his poverty-stricken country. The result would be the most extensive clearance – and destruction – of tombs and temples the Nile Valley has ever witnessed. Those same monuments reverentially drawn and measured by Napoleon's scholars were now dismantled as handy sources of building materials for new factories; while the more fortunate of these 'old stones' would be used as diplomatic levers to further Muhammad Ali's modernizing ambitions.

Enter Belzoni

The successors to the French scholars were a rough lot of adventurers and opportunists – Egyptology's advance guard. Theirs was a bare-knuckle world, for a time dominated (in the practical aspects at least) by two men: the French Consul-General, Bernardino Drovetti (•p. 29), and Giovanni Battista Belzoni, a native of Padua.

Belzoni, a would-be hydraulic engineer and one-time circus strongman, had been persuaded to visit Egypt in 1815, at the age of 25 and in the company of his spirited Irish wife, Sarah, by the dream of making his fortune selling a new water-lifting device to the Pasha. In this ambition he was to be disappointed: not because the contraption failed to work, but because the Pasha would lose face if he were seen to be economizing on man-power or oxen, twin symbols of his prestige. But alternative employment soon beckoned. During his stay in Cairo, Belzoni had met and befriended Johann Ludwig Burckhardt; and it was Burckhardt who introduced him to Henry Salt, British Consul-General in Cairo between 1816 and his death in 1827.

This was the key moment in British Egyptology. Under Burckhardt's influence, Salt determined to put

together a collection of ancient Egyptian antiquities for eventual sale in Europe – and Belzoni, with his remarkable combination of strength and intelligence, was just the man he needed to carry this plan through to fruition.

After sundry small-scale investigations and discoveries in the tombs and temples of Thebes, Belzoni embarked on his first journey up the Nile, travelling as far as Abu Simbel (where he would later clear the huge temple of Ramesses II discovered by Burckhardt some months

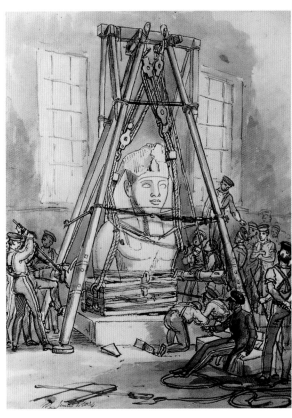

(above) Installing the 'Young Memnon' in the sculpture gallery of the British Museum. Belzoni achieved the removal of this monumental (2.75 m, 9 ft high) and exceptionally well-preserved bust from the mortuary temple of Ramesses II – the Ramesseum at Thebes – with consummate skill and just in time. Drovetti, too, had shown an interest in the piece, and drilled it for the insertion of dynamite to reduce the mass. The hole can still be seen in the statue's right shoulder.

After 1816
The Durham
Servant Girl

Fine examples of Egyptian art collected during the swashbuckling days of Drovetti, Salt and their peers are commonplace; those still preserving some indication of their original findspot are, by the very nature of the collecting methods of the period, among Egyptology's rarest birds.

One such piece, acquired at Thebes after 1816 by Lord Algernon Percy, 1st Baron Prudhoe and 4th Duke of Northumberland, is this small boxwood cosmetic

vessel in the form of a servant-girl, now in the Durham University Oriental Museum (N 752). Beautifully carved and exceptionally well preserved, this charming statuette, delicately balancing its awkward load, breaks every convention in the strict rule book of Egyptian art.

It came from a pit in the vicinity of Giovanni d'Athanasi's house, above tomb TT52 at Sheikh Abd el-Qurna, and originally belonged to a well-known historical personage of the reign of Amenophis III – the first prophet of Amun, Meryptah.

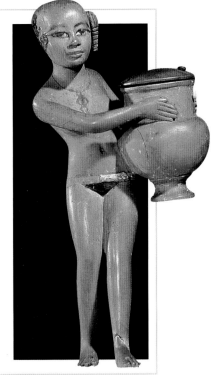

1813–17
Abu Simbel

Johann Ludwig Burckhardt, a Swiss scholar, first travelled to Egypt in 1812 and remained there until 1817. Fluent in Arabic, he was able so convincingly to pass

himself off as a Muslim (Ibrahim Ibn Abdalla, or 'Sheikh Ibrahim') that he eventually gained access to Mecca and Medina, Islam's holiest shrines, which were barred to non-believers.

Burckhardt visited the site of Abu Simbel in deepest

Nubia in 1813 with the intention of seeing the small temple of Hathor. He achieved his aim, and much more besides – in the form of a second and yet more magnificent temple cut into the rock for Ramesses II, today recognized as one of the

greatest monuments of the ancient world. Despite the temple's enormous scale, its existence had passed without comment. Burckhardt's disguise prevented him from showing too great an interest in the monument – he would have been killed for doing so –

though he was keen to know more. Instead he persuaded Salt to have it dug from the sand. This was accomplished in 1817 by Giovanni Battista Belzoni – the task taking over a month. This painting, by Linant de Bellefonds, is of a subsequent clearance in 1819.

---

before) and beyond to Wadi Halfa. All the way he was gathering pieces for Salt's collection (mostly sculpture, but papyri too) – to the great and undisguised suspicion of the locals:

> '"But pray", added [the Bey], smiling, "have you a scarcity of stones [as well as corn] in Europe, that you come here to fetch them away?" I answered that we had plenty of stones, but we thought those of Egypt were of a better sort. "O ho!" replied he, "it is because you find some gold in them perhaps, thank God!"'

But there would be no gold, or significant finds – yet. Not until his return to Luxor did Belzoni embark upon the round of inspired discoveries which would make his name and, sad to say, ultimately provoke his employer's jealousy and ire.

Success in the Valley of the Kings

At the end of 1816, Belzoni was directed by Salt to arrange the removal of the bottom part of a fine, decorated sarcophagus (Louvre D1=N337) from what we now recognize as the tomb of Ramesses III. The lid (now in the Fitzwilliam Museum, Cambridge, E.1.1823), unknown to Salt, was buried under the heaps of rubble that filled the burial chamber, and this Belzoni claimed for himself. His curiosity for discovery sparked by this find, Belzoni decided to turn his hand to a spot of fresh digging – and stumbled upon a new tomb almost at once.

'I cannot boast of having made a great discovery in this tomb,' Belzoni was later to write, 'though it contains several curious and singular painted figures on the walls'. It proved to be the burial place of Ay, successor to Tutankhamun, subsequently numbered 23 in J. Gardner

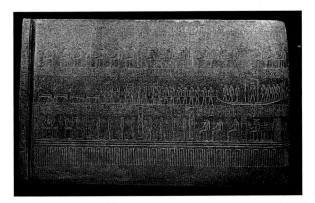

The wonderfully carved lid (opposite, below) and coffer (top) of the granite sarcophagus removed by Belzoni from the tomb of Ramesses III in the Valley of the Kings.

(above) The granite sarcophagus found by Belzoni in the West Valley tomb of Ay, as lit by magnesium flare in a photograph taken at the end of the 19th century.

The tomb of Sethos I

It was an impressive total achieved in a remarkably short space of time; but the excavator's greatest find was still to come – on 18 October 1817:

'I perceived immediately by the painting on the ceiling, and by the hieroglyphics in basso relievo, which were to be seen where the earth did not reach, that this was the entrance into a large and magnificent tomb. At the end of this corridor I came to a staircase twenty-three feet long .... From the foot of [this] I entered another corridor .... The more I saw, the more I was eager to see ...: but I was checked in my anxiety at this time, for at the end of this passage I reached a large pit, which intercepted my progress ....

On the opposite side of the pit facing the entrance I perceived a small aperture ....

When we had passed through the little aperture, we found ourselves in a beautiful hall ... [with] four pillars .... Proceeding farther, we entered a large hall ... I termed the Hall of Pillars ....'

Belzoni had penetrated the innermost recessess of KV17, the lost tomb of pharaoh Sethos I, father of Ramesses II (the Great), and the best-preserved example of ancient Egyptian tomb architecture yet brought to light. The bold and brilliant colours of the decorated walls were preserved in pristine condition, their original sheen reflecting still in the light of the explorers' firebrands.

Sethos himself was long gone. As Egyptologists now know, he had shared his tomb for a while with the bodies of his son, Ramesses II, and his father, Ramesses I, transferred there for safekeeping at the end of the New Kingdom. The entire group had then been removed for reburial in the tomb of Inhapy, with at least two of the three turning up among the cache of mummies found at Deir el-Bahri in 1881 (•p. 64). Yet what the ancients had left was more than sufficient to generate immense interest and excitement; for, lying across the entrance to a

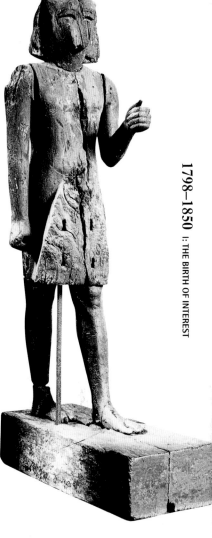

(above) Life-sized wooden 'guardian' statue, one of a series of funerary images recovered by Belzoni from the tomb of Ramesses I. Similar figures, in pristine condition, would be brought to light a century later in the tomb of Tutankhamun (•p. 160).

Wilkinson's roster of Theban royal tombs. It was fully cleared only in 1972 by the American Egyptologist Otto Schaden.

Ay's tomb was to be the first of eight uncovered by Belzoni in the coming months. The list also included: the unfinished tomb WV25, re-employed as a convenient burial place by a private family in the 22nd Dynasty and entered by Belzoni with the persuasive help of a battering-ram in August–September 1817; KV19, the beautifully painted tomb of the Ramessid prince Mentuherkhepshef; the 18th-Dynasty KV21, with its two female mummies; and then, on 10/11 October 1817, the tomb of Ramesses I, KV16, still containing its sarcophagus and a few scraps of the original burial equipment. The presence of two lesser tombs – KV30 and KV31 – Belzoni generously pointed out to the Earl of Belmore, who was then visiting the site and eager to do a little digging of his own.

(left) Pharaoh Ramesses I flanked by the 'souls' of Nekhen (left) and Pe (right): a detail of a scene in the burial chamber of the king's beautifully painted and well-preserved tomb at Thebes, which was entered by Belzoni on 10/11 October, 1817.

21

Belzoni's plan and section of the tomb of Sethos I (below left) conveyed a reasonably accurate impression of the actual monument – unlike his published copies of the tomb's extensive wall and pillar decorations (left). In comparison with the superb composition, cutting and colour of the original scenes (below), Belzoni's documentation was extremely poor, even for its day.

SECTION of the TOMB of SAMETHIS in THEBES.
Discovered and Opened by G. BELZONI, 1820

(left) The alabaster sarcophagus trough from the tomb of Sethos I in the Valley of the Kings – as displayed among other remnants of antiquity in the basement of the architect Sir John Soane's eccentric home in Lincoln's Inn Fields, London, where it can still be seen today. Fragments of the monument's shattered lid are arranged on the floor beneath.

(below) Colossal statue of Amenophis III, dug up by Belzoni on the site of the king's mortuary temple at Kom el-Heitan, Thebes, 'on the very second day of my researches ... [and] the finest of the kind I had yet found. It is ... nearly ten feet high, and of the most beautiful Egyptian workmanship'.

subterranean passage cut into the floor of the royal burial chamber, was the base (together with a few fragments of the lid) of Sethos' beautiful anthropoid outer sarcophagus. Carved from a single block of honey-coloured alabaster, its discovery was to be Belzoni's greatest moment.

Salt was delighted, and arrangements were soon made for the piece to be added to his collection for shipment back to England. Offered first to the British Museum, after protracted discussion the sarcophagus was eventually rejected as too expensive; it was immediately snapped up by the architect Sir John Soane, to embellish the basement of his bizarre Lincoln's Inn Fields house in London, where it still resides.

Sadly, the wonderful freshness of Sethos I's tomb was to prove a transient glory: a flash flood soon after the discovery, and the taking of wax impressions of the reliefs by Belzoni and his helpers in order to communicate to a wider audience the wonders of the tomb, resulted in the loss of much ancient colouring. Subsequent visits by thousands of 19th-century tourists, with their soot-producing torches and oil lamps, successfully obscured what was left. Adding injury to insult, Champollion, Ippolito Rosellini, Karl Richard Lepsius – scholars all – as well as others unknown, were to disfigure the monument still further by the brutal removal of entire sections of decoration (•p. 34). These were acts carried out in the names of science and preservation, at a time of uncertainty for

Egypt's ancient past; but they left terrible scars, still clearly visible today.

For Belzoni, as well, the discovery was to prove a decidedly two-edged sword, terminally souring his relations with Henry Salt. Resentment as to whom the discovery of the Sethos I tomb actually belonged – employer or employee – was growing and would, predictably, end in tears on both sides.

Digging at the pyramids

Belzoni's explorations ranged the length and breadth of Egypt, and inevitably included a spot of digging at the famed Giza pyramids. Here too the Paduan was lucky, in the spring of 1818 locating the upper entrance to the second pyramid, of Khephren, on its north face, closed with a portcullis slab. Several weeks later, on 2 March, Belzoni was able to enter the burial chamber itself:

'My torch, formed of a few wax candles, gave but a faint light; I could, however, clearly distinguish the principal objects. I naturally turned my eyes to the west end of the chamber, looking for the sarcophagus ... but I was disappointed when I saw nothing there .... On my advancing towards the west end, [however,] I was agreeably surprised to find, that there was a sarcophagus buried on a level with the floor.'

23

After 1819
An Early Glimpse of Amarna Art

The inevitable break between Belzoni and his employer, Henry Salt, came soon after the Paduan's triumphal return to England in 1819 and the launch of the exhibition and book documenting 'his' discoveries in the land of the pharaohs. Salt, apoplectic with rage, determined to outdo his former employee, and embarked upon further excavations under the direction of another 'servant', the Greek Giovanni d'Athanasi (Yanni Athanasiou) (•p. 32).

Although the headline-hitting discovery Salt sought seems to have eluded him, much else of value and importance was brought to light – including this exceptional yellow limestone statue of an Amarna pharaoh (Louvre N831), provenance unknown. It is the most visible manifestation of that extraordinary era in the years before the excavations at el-Amarna by Flinders Petrie in 1891 (•p. 83).

The Salt statue – usually identified as an image of the pharaoh Akhenaten himself – as restored stands some 64 cm (25 in) high. The remains of an arm around the king's waist indicates the original presence of a queen, seated on his right. The state of preservation of the face is exceptional, and perhaps represents the most true-to-life portrait we have of this strange, controversial pharaoh.

He hurried across to take a peek – but no royal body was to be seen. A handful of cattle bones lay in its place, the king's burial treasures having been carried off long years before: Belzoni had been beaten to it by earlier explorers bravely forcing another route through the pyramid structure and leaving their lunch behind them. Above the sarcophagus, on the wall, was an Arabic inscription commemorating this visit more than a thousand years before:

> *'The Master Mohammed Ahmed, lapicide, has opened them; and the Master Othman attended this [opening] and the King Alij Mohammed at first [from the beginning] to the closing up.'*

(right) Medal issued to commemorate Belzoni's entry into the Second Pyramid at Giza; the event is imaginatively depicted in this plate from a 19th-century account for children, *Fruits of Enterprize.*

After 1816
The Late Ramessid Letters

Among the many papyri sent back to Europe by Henry Salt in 1818 were several items from the Deir el-Medina family archive known collectively as the Late Ramessid Letters. A new interpretation of one of these (no. 28) has recently shed important light on the fate of the tombs in the Valley of the Kings and elsewhere, and the moving of the royal mummies (•p. 66), at the end of the New Kingdom. The text reads as follows:

> *'To the fan-bearer on the king's right hand, royal scribe and general, high priest of Amun-Re, king of the gods, viceroy of Kush [Nubia], ... Paiankh, from the two chief workmen, the scribe of the necropolis, Butehamun, the guardian Kar, and*
> *[...] In life, prosperity, and health and in the favour of Amun Re, king of the gods ....We have noted all matters about which our lord has written us ... saying, "Uncover a tomb among the tombs of the ancestors and preserve its seal until I return", so said he, our lord. We are executing commissions. We shall cause you to find [the seal] still affixed. Made ready is that [of] which we know ....'*

Paiankh was clearly dipping into Egypt's buried riches to finance his campaigns against the viceroy of Nubia, Panehsy, in the south – the start of the official despoliation of the Theban necropolis, for long regarded as the work of 'independent' bands of tomb robbers.

Before and after 1816 Sekhmet and her Many Statues

'Mr. Belzoni has done much; but the surface of Thebes is hardly scratched, its mine of diamonds remains unexplored'
ROBERT RICHARDSON

The lioness-headed goddess Sekhmet, despite her amiable facial appearance, enjoyed in antiquity a reputation as one of the fiercer members of the Egyptian pantheon. Her statues, in which she is represented either seated or standing, are among the masterpieces of Egyptian sculpture in the round.

The first recorded excavation of one of these statues dates back to around 1760, with the visit to Thebes of the naturalist Vitaliano Donati, a scientist sent out by the King of Savoy, who was prepared to pay a fortune for a souvenir to take home with him.

Four decades later, the scholars of Napoleon's Expedition chanced upon a further 15 whole and fragmentary examples (ceded to the British in 1801); and in 1816 Belzoni, digging at Karnak on behalf of Henry Salt, uncovered a further 18, of which 6 were substantially intact. Subsequent digging by Belzoni and Salt in 1817–18 uncovered around 20 more, 5 of which were in a good state of preservation.

The discovery of a series of closely similar Sekhmet sculptures set up at Amenophis III's mortuary temple, Kom el-Heitan (a find claimed by Belzoni, but in fact made by Drovetti a few years previously) seems

to indicate the original location of the statues.

The number of Sekhmet statues thought to have been (re-)erected at Karnak is staggering. Auguste Mariette, in the middle years of the 19th century, put the total at 572. Of these the English Misses Margaret Benson and Janet Gourlay, digging in the Mut temple in 1895–97, identified the remains of 188 still in place. Today the count runs to over 700. The majority are inscribed for Amenophis III; others carry the cartouches of the 19th-Dynasty king Ramesses II, the 21st-Dynasty 'priest-king' Pinudjem I, and the 22nd-Dynasty pharaoh Shoshenq I – though most of these later inscriptions probably represent usurpations of sculptures of the 18th-Dynasty ruler.

The collection has been described as 'a monumental litany' in stone, intended to conjure 'the dangerous goddess' in pharaoh's eternal defence – perhaps at his time of greatest vulnerability, during the *sed*-festival (jubilee), but not impossibly against the plague raging throughout the Near East in the 14th century BC.

CAPTAIN CAVIGLIA
AND THE COLOSSUS OF RAMESSES II

Discovery/excavation
1820
by
Giovanni Battista Caviglia

Site
Memphis (Temple of Ptah)

Period
New Kingdom, 19th Dynasty,
reign of Ramesses II,
1290–1224 BC

'Very many years ago, [this statue] was given to England; but the government that could cheerfully waste £21,000 in trying to make a clock ['Big Ben']strike at Westminster, has never been rich enough to carry from Egypt any important gift ....'
FREDERICK WILLIAM FAIRHOLT

Belzoni and d'Athanasi were not the only agents employed by Henry Salt in his insatiable quest for Egyptian antiquities; less well-known, though equally colourful, was the Genoese sea-captain Giovanni Battista Caviglia. Employed by Salt from 1816 on, Caviglia would later find work with Howard Vyse, dynamiter of the Giza pyramids (•p. 36). Vyse and Caviglia soon fell out, however, with the latter, before he left, famously flinging down an unused advance of £40 'tied up in an old stocking'. This repulsive garment Vyse, with admirable sang-froid, 'carefully returned with my best compliments, as soon as I had taken out the money'.

Such glorious moments were still in the future, however, when, in 1820, Caviglia was instructed by Salt to investigate the ruins of Memphis, a moonscape wasteland which in better days had functioned as ancient Egypt's first capital. Caviglia's main find here was the colossal statue of Ramesses II known as Abu'l-Hol ('Father of terror') – a name confusingly applied to several Egyptian monuments, including the Great Sphinx at Giza.

Caviglia's statue – today a principal attraction for visitors to Memphis – originally stood at the south entrance to the great temple of Ptah, of which little now remains. The colossus had fallen face down and the pharaoh's perfectly preserved facial features were obscured. In an attempt to gain political favour, the monument was presented by Muhammad Ali to the British Government, but no attempt was made to collect it. The extraordinary scale of the sculpture perhaps explains why: even in its damaged state it approaches 11 m (36 ft) in height, while the weight is estimated at around 100 tonnes.

The statue's platform was uncovered by an Armenian engineer-archaeologist, Joseph Hekekyan, in 1852, and 35 years later the sculpture was raised and turned over. The beauty of the piece was now clear to all, and the British began at last to talk of collecting their prize. But too late. Politics again intervened: '[Since] its removal would annoy the French ... Sir E. Baring [asked] if the British Museum would abandon all claim'. In the interests of delicate Anglo-French relations, the sculpture was allowed to lie.

GIOVANNI BATTISTA CAVIGLIA (1770–1845)

- Born, 1770, Genoa
- Anglophile master mariner based on Malta and working the Mediterranean Sea
- Excavates at Giza for Henry Salt (•p. 19), 1816–19, and for Colonel Howard Vyse, 1835-36
- Dies Paris, 7 September 1845

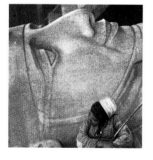

(above) The exquisitely preserved face of 'Abu'l Hol', revealed in 1887 when the limestone statue was eventually turned over by Major A. H. Bagnold of the British Army's Royal Engineers.

(left) The colossal statue of Ramesses II, as found by Captain Caviglia, lying face down in the mud with its badly weathered back exposed: a photograph taken before 1887.

PASSALACQUA AND THE TOMBS OF TWO MENTUHOTEPS

1820s Papyrus Treasures of Bernardino Drovetti

THE TOMB OF QUEEN MENTUHOTEP

Discovery/excavation
1822–25
by
Giuseppe Passalacqua

Site
Thebes (Dra Abu'l-Naga)

Period
Second Intermediate Period,
17th Dynasty, reign of
Djehuty, c. 1600 BC

THE TOMB OF MENTUHOTEP THE STEWARD

Discovery/excavation
1823
by
Giuseppe Passalacqua

Site
Thebes (Asasif)

Period
Middle Kingdom, 12th
Dynasty, 1991–1783 BC

Although the field of antiquities collecting was dominated by the likes of Drovetti and Salt during the opening years of the 19th century, there was room, too, for smaller fish. One of these lesser diggers, the Trieste-born adventurer Giuseppe Passalacqua, had first visited Egypt with the idea of setting up business as a horse dealer; before long, however, he found himself swept up in the general hysteria for exploration. Passalacqua's name is associated with two particularly interesting Theban finds: an intact private burial of Middle Kingdom date; and the undisturbed tomb of Queen Mentuhotep, wife of the obscure 17th-Dynasty king Djehuty.

The tomb of Queen Mentuhotep

The tomb of Queen Mentuhotep was uncovered at Dra Abu'l-Naga sometime between 1822 and Passalacqua's departure from Egypt in 1825. As frequently at this date, the tomb had first been entered by local diggers, who appear to have removed at least one important item before Passalacqua was able to view the discovery. What Passalacqua was shown were the coffined mummy of the queen and a canopic chest; this last had originally been prepared for the use of her husband, King Djehuty himself, but, according to a later text on the front of the chest, was subsequently presented by him to the queen's burial. Mentuhotep's chest, possibly employed in the burial as a cosmetic box, was removed from the tomb at once, later to be sold on to the Berlin Museum with the rest of Passalacqua's collection.

The queen's massive coffin, too heavy or too ugly to be deemed worth the effort of shifting, was evidently left in place. Here it was later examined by John Gardner Wilkinson, in 1832, who carefully copied its '10 hieratic tablets [columns]' of inscription – the earliest recorded texts of the Book of the Dead. Although the present location of the coffin itself is unknown – the chances are that it was broken up for firewood not long after Wilkinson's visit – these copies survive among this early Egyptologist's papers in the Bodleian Library, Oxford and the British Museum (EA 10553). As the inscriptions reveal, Mentuhotep was a daughter of the vizier Senebhenaef and the 'hereditary noblewoman' Sebekhotep.

There was a curious postscript to the Mentuhotep find in 1996. With the death of an English private collector an unheard of rarity came to light – an unrecorded 17th-Dynasty royal funerary diadem in silver. The recent history of this crown could plausibly be traced back through its previous owners to the first half of the 19th century, and its original discovery, by extension, to the excavations carried out at that time in the royal necropolis at Dra Abu'l-Naga. In style, the newly discovered crown is closely similar to the headpiece of King Nubkheperre Intef (•p. 32) in Leiden, but for the significant fact that it is fitted with *two* brow serpents rather than a single uraeus – which points to queenly rather than kingly employment. Given the paucity of competing candidates, a good case can be made for identifying it as the crown of Passalacqua's Queen Mentuhotep, found in place outside the bandages of the mummy and carried off by his diggers for sale before Passalacqua himself was shown the tomb.

GIUSEPPE PASSALACQUA (1797–1865)

- Born Trieste, 1797
- Visits Egypt to trade horses; recognizing the greater potential of antiquities, he turns to digging
- Exhibits his collection in Paris, 1826; refused by the Louvre (at 400,000 francs), the antiquities would be acquired by Berlin Museum (100,000 francs), 1826, followed by Passalacqua as curator, 1827
- Dies Berlin, 1865

(left) The newly discovered funerary diadem of Queen Mentuhotep. The headpiece is fashioned in silver, and chased with a typical, 17th-Dynasty basketwork design; the detail of the twin uraei and pendant streamers, however, is engraved – one of the earliest attested instances of this technology.

(below) King Djehuty's painted wooden canopic chest, apparently employed as an *ad hoc* cosmetic box for the burial of his wife, Mentuhotep.

4000 BC
3000 BC
2000 BC
1000 BC
0
AD 700

27

THE BURIAL EQUIPMENT OF QUEEN MENTUHOTEP

rectangular coffin, wood, inscribed (lost)

mummy (lost)

diadem with twin uraei, silver (private collection)

canopic chest containing cosmetic objects (Berlin 1179)

    canopied chest on stand, reed

    spoon, wood

    vessel, faience

    vessels, serpentine (1), alabaster (5)

    plant remains

(above) John Gardner Wilkinson's watercolour sketches (now in the Bodleian Library, Oxford) of Queen Mentuhotep's wooden coffin – a valuable record of a lost object.

The tomb of Mentuhotep the Steward

'Dec. 4 [1823]. … Just before sunset, I was hailed by Signor Passalacqua to go to the place he was then excavating, to see his discoveries. He had dug a considerable depth, when a doorway, or entrance to a tomb was announced. He was fortunate; the place evidently having never been disturbed. Delighted with his discovery, he descended and entered with the Arabs he employed, carrying flambeaux ….'
JOHN MADOX

Passalacqua's best-known discovery at Thebes was made on 4 December 1823, and documented not only by Passalacqua himself but also by an observer to the proceedings, the English traveller John Madox. Madox describes the sight that met his eyes as he peered into the newly discovered burial pit:

'The chamber was spacious, but there was only one large sarcophagus, with two small figures in either side in wood, with ornaments on their heads, and in one corner was the head of an ox, perfect and blanched. There were also two small models of boats, one with men in the act of rowing,

neatly carved, and the rigging all complete. The other boat showed the manner of bringing the dead by water to this place for interment ….'

The next day, when the unpacking of the tomb began in earnest, Madox could expand on his earlier description:

'Passalacqua's men got out the sarcophagus, resembling a large long box, square at the ends, and different from most others that have been found. There were three cases, one within another, which is usual with a mummy of the first class, all more curiously than beautifully painted; the inside was covered with a kind of parchment, on which were hieroglyphic characters from one end to the other.'

Passalacqua had discovered the intact burial of a Middle Kingdom steward who, by chance, shared the same name as the queenly occupant of the previous tomb described – Mentuhotep, 'the (Theban) god Montu is content'. The steward's was the first Middle Kingdom burial to have been uncovered at Thebes and, although numerous interments of the same sort would later be found elsewhere, at the time it was such a novelty that 'a dispute arose between Janni [Giovanni d'Athanasi (•p. 32), agent of Henry Salt] and Passalacqua …. [This] at length extended from the principals to their men, one of Passalacqua's commencing the disturbance by beating one of Janni's, when all were soon up in arms'. Egyptology, in the early years of the 19th century, was a passionate business.

The contents of the new tomb thankfully survived the fracas, accompanying their rough-neck discoverer to his new position in charge of the Berlin Egyptian collection in 1826–27.

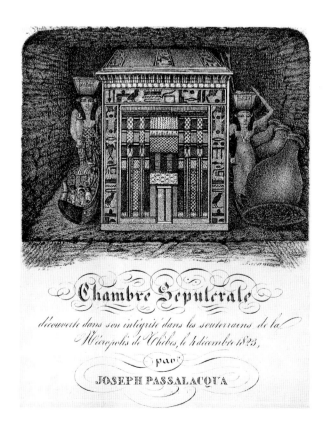

(right) 'Passalacqua's tomb' as first uncovered – the frontispiece to the excavator's *Catalogue raisonné et historique des antiquités découvertes en Égypte*, by means of which the discoverer attempted to market his finds in Paris. The French turned up their noses, and, in 1826, the collection– followed by its collector – would be acquired by Berlin.

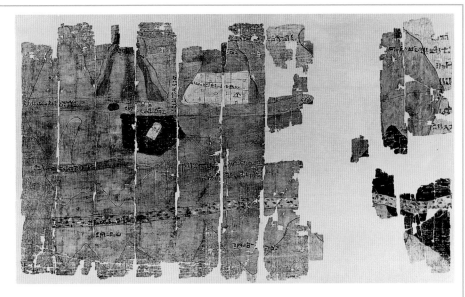

1820s
Papyrus Treasures of Bernardino Drovetti

Henry Salt's greatest competition in the search for portable Egyptian antiquities came from the Piedmont-born French Consul-General Bernardino Drovetti (*above*), who had been active in his single-minded pursuit for some years prior to the British Consul's appointment in 1815. Rivals the two might have been, but pragmatists also: and so, to avoid undue conflict, they divided the country between them for its more efficient exploitation.

Beyond the odd allusion in contemporary publications and surviving letters, the context of what Drovetti dug up is now, for the most part, lost. This is a tragedy, because the French Consul-General (one of the most important figures in Muhammad Ali's domain,

and the brain behind Egyptian–Western cultural exchange and the modernization of Egypt) was arguably one of the most experienced explorers Egypt has ever seen. He supervised digging over an extended period when intact tombs were not infrequent and the most amazing finds still to be made.

The antiquarian potential of the country at this time is illustrated by the magnificence of the European collections of Egyptian art Drovetti was instrumental in establishing – that now in Turin (based on Drovetti's first collection, acquired by Charles Felix, King of Sardinia, in 1824); that in the Louvre (formed around Salt's and Drovetti's second collections, which were acquired by Charles X of France in the 1820s); and that in Berlin (acquired at the instigation of Karl Richard Lepsius in 1836 to build upon the collection begun by Giuseppe Passalacqua and another acquisitive traveller, Baron von Minutoli).

The first of these collections is particularly rich in that most fragile of treasures, papyrus, of which Vivant Denon had made the first historic find in 1799 (•p. 16). While the Denon text was a common-or-garden

Book of the Dead, however, the collection Drovetti sold to Charles Felix included such rarities as the Turin Royal Canon, or king list (*right*), an ancient ground-plan of the tomb of Ramesses IV in the Valley of the Kings (*below*), and the goldmines map (*above*), all from Deir el-Medina.

It is believed by some scholars that these and other documents – including the famous Judicial Papyrus recording a plot against Ramesses III (P. Turin 1875), as well as texts later acquired by Anthony Charles Harris (•p. 45) – had once formed part of the same state archive at Medinet Habu, the administrative headquarters of western Thebes at the end of the New Kingdom.

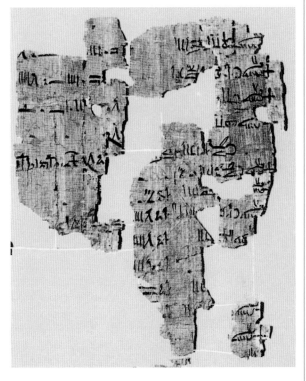

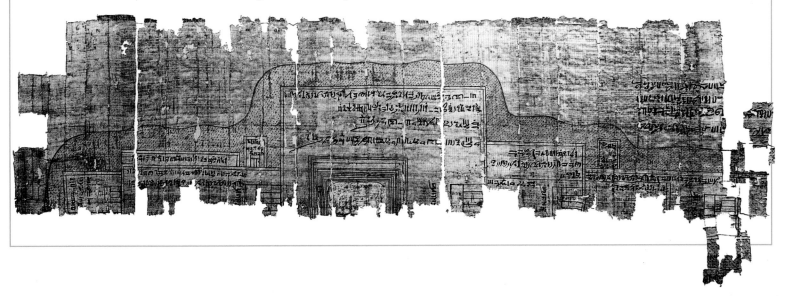

THE TOMB OF AN EGYPTIAN HERO: GENERAL DJEHUTY

Discovery/excavation
1824
by
Bernardino Drovetti

Site
Saqqara

Period
New Kingdom, 18th Dynasty,
reign of Tuthmosis III or later,
after 1479–1425 BC

'And he caused two hundred baskets, which he had had fabricated, to be brought and caused two hundred soldiers to descend into them ... They were told: As soon as you enter the town, you shall ... seize hold of all persons who are in the town and put them in rope bonds straightaway.'

EXTRACT FROM THE CAPTURE OF JOPPA

Bernardino Drovetti's excavations were not restricted to the seemingly inexhaustible archaeological wealth of Homer's 'Hundred-gated Thebes', but encompassed other sites as well. A particularly rich hunting-ground was Saqqara, necropolis of Egypt's ancient capital, Memphis. Here Drovetti and his agents worked to particularly good effect; and it was at Saqqara that one of Egyptology's most remarkable discoveries would be made.

The ancient Egyptians were a proud people, and revelled in the martial achievements which, under the 18th Dynasty, had brought much of the ancient world under their sway. The military exploits of pharaoh Tuthmosis III (during whose reign the Egyptian empire reached its greatest extent – from the Euphrates in the north to Gebel Barkal in the south) were a particular source of inspiration, and commemorated not only in the 'historical' inscriptions set up in the temples for the benefit of the gods but in popular folklore as well.

One famous literary composition of the period, recorded on a papyrus in the British Museum (EA 10060), recounts a notable episode in Tuthmosis III's Syrian campaign, a tale nowadays known as 'The Capture of Joppa'. The hero of this story was one of Tuthmosis III's principal generals, Djehuty. Djehuty's achievement was to infiltrate the rebellious stronghold of ancient Jaffa on the coast of southern Palestine by concealing himself and two hundred of his men in large baskets. It proved such a breathtakingly successful stratagem that it would live on in popular tradition – as the tale of Ali Baba and the forty thieves in *The Thousand and One Nights*.

Djehuty's tactics ensured for him a place as one of the great generals of world history, and it is all the more remarkable that the actual burial of this historical figure should have survived intact until Drovetti's time. The Egyptologist Joseph Bonomi, writing in 1843, recorded what he knew of the circumstances of the find:

(below) Gold-mounted heart-scarab on its original gold chain, from the burial of General Djehuty. The base carries a spell from chapter 30B of the Book of the Dead, intended to prevent the heart from testifying against its owner at the final judgment.

(below) Statue of Tuthmosis III, the great martial pharaoh under whom General Djehuty served.

THE FUNERARY EQUIPMENT OF GENERAL DJEHUTY

canopic jars*, calcite (4) (Florence 2222–2225)

ointment vessels*, calcite (7) (Leiden AAL 37, L VIII 20; Louvre N1127; Turin 3225–3228)

bowls*, gold (1), silver (1) (Louvre N 713, E 4886)

scribal palettes*, schist (1), calcite (1) (Leiden AD 39; Turin 6227)

heart scarab*, green stone in gold mount with gold chain (Leiden AO 1a)

ring, gold (British Museum EA 71492)

?ring, gold (Liverpool M 11437)

bracelet, gold (Leiden AO 2b)

dagger*, bronze with inlaid wood grip (Darmstadt Ae 1,6)

*Objects inscribed specifically with Djehuty's name and titles. Other items which may have originated in Djehuty's tomb are to be found in Bologna, Florence, Leiden, London and Paris.

(above) Shallow bowl of solid gold from Djehuty's burial, its inner surface decorated in repoussé with lotus blossoms and fish; the outer edge of the vessel is chased with the names and titles of the owner, and allusions to his victories in the north. It was accompanied by a second bowl, of silver, of the same general type but less well preserved.

(above right) The Ashburnham ring – a stray find from Djehuty's burial acquired by the British Museum a few years ago. The swivel bezel is inscribed with the prenomen of Tuthmosis III (Menkheperre), 'beloved of Ptah-beautiful-of-face', the Memphite city god.

'In the winter of 1824 a discovery was made in Sakkara, [Saqqara] of a tomb enclosing a mummy entirely cased in solid gold, (each limb, each finger of which, had its particular envelope inscribed with hieroglyphics,) a scarabaeus attached to a gold chain, a gold ring, and a pair of bracelets of gold, with other valuable relics. This account was wrested from the excavators à coups de bâton administered by Mohammed Defterdar Bey; by which means were recovered to Sigr. Drovetti, (at whose charge the excavation was made,) the scarabaeus and gold chain, a fragment of the gold envelope, and the bracelets, now in the Leyden Museum ....'

(right) One of Djehuty's two gold bracelets, now in Leiden, doubtless a gift from the king whose cartouche it carries – Tuthmosis III.

Regrettably, the contents of the tomb were dispersed by Drovetti and his diggers without record, and the location of the tomb was lost. Today only a small proportion of the general's burial equipment – for the most part those pieces actually inscribed with Djehuty's name – is recognizable from the mass of unprovenanced funerary material brought to light in Egypt at the time and shipped to Europe. But these few objects (see table above) are sufficient to establish beyond any shadow of a doubt that the general's burial, when found, was undisturbed, and heroically provisioned.

We can only hope that the tomb itself – and anything Drovetti's men may have missed – will be uncovered in years to come.

31

THE FIRST INTACT BURIAL OF AN EGYPTIAN KING: NUBKHEPERRE INTEF

1828 The Metternich Stela • 1828–29 The Franco-Tuscan Expedition

Discovery/excavation
1827
by
Egyptian locals

Site
Thebes (Dra Abu'l-Naga)

Period
Second Intermediate Period,
17th Dynasty, c. 1635 BC

(below) Funerary diadem
associated with King Intef,
crudely fashioned of sheet
silver with a gold cobra on the
brow and faience-inlaid knot
and streamers to the rear.

4000 BC
3000 BC
2000 BC
1000 BC
0
AD 700

The year 1827 saw the discovery of Egypt's first recorded kingly burial: that of the 17th-Dynasty Theban ruler Nubkheperre Intef – though his identity was unrecognized at the time. The circumstances of the find were not pieced together until some eight or nine years after the event by Henry Salt's Greek excavator, Giovanni d'Athanasi, who had himself acquired some of the objects from it. Athanasi described how locals had found the tomb:

'during the researches made by the Arabs in the year 1827, at Gourna … in the mountain … Il-Dra-Abool-Naggia, a small and separate tomb [was uncovered], containing only one chamber, in the centre of which was placed a sarcophagus, hewn out of the same rock, and formed evidently at the same time as the chamber itself …. In this sarcophagus was found [the coffin of Nubkheperre Intef], with the body as originally deposited. The moment the Arabs saw that the case was highly ornamented and gilt, they immediately … knew that it belonged to a person of rank. They forthwith proceeded to satisfy their curiosity by opening it, when they discovered, placed around the head of the mummy, but over the linen, a diadem, composed of silver and beautiful mosaic work, its centre being formed of gold, representing an asp, the emblem of royalty. Inside the case, alongside the body, were deposited two bows, with six arrows …

The Arabs … immediately … proceeded to break up the mummy … for the treasures it might contain, but all the information I have been able to obtain as to the various objects they found, is, that the Scarabæus … was placed on the breast, without having … any other ornament attached to it.'

Despite d'Athanasi's detective work, the context of the finds was forgotten almost at once; though, thanks to their extraordinary nature, the principal pieces from the assemblage could later be re-identified. The coffin of Nubkheperre Intef (its significance lost and with a new, female occupant) would find its way to the British Museum (EA 6652) via the sale of Henry Salt's third collection at Sotheby's in 1835. With it travelled the heart scarab of a king Sebekemsaf (EA 7876), evidently the same piece as that mentioned by d'Athanasi. As for the diadem, this reached Europe separately, the year after the discovery, and is now in the Rijksmuseum van Oudheden, Leiden (AO11a).

The actual location of Nubkheperre's tomb was established by Auguste Mariette (•p. 40) in 1860, marked by two small obelisks. The site was relocated by Herbert Winlock (•p. 156) in 1919, close to the Ramessid private tomb of one Shuroy. This is almost certainly the tomb of the overseer of offerings *Iuroy* (an easy confusion in the hieratic script) mentioned in an ancient necropolis inspection record (Papyrus Abbott) drawn up in Year 16 of Ramesses IX. The document records how an attempt had been made by robbers to burrow into the tomb of Intef from that of Shuroy/Iuroy, but had proved unsuccessful. The king had had a lucky escape, and between that date and 1827, it seems, had lain in his tomb undisturbed.

GIOVANNI D'ATHANASI
(YANNI ATHANASIOU)
(1798–1854)

• Born 1798, on the Greek island of Lemnos
• Joins his father, a merchant, in Cairo, 1809; servant to Ernest Missett, British Consul-General in Egypt, 1813–15, and to his successor, Henry Salt, 1815–27; assisting the latter and his successor, John Barker, in their antiquities collecting
• Independent operator until 1835, disposing of his collection in three sales at Sotheby's, London, 1836, 1837 and 1845
• Failed picture dealer, London, 1849-50
• Dies in poverty, London, 19 December 1854

(below) With the Intef coffin when it arrived in London was this gold-mounted green stone scarab. Though d'Athanasi associates it with the burial, probably rightly, the jewel is inscribed around the edge for Sebekemsaf, an earlier king.

(opposite) Intef's gessoed and gilded wooden *rishi* ('feathered') coffin; the lifelike eyes are inlaid with alabaster and obsidian, and set in copper-alloy frames. Though the original body had been removed by the time the coffin reached the British Museum, fragments of linen from the mummy, as well as papyrus, were still attached to the resins within.

1828
The Metternich Stela

'One day in the reign of Nectanebo II, the last of the Pharaohs, a priest called Nesu-Atum … visited the burial place of the Mnevis bulls, the bulls sacred to Atum, at Heliopolis. Nesu-Atum was a man of antiquarian tastes – a fashionable foible at the time – and apparently had the means to indulge them. He noticed certain "writings" among the inscriptions in the necropolis which appealed to him particularly, and he gave orders to have them copied for a monument he wished to set up in honour of Mnevis and the Pharaoh … '
NORA SCOTT

The tangible result of Nesatum's piety was a large

and elegantly proportioned greywacke stela, carved with extraordinary, precise detail and presumably set up at Heliopolis during his lifetime – that is, in the mid-4th century BC. Surviving the Persian conquest, it was carried off in Greco-Roman times for re-erection at Alexandria.

Centuries later, in 1828, during the digging of a well for a Franciscan monastery, Nesatum's monument was once again brought to light, and, amazingly, in its original, pristine state. Presented as a gift by Muhammad Ali to the Austrian Chancellor, Prince Clemens Metternich-Winneberg, it was borne away yet again – this time to Schloss Metternich at Königswarth, Bohemia. And in 1950, the Metternich Stela (as it is now generally known) was finally acquired by the Metropolitan Museum of Art in New York (MMA 50.85).

In antiquity, the Metternich Stela's magical role was to protect against the evil ways of wild animals, scorpions and serpents. Dominated by a delicately carved vignette showing Horus the child pacifying a variety of noxious beasts ('Horus on the crocodiles'), the remainder of the monolith is covered, in its entirety, with a collection of potent spells. Water poured over these texts would absorb their power, and could be used medicinally to miraculous effect – as the texts themselves say, 'to seal the mouth of all reptiles in heaven or earth or in the water, to save the people, to pacify the gods, to glorify Re'. For those already stricken, the magic was equally efficacious:

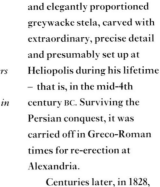

'Flow out, poison …. It is Horus who exorcises you; he cuts you to pieces, he spits you out …. Arise, you who were tormented – Horus has returned you to life; he who is newly born has come forth himself and has overthrown his enemies who sting …. Turn, snake, take away your poison …. Flow out, enemy! Back, poison!'

Such dangers were ever-present in ancient Egypt, and small versions of the Metternich Stela – popularly known as 'cippi (shields) of Horus' – containing a more restricted range of texts, were common and necessary items of domestic equipment from the 25th Dynasty on (*above*). Earlier examples are distinguished by the head of the god Bes protruding above the outline of the shield; later ones by its inclusion within the frame. The Metternich Stela is by far the largest and finest monument of the class, and certainly the most comprehensive in its range of spells. By its creation, the priest Nesatum was performing a singular public service; it would be pleasing to think that his wish for a long and happy life was in turn granted by the gods in whose powers he placed such unquestioning faith.

1828–29
The Franco-Tuscan Expedition

'Into this Egypt already so impoverished by Musselman devastators and European speculators, learned society has now descended like an invasion of barbarians to carry off what little remains of [the country's] admirable monuments.'
ÉMILE PRISSE D'AVENNES

The brutal exploitation of Egypt's ancient past by adventurers such as Drovetti, Salt and Belzoni was thankfully a passing phase, and a return to more cautious investigation and recording was on the way.

This new beginning was signalled by the arrival on the scene, in 1821, of John Gardner Wilkinson, famed for his later, multi-volume work *The Manners and Customs of the Ancient Egyptians*, and by James Burton and Robert Hay, antiquarians who worked in Egypt from the mid-1820s to the mid-1830s. The interest of these men was not in the wholesale removal of antiquities, but in the scientific recording of the monuments *in situ*.

The spirit of the Napoleonic Expedition reborn, a second scientific survey of Egypt's standing antiquities was organized in 1828–29 under the joint direction of Champollion (seated in the centre *below*) and the Tuscan scholar Ippolito Rosellini (standing next to Champollion). The team consisted of 12 architects and draftsmen, including the young artist Nestor L'Hôte – whose papers were to have the greatest influence on the course Egyptian archaeology would take in coming years (•p. 40). The expedition's guide was Alessandro Ricci, who had assisted Belzoni in his somewhat primitive (though sincere) documentation of the tomb of Sethos I in 1817 (•p. 21).

New discoveries were few: the aim of Champollion and his colleagues was to collect and document what had already been uncovered – and of this there was no shortage. Inevitably, perhaps, there were excesses: souvenirs of the trip included two wall-reliefs from the luckless tomb of Sethos I in the Valley of the Kings – though these had been removed, as the Frenchman would defensively proclaim, in these troublesome times, not as booty but solely for their continued preservation.

THE GOLD OF MEROE: FERLINI'S TREASURE

1837 Blasting at Giza: Howard Vyse and the Pyramid of Menkaure
1842–45 Lepsius and the Prussian Expedition

Discovery/excavation
1834
by
Giuseppe Ferlini
and Antonio Stefani

Site
Meroe (North Cemetery,
Pyramid Beg N6)

Period
late 1st century BC

'The discovery of Ferlini is still remembered by most people, and has since that time caused the ruin of many Pyramids. They were also full of it at Chartûm [Khartoum], and more than one European, besides the Pascha himself, imagined they might still find treasures there ....'
KARL RICHARD LEPSIUS

Nubia, the land to the south of Egypt beyond the first cataract, was ancient Kush, gateway to Africa and a source of gold and precious materials including ivory and animal skins. It was a land in which the Egyptians maintained a keen interest from the Old Kingdom on – casual exploitation developing into virtual annexation when, during the New Kingdom, the country was thoroughly Egyptianized and placed under the control of a viceroy based at Aniba. With the collapse of active Egyptian involvement in Nubian affairs around 1000 BC, Nubian culture was allowed to develop under its own steam – and to impressive effect.

GIUSEPPE FERLINI
(c. 1800–70)

- Born Bologna, around 1800
- Surgeon-Major to the Egyptian army, 1830, serving in the Sudan
- Retires from the army, 1834, to excavate at Meroe in partnership with Antonio Stefani; finds sold and now in Munich and Berlin
- Dies Bologna, 29 December 1870

4000 BC

3000 BC

2000 BC

1000 BC

0

AD 700

(right) Reconstructed broad collar of Queen Amanishakheto in stone, faience and glass, from the Ferlini Treasure. The necklace is composed of recognizable though debased forms of Egyptian dynastic amulets, including the *ankh*-sign ('life'), the *wedjat* or 'eye of Horus', fish and scarabs.

(below) One of the Queen's enamelled gold bracelets, decorated at the hinge with an image of the goddess Mut, consort of Amun.

(below) A finger-ring from the treasure with a shield-shaped bezel decorated with pendant beads and surmounted by the crowned head of a ram – the traditional animal-manifestation of Amun. The cloisons are filled with blue glass.

35

(above) A drawing of the decorated pylon entrance of Queen Amanishakheto's pyramid. Prepared in 1844 by Ernst Weidenbach, it is an excellent example of the precise epigraphic work produced by the Prussian Expedition under Karl Richard Lepsius (•p. 37).

hundreds of their sacrificed servants. And it was here that Giuseppe Ferlini found buried treasure.

Ferlini was an Italian physician serving with the Egyptian army of occupation in the Sudan who gradually became obsessed with the idea of excavating the ancient sites with which the upper Nile abounds. He realized this ambition in 1834, when he retired from military life and teamed up with a Khartoum-based merchant of Albanian origin, Antonio Stefani. After several fruitless explorations as they progressed downstream, Ferlini and Stefani arrived at Meroe.

Ferlini's mind was focused on digging – in practice demolishing – the cemetery's smaller pyramids in search of valuables. Unsuccessful in this search, he turned his attention to one of the largest funeral monuments in the northern cemetery – the well-preserved pyramid of Queen Amanishakheto (Begarawiya North 6), some 27 m (88 ft) high. Amanishakheto, as we now know, held the title of *kandake* – indicating not only that she ran a close second in the royal pecking order, as mother of the king, but could – and did – wield power in her own right. Clearly an important figure – a female enemy of the Roman emperor Augustus, a second Cleopatra – it soon became clear that she had been interred in some style.

Ferlini directed his 30 men to climb the queen's pyramid, and set them to pulling it apart, block by block, from the top down, in search of a way in. Within a short time, Ferlini claims, a cavity came into view:

In the earlier phases of the Kushite kingdom, the religious centre and principal burial ground was Napata – represented today by the archaeological sites of Gebel Barkal, el-Kurru and Nuri (•p. 147). From the 4th century BC on, Meroe, situated on the east bank of the Nile some 200 km (125 miles) northeast of modern Khartoum, assumed the pre-eminent role. Developing a form of writing based on Egyptian demotic (but conveying a still unknown language), Meroe soon extended its influence over a wide area. The years spanning the mid-3rd century BC and the mid-4th century AD witnessed the burial at this site of over 40 kings and queens – and many

1837
Blasting at Giza: Howard Vyse and the Pyramid of Menkaure

Belzoni was not the only European of his time to show an interest in the Giza pyramid plateau (•p. 23). In 1837 the British military officer Richard William Howard Vyse, working with the civil engineer John Shae Perring, carried out intensive investigations in both the Great Pyramid of Khufu and the Second Pyramid of Khephren, though with little to show for their appalling destruction.

The Third Pyramid, of the 4th-Dynasty King Menkaure, which the excavators blasted with gunpowder and eventually entered on 29 July, proved more productive. Here, in the burial chamber *(left)* was an exquisite basalt sarcophagus (subsequently lost at sea, either off Malta or close to Cartagena, when the ship carrying it to England sank). Fragments of a wooden coffin *(right)* of the 26th Dynasty (British Museum EA 6647) were also found, from a later reburial of the king. Human remains also in the British Museum, (EA 18212), once believed to be those of Menkaure himself, are now thought to be much later in date.

THE GIZA PYRAMIDS BEFORE HOWARD VYSE

PYRAMID	OWNER	INTERNAL ELEMENTS KNOWN
Great	Khufu	all, excepting the first room above the King's Chamber
Second	Khephren	upper Descending Passage only
Third	Menkaure	none

1842–45
Lepsius and the Prussian Expedition

The Prussian Expedition, sponsored by Friedrich Wilhelm IV and led by the great Karl Richard Lepsius, shared the same lofty aim as the Franco-Tuscan Expedition (•p. 34), an aim it achieved with even greater success: while the Champollion-Rosellini reports occasionally prove useful to Egyptologists today, Lepsius's *Denkmäler aus Aegypten und Aethiopien*, issued in 12 volumes (1849–59, with five volumes of text 1897–1913), is fundamental.

Nor did the Prussians return empty-handed: their luggage bulged with 15,000 artifacts and casts, including a dynamited column from the ill-fated tomb of Sethos I (• p. 21) and sections of tiled wall from Djoser's Step Pyramid at Saqqara (•p. 169) – a gift from Muhammad Ali in thanks for a dinner service presented by the Prussian king. Such acts were perhaps inevitable: for, as A. H. Rhind observed, with 'so much expenditure so many tangible returns were expected'. The Expedition here celebrates the Prussian king's birthday on top of Khufu's pyramid, in a painting by Georg Frey.

'The exposed opening was formed of poorly laid stones and permitted us a view into a cavity and its contents …. We had the large blocks that lay above it removed, exposing a rectangular chamber … roughly five feet high and six or seven feet square. The first thing we saw was a large object covered by a white cloth of cotton or linen, which fell into shreds at a mere touch. Beneath it there emerged a four-sided bed or bier …. Under this bier I found a [bronze] vase, which contained objects wrapped in cloths …. On the floor of the chamber next to the vase lay bits of glass paste and stones strung on threads into chains, also amulets, little idols, a metal case, little turned boxes, a saw, a mallet, and numerous other objects ….

I gathered up everything I had found and packed it into leather satchels and in this manner hid the gold from the Arabs ….'

In the relative security of their tent, Ferlini and Stefani examined what they had found. Ferlini's 'soul filled with joy. I admired the goldwork, and upon seeing the quantity of it, I realized it had to exceed greatly all that which I knew was spread throughout the museums of Europe ….'

Following their exhibition in Europe in 1837, Ferlini's finds eventually found their way to Munich, via the extraordinary collecting instincts of King Ludwig I of Bavaria, who purchased a selection of pieces from the finder in 1840; the remainder of the hoard was acquired by the Berlin Museum four years later, at the recommendation of Karl Richard Lepsius himself.

The Ferlini Treasure attracted controversy from the very start. For many at the time, the debased forms and crudeness of the work marked out the jewels as obvious fakes. Nowadays the debate tends to be concentrated not on the jewelry's authenticity, which is undisputed, but

upon its supposed context – the problem being that there is insufficient space in the demolished part of Amanishakheto's pyramid to have accommodated a chamber of the dimensions specified in Ferlini's account. In fact, as Yvonne Markowitz and Peter Lacovara persuasively argue, there seems every likelihood that, by his claims, Ferlini was attempting to cover his tracks – that in fact he had discovered the queen's jewelry not in the summit of the pyramid proper but in its subterranean burial chamber. This chamber was unknown to scholars until cleared by George A. Reisner in 1921 during the course of his excavations at the site, when fragments were brought to light of a painted linen shroud, pieces of wood and further items of jewelry associated with Ferlini's hoard.

(below) The pyramid of Queen Amanishakheto in 1821 – an engraving from Frédéric Cailliaud's *Voyage à Meroe*. As this engraving makes clear, the monument had suffered damage even before Ferlini's attack on the summit.

SECTION II
THE FIRST ARCHAEOLOGISTS

*'The interest of … science demands not that the excavations be broken off …
but that the excavators be subjected to such regulation that the conservation
of the tombs discovered today and in the future might be fully assured and
guaranteed against the blows of ignorance and blind cupidity.'*
JEAN FRANÇOIS CHAMPOLLION

By the middle years of the 19th century it was becoming increasingly clear
to an enlightened few that Egypt's ancient past was a finite and rapidly
dwindling resource. The country's monuments were under siege as never
before, with the relentless pressures of modernization adding to the chaos
wrought by the unchecked enthusiasms of Drovetti, Salt and others.
Much that had survived for millennia, and ought to have been treasured,
was irretrievably lost in a matter of decades.

But the tide of needless destruction was on the turn: Champollion's
pleading had resulted in the issuing of a government ordinance in 1835
aimed at the protection of Egypt's pharaonic past and the establishment of
a 'Service for the Conservation of Antiquities'. Only in 1850, however,
with the appearance in Cairo of another Frenchman, Auguste Mariette,
would these high-flown aspirations finally be put into real, practical
effect. A tough, uncompromising, dynamo of a man, Mariette would be
the monuments' first true champion and the dominant force in Egyptian
exploration for 30 years to come.

As Mariette ripped through the land on an unprecedented scale, clearing and recording, discovery followed ever more brilliant discovery to
stoke the fires of public awareness. And the finds would be kept, studied
and cared for – with an Egyptian national museum as Mariette's ultimate
aim and achievement.

From the perspective of a somewhat bleak past, the future looked
increasingly bright. Technique remained as poor as ever – for archaeology,
these were early days still; but losses, from now on, would be sustained in
the names of Egypt, science and progress, rather than in the narrow
pursuit of personal gain.

Detail of an inlaid gold
pectoral ornament of
Ramesses II, from Mariette's
excavations at the Serapeum
(●p. 40).

THE BURIAL PLACE OF THE APIS BULLS: MARIETTE AND THE SERAPEUM

1850 The Louvre's Seated Scribe

Discovery/excavation
1851
by
Auguste Mariette

Site
Saqqara

Period
New Kingdom, 18th Dynasty-Ptolemaic Period, 1391–30 BC

'M. Mariette proposes also to undertake excavation at particular points in ancient Egypt, as yet imperfectly explored, in order to enrich our museum with the products of his researches.'
CHARLES LENORMANT

In 1821, a year after the publication of Belzoni's *Narrative*, François Auguste Ferdinand Mariette was born in Boulogne-sur-Mer. It was the start of a life which set the study of pharaonic Egypt on an organized footing for the first time. Yet Mariette's destiny was not immediately apparent – until a chance encounter, in his third decade, with the writings and drawings of a relative, the artist Nestor L'Hôte. L'Hôte had accompanied the Egyptian expedition of Champollion and Rosellini as a wide-eyed youth in 1828 (•p. 34), and the enthusiasm conveyed by his letters home was almost tangible. As the young Auguste turned the pages, and read and wondered, his fate was sealed.

In thrall to this new passion, Mariette settled down to serious study and in 1849 was accepted into the Louvre as a junior curator. A year after that, aged 29, he found himself in Cairo at last – sent on behalf of the Bibliothèque Nationale, in a fit of nationalistic pique, to search out Coptic texts to match those recently acquired by the British.

Mariette's first experience of Egypt would be a memorable one; Coptic texts were soon forgotten as news spread of the young man's discovery of the legendary Serapeum, catacomb of the sacred Apis bulls. It was the greatest find since the tomb of Sethos I (• p. 21); and, for Egypt, it would mark the first, decisive step down the road to a national programme of excavation, salvage and preservation.

The task of searching out pharaonic objects for the Louvre had always been an aim, if a subsidiary one, of Mariette's 6-month mission to Egypt; the Coptic Patriarch's unwillingness to part with further precious texts (after Lord Curzon in 1833–34 and Henry Tattam in 1839 had so thoroughly plundered the Church's holdings in the Wadi Natrun) now permitted the Frenchman to focus his attentions fully in that direction. But where to begin?

The more he ruminated on the possibilities, the more Mariette found himself drawn to the vast Saqqara burial ground – the source, he was told, of a series of sphinxes he had noticed and admired in Cairo (with Antoine Clot, Louis Linant de Bellefonds and others) and Alexandria (at the house of Count Stephan Zizinia) shortly after his arrival. And so:

'One day, walking across the necropolis, metre-rule in hand, seeking to disentangle the plans of the tombs, my eye fell upon another of these sphinxes. It was a revelation. Although three-quarters buried, it was clear that this sphinx was in its ancient location. The avenue which had furnished the collectors of Cairo and Alexandria with so many monuments was therefore found.'

(below) In pursuit of the Serapeum: Mariette's excavations in progress in a plate from the excavator's publication of the discovery, showing a deep trench cut across the ancient processional route described by Strabo. The 135th sphinx is seen at the bottom.

FRANÇOIS AUGUSTE FERDINAND MARIETTE (1821–1881)

- Born Boulogne-sur-Mer, France, 11 February 1821
- Teaches French and drawing in Stratford, England, 1839–40; ribbon designer, Coventry, 1841
- Bacc.-ès-Lettres, Douai, 1841; teacher of French, Collège de Boulogne, 1843
- Begins to study Egyptology aged 21; catalogue of Boulogne Egyptian collection, 1847
- Minor position in the Louvre, 1849
- Visits Egypt to acquire Coptic manuscripts, 1850; he employs his funds for excavation
- Discovery of the Serapeum, 1850; Valley Temple of Khephren, Giza, 1853; excavations at Saqqara, Giza, Thebes, Abydos, Elephantine
- Assistant conservateur in the Louvre, 1855–61 (honorary after)
- Appointed Director of Egyptian Monuments, 1858, carrying out extensive, large-scale excavations throughout Egypt, especially before 1863
- Discovery of the Ahhotep treasure, 1859 (• p. 50)
- First Museum of Egyptian Antiquities at Bulaq, 1863
- Death from cholera of Mme Mariette, Cairo, 1865
- Contributes to the libretto of Verdi's opera Aïda, first performed in Cairo, 1871
- Dies at Bulaq, 18 January 1881; now buried in the grounds of the Cairo Museum

The situation was rapidly developing from one of extraordinary coincidence to major discovery. For Mariette was well aware that the Greek author Strabo, writing in the 1st century BC, had mentioned a sanded-up avenue of sphinxes leading to the famous Serapeum, burial place of the sacred Apis bulls – a site for which many, including Napoleon's Expedition, had searched in vain. These sphinxes seemed to be the evidence which Mariette's predecessors had missed. The Frenchman decided to test the theory – though dispensing, in his haste, with the need to arrange the necessary *firman* (official permission).

Before long, to Mariette's delight, his hurriedly assembled team of diggers had uncovered over a hundred more sphinxes – lining a great processional way. And as the excavations continued over the following weeks, so did this avenue, until it eventually came to a halt in front of a buried temple courtyard.

(left) One of the tell-tale limestone sphinxes which alerted Mariette to the potential of the Saqqara site – lion-bodied with the head of a king, still resting on its ancient plinth.

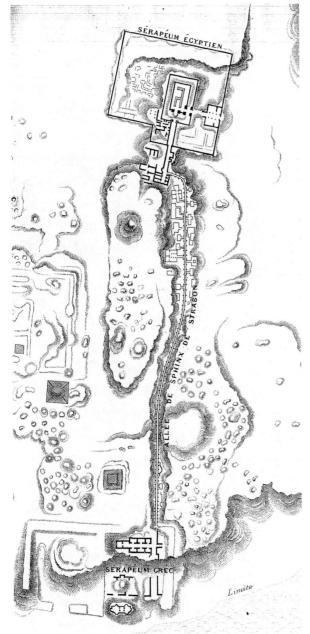

The inscriptions of the newly discovered temple revealed that it had been dedicated to the god Osiris-Apis (Greek 'Osorapis'), the deceased form of the sacred bull of Ptah. The young Frenchman was clearly on the right track, and, as the digging continued, a paved and walled processional way gradually revealed itself – the so-called *dromos* – leading directly to the Serapeum temple itself.

Bull burials and the 'tomb of Khaemwaset'

Entry to the sacred catacomb beneath this temple was at last achieved on 12 November 1851, almost a year after Mariette's inspired search began. The official opening took place three months later – by which time Mariette had emptied the sepulchre of its principal finds in an attempt to preserve them from the clutches of Abbas Pasha, ruler of Egypt at that time. Abbas – already irritated by Mariette's lack of regard for the due formalities (neglecting to seek permission to carry out his work) – was again proving difficult. The Pasha's interest in such discoveries was limited to their potential as bribes and gifts to visiting potentates – a sad fate for such a significant find, and an outcome which Mariette was determined to avoid at all costs.

The subterranean sections of the Serapeum proved to consist of a long gallery inset with numerous votive stelae and sealed by a huge sandstone door, with side-chambers containing 24 magnificent granite sarcophagi (each up to 65 tonnes in weight). These had been prepared between Year 52 of Psammetichus I of the 26th Dynasty and the end of the Ptolemaic period to contain the mummified remains of the Apis bulls – the earthly incarnations of the city god of Memphis. Only three of these bull sarcophagi were inscribed – with the names of Amasis, Cambyses and, on an unused lid abandoned in the corridor, with the

(left) Plan from Mariette's report, showing the Serapeum site as revealed by his excavations.

cartouche of Khababash, Egypt's last native ruler before the brief reappearance of the Persians and the advent of Alexander the Great. All the sarcophagi in this gallery, without exception, had been opened and emptied in antiquity.

In spring 1852, however, further galleries were found – the so-called lesser vaults – with similar rock-hewn chambers which this time proved to have contained wood-coffined bull-burials dating from Year 30 of Ramesses II down to the 22nd Dynasty. And, in one of these chambers (to gain access to which Mariette was obliged to resort to that favoured technique of his predecessors – explosives), the burial, made in Year 55 of Ramesses II, had miraculously survived intact.

For the excavator, as for many Egyptologists since, the wooden coffin within was thought to contain the remains of a man – from the inscriptions Prince Khaemwaset, Ramesses II's antiquarian-minded son (•p. 57). Appearances, however, were to be deceptive, as we now know: for

(top) The subterranean 'Greater Vaults' of the Serapeum. To Mariette's dismay, the tourists would descend in their thousands: '...nothing can give you any idea of the trouble and inconvenience these visits have caused me. It is the eighth plague of Egypt'.

(above) Inscription of the last native Egyptian king, Khababash – a lid intended for one of the Apis bull burials, abandoned at the entrance to the Greater Vaults at the time of the Persian invasion.

(right) Despite their monumental remains, most of the bull sarcophagi had been plundered in antiquity simply by pushing the lids to one side.

1850 The Louvre's Seated Scribe

Mariette's search for the Serapeum yielded many impressive finds, including several masterworks of Egyptian art. One of these was the famous statue of the seated scribe now in the Louvre (E3023), discovered in a mastaba tomb (Mariette C20) bordering the avenue leading to the Serapeum. Extraordinarily well-preserved, with eerily life-like eyes rimmed with copper and inlaid with quartz, rock crystal and ebony, the sculpture represents one of ancient Egypt's most enduring images. Its identification, however, like the circumstances of its discovery, remains uncertain. Recognized by some authorities as a sculpture prepared for the high official Sekhemka, for others its subject is the provincial governor Kay, a block-seated statue of whom is also in Paris (Louvre A106) – though this attribution is somewhat weakened by the fact that Kay is evidently left- and the scribe right-handed. Mariette himself often referred to the statue as the vizier Pahernefer, perhaps based on unpublished evidence. Whatever its true identity, the sculpture dates in all probability from the early years of the 5th Dynasty.

Peering into the gloom of this latest find, Mariette was able to make out a decorated chamber containing two huge, resin-painted rectangular coffins embellished with gold leaf or white paint. Alongside stood four large canopic jars (for the embalmed viscera), carved in alabaster and with human-headed stoppers, and a tall, standing image of Osiris in gilded wood. Close by were two shrines, decorated with scenes of Ramesses II and Khaemwaset making offerings before the Apis bull and topped with figures of Anubis; each shrine contained four faience statues inscribed and dedicated by the vizier Paser. Two large, painted sandstone *shabtis* of Khaemwaset were set into a niche in the south wall; niches in the opposite wall contained two magic bricks, a *djed*-amulet and fragments of gold leaf, while further cuts in the chamber floor proved to contain a further 247

(above) Mask of sheet gold found within the coffin of Apis XIV. Its anthropoid form, and the presence among the burial debris of items of inscribed jewelry, misled Mariette into believing the burial to be that of Khaemwaset, a son of Ramesses II.

(right) Splendid pectoral ornament with which one of the sacred bulls (Apis IX) had been equipped in death: a ram-headed falcon of gold, the cloisons of its upper surface originally set with inlays of glass and semiprecious stone.

despite the named jewels and an anthropoid mask, what Mariette had found was probably not human at all, but an intact (if exceptionally decayed) bull-burial – that of Apis XIV. And it is for 'Osiris-Apis' that the burial's scarab, *wadj*-amulet and 18 human-headed *shabtis* are actually inscribed.

The isolated Apis burials

'Although 3700 years had elapsed since it was closed, everything in the chamber seemed to be precisely in its original condition. The finger-marks of the Egyptian who had tested the last stone in the wall built to conceal the doorway were still recognizable on the lime. There were also the marks of naked feet imprinted on the sand which lay in one corner of the tomb-chamber. Everything was in its original condition ....'

Mariette's work at the Serapeum continued throughout 1852, and resulted in the discovery of a third series of smaller bull burials – the earliest yet uncovered – ranging in date from Amenophis III of the 18th Dynasty down into the 19th Dynasty. One of these burials was again, miraculously, found intact.

shabti-figures in hard stone, calcite and faience dedicated, following the bulls' deaths in Years 16 and 30, by several other functionaries of Ramesses II's long reign. The sight was extraordinary, and Mariette was dumbfounded – as much by the ancient priests' time-bridging footprints still clearly visible in the sand of the floor as by the splendours of the treasures themselves.

Close examination of the finds from this chamber revealed the fact that the corpses of both bulls had been broken into small pieces – the more imaginative believe that the animals were ritually cooked and eaten – before being wrapped and liberally coated with resins; in consequence, there was very little left to see of the bodies themselves. From among the debris of one of the burials (Apis IX), however, which had been contained within three rectangular coffins and covered by an anthropoid lid with gilded face (like that of 'Khaemwaset'), Mariette did retrieve a number of interesting funerary items. These included 15 bull-headed *shabti*-figures, 10 items of

43

(right) An inlaid gold pectoral from Apis VII, modelled in the form of a shrine containing images of the goddesses Wadjyt (cobra) and Nekhbet (vulture), with a ram-headed *ba*-bird above. The prenomen within the cartouche is that of Ramesses II – Usermaatre-setepenre. Curiously, while the signs are correctly orientated to face the divinities, the cartouche itself is reversed.

gold jewelry (some again dedicated by Khaemwaset), and a range of hardstone amulets. The companion burial (Apis VII), which was the earlier, yielded an inlaid gold pectoral of Ramesses II and six further Apis-headed *shabti*-figures.

It was not long before some 230 cases of antiquities were *en route* to the Louvre, in Paris; sufficiently impressed by the return on their modest, 6,000 Fr investment, increased funding from his sponsors was guaranteed, as the excavator had hoped, for a return and further exploration.

THE APIS BULL BURIALS

ISOLATED TOMBS		LESSER VAULTS		GREATER VAULTS	
MARIETTE NO.	DATE	MARIETTE NO.	DATE	MARIETTE NO.	DATE
I	Amenophis III	X–XIV	Ramesses II	XXXVIII	Psammetichus I, Year 52
II	probably 18th	XVI	Ramesses VI	XXXIX	Necho II, Year 16
	Dynasty	XVII	Ramesses IX	XL	Apries, Year 12
III	Tutankhamun	XXVII	Osorkon II,	XLI	Amasis, Year 23
IV–V	Horemheb		Year 23	XLII	Cambyses, Year 6
VI	Sethos I	XXVIII	Takelothis II, Year 14	XLIII	Darius I, Year 34
VII	Ramesses II,	XXIX	Shoshenq III, Year 28	XLIV	Darius I, Year 4
	Year 16	XXX	Pami, Year 2	XLV	Darius I
IX	Ramesses II,	XXXI	Shoshenq V?, Year 4?	unnumbered	Nepherites I, Year 2
	Year 30	XXXII	Shoshenq V, Year 11	XLVI	Khababash, Year 2
		XXXIII	Shoshenq V, Year 37	LV	Ptolemy VI Philometor,
		XXXIV=XXXV	Bocchoris, Year 6/Shabaka,		Year 17
			Year 2	LVII	Ptolemy VIII Euergetes II,
		XXXVI	Taharqa, Year 24		Year 52
		XXXVII	Psammetichus I, Years 20/21	unnumbered	unknown

THE HARRIS PAPYRI:
THE GREATEST COLLECTION EVER FOUND

1860 Rhind's Tomb

Discovery/excavation
before 1855
by
Egyptian locals

Site
Thebes (unidentified tomb
near Medinet Habu)

Period
New Kingdom, 20th Dynasty,
1196–1070 BC

While Mariette was beginning to make his mark in the official archaeological sphere, life in the unofficial sector went on much as before. The diggers of *sebakh* – the decayed mud-brick used as a fertilizer in the fields – worked their ruins; and the professional robbers plundered their tombs. Buyers were few but keen, and of interesting finds there was no lack – except for good papyri, which had always been in short supply. From the 1830s onwards, these were being faked by sticking loose fragments from one or more texts around a bundle of reeds so as to resemble unopened rolls; and it was not long before the notorious forger Constantine Simonides, in Europe, began to experiment with entire Greek texts.

Several names are associated with the collecting of ancient Egyptian papyri. The French initiated the process (•p. 16), while Belzoni and Salt had recovered not a few (•p. 24). The Greek merchant Giovanni Anastasi, Swedish-Norwegian Consul-General in Egypt, was another avid collector – his haul including an impressive group (now scattered throughout a number of collections) of Greek and demotic magical texts from a single library at Thebes. Few, however, could compete with Anthony Charles Harris; the quality of his acquisitions was stupendous, and eclipsed anything found before or since.

Harris was a British commissariat official in Alexandria during the middle years of the 19th century, and a partner (with his brother) in the trading house of Harris and Company. A keen buyer of pharaonic antiquities since the 1830s, in February 1855 he was offered a collection of up to 20 papyri (see table) which were said to have been found together the previous winter behind the temple of Medinet Habu. He was sorely tempted by the group, but, lacking the resources to keep them all, concentrated on what seemed to him the best – the remainder he reluctantly let slip through his fingers. The list of those he retained is awesome nevertheless, and pre-eminent among them is the so-called Great Harris Papyrus – a magnificent, illustrated list of temple donations made by Ramesses III, at 40.5 m (133 ft) long the longest known papyrus from ancient Egypt. The remainder included three documents from the famous group of texts documenting the trials of those who had robbed the royal tombs and Theban temples between the reigns of

ANTHONY CHARLES
HARRIS (1790–1869)

- Born London, 1790
- Establishes with his brother Harris and Company, general merchants in Alexandria
- Collector of Egyptian antiquities, with a particular interest in papyri – his acquisitions including the Harris Papyri and tomb robbery documents
- Dies Alexandria, 23 November 1869
- Harris collection sold to the British Museum by his daughter, Selima, in 1872

4000 BC

3000 BC

2000 BC

1000 BC

0

AD 700

(right) A page from the Great Harris Papyrus, a posthumous list of donations made by Ramesses III to Amun and his priesthood. The penmanship of this magisterial document – the work of four separate scribes – is among the finest to have survived from ancient Egypt.

(left) A vignette from the Great Harris Papyrus: Ramesses III, wearing the white crown of Upper Egypt and dressed in a diaphanous white robe, stands before Re-Harakhty, 'great god, lord of heaven' – the first in a procession of Heliopolitan gods which prefaces this section of the document.

A RECONSTRUCTION OF THE 1855 PAPYRUS FIND

PRESENT LOCATION	MUSEUM NO.	ALTERNATIVE NAMES
London	BM EA 9999	P. Harris I=P. Great Harris
London	BM EA 10221*	P. Abbott
London	BM EA 10052*	
London	BM EA 10053*	P. Harris A=P. Harris 499= P. Amherst VII
London	BM EA 10054*	
London	BM EA 10068*	
London	BM EA 10403*	
Liverpool	M 11162*	P. Mayer A
Liverpool	M 11186*	P. Mayer B
London	BM EA 10383*	P. de Burgh
Rochester New York (Pierpont Morgan Library)	MAG 51.346.1*	P. Amherst VI*
Brussels	E 6857*	P. Leopold II

* Robbery documents

Ramesses VI and XI. These selected documents, together with the rest of Harris's rich collection, were eventually acquired – despite competition from Mariette – by the British Museum in 1872, via the collector Henry Abbott and Harris's daughter, Selima.

The precise findspot of this haul was said by a near-contemporary – the Egyptologist A. A. Eisenlohr – to have been a tomb which, 'when opened, was found full of mummies which had been torn to pieces and destroyed in recent times. In this grotto, under the mummies, was a rude hole in the rock, in which the rolls of papyrus were found deposited together. This hole was covered with potsherds, which were held together with mortar'. The circumstances are reminiscent of an ancient discovery referred to in Papyrus Ambras (P. Vienna 30), which records the purchase 'from the people' during the 20th Dynasty of a similar group of official documents found concealed within two jars. Not impossibly, the assemblage from which Harris made his selection was another official cache, deposited for safety at the politically unstable close of the New Kingdom around 1000 BC.

1860
Rhind's Tomb

Although Auguste Mariette's role as saviour of Egypt's ancient past is loudly, and justly, proclaimed, he was not alone in his desire to prevent the needless destruction and loss of archaeological information. Alexander Henry Rhind, a young Scottish lawyer who visited Egypt several times between 1855 and 1863, carried out a number of important excavations among the myriad shafts and passages cut into the hills of the Theban west bank.

His most celebrated discovery here was an intact group-burial of the late Hellenistic–early Roman period at Sheikh Abd el-Qurna, in an abandoned tomb of 18th-Dynasty date – an interesting and at that time unparalleled find. More remarkable still was the speed with which Rhind's careful records of his work appeared in print: a memoir in 1862 (right), and facsimiles of the two papyri found in 1863. Had Mariette documented so meticulously, and published so promptly, Egyptologists would today be very much more in his debt.

FUNERAL CANOPY FROM THE UPPER CHAMBER OF THE TOMB

PRINCE PLONPLON AND THE BURIAL OF KAMOSE

Before 1858 The Boston Pectoral • After 1858 The Montu Priests
1858 The Queen of Punt

Discovery/excavation
1857
by
Auguste Mariette

Site
Thebes (Dra Abu'l-Naga)

Period
Second Intermediate Period,
17th Dynasty, c. 1555–1550 BC

'Few excavations have been more brilliantly planned out beforehand – and less adequately published afterwards.'
HERBERT WINLOCK

Mariette returned to the Louvre on 24 September 1854, on the eve of the Crimean War; but life behind a Paris desk little suited him, and within three years he was back in the field. The return was in fact orchestrated by Mariette's new mentor, Ferdinand de Lesseps of Suez Canal fame. De Lesseps made sure that word reached Egypt of a planned visit by Prince Napoleon, the restless cousin of Napoleon III of France. It prompted the usual diplomatic flurry and a curious order: 'Said Pâshâ wanted every step of the visiting prince to sprout antiquities, and to assure a fertile crop and save "Plonplon's" time, Mariette was to proceed up river, dig for antiquities and then bury them again all along the proposed itinerary'. (The 'salting' technique was repeated in 1868–69, for the visit of Edward, Prince of Wales – the future King Edward VII – who was fortunate enough to 'discover', in the Theban tomb of Amenkha, a group of 30 coffins which had been similarly planted by Mariette but a short time before.)

So it was that Mariette, in October 1857, was summoned back to Egypt by Said to make all necessary arrangements for Plonplon's visit. Setting his men to work at several promising sites up and down the country – Giza, Saqqara, Abydos and Elephantine – the diggers' haul promised to be a good one. The most important discovery, however, would be made at Thebes, in the area known as Dra Abu'l-Naga.

(below) The bronze dagger, with silver grip and gold-covered pommel, recovered from Kamose's coffin. It seems originally to have been suspended from the neck of the king's mummy on a papyrus cord.

Before 1858
The Boston Pectoral

This spectacular vulture ornament, perhaps once attached to a coffin, was virtually unknown to Egyptologists until its appearance at auction in New York in 1981 (with tales of murder and dubious dealings trailing in its wake). The jewel is made up of three separate and exquisite gold and silver sections inlaid with precious stones and coloured glass, and measures an impressive 38 cm (15 in) from wing tip to wing tip. Acquired by the Museum of Fine Arts, Boston (MFA 1981.159), subsequent research showed the piece to have been bought in Egypt as long ago as 1858, improbably associated with a Ptolemaic period papyrus (now Lafayette College, Mass.), a (suspect) scarab of Shoshenq III (Metropolitan Museum of Art MMA OC 924), and other items. It was most probably a stray from the Second Intermediate Period royal burial-ground at Dra Abu'l-Naga, which had already yielded so much of interest to official excavator and private digger alike.

(left) Elements detached from a gold bracelet similar to one later found with Queen Ahhotep (•p. 50): a cartouche of King Ahmose flanked by two gold lions.

PRINCE PLONPLON AND THE BURIAL OF KAMOSE

Neither the simple, painted-wood coffin nor the rough hole into which it had been carelessly dropped seemed to offer any indication that this was a particularly significant find, while the mummy itself fell to pieces almost as soon as it was exposed to the air. But from among the bandages and bones Mariette's men were able to extract a range of impressive funerary items: a bronze and gold dagger (now in the Bibliothèque royale, Brussels), suspended on a papyrus cord in the vicinity of the left arm; two lion amulets in the area of the chest together with a cartouche-shaped box inscribed with the name of a king, Ahmose (these three items, Louvre E7167–68, actually parts of a bracelet); a bronze mirror (Louvre E3458); and a scarab and some amulets (now lost).

The material promised to supplement nicely the other 'discoveries' Mariette's men had procured for their royal guest – when Plonplon's visit was unexpectedly cancelled. The excavator, however, his eye set firmly on remaining in Egypt, nevertheless assembled a few souvenirs of the failed trip for Said Pasha to despatch to the Prince in Paris. It was a shrewd move on Mariette's part: as a result he would be able to count upon the grateful Prince Napoleon's future support, and Said's acquiescence, in his attempts to secure full and formal control over Egypt's ancient monuments.

While the bulk of the contents of the Dra Abu'l-Naga burial were duly shipped off to France, the stuccoed and painted sycamore coffin (JE 4944) was placed in store and forgotten. It was not examined properly until fifty years later, when the museum curator Georges Daressy managed to make out for the first time the correct reading of the owner's name: 'King Kamose'; Mariette had assumed the burial to be that of an unknown Ahmose (based on the name on the bracelet elements) of the 11th Dynasty, to which period he assumed all *rishi*, or feather-decorated coffins belonged. Without realizing it, Mariette had discovered – and given away! – the burial equipment of one of Egypt's most celebrated rulers: the same Kamose who had initiated the expulsion from Egypt of the Hyksos 15th Dynasty (•p. 202), which ushered in Egypt's golden age – the New Kingdom. Ironically, this was a period with which Mariette was very much taken, and to whose documentation he would over the years contribute a great deal.

Nevertheless, Kamose's coffin seemed ill-suited to such a significant ruler, being of execrably poor quality and with the name written simply, without cartouche or prenomen. It was, doubtless, an ancient replacement, prepared at the time Kamose's original tomb – mentioned as still intact in the 20th Dynasty Abbott Papyrus (one of the documents which A. C. Harris let slip (•p. 45)) – was dismantled at the end of the New Kingdom.

'The safety of the monuments'

On 1 June, 1858 Auguste Mariette found his position as Said's hunter of antiquities formalized at last in a new, long hoped-for post – *mamur*, or director, of ancient

(below) The modest, painted coffin containing the mummy of Kamose – though contemporary, presumably a replacement furnished at the time of the king's reburial under the 20th or 21st Dynasty.

After 1858
The Montu Priests

The priests of Montu, the ancient god of Thebes, had been buried in a honeycomb of tombs beneath the temple of Queen Hatshepsut at Deir el-Bahri during the first two-and-a-half centuries of the Third Intermediate Period. Between 1858 and 1866, Mariette discovered around a hundred of these burials, and further tombs of the same type have occasionally come to light since. The precise circumstances of Mariette's finds remain obscure, but the discovery of the cache(s) proved timely for promoting his cause. Many of the priests travelled to Paris for the Great Exhibition of 1867, where their gruesome remains were greeted with appalled enthusiasm by the French populace, this enthusiasm culminating in the unwrapping of one of the group in a ceremony presided over by Emperor Napoleon III and Ismail Pasha. While the coffins (inc. Cairo CG 41001–72) later returned to Egypt, the occupants remained in France, where they are today prized possessions of the Musée de l'Homme in Paris.

monuments. His wide-ranging powers as guardian of Egypt's pharaonic past were neatly summed up in the letter of appointment he had received from Said at the time of his original engagement: 'You will ensure the safety of the monuments, you will tell the governors of all the provinces that I forbid them to touch one single antique stone; you will imprison any peasant who sets foot inside a temple'.

In the years to follow, Mariette extended his excavations throughout Egypt and beyond, the work variously directed by his right hand man Bonnefoy, his assistant Matteo Floris, and later by Luigi Vassalli, Théodule Devéria from the Louvre, and Charles Edmond Gabet

and Louis Chaillan. Often the excavations were carried out with no supervision at all. System was absent, and recording generally poor since the rate of work was so frenetic; while, tragically, many of the records which were made appear to have been lost when Mariette's house at Bulaq was flooded in 1878.

For his enemies, Mariette was 'a whirlwind which is going to destroy Egypt'; but his position now was unassailable. The Frenchman's one pressing obligation was to dazzle Said with ever-more-wonderful finds – to repose in his cherished dream of a national museum of pharaonic civilization. The digging would continue, strengthening Mariette's position and his influence for good.

1858
The Queen of Punt

Among Mariette's greatest discoveries at Deir el-Bahri was this relief, one of two depicting Ity, the enormous wife of Parahu, chieftain of far-distant Punt.

The mysterious land of Punt – seemingly stretching from eastern Sudan down into northern and western Ethiopia – was an important source for the Egyptians of resins, gold and electrum. To obtain these commodities, Queen Hatshepsut of the 18th Dynasty despatched a trading mission, which was recorded in detail in splendid reliefs decorating her mortuary temple. It is not impossible that the Punt expedition was commemorated in such splendid style to bolster Hatshepsut's dubious status – her assumption of pharaonic prerogatives during the middle years of the 18th Dynasty being highly irregular.

This block Mariette found still in place on the south wall of the temple's middle colonnade in 1858, but it was removed soon after by philistine souvenir-hunters. Fortunately it was recovered and placed in safe-keeping (Cairo JE 14276), a cast now occupying its position in the temple itself.

The Deir el-Bahri scenes were evidently celebrated as much in antiquity as they are today, with one New Kingdom admirer sufficiently intrigued by Punt's exotic queen that he prepared a quick sketch on limestone to impress his friends (*below, right*). This ostracon, with its overtones of the modern seaside postcard, was rediscovered at the nearby workmen's village of Deir el-Medina and is now in the Berlin Museum (21442).

49

AN EGYPTIAN QUEEN:
THE COFFIN AND JEWELS OF AHHOTEP

1859 Mariette's Abydos Burial • 1859 'Hyksos' Sculptures
1860 The Sheikh el-Beled • 1860 The Statue of Khephren

Discovery/excavation
1859
by
Auguste Mariette

Site
Thebes (Dra Abu'l-Naga)

Period
New Kingdom, 18th Dynasty,
reign of Ahmose,
1550–1525 BC

Just two years after discovering the burial of Kamose (•p. 47), Mariette's workmen, digging in the same part of the Theban necropolis on 5 February 1859, again struck it rich. On learning of the find, Mariette's associate, the Luxor dealer Galli Maunier, promptly sent the following report to Cairo:

'I have pleasure in advising you that your [overseers] at Gourneh have found at Dra-Abou-Naggi, a magnificent mummy case, and a chest containing four alabaster vases, of varying forms, without covers or inscriptions, found by the side of the mummy case. The mummy case has the lid entirely gilded, a longitudinal inscription ... [and] the eyes ... of enamel framed with gold; on the head is a uraeus serpent in relief, [though] unfortunately the head of the serpent is missing ....'

The assemblage represented an important and clearly intact burial in its original coffin – according to one of Howard Carter's sources, within a brick-lined vault – with its accompanying embellishments far richer than those found with Kamose. The coffin's owner and occupant proved to be a queen, Ahhotep, whose funerary equipment included military weapons and a necklace of golden flies – traditionally awarded for valour in battle. These finds prompted her initial identification as a wife of Kamose, buried, it was suggested, with these martial symbols in recognition of her part in the expulsion of the Hyksos. Today, scholars are less certain.

In Mariette's absence the find was carried off to Qena in its entirety, to be eagerly opened by the local chief, Fadil Pasha; the mummy was rifled, the bones and linen discarded, and the 2 kg (4 lb) or so of solid gold jewelry and other funerary objects despatched, obsequiously but no doubt with great reluctance, to Said Pasha in Cairo.

Mariette rightly suspected that the queen's treasure was in grave danger of being melted down, or broken up and distributed as trinkets among the members of Said's harim; he also feared that the hard-won monopoly on excavation which he currently enjoyed would be undermined if he did not act decisively to retrieve the situation. Mariette therefore took prompt action, as his French colleague, Théodule Devéria, describes:

'We had just about gone as far as [our steam boat] the Samannoud would make it [owing to the low level of the Nile], when we saw the boat carrying the treasure from the

(above) A hinged armlet, one of several such ornaments buried with Queen Ahhotep, modelled in the form of the vulture goddess Nekhbet. Though the material is gold, of the highest purity and embellished with inlays of semiprecious stones, the style is delightfully naive.

(left) Queen Ahhotep's richly decorated coffin lid (the base is lost), decorated over its entire surface with thick gold leaf and with the eyes, most unusually, set in frames of massive gold. The wood is an imported, coniferous species.

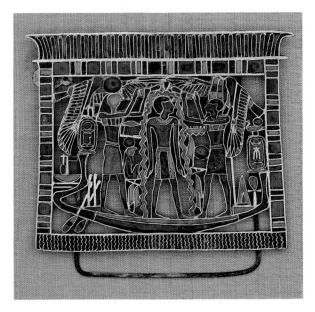

(left) The queen's inlaid gold pectoral, with a scene showing the 'baptism of pharaoh' – Ahmose – by the gods Re and Amun. In comparison with the extraordinary jewels produced in the Middle Kingdom (•pp. 88, 138, 233), the clumsiness of the workmanship is apparent.

pharaonic mummy coming towards us. At the end of half an hour the two boats were alongside each other. After some stormy words, accompanied by rather lively gestures, Mariette promised to one to toss him overboard, to another to roast his brains, to a third to send him to the galleys, and to a fourth to have him hanged. At last they decided to place the box containing the antiquities on board our boat, against a receipt....'

A desperate and strictly illegal action, it was the only chance the *mamur* had to preserve the burial-group relatively intact. But the gamble paid off handsomely. Impressed as much by Mariette's daring as by the

(below) A second armlet from Ahhotep's treasure, taking the form of an archer's 'bracer' modelled in solid gold and inlaid with carnelian, lapis and feldspar. The vertical projection was intended to protect the inner wrist from the released bow-string.

QUEEN AHHOTEP:
the principal finds

CAIRO CG NO.	DESCRIPTION	INSCRIPTION
28501	gilded wooden anthropoid coffin	Ahhotep
18478-80, 18482	alabaster cylinder jars (4)	
52004	inlaid gold pectoral	Ahmose
52672-73, 52713, 52733	gold and carnelian broad collar elements	
52671	gold necklace with three large flies	
52692	small electrum flies (2)	
52670	gold necklace with scarab	Ahmose
uncertain	gold-mounted bead pendant	
52693?	gold aegis amulets (2)	
52642	gold 'bracer', with sphinxes	Ahmose
52068	inlaid gold vulture armlet	
52069	inlaid gold armlet with coronation scene	Ahmose
52071-72	gold, carnelian, turquoise and lapis wristlets (2)	Ahmose
52070	gold, carnelian, turquoise and lapis wristlet	Ahmose
52073-88	gold/electrum bracelets/armlets (16)	
52688	gold bracelet elements	
52664	bronze mirror, with handle	
52705	wooden fan, gold foil decoration	Kamose
52662	'staff', gold foil decoration	
52666	gold and silver model boat	
52667	silver model boat	
52668	wood and bronze model wheeled vehicle	
52703-04	lion gaming pieces, gold (1) and bronze (1)	
52645	bronze axe, with handle, richly decorated	Ahmose
52647	bronze axe, with handle, gold foil decoration	Kamose
52646	bronze axe, with handle, undecorated	
52648	bronze axe-blade	Kamose
52649-57	gold (3) and silver (6) model axes	
52658-59	bronze and gold dagger and scabbard, richly decorated	Ahmose
52660	bronze and gold dagger	
52661	bronze and gold dagger	

The three massive fly amulets found suspended from the neck of Ahhotep's mummified body. Acknowledging the tireless persistence of the insect, jewels of this type were awarded by the king for valour on the field of battle.

magnificence of Ahhotep's jewels, Said Pasha at last agreed to the setting up of a formal museum to replace the warehouse which had served this purpose since the ordinance of 1835. This museum opened in October 1863 to receive the Frenchman's ever-growing pile of treasures for posterity – or, as Said more likely saw it, until they might come in useful for oiling the wheels of international diplomacy.

Ominously, such a moment arrived in 1867, following the exhibition of Ahhotep's jewelry in Paris alongside the rather less appealing Montu priest mummies (•p. 48). Empress Eugénie, wife of Napoleon III, cast a covetous eye and let it be known that she would be more than happy to receive the collection as a gift. Said's successor, Ismail, anxious to curry French favour, was not averse to the idea, though graciously conceded that he would have to consult his French antiquities chief first. This was not to prove the formality Ismail had envisaged. Mariette – perhaps still smarting from Said's offer to Archduke Maximilian of Austria a decade before to take whatever he liked from the Egyptian state collections – refused to entertain the idea. The rightful home of the jewels, Mariette insisted, was Egypt. However noble, it was a stand which would do little to endear him to his masters: the Frenchman's funds, for a time, were cut off by the furious Ismail, while the support of his emperor was lost for good.

1859
Mariette's Abydos Burial

Abydos was a sacred site of great antiquity and an important focus of pilgrimage throughout dynastic history. Here Mariette maintained a force of 30 men who dug continuously for 18 years, much of their effort taken up with clearing the magnificent mortuary temple of Sethos I. But other work was undertaken as well, and not far from this temple, in June 1859, an intact limestone sarcophagus was brought to light:

'A large wooden coffin, with the face of a mummy, lay within ... so completely perished that it gave way at the slightest touch. The mummy, for its part, was in no better condition. Hardly had the coffin been opened than it collapsed onto itself and, after a few minutes, turned to dust ....'

Among the fragments of the disintegrated corpse was a splendid pair of light, tinkly earrings of gold (Cairo CG 52323–4), inscribed for Ramesses XI, and some 78 further items of precious jewelry, untouched since the day of the funeral more than three thousand years before. To whom the jewels belonged, and even the sex of the corpse, remain imponderables, however.

Mariette's ambitious style of excavation left a trail of many such casualties in its wake, and was frowned upon by the succeeding generation of Egyptologists. Flinders Petrie (•p. 67) records why:

'[Mariette] only visited his excavation once in a few weeks and left everything to native reises, just ordering a particular area to be cleared out. The reises often did not go to the work all day, and the workers did no more than they could help....

They were much afraid of the work being stopped, so when their digging did not produce enough results to be encouraging, they used to buy from dealers, in Cairo and elsewhere, sufficient miscellaneous antikas to keep up Mariette's interest in the place. Of course it goes without saying that a good find was kept back so far as was prudent ....

The bulk of Mariette's excavating frenzy was undertaken during the period 1858–63 and, to give one instance of the scale, in 1861 some 35 sites were being explored simultaneously. His critics clearly had a point. But Mariette's aim was to make a mark, to establish in the minds of the Egyptians, as thoroughly and in as short a time as possible, the principle and the value of official excavation. And in this he would succeed famously.

MARIETTE'S EXCAVATIONS:
A Snapshot, May 1858

SITES	NO. OF WORKERS
Beni Suef, Mit Faris, Qerdan	130
Qena, Qurna, Karnak	300
Galioubia, Tell el-Yahudiya, Manshiyet Ramla	150
Girga, Abydos	50
Giza, Saqqara, Memphis	400
el-Minya, Tuna el-Gebel	100
Esna, Medinet Habu, Edfu	5,200
Gharbia, Sais	500
Total no. of workers employed	7,280

1859
'Hyksos' Sculptures

Digging among the ruins of the great Amun temple at Tanis (biblical Zoan) in 1859, Mariette uncovered a series of superb black granite royal sculptures of somewhat bizarre type which he mistakenly assigned to the Hyksos period of Asiatic rule (now in Cairo, including CG 392–94, 530). Egyptologists today recognize in the faces of these masterworks the powerful 12th-Dynasty ruler Ammenemes III.

Frustrated by the lack of archaeological documentation for these sculptures, scholars share the feelings of the *mamur's* assistant, Charles Gabet, who wrote: 'You see, Monsieur, that your hopes for Sân were well-founded and that your predictions have been realized. Only what a pity the works in this locality were not better supervised'.

1860
The Sheikh el-Beled

Mariette's excavations at Saqqara uncovered much great sculpture, one of the most celebrated works being this extraordinary wooden statue of the 5th-Dynasty high official Kaaper (*left*), recovered from mastaba C8 at Saqqara in 1860. The statue was named by the workmen 'Sheikh el-Beled', after their local village headman whom it resembled. It was originally covered with painted gesso, which has now fallen away to reveal the extraordinary modelling.

Two associated striding statues of similar scale, also in wood and depicting a young man (Cairo CG 32) and a woman (CG 33), are generally identified as representations of Kaaper as a young man, and of his dutiful wife (*right*).

As Mariette discovered, the value of such powerful works of art as icons in a rapidly emerging field was immeasurable.

1860
The Statue of
Khephren

*'[The statues] are seven in
number and all represent king
Chephren [Khephren]. Five of
them are mutilated; but the two
remaining are entire, and one of
them is in such a perfect state of
preservation that it might be
thought to have come from the
hand of the sculptor only
yesterday.'*
AUGUSTE MARIETTE

The year 1860 found Mariette
working at Giza, exploring
beneath the paving of the
'Long Vestibule' of
Khephren's valley temple
(*right*) to investigate a
rumour reported by the late
Alessandro Ricci that
the Sphinx was actually
a tomb.

Although no evidence
was forthcoming to prove
the claim, in the course of
his investigations Mariette
encountered a pit containing

several statues of the
building's 4th Dynasty
owner. The find represented
a mere handful of the many
sculptures which had once
adorned the temple and
which were later (though
still during Old Kingdom
times) broken up to make
stone vessels.

The prize of the group
was this wonderfully
preserved image of
Khephren protected by the
Horus falcon, a masterwork
of Old Kingdom sculpture –
and indeed of Egyptian art

during any age – which
was destined to become
one of the principal
exhibits of the museum
at Bulaq (now Cairo
CG 14).

And Egypt could so
easily have lost it: 'A few
hundred francs more,'
the excavator was wont
wickedly to remark in
reference to the untimely
halt in his earlier
explorations of 1853–54
owing to lack of funds 'and
the statue ... would today be
in the Musée du Louvre'.

FINDING THE TOMB OF HESYRE, CHIEF ROYAL SCRIBE

1863 Statues from the Tomb of Psamtek • 1864 The Tale of Setne-Khaemwaset
Before 1862 The Edwin Smith Papyri • Before 1865 The Palermo Stone
1871 The Meidum Sculptures • 1871 The Tomb of Ti • 1874 The Karnak Taweret

Discovery/excavation
1860
by
Auguste Mariette;
James Edward Quibell

Site
Saqqara (tomb S2405 [A3])

Period
Early Dynastic Period, 3rd
Dynasty, reign of Djoser,
2630–2611 BC

'The tomb of Hosi [Hesyre] is constructed in yellowish brick and the principal chamber is a long corridor pierced with numerous rectangular niches. It was from the back of ... these niches that we took the precious panels ....'
AUGUSTE MARIETTE

By 1860 Mariette had transferred his principal effort south from Giza to Saqqara, to be rewarded by the discovery of the mastaba-tomb of Hesyre, 'head of royal scribes', who lived during the reign of Djoser, builder of the Step Pyramid, in the early days of united dynastic rule. Digging down into the mud-brick superstructure of Hesyre's tomb, Mariette was able to come away with five extraordinary wooden panels, each 1 m (3¼ ft) high and carved in delicate, raised relief (Cairo CG 1426–30). These were, by any standards, masterworks, and would feature prominently in Mariette's lavish *Album du Musée de Boulaq*, an early publication of his new museum issued a decade later.

Whatever the celebrity of the reliefs, the precise location of Hesyre's tomb was soon forgotten; for it was Mariette's far-sighted practice, having once explored a tomb, to cover it again to protect it from robbers, vandals and the elements. Passed over in silence on Jacques de Morgan's map of the Saqqara necropolis published in 1897, the monument was considered lost for good until accidentally stumbled upon during excavations carried out by James E. Quibell (•p. 97) in 1911–12 to the north of the Step Pyramid. Under Quibell's direction, the tomb was properly cleared, measured and at last published. Mariette's wooden reliefs could now be seen in context.

A remarkable tomb

The tomb of Hesyre was extraordinary on at least three counts. Its date – 3rd Dynasty – was significantly early; its size was imposing – the mastaba superstructure was essentially of solid mud-brick, measured 43 m (141 ft) long and at one point still stood more than 5 m (16½ ft) high; and its decoration, severely archaic in style, was extremely fine.

The main room of the tomb was a long narrow passage or corridor, along the length of which, on its western side, stood a series of 11 niches into which the tomb's wooden panels had originally been set: five (at the south end) recovered by Mariette; a fragmentary example removed by Quibell (at the north end); and the remains of a further five panels abandoned during Quibell's reclearance as not worthy of salvage. The wall itself was decorated with bold geometric designs in black, red, yellow and green, clearly intended to imitate wall-hangings.

The decoration covering the other side of this narrow passage was equally noteworthy, though Mariette and his men had seemingly missed it. Quibell's description is as follows:

'There were no scenes of bearers of offerings, no figures of butchers with little explanatory texts above them, no human figures, nor animals, indeed, at all, but a long row of oblong frames on a background of matting, looking much like pictures in a gallery.'

(above & left) Two of the finest of the panels recovered by Mariette from the mastaba of Hesyre at Saqqara. The tomb owner is represented on each, though pose and wig differ; his scribal equipment – the symbol of his rank – are given due prominence, though the man's specialist skills included medicine and dentistry.

The subject-matter of these 'pictures', each divided into three registers, was the deceased's funerary accompaniments, including (the lower part of) a statue of the tomb owner, a 'serpent' board and other games, wood and copper measures and a range of bedroom furniture. The paintings (which were subsequently reburied) possessed a character quite distinct from that of the wall decorations found in later tombs, as the copies prepared by Quibell and his wife in watercolour and line reveal.

The burial apartments

Thanks to Quibell's report, the underground portions of the tomb can be seen to have occupied three levels (the uppermost closed with a stone 'portcullis' sliding in a groove). Predictably, they had been plundered in antiquity and little was left save a scattering of human bones, potsherds, a few broken stone vessels in a range of Early Dynastic forms, and a bone handle carrying the name of Hesyre. A fragmentary mud seal with the name of Netjerykhet-Djoser, builder of the Step Pyramid complex, confirmed and clarified the tomb's 3rd-Dynasty date.

The reliefs

Hesyre's wooden tomb reliefs were clearly far from unique (other fine monuments in wood include a lintel-stela of one Nedji and the wooden false door of Ika – Cairo JE 72201 – found at Saqqara in 1940), but the material is uncommon in the archaeological record. This state of affairs perhaps owes less to the depredations of the white ant than to the general scarcity in Egypt of good timber, as a result of which salvage and reuse have always been the norm.

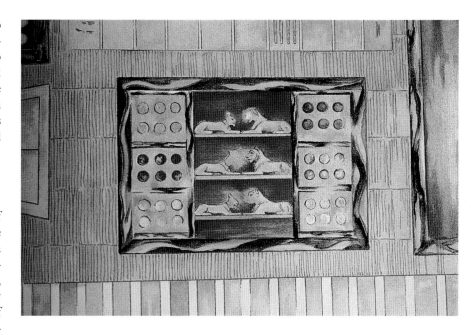

Whatever their status in antiquity, however, the Hesyre reliefs are without doubt the masterpieces of the genre, distinguished not only by the quality of their carving but more remarkably, at such an early period, by the subtlety of the drafting. As has elsewhere been remarked, the generous spacing given over to the hieroglyphic signs – any one of which might stand as a masterpiece in its own right – cleverly disguises the vertical columns into which the texts are divided; while the image of the owner, positioned at the end of the final column, for all its size, is no more than an elaborate determinative of the name. Already, by the 3rd Dynasty, the blending of image and inscription, which was to become a characteristic feature of Egyptian art throughout its long history, had found full expression.

(above) A detail of one of the wall-paintings found in the superstructure of Hesyre's mastaba tomb – a selection of gaming pieces. To the excavator, the paintings resembled nothing so much as 'pictures in a gallery'.

1863
Statues from the Tomb of Psamtek

Sweeping around south of the causeway of Unas (•p. 187) at Saqqara in 1863, Mariette uncovered yet more treasures concealed in a pit giving access to an important triple tomb which had previously been noted by his early 19th-century precursor, James Burton.

On the east side, this underground burial-complex had been employed by two high officials who shared the same name – Psamtek – and on the west, by a 26th-Dynasty king's daughter and king's wife called Khedebneitirtbint.

The pit itself proved to contain three large-scale, greywacke sculptures, each a little under 1 m (3 ft) in height: a seated Isis (Cairo CG 38884; *right*); a seated Osiris (Cairo CG 38358); and an image of the owner standing before and protected by the Hathor cow (Cairo CG 784; *left*). The last is very reminiscent of – and may indeed have been modelled on – the more famous image which would later be brought to light at Deir el-Bahri by Édouard Naville (•p. 128).

The owner of the statues, whose name they carry, was clearly one of the Psamteks of Burton's tomb – a 'Chief Scribe', 'Overseer of Seals', and 'Governor of the Palace' who exercised power during the 26th Dynasty, and in all probability under the pharaoh Amasis.

What they lack in soul, Psamtek's statues amply make up for in modelling of unmatched crispness and precision, virtual perfection in the choice and finish of material, and faultless Saite proportions and style.

1864
The Tale of Setne-Khaemwaset

Besides the usual range of statues, stelae and coffins, diggers during the 19th century uncovered a fair number of oddities – including the 3rd-century BC text of one of demotic literature's most famous stories, 'The tale of Setne-Khaemwaset'. Curiously, this was found with other 'heathen' texts of the pharaonic period in the tomb of a Coptic monk at Deir el-Medina in 1864. Subsequently bought by Mariette for his museum (now Cairo CG 30646), the papyrus comprises four (of an original six) numbered pages of the first story of the cycle referred to as Setne I.

It was to prove an important find: 'Up to that time,' Gaston Maspero later noted, 'the study of demotic writing had not been very popular among Egyptologists; the tenuity and indecision of the characters that compose it, the novelty of the grammatical forms, and the dullness or feebleness of the subjects dealt with, alarmed or repelled them'. With the discovery of Setne-Khaemwaset (a second episode of which would be published in 1909 from a papyrus in the British Museum, EA 10822), all that changed for good.

The Setne Khaemwaset of the title was none other than the *setem*-priest Khaemwaset, high priest of Ptah at Memphis and son of Ramesses II (• p. 41), around whose antiquarian exploits the imaginary tale had been woven. Khaemwaset's quest in Setne I is for the magical book of Thoth, which will confer upon its owner untold powers over the natural order of the world – more than a hint, perhaps, that the historical prince's funerary researches were inspired less by the wish to celebrate his long-dead ancestors than facilitate the rifling of their eternal belongings.

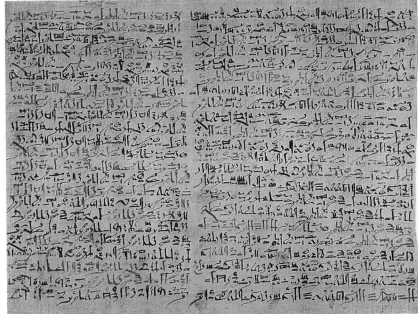

Before 1862
The Edwin Smith Papyri

Edwin Smith, an American, came to Luxor at the age of 36 in 1858, setting up as a money-lender and dealer. He acquired four of the most important scientific texts ever found: the Rhind mathematical papyrus (British Museum EA 10057–58 + Brooklyn 37.1784E); the British Museum mathematical leather roll (EA 10250); the Ebers medical papyrus (Leipzig); and the Edwin Smith surgical papyrus (New York Academy of Medicine; *above*). All originated in a single tomb of the early 18th Dynasty, plundered by locals and sold on for immense profit: his text alone cost the German professor George Ebers the enormous sum of $8,000.

Before 1865
The Palermo Stone

An important piece in the jigsaw puzzle of ancient Egyptian chronology is the fragmentary annals text popularly known as the Palermo Stone. It is named after the museum in which it is now kept and was found, presumably, in Sicily (to which it may have travelled as ballast) some time before 1865. This and smaller related fragments now in Cairo (inc. JE 39734–5, 44859–60, the first three said to have been found at el-Minya) and at University College, London (Petrie Museum UC 15508, acquired at the time of Petrie's Memphis excavations) chronicle the principal, primarily ritual, events of the Egyptian state calendar, together with Nile flood levels, beneath the name of the king in whose reign they occurred.

The complete text appears to have spanned the period from the unification of Egypt down to the 5th or even 6th Dynasty. The enormous potential of its tantalizing and much discussed fragments has, it seems, yet to be fully realized.

1871
The Meidum Sculptures

This remarkable pair of life-sized sculptures of painted limestone was discovered at Meidum in 1871 in the mastaba of Rahotep and Nofret by Mariette's assistant, Albert Daninos.

Although buried more than four and a half thousand years before, in the reign of the 4th-Dynasty king Snefru, their condition was almost perfect – so much so that the Egyptian employed in digging out the tomb (no. 6) soon reappeared, terrified

and jabbering incoherently. As Daninos explains: 'He had found himself in the presence of two heads of living human beings whose [crystal] eyes stared back at him'.

The extraordinary statues of prince Rahotep and princess Nofret (Cairo CG 3–4) were not the only surprises in store at Meidum. Further work, in the tomb of Nefermaat and Itet (no. 16) revealed several unique, paint-filled reliefs and that most famous of all Egyptian tempera paintings, the Meidum geese (*above*).

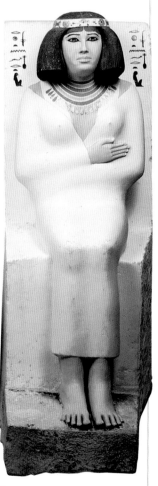

1871
The Tomb of Ti

Ti, overseer of the pyramids of the 5th-Dynasty kings Neferirkare and Niuserre, and of the sun-temples of Sahure, Neferirkare, Raneferef and Niuserre at nearby Abusir, was one of the most important men of his time, and his house of eternity at Saqqara was a large and impressive one.

The tomb (D 22) is famed today – as it evidently was in antiquity – for the quality and range of its wall scenes. Its reliefs inspired a number of non-Memphite artists working at Meir, Deir el-Gebrawi and el-Hawawish. The walls seem, when first uncovered by Mariette, to have retained a good deal of their original colour – until the taking of wet-squeeze copies by a Dr Reil during the 1870s.

The subject-matter of Ti's wall-decorations – which were intended magically to come to life and perpetuate the deceased's worldly estates for his enjoyment after death – is rich and imaginative, beautifully drafted and cut, and provides an immeasurable amount of information about daily life in 5th-Dynasty Egypt. As one Egyptologist earlier last century speculated:

'I have sometimes thought, that if one could imagine a general destruction of the

monuments of Egypt, out of which it was possible to save one thing only, that one thing would be the large room in the tomb of Ti ... [T]he artistic merit of [the tomb's] reliefs has had bare justice done to it.'
A.A.QUIBELL

Other tombs have been discovered which rival Ti's. These include the nearby and almost contemporary tomb of Ptahhotep and Akhethotep (D64), another Mariette find which was fully cleared by students of Flinders Petrie; and the great 5th-Dynasty tombs of Kagemni and Mereruka

discovered by de Morgan (•p. 86). The artistic achievement of these monuments is at last being revealed, in breathtaking detail, by the superb photography of the Oxford Expedition to Egypt under the direction of Yvonne Harpur.

As in all Egyptian tombs, there were statues too. According to Mariette, Ti's

principal *serdab* – a hidden feature of the Old Kingdom tombs first noted during the course of the Frenchman's work here – contained around 20 such images, though only one of these sculptures was found intact; now removed to the Cairo Museum (CG 20), its original position is today occupied by a cast.

1874
The Karnak Taweret

The best Egyptian sculpture of the Saite period is characterized by a perfection of form and execution – and perhaps the finest Saite sculpture of all is this exquisite statue of the goddess Taweret (Cairo CG 39145). Dedicated by the high priest Pabasa, chief steward of the 26th-Dynasty god's wife of Amun, Nitocris, the sculpture was discovered by locals digging at Karnak in 1874 and promptly confiscated by Mariette for his museum.

It owes its excellent state of preservation to having been enclosed within a limestone shrine open only at eye level for limited communication with the outside world – the reception of prayers. The statue's beauty would be known only to the goddess herself.

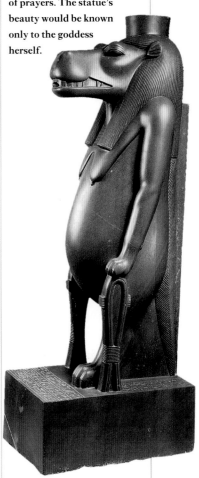

THE PYRAMID TEXTS:
THE WORLD'S OLDEST RELIGIOUS LITERATURE

1881 A Votive *Shabti* of Ptahmose, Mayor of Thebes
1881 The Wilbour Plaque

Discovery/excavation
1881

by
Heinrich &
Émile Brugsch

Site
Saqqara

Period
Old Kingdom, 5th–6th
Dynasties, 2356–2150 BC

'O ye who are set over the hours,
ye who go in front of Re,
prepare a way for Unas,
that Unas may pass through the guard [of demons] with terrible faces!'
PYRAMID TEXTS, UTTERANCE 251

Early in 1881, as the English Egyptologist E. A. Wallis Budge (•p. 72) would later recall, Gaston Maspero (•p. 64), then Director of the French Institute in Cairo, was shown by the now-ailing Mariette a series of paper squeezes – impressions of a long religious hiero-glyphic text arranged in neat, vertical columns. The squeezes had been brought to Mariette by the brilliant Heinrich Brugsch and his wayward brother Émile, who had dis-covered the texts inscribed on the walls of a tomb chamber at Saqqara. The findspot, Mariette declared, was an Old Kingdom mastaba-tomb prepared for a man by the name of Pepipen; but this, as Maspero quickly understood, was mere bravado on the old man's part. For it was clear that 'Pepipen' was in fact a writing of 'this Pepi' – a reference to king Pepy I of the 6th Dynasty; and, as the discoverers themselves had clearly seen, the tomb upon whose walls the texts had been inscribed was no mastaba but the interior of Pepy I's crumbling pyramid at Saqqara.

Mariette's reluctance to admit the identification, even to himself, was caused by his stubborn adherence to one of his 'golden rules' of Egyptian archaeology: that of the 'silent pyramid'. Pyramid tombs, Mariette had always maintained, were never inscribed. Only with the discovery of a second pyramid, belonging to Pepy I's successor, Merenre (and still containing the remains of the original owner – the oldest known royal mummy),

**ÉMILE CHARLES
ADALBERT BRUGSCH**
(1842–1930)

- Born Berlin, 24 February 1842
- Joins his brother, the philologist Heinrich Brugsch, as Assistant in the Khedive's School of Egyptology in Cairo, 1870–79
- Assistant to Mariette, and Assistant Conservator, Bulaq Museum, 1871; subsequently promoted to Keeper, Bulaq/Giza/Cairo museums, 1883, resigning 1914
- Works with brother Heinrich on Mariette's behalf at Saqqara, discovering the Pyramid Texts, 1881; clears the Deir el-Bahri cache, 1881 (•p. 64)
- Skilled lithographer and photographer; extracurricular activities said to have included the surreptitious sale of museum objects in his charge – perhaps to keep the institution afloat
- Dies Nice, 14 January 1930

(far left) Gaston Maspero, the excavator, standing before the basalt sarcophagus in the burial chamber of the pyramid of Unas. The walls of the antechamber (left), are entirely covered in carefully cut columns of hieroglyphs conveying the various spells of the Pyramid Texts.

THE DISCOVERY OF THE PYRAMID TEXTS

PYRAMID OWNER	DYNASTY	DATE OF CLEARANCE
Unas	5th Dynasty	c. 14–28 February 1881
Teti	6th Dynasty	18 April–29 May 1881
Pepy I	6th Dynasty	May 1880–Feb./March 1881
Merenre	6th Dynasty	c. 1–14 January 1881
Pepy II	6th Dynasty	Feb.–March 1881

was Mariette obliged to admit defeat. This was a matter of weeks before his final illness and death on 18 January 1881.

'The pyramids of Gizeh belonged to the Pharaohs of the Fourth Dynasty, and those of Abooseer to the Pharaohs of the Fifth. The five pyramids of Sakkarah, of which the plan is uniform … are contemporary with the mastabas with painted vaults …. One is not astonished, therefore, to find them inscribed and decorated.'

The columns of inscription which the Brugsch brothers had found are known, appropriately, as the Pyramid Texts. And, following the discovery of the first series in Pepy I's and Merenre's burial chambers, others, at Maspero's urging, were uncovered in quick succession.

In the clearance of these tombs Maspero took a very hands-on approach – and it very nearly cost him his life. During the excavation of the pyramid of Pepy II, 'at the expense of Mr. John Cook [of Thomas Cook and Sons] in 1881 Maspero … was buried by a fall of masonry in one of the chambers, and was only dug out with the greatest difficulty by E. Brugsch Bey …'. Fortunately he survived, and subsequently studied and published the texts in what Budge has described as 'one of the greatest triumphs of Egyptian decipherment'.

What were these texts? As Maspero saw, they describe or allude to the different stages in the rebirth of the king (or queen) into a uniquely royal hereafter within his (or her) Netherworld pyramid, and were arranged on the walls as if to be read by the deceased from beyond the grave. As with the spells of the later Coffin Texts and the Book of the Dead (which incorporate much of the earlier Pyramid Texts' content), there is no single, standard edition. Each pyramid employed a different selection drawn from what was evidently a much larger body of texts. All told, Maspero's collation included more than 4,000 lines of this corpus – the earliest, most important and extensive expression of religious thought to have survived from anywhere in the ancient world.

Later, further royal burial chambers decorated with Pyramid Texts were uncovered, including four brought to light by Swiss archaeologist Gustave Jéquier between 1926 and 1933 (belonging to the obscure, 8th-Dynasty King Ibi, and the 6th-Dynasty queens Wedjebten, Neith and Ipuit). And, as the recent find of Ankhesenpepi at Saqqara suggests, there are doubtless more.

(below) Detail from the antechamber, south wall, pyramid of Unas. The columns of hieroglyphs contain portions of Utterance 262, calling on the gods to recognize the deceased king.

1881
A Votive *Shabti* of Ptahmose, Mayor of Thebes

This exceptional, polychrome faience *shabti* figure (Cairo CG 48406), dating from the reign of Amenophis III, comes not from the tomb of its owner, the mayor and vizier Ptahmose, but from the North Cemetery at Abydos. Ptahmose had dedicated it here in the hope of benefiting from a closer association with the local god, Osiris. In perfect condition, it was found by Mariette's workers in 1881.

The primary interest of the piece is artistic and technical: *shabti* figures of this sophistication are seldom encountered. Two comparable examples, made for the lady of the house Sati, in Brooklyn (37.123E; 37.124E), are reported to have been discovered at Saqqara; while a third, prepared for the god's father Ay, Tutankhamun's successor, before his accession, has been in private hands for many years.

1881
The Wilbour Plaque

The American journalist and amateur Egyptologist Charles Edwin Wilbour wintered regularly in Egypt from 1880 until his death, copying inscriptions and collecting the odd antiquity. This spectacular object (Brooklyn 16.48) – a sculptor's trial depicting Akhenaten and Nefertiti – was kicked up at el-Amarna by a local villager; Wilbour bought it for the princely sum of 22 piastres on 22 December 1881 as an early Christmas present to himself. It was one of the first significant pieces of portable Amarna art to surface since the days of Lepsius but, with the systematic exploration of the site by Flinders Petrie and others (•pp. 83, 134), would mark the beginning of a veritable flood of sculpture over coming decades.

1881–1914
SECTION III
THE GLORY YEARS

Auguste Mariette died in 1881, to be succeeded by his nominated heir and assistant, Gaston Camille Charles Maspero. The new director was cast in quite a different mould from his gruff predecessor: Professor of Egyptology at the Collège de France, Paris, since 1874, and Director of the French Archaeological Institute in Cairo, Maspero was a man of great charm, combining the skills of the true scholar with those of an immensely capable administrator and diplomat. Following his first meeting with the young Egyptologist at the 1867 Paris exhibition, Mariette had presciently remarked: 'He will go far'.

Maspero's inheritance seemed initially an uncertain one. Egypt, deep in debt as a result of Khedive Ismail's high-spending, had been placed under dual Anglo-French rule in 1879 – with English control of the country's finances under Sir Evelyn Baring, and French direction of culture (law, education and archaeology) through the Ministry of Public Works. Now, in 1882, increasing nationalist unrest threatened to upset the apple cart – resulting in the infamous bombardment of Alexandria by the British and French navies to quell what had rapidly broken into open revolt. This action was followed by the reinstallation of the Khedive and the imposition of British military rule, destined to remain in place for the next three-quarters of a century; the pay-off for the French would be their continuing control over Egypt's ancient past.

Ultimately, therefore, Maspero's position was secured, his office properly financed for the first time, and the scene set for a massive expansion in controlled excavation. Under his increasingly relaxed supervision – spanning the years 1881–86 and 1899–1914, sandwiching the directorships of a stream of lesser men – the archaeological exploration of the Nile Valley was set on an international footing, with generous official divisions of 'duplicates' from what was found to act as an incentive to further work. This was to be Egyptology's golden age – the era of Flinders Petrie and Wallis Budge, Theodore Davis, Lord Carnarvon and Howard Carter; a time of tourists and grandees, collectors and forgers, scholars, rogues and some of the greatest discoveries the world has ever seen.

Prince Mesehti's formidable Egyptian bodyguard – a wooden model from his 11th-Dynasty tomb uncovered by locals at Asyut, Middle Egypt (•p. 87).

ROYAL MUMMIES:
THE DEIR EL-BAHRI CACHE
Before 1881 New Light on Egyptian Medical Science

GASTON CAMILLE CHARLES MASPERO
(1846–1916)

'He was not only an accomplished Egyptologist, but he possessed all the tradition of his great predecessor Mariette. He understood the natives very well, and he could talk colloquial Arabic as well as a donkey-boy, and used tact and sympathy in dealing with them, except on a few occasions – e.g. the torturing of natives at Kanâ [in connection with the finding of the royal mummies].'
E. A. WALLIS BUDGE

- Born Paris, 24 June 1846
- First becomes interested in Egyptology age 14; introduced to Mariette in 1867
- Professor, Écoles des Hautes Études, Paris, 1869; doctorate 1873; Professor of Egyptian Philology and Archaeology, Collège de France, 1874
- Director of French archaeological mission, Cairo, 1880
- Director of Antiquities and Bulaq Museum, 1881–86 and 1899–1914, involved in several important discoveries – including the Pyramid Texts (•p. 60), the first cache of royal mummies, the tomb of Sennudjem (•p. 69), and excavations in the Valley of the Kings (•p. 113)
- Dies Paris, 30 June 1916

Discovery/excavation
before 1881
by
Émile Brugsch

Site
Thebes (Deir el-Bahri, tomb DB320)

Period
Second Intermediate Period–Third Intermediate Period, 17th–22nd Dynasties, c. 1500–c. 900 BC

'For the last ten years or more it had been suspected that the Theban Arabs (whose main occupation is tomb-pillage and mummy-snatching) had found a Royal sepulchre. Objects of great rarity and antiquity were being brought to Europe every season by travellers who had purchased them from native dealers living on the spot; and many of these objects were historically traceable to certain Royal dynasties which made Thebes their capital city. Some of the travellers were also dealers, and resold their purchases to the British Museum and the Louvre. At length suspicion became certainty ....'
AMELIA B. EDWARDS

The discovery in 1881 of a tomb containing the mummies of some of ancient Egypt's greatest rulers was made quite by chance, in the bay of the Deir el-Bahri cliffs on the Theban west bank, by the straying goat of a local family. Attracted by the animal's bleating, Ahmed Abd el-Rassul found that the creature had fallen down one of the vertical tomb-shafts which honeycomb the area. Cursing, he descended after it to find himself in a cramped corridor cluttered with dark shapes; lighting a candle, the shapes came into focus – an amazing vision of dusty wooden coffins, stretching as far as the eye could see, heaped one upon another. Nor were these ordinary coffins: the occasional *uraeus*, the royal cobra, mounted on the brow, and several cartouches in the identifying texts inscribed on the lids, showed clearly that Abd el-Rassul's goat had stumbled into a tomb filled with kings.

Ahmed and his brothers Muhammad and Hussein managed to keep their find secret for several years. The quantity of important objects leaking out on to the Luxor antiquities market, however – including papyri, *shabti*-figures, bronze vessels, inscribed wrappings and at least one mummy (perhaps that of the missing Ramesses I), said to have been thrown into the Nile by its faint-hearted purchaser – inevitably brought the discovery to the attention of the authorities. The trail led directly to the door of the Abd el-Rassuls; and, following a brutal interrogation of the brothers (one of whom, Hussein

(above) The simple, white-painted coffin prepared for the reburial of Tuthmosis II at the end of the New Kingdom.

(opposite above) Unpacking the royal dead in the Bulaq Museum: an early photograph showing the 18th-Dynasty coffin of Ahmose, its lid removed to reveal the wrapped and heavily garlanded mummy within.

(left) Émile Brugsch, Gaston Maspero and the Abd el-Rassuls at the entrance to the Deir el-Bahri tomb shaft.

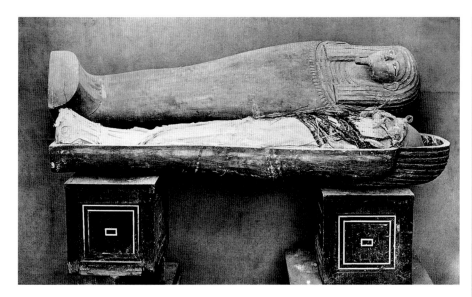

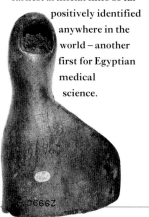

Abd el-Rassul, is never heard of again) by Daoud Pasha, *mudir* of Qena, Muhammad decided to confess. The family had already profited handsomely from the discovery, and there was, after all, more cash to be had for information on the find.

Gaston Maspero, the newly appointed Director of Mariette's Service des Antiquités, was absent in France when the *dénouement* finally came, and the investigation of Muhammad Abd el-Rassul's claims fell to Émile Brugsch (•p. 60), then an assistant in the museum at Bulaq. The date was 6 July 1881, with the heat of the Egyptian summer at its most merciless. Lowered down into the crumbling tomb-shaft, Brugsch soon forgot any discomfort as he surveyed the scene which met his eyes: he recalled how he found himself, as if in a dream, in a low corridor piled high with 'cases of porcelain funerary offerings, metal and alabaster vessels, draperies and trinkets, until, reaching [a] turn in the passage, a cluster of mummy cases came into view in such numbers as to stagger me'.

> '*Collecting my senses, I made the best examination of them I could by the light of my torch, and at once saw that they contained the mummies of royal personages of both sexes; and yet that was not all. Plunging on ahead of my guide, I came to the [end] chamber ... and there standing against the walls or here lying on the floor, I found even a greater number of mummy-cases of stupendous size and weight.*
>
> *Their gold coverings and their polished surfaces so plainly reflected my own excited visage that it seemed as though I was looking into the faces of my own ancestors.*'

The find was unprecedented and, as rumours of the discovery quickly spread, the locals grew restless. Brugsch realized that swift and decisive action was called for, and within a matter of days the tomb was emptied and its occupants – in excess of 50 kings, queens, lesser royals and courtiers, together with almost 6,000 accompanying objects – sent on their way by museum steamer (taxed *en route* as dried fish) to Bulaq.

(below) Among the smaller objects recovered from the cache were cups of faience and glass, *shabti*-figures and a varied range of containers for the embalmed viscera of the royal and noble dead.

(right) The location of the cache in relation to Hatshepsut's famous mortuary temple, and (at a larger scale) the sketch plan published by Brugsch and Maspero which shows the peculiarly attenuated form of the tomb.

Before 1881 New Light on Egyptian Medical Science

This rare medical appurtenance – a prosthetic big toe showing signs of having been worn in life – was found at Thebes in position on a mummy sometime before 1881, when it was acquired by the British Museum (EA 29996). The splicing discernible in the threads of the cartonnage's linen base suggest a date before *c.* 600 BC; it is very probably several centuries older still. Together with a closely similar prosthesis in wood recently discovered by a German team on an intrusive mummy of probable Third Intermediate Period date from Sheikh Abd el-Qurna tomb TT95, it represents the earliest artificial limb so far positively identified anywhere in the world – another first for Egyptian medical science.

KINGS IN THE DEIR EL-BAHRI CACHE
(Lesser royals, high priests and private individuals omitted)

NAME	MUMMY	COFFIN	NAME	MUMMY	COFFIN
Seqenenre-Taa	•	•	Ramesses I		•
Amosis I	•	•	Sethos I	•	•
Amenophis I	•	•	Ramesses II	•	•
Tuthmosis I	•?	•*	Ramesses III	•	•
Tuthmosis II	•	•	Ramesses IX	•	
Tuthmosis III	•	•			

*Original coffins reused for the reburial of the high priest of Amun Pinudjem I

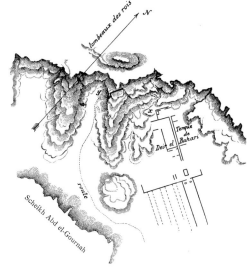

The history of the cache

The discovery of so many kings, lesser royals and retainers within a single tomb came as a surprise to the scholarly community, who were equally puzzled by the poor quality and condition of the coffins in which the royal dead were contained, as well as the general lack of associated burial furnishings – for the pre-21st-Dynasty mummies at least. Study of the dockets which a number of the coffins and bandaged mummies carried eventually revealed all:

'Year 15, 3rd month of akhet-season, day 6: Day of bringing the Osiris king Usermaatre-setepenre [Ramesses II] life! prosperity! health! to renew him and to bury him in the tomb of the Osiris king Menmaatre-Sety [I] life! prosperity! health! by the high priest of Pinudjem.'

This docket, written in ink on the bandages of the mummy of Ramesses II, indicated clearly what had occurred: the king's mummy had in antiquity been removed from his own tomb for reburial in that of Sethos I, KV17 (•p. 21), nearby; and, as other dockets associated with these two kings would reveal, they and the mummy of Ramesses I had subsequently been removed from the tomb of Sethos I for reburial within the tomb of Queen Inhapy. The reason Egypt's greatest kings were so shoddily presented was that they had been unceremoniously moved around over a period of several hundred years at the start of the first millennium BC, losing most of their original burial equipment along the way.

The final resting place of the New Kingdom royal dead, DB320, is now recognized as the family vault of the Theban high priest Pinudjem II, whose relations – their mummies for the most part undefiled and contained in coffins glinting still with thick gold leaf – occupied the end chamber of Abd el-Rassul's tomb. The battered mummies which later joined them were introduced several decades later, after Year 11 of Shoshenq I of the 22nd Dynasty.

For Maspero, who published his report on the royal cache – *Les momies royales de Déir el-Baharî* – in 1889, the repeated moves and cachings had been prompted by the ceaseless attentions of robbers at the end of the New Kingdom. Egyptologists today, however, recognize that the stripping of the dead was the work not of local robbers, but of the state, hungry for bullion at a time of serious economic decline. Not a few of the earlier kings' funerary jewels and equipment would later turn up, reused, in the Tanis burials of their 21st- and 22nd-Dynasty successors (•p. 189).

The discovery of the royal mummies caused an international sensation. Archaeologists could hardly believe their good fortune. Before 1881, the kings of Egypt had been mere names attached to statues, reliefs and the odd papyrus; now it was possible to gaze upon the face, even touch the skin, of Pharaoh himself. And there were further discoveries of this same sort still to come (•p. 103).

(below) The well-preserved coffin of Astemkheb, daughter of the high priest Menkheperre and probably a lesser wife of the high priest Pinudjem II – discovered with the bulk of the Third Intermediate Period dead within the principal burial chamber of the DB320 cache.

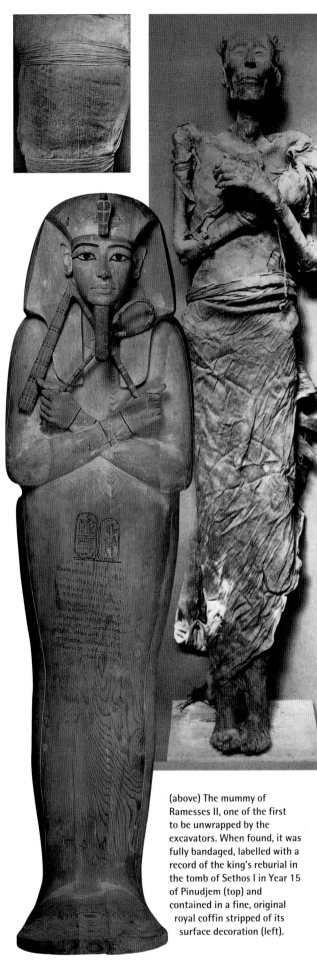

(above) The mummy of Ramesses II, one of the first to be unwrapped by the excavators. When found, it was fully bandaged, labelled with a record of the king's reburial in the tomb of Sethos I in Year 15 of Pinudjem (top) and contained in a fine, original royal coffin stripped of its surface decoration (left).

GREEKS IN EGYPT: NAUKRATIS

Discovery/excavation
1883
by
W. M. Flinders Petrie

Site
el-Nebira (Naukratis)

Period
Late Period, 26th Dynasty,
reign of Amasis, 570–526 BC,
and after

'[Here at el-Nebira] I met a sight which I had never hoped for – almost too strange to believe. Before me lay a long low mound of town ruins, of which all the core had been dug out by the natives for earth …. Wherever I walked in this crater I trod on pieces of archaic Greek pottery ….'
W. M. FLINDERS PETRIE

William Matthew Flinders Petrie, a brilliant young Englishman of a strongly practical turn of mind, first visited Egypt in 1880 to test the veracity of the theories of that band later labelled 'pyramidiots' – those who, like the Astronomer Royal of Scotland, Charles Piazzi Smyth, sought in the dimensions of the Great Pyramid some hitherto unrecognized divine truth. Petrie's sober measurements and calculations soon laid to rest that fantasy, and the young excavator, his eyes now opened to the potential of Egyptian exploration, set off in search of new challenges in this land of antiquarian opportunity.

Petrie's appearance on the Egyptological scene was like a breath of fresh air. His predecessors had had as their aim, without exception, the discovery of monuments and large statues; what attracted Petrie were the lesser finds – the broken detritus of everyday living, the pots, pans, beads, amulets and other curiosities which were generally passed over without comment or missed altogether in the massive earth-moving operations of the day (at which Petrie's early rival, the Swiss Édouard Naville, was a master). Petrie instinctively recognized the immense potential of such modest material – and later brilliantly proved, through his development of sequence dating (•p. 94), how valuable such mundane, repetitive finds, properly studied, could be.

The results of Petrie's first decade of work, carried out in part independently (with private sponsorship) and in part for the Egypt Exploration Fund, were in due course published in his eminently readable *Ten Years' Digging in Egypt, 1881–1891*. And of the many magical moments this book records, none displays the man's enviable combination of luck and intuition better than his finding of Greeks in the Nile Delta.

Flinders Petrie first came across his Greek settlement mound, littered, as it seemed, with the 'smashings of the Museum's vase-rooms', close to the villages of el-Nibeira, el-

(right) Restored pottery cup with multiple eyes –
c. 575–550 BC, from Naukratis. The vessel carries a scratched dedication to Aphrodite by a certain Rhoikos – who has been identified as the architect of the temple of Hera on Samos.

WILLIAM MATTHEW FLINDERS PETRIE
(1853–1942)

'T. E. Lawrence, who was one of his students, commented that "a Petrie dig is a thing with a flavour of its own"; the same remark could apply to his whole life …'
MARGARET S. DROWER

- Born Charlton, 3 June 1853
- Inspired by the Astronomer Royal of Scotland, Charles Piazzi Smyth, visits Egypt in 1880 to survey the Giza pyramids; converts from pyramidology to archaeology
- Digs for the Egypt Exploration Fund, 1884–86, as assistant to Édouard Naville
- Independent fieldwork 1887 on; establishes Egyptian Research Account, 1894, subsequently British School of Archaeology in Egypt; rejoins EEF, 1896–1905
- First Edwards Professor of Egyptology, University College London, 1892–1933
- Excavator of numerous sites in Egypt and Palestine, and author of more than 1,000 books, articles and reviews; founder and editor of the journal *Ancient Egypt*; his massive collection of Egyptian antiquities is now in the Petrie Museum at University College London
- His many triumphs include the discovery of Naukratis, the invention of sequence dating (•p. 94), the salvage of the Abydos archaic royal tombs (•p. 109), the proto-Sinaitic script (•p. 124) and the el-Lahun jewels (•p. 138)
- Dies Jerusalem, 28 July 1942; his head detached and returned for study to England

4000 BC
3000 BC
2000 BC
1000 BC
0
AD 700

Gieif and el-Niqrash in 1883 in the course of following up a lead offered by the chance purchase in Cairo of an Archaic Greek statuette. Nothing like the site had ever been found before, and Petrie's imagination raced at the prospects. Not until 1884, however, was he able to return with his young acolyte, Francis Llewellyn Griffith, to explore the place on behalf of the Egypt Exploration Fund, 'determined to understand its history'.

As it happened, the secret of the mound would be revealed to Petrie far sooner than he could have hoped:

'The only place that I could find to live in about there was an old country house of a pasha; and, while looking at it, I noticed two blocks of dark grey stone by the side of the entrance. Turning one of them over, I there saw ... a decree of the city of Naukratis ... [T]he unknown town now had a name ...'

Naukratis! The Greek trading centre mentioned by the Greek historian Herodotus, which the great Heinrich Schliemann, excavator of Troy, had himself been anxious to find and dig up. 'All that day "Naukratis" rang in my mind, and I sprang over the mounds with that splendid exultation of a new discovery, long wished for and well found.'

Herodotus, who visited the town in the middle years of the 5th century BC, devotes several paragraphs to a description of it. He records that the Egyptian king Amasis (570–526 BC) gave Naukratis to his Greek mercenaries 'as a commercial headquarters for any who wished to settle in the country' and 'made grants of land upon which Greek traders who did not wish to live permanently in Egypt might erect altars and temples'. An existing settlement with an established, largely East Greek presence dating back perhaps to Psammetichus I, in the 7th century BC, the city was in effect granted a monopoly on Greek trade – primarily silver and other Mediterranean commodities (such as olive oil) in return for Egyptian

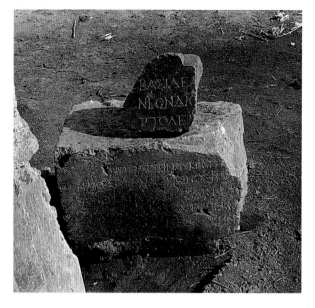

(left) Block recording (in Greek) the dedication of a statue to Heliodorus by the inhabitants of Naukratis – key to the identity of Petrie's extraordinary site.

(below) Evidence of Greek occupation: fragments of classical architectural ornamentation recovered by the Egypt Exploration Fund from the site of the second Apollo temple.

corn, linen and papyrus. And Naukratis certainly flourished – not only under the Saite kings but through the Persian period as well, until eventually superseded by the new foundation of Alexandria (•p. 232) in the 4th century BC.

Material finds would be numerous, but perhaps the most intriguing were the inscriptions incised with a point or inscribed in ink on vessels dedicated at one or other of the town's several Greek sanctuaries – of Apollo, Aphrodite, Hera and the Dioskouroi. A number of these vessels were seemingly offered by individuals well-known from history, with texts (we may guess) actually written in their own hands. The list includes not only the architect of the temple of Hera on Samos, Rhoikos, and the mercenary Phanes of Halicarnassus (whom Herodotus records as deserting Amasis for the Persians) but – the most amazing of all – an autograph of the father of history himself, Herodotus: a fragment of an Attic cup with his name on was found in 1903 by one of Petrie's successors at the site, D. G. Hogarth, during his excavation of the Hellenion.

(above) Inscription from the base of an Attic cup with the name 'He[ro]dotus' – conceivably the famous Greek historian who visited and wrote on this site during the 5th century BC.

(left) Unfinished sandstone relief of a warrior wearing a crested Corinthian helmet and carrying a shield and spear. Found near a shrine of Aphrodite in the Hellenion precinct during a later season at the site, 1899.

THE TOMB OF SENNUDJEM,
SERVANT IN THE PLACE OF TRUTH

Discovery/excavation
1886
by
Salam Abu Duhi; Gaston
Maspero

Site
Thebes
(Deir el-Medina, tomb TT1)

Period
New Kingdom, 19th Dynasty,
reign of Sethos I,
1306–1290 BC

'At five in the evening, 1st February [1886], just as we had returned from an excursion to the nearby ruins of Karnak, a miserable-looking bedouin, burned by the sun and his body barely covered … presented himself …. He had come to inform us of the discovery, made a few hours previously in the Theban necropolis, of an intact tomb still closed by the same door … the ancient Egyptians had pushed to after depositing the last body ….'
EDUARDO TODA Y GÜELL

The tomb of Sennudjem (no. TT1) ranks with the royal mummies at Deir el-Bahri (•p. 64) as one of the great discoveries of Maspero's first period as Director of the Egyptian Antiquities Service. The find was made by a bedouin, Salam Abu Duhi, and two companions who, after seven days of digging under Government license, entered the underground chambers of an intact tomb concealed beneath the debris of later burials. Maspero, together with the Spanish Consul-General, Eduardo Toda y Güell (to whom we owe an important account of the discovery), hurried to investigate, with fellow guests Urbain Bouriant and the dealer/photographer Jan Herman Insinger.

The only feature visible at ground level was the opening of the tomb's rock-cut entrance pit, just 4 m (13 ft) deep, with ancient hand-holes cut into two sides to facilitate the ancients' ascent and descent. At the bottom of this pit the explorers were faced with a narrow, sloping passage; beyond lay a small, undecorated chamber cut in very poor rock. Another pit, cut close to the west wall of this chamber, gave access to a second gallery, at the end of which lay the burial chamber itself. 'It was clear', wrote Toda, 'that we were in the presence of one of those rare tombs which … had escaped the depredations of the Romans, the Copts and the Arabs': for the beautifully painted wooden door (now Cairo JE 27303) separating death from the world of the living was still in place, closed with a sealed bolt, perfect and untouched by the passing of more than three millennia.

Hurriedly making notes in the airless, 48°C (118°F) heat, Maspero and his colleagues dismantled the door frame and entered the realms of the dead. The silent burial chamber was small, no more than 5 m (16½ ft) in length and half as wide, with a vaulted ceiling. Toda vividly records what the excavators' trembling candles revealed:

'The ground was covered with bodies: nine of them enclosed in their sycamore caskets, and eleven stretched out on the sand. In the corners one could see piles of pottery vases, bread, fruit, furniture, of garlands of desiccated flowers. Close to the wall were placed two funerary sleds, probably those left by the retinue of the last interment wishing to leave the tomb as quickly as possible. But our attention was principally drawn by the paintings decorating the four walls and the ceiling of the sepulchre, which had been preserved as fresh and intact as the day, long ago, they were first made.'

(left) The west wall of the small but exquisite vaulted burial chamber prepared for the family of Sennudjem: the deceased and his wife, Iyneferti, raise their hands in adoration before the gods of the Underworld.

4000 BC

3000 BC

2000 BC

1000 BC

0

AD 700

69

This tomb was, in fact, the first substantial, intact burial of dynastic date to have been found in Egypt since the days of Drovetti (•p. 29) – who had recorded virtually nothing coherent of his many discoveries. Sixty years later, and well aware of their predecessors' deficiencies, Maspero and his team worked methodically, taking notes, clearing the chamber systematically and arranging the removal of the tomb's occupants to the Museum boat for transport, with the tomb door, to Cairo. Despite their caution, however, there were extensive losses: a number of pieces were stolen, damaged or destroyed completely *en route* to Maspero's steamer – and of the 11 fragile, uncoffined mummies, only the heads reached the shore.

Whose tomb?

The principal owner of Salam Abu Duhi's tomb, as the inscriptions and the wall decorations revealed, was the 'servant' (literally 'one who hears the call') 'in the Place of Truth, Sennudjem', a workman employed on the cutting, decoration and equipping of the royal tombs in the Valley of the Kings and the Valley of the Queens. Moderately well off by local standards, he and his family – a wife, seven sons, four daughters, two daughters-in-law and several grandchildren – were able to call upon the skills of the talented fellow craftsmen with whom they shared their lives in the workmen's settlement at Deir el-Medina (•p. 174). And, as we see today from the tomb's wonderful burial furniture, Sennudjem's contacts served him well.

(left) Although the bulk of the antiquities recovered from the Sennudjem family vault are now in Cairo, objects from the burial are also in the Berlin Museum, the Metropolitan Museum of Art, New York (which acquired 29 objects in the discovery year), the Pushkin Museum in Moscow, and Madrid. Here we see the upper part of the inner coffin lid of Khonsu, Sennudjem's son, now in New York.

(left) Detail from the funerary sledge containing the coffined mummy of Sennudjem's son, Khonsu: the mummified deceased is tended by Anubis, god of embalming, under the watchful gaze of the divine sisters Isis and Nephthys.

Sennudjem and his family lived during the reign of the 19th-Dynasty pharaoh Sethos I (with the preparation of whose tomb – •p. 21 – the man was no doubt closely involved), a period for which surviving burials are uncommon. Despite its less than perfect salvage, therefore, the discovery sheds important light on the funerary customs of the period's would-be middling classes. An interesting comparison may be made with the tomb of Kha (•p. 126), a better-off and rather more privileged predecessor of Sennudjem, with its abundance of precious and not so precious metals, cosmetics and linens – though we may speculate as to what, of these commodities, originally placed in the Sennudjem family vault, had been stolen by successive burial parties as and when later bodies were added to the tomb.

The arrival of Grébaut

Shortly after the discovery of Sennudjem's tomb, Gaston Maspero returned to France due to ill-health. Though his wish was to be succeeded by the Swiss Édouard Naville, the candidate's nationality ruled against him; Maspero's place was instead taken by another Frenchman, Eugène Grébaut, a former student who had held the post of Director of the French Archaeological Mission in Cairo since 1883. It was to prove an unhappy choice.

As Egyptology's official biographical record remarks, Grébaut's 'appointment was unfortunate as he was by nature unsuited to the work and' – simply by applying the rules – 'caused much ill feeling both with Egyptologists and local Egyptians'. His contemporaries were more forthright: for Petrie, he was anti-English and 'out of all reason'; while for Budge, 'all those who had at heart the progress of Egyptology, and the welfare of the National Collection in Egypt, regretted the appointment'.

One of Grébaut's main accomplishments was the transfer of Mariette's collection from Bulaq to a new museum at Giza. But much was 'lost' on the way. Politically, it was an unhappy time for all – but in the field it was business as usual.

(below) Sennudjem, servant in the Place of Truth, ploughs the fields of the mythical hereafter, accompanied by his wife Iyneferti.

THE FAMILY VAULT OF SENNUDJEM

NAME	STATUS	DESCRIPTION OF OBJECTS
Amennekhu		mummy, *shabti*
Hathor		coffin, mummy
Hetepu		mummy, *shabti*
Isis		coffin, mummy, canopic chest, box
Iyneferti	wife of Sennudjem	coffins (2), mask, mummy, canopic chest, *shabtis* (4), boxes (6), stools (2)
Khabekhenet		mummy, canopic chest, *shabti*-coffins (2), *shabtis* (2), boxes (6)
Khonsu	son of Sennudjem	outer coffin on sledge, coffins (2), mask, pectoral, mummy, canopic chest, *shabti*-box, *shabtis* (13), boxes (4), staves (3)
Mose		mummy, *shabtis* (5), stools (2)
Paraemnekhu		mummy, *shabti*-box
Parahetep		coffin, mummy, *shabti*
Ramose		coffin, mummy, *shabti*-box, *shabtis* (3), box
Sennudjem	tomb owner	outer coffin on sledge, coffins (2), masks (2), pectorals (3), mummy, canopic chest, *shabti*-coffins (4), *shabtis* (9), bed, chair, stool, pottery vessels (5), staves (6), architect's instruments (4)
Tameket	wife of Khonsu	coffins (2), mummy, canopic chest, *shabtis* (4)
Tashesen		coffin, mummy, *shabti*
ownership uncertain		coffins (2), pectoral, mummies (6), *shabti*, *shabti*-boxes (7), stool, offering table, pottery vessels (7), baskets (2), fringed textile, linen, sandals (pair), architect's instruments (3), box, limestone ostracon with 'Story of Sinuhe', food provisions (bread, biscuits, eggs, dates, dom-fruits, corn, water, milk, wine), floral garlands (3)

1887
PHARAOH'S DIPLOMATIC ARCHIVE: THE AMARNA LETTERS

Before 1887 The Berlin Green Head
1888 The Statue of Hetepdief • 1887 Foreign Tribute
Before 1888 Wallis Budge and the Book of the Dead

ERNEST ALFRED THOMPSON WALLIS BUDGE (1857–1934)

- Born Bodmin, 27 July 1857
- Studies Egyptian under Samuel Birch at the British Museum, 1870–78
- Christ's College, Cambridge, 1879–82; enters British Museum 1883, Keeper Department of Egyptian and Assyrian Antiquities, 1894–1924
- Excavated Aswan, and Gebel Barkal, Meroe, Semna and other Nubian sites; also at Nineveh and Der, Iraq
- Prolific author – his books alone exceeding 140 titles
- Dies London, 23 November 1934

Discovery/excavation
1887
by
Egyptian local

Site
el-Amarna (Records Office)

Period
New Kingdom, 18th Dynasty, reigns of Amenophis III-Tutankhamun?, 1391-1323 BC

'Whilst the official arrangements for my Mission to Baghdâd were being made, I received information from a native in Egypt that some very important discoveries ... had [recently] been made ... [A] native woman had discovered at Tall al-'Amârnah, by accident, a large box full of pieces of clay, with what [the informant] thought was writing on both sides of each piece. He and his friends had secured a great many of them, and some dealers said that the pieces of clay were like the little blocks of clay which had been brought to Cairo from Baghdâd a few years ago, and that the marks on back and front were kitba mismârî, *"nail-writing",* i.e. *cuneiform ....'*

E. A. WALLIS BUDGE

The discovery of the el-Amarna archive – more than 300 pillow-shaped clay tablets (since augmented by subsequent finds to a current total of 382) bearing inscriptions in the impressed, wedge-shaped script of Egypt's Near Eastern neighbours – reads, as so much in the history of Egyptian exploration, like a fairy story. Nothing of the kind had ever before been found on the banks of the river Nile, and, because the clay tablets looked so unpromising – in appearance they are not dissimilar to stale dog biscuits – the discoverer had been pleased to sell those she did not destroy to a neighbour for a modest 10 piastres.

(below) Amarna letter EA 19, from Tushratta, king of Mitanni, to Amenophis III: 'May my brother send me ... much more gold than he did to my father. In my brother's country, gold is as plentiful as dirt'.

(right) 'To the king [Akhenaten], my lord, my god ... Message of Yapakhu, ruler of Gazru [Gezer] ... May the king, my lord the Sun from the sky, take thought for his land ... lest the Apiru destroy us' Amarna letter EA299.

(below) Petrie's own plan of the building which he excavated and identified as the findspot of the Amarna archive.

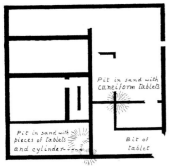

(below) Complex of buildings, the walls still remarkably well preserved, close to the virtually destroyed Records Office where the Amarna letters were first found.

At the time of the discovery the man best equipped to pass comment on such a find, the Revd Professor Archibald Henry Sayce, was absent from Egypt; a few samples were therefore taken to France to be shown to the eminent but by then virtually blind French Assyriologist Jules Oppert, who dismissed them as obvious fakes.

Others, optically better equipped than the elderly M. Oppert, were more astute in their assessment – among them the wily E. A. Wallis Budge, then an Assistant Curator at the British Museum. Unusually for an Egyptologist, Budge had a working knowledge of cuneiform, and, unlike his older colleague, he realized at once the significance of what he was looking at, as he recorded in his memoirs:

'On the largest and best written ... I was able to make out the words "A-na Ni-ib-mu-a-ri-ya," i.e., "To Nib-muariya", and on another the words "[A]-na Ni-im-mu-ri-ya shar mâtu Mi-is-ri," i.e., "to Nimmuriya, king of the land of Egypt" .... I felt certain that the tablets were both genuine and of very great historical importance.'

The king in question was Amenophis III, father of the 'heretic' pharaoh Akhenaten (Amenophis IV) by whose command the new city of Akhetaten had been built on the el-Amarna plain.

Budge decided at once to purchase what he had been shown, and in this his instincts were good: for what the unknown Egyptian woman had uncovered turned out to be part of a unique diplomatic archive dating from the middle years of the 2nd millennium BC. Following Budge's authentication, news of the tablets' significance quickly leaked out – and the remaining pieces from the hoard were immediately snapped up by the Berlin Museum, the Louvre, and the Egyptian Museum at Bulaq.

The first Egyptologist to locate the actual findspot of the tablets was Flinders Petrie (•p. 67). Digging at el-Amarna in 1891 (•p. 83), close to the King's House (the private quarters of Pharaoh), Petrie turned his attention to a building which had been 'shewn to Prof. Sayce in a previous year as the place where the tablets were found'. The identification of this building as the original location of the tablets was confirmed when Petrie turned up yet more 'in a chamber, and two rubbish pits'.

It was not until some years later, however, that the precise nature of the building Petrie had dug was revealed. Both Percy Newberry, during a visit to the site made in 1895, and J. D. S. Pendlebury, digging on behalf of the Egypt Exploration Society in 1933–34, subsequently observed that it had been built with mud-bricks stamped 'The House of Correspondence of Pharaoh, life! prosperity! health!'. What Petrie had uncovered – no less – were the ruins of the ancient Egyptian foreign office

Sadly, even by Pendlebury's time 'It has been much ruined owing to the hopes of successive generations that more tablets would come to light. The walls are so broken that it is hard to see where the original entrance was situated and the walls have almost entirely disappeared'.

Before **1887**
The Berlin
Green Head

Dating from the 1st century BC, this extraordinary head (Berlin 12500), carved in green stone, is without doubt the masterpiece of its type. It was discovered by local Egyptians, but where and precisely when are unrecorded.

By 1887 it was in the collection of Prince Ibrahim Hilmy, and passed in that same year to the faience connoisseur Henry Wallis. Egyptologists still hope that the statue from which it came will one day turn up, to fill in at least some of the gaps in the history and understanding of the piece.

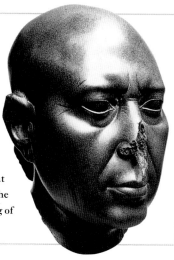

THE AMARNA LETTERS:
What is where now?

LOCATION	NO. OF TABLETS/ FRAGMENTS
[Arkeoloji Müzeleri, Istanbul	1 (found at Tell el-Hesi, Palestine)]
Ashmolean Museum, Oxford	22
British Museum, London	94 (+ 1 fragment belonging to a Berlin tablet)
Cairo Museum	49/50 (+ 1 fragment belonging to a BM tablet)
Louvre, Paris	7
Metropolitan Museum of Art, New York	2
Musée du Cinquantenaire, Brussels	1
Oriental Institute, Chicago	1
?Pushkin Museum, Moscow	3?
Vorderasiatisches Museum, Berlin	202/203 (+ 3 fragments belonging to BM tablets and other unnumbered fragments)
lost (ex-collections Lord Amherst; Jules Oppert)	2

•Of the main Amarna group, A. H. Sayce estimated (perhaps excessively) that as many as 150–200 tablets were destroyed at the time of the discovery

The subject–matter of the tablets

TABLET TYPE	QUANTITY
letters, or inventories attached to letters	350
mythical or epic texts	6
syllabaries	3
lexical texts	5
list of gods	1
tale of Hurrian origin	1
list of Egyptian words in syllabic cuneiform with Babylonian equivalences	1
amuletic text	1
uncertain	14

•Total number of tablets extant: 382

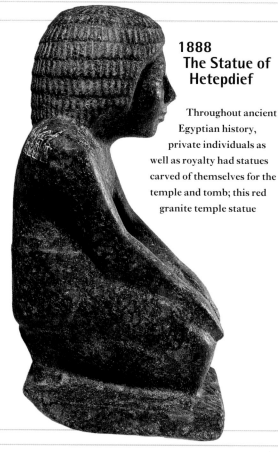

1888
The Statue of
Hetepdief

Throughout ancient Egyptian history, private individuals as well as royalty had statues carved of themselves for the temple and tomb; this red granite temple statue (Cairo CG 1) of a nobleman and functionary by the name of Hetepdief, son of Merydjehuty, holds pride of place as one of the oldest extant. Discovered at Memphis in 1888 and dating from the late 3rd Dynasty, the statue is distinguished by the series of *serekh*-framed names of the first three kings of the preceding 2nd Dynasty – Hetepsekhemwy, Raneb and Ninetjer – carved on the right shoulder. These establish both the cults with which Hetepdief was associated during his lifetime, and, it is usually assumed, the order of succession of these three early rulers.

1887
Foreign Tribute

While we know from various documents, especially the Amarna letters, that politics in the ancient world was driven by diplomatic exchange and the giving of gifts, little physical evidence for the practice has been identified in the archaeological record. Tutankhamun's iron dagger (Cairo JE 61585) is perhaps the most famous object of the class, while another might be the spectacular red jasper lid in the form of a lion-mauled bull (*left*), apparently of mid-2nd millennium BC date, found at el-Amarna and now in the British Museum (EA 22866).

The small head (*right*) of inlaid shell, possibly turbinella, perhaps the stopper from a high-status Syrian oil horn, may be a further import of the same kind. Acquired by the English collector William Joseph Myers in the Luxor area in November 1887, it is now at Eton College (ECM 820).

The contents of the archive

'Send me much gold. And you, for your part, whatever you want from my country, write to me so that it may be taken to you.'
BURRA-BURIYAS, KING OF BABYLON, TO AKHENATEN
(OR TUTANKHAMUN)

There has been much discussion about the content of the Amarna letters. Predominantly written in a provincial form of Babylonian (with a sprinkling of letters in Assyrian, Hurrian and Hittite), the correspondence divides into two principal groups. The first is that with pharaoh's equals – Babylonia, Assyria, Mitanni, Arzawa (to the west of Cilicia), Alashiya (Cyprus) and the land of the Hittites, for the most part seeking to maintain the status quo by the mutual exchange of gifts and the receipt of women into the king's harim.

The second and larger group (including a single tablet subsequently found at the site of Tell el-Hesi) documents the petty rivalries and disputes among Egypt's vassal states in Syria and Palestine. Interestingly, several of the tablets – perhaps the majority if recent analysis of their clay proves accurate – represent copies prepared in Egypt for the files. Syllabaries and lexical texts necessary for the process of composition and interpretation, together with other background reading, were included in the haul.

The el-Amarna archive is generally believed to span a period of between 15 and 30 years, beginning in about Year 30 of Amenophis III (1391–1353 BC); the tablet Budge had first been shown was thus one of the earliest. The letters between equals mention the recipient king by name, revealing that the bulk of this correspondence dates from late in the reign of Amenophis III and continues through the reign of Akhenaten (though perhaps not far beyond). Unfortunately the letters from Egypt's vassals, since they do not mention the Egyptian recipient by name, have to date proved rather more difficult to classify.

Before 1888 Wallis Budge and the Book of the Dead

Despite Egypt's generosity during the late 19th and early 20th centuries in allowing foreign archaeologists to retain a proportion of their excavated finds – the system of division – the purchasing activities of the world's leading museums was to continue virtually unchecked; for it is a sobering fact that the finest antiquities are rarely brought to light in controlled excavation.

One of the most active European buyers of non-excavated pieces was E. A. Wallis Budge, on behalf of the British Museum. Of Budge's many purchases, few can match his acquisition of three of the New Kingdom's finest Books of the Dead – those of Any ('true scribe of the king, his beloved, scribe who reckons the divine offerings of all the gods, overseer of the double granary of the lord of Tawer'); Nu ('estate overseer of the treasurer'); and Anhai ('chantress of Amun … leader of the musicians of Osiris, Nebtu and Khnum'), all now in the British Museum (EA 10470, 10477, 10472).

The 'Book of the Dead' was not a single text but an assortment of spells or 'chapters', with accompanying vignettes, written on rolls of papyrus, vellum or leather. Its purpose was to enable the deceased to pass through the underworld in safety and achieve a carefree existence in the hereafter. Because of the text's importance, great care was often lavished upon it.

Budge's beautifully illuminated manuscripts came to England in 1888, and with a story. Sadly, little credence can be attached to it – they date from three different dynasties: Nu the 18th, Anhai the 19th and Ani the 20th, and so it is unlikely that they come, as Budge claimed, from the same tomb. Equally dubious is his account of what happened next: how, after a brief period of confiscation by the authorities, our rotund and reckless hero retrieved the papyri by digging through the wall of the mud-brick storeroom in which they were being held on the orders of the Antiquities Service chief; or how Budge reached Cairo just one step ahead of his pursuers to place the documents in the hands of the British military; and how, thanks to British Government protection, they eventually reached England.

No more and no less, Budge was the teller of a remarkably good tale – to the amusement, but also distraction, of scholars today.

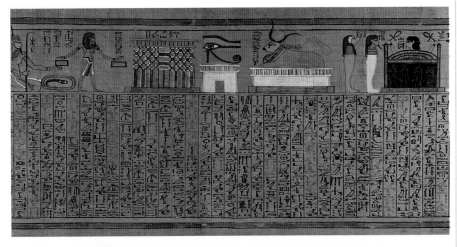

1888

FACES FROM THE PAST: THE FAIYUM PORTRAITS

1888 The Labyrinth • 1888 A Colossal Head of Ammenemes III from Bubastis
1888 The Palace of Amenophis III • 1888 Artists' Sketches from the Valley of the Kings
1889 The Kahun Papyri

Discovery/excavation
1888, 1910–11
by
W. M. Flinders Petrie

Site
Hawara

Period
Roman Period, 1st–3rd
centuries AD

Thanks to several recent exhibitions, the 'Faiyum' portraits – lifelike paintings once bandaged in place over the face of the mummy – are now well established in the popular perception of ancient Egyptian art. Nevertheless, though the first examples were brought back from Egypt as early as 1615 (by the Italian traveller Pietro della Valle; and later, from Thebes, by Henry Salt), it was not until the paintings literally flooded the art market in the 1880s that they caused much of a stir. It was all skilfully stage-managed by an Austrian antiquities dealer, Theodor Graf, who had had the foresight to buy up and exhibit around the world all the portraits dug up by locals in the vicinity of the Faiyum town of el-Rubaiyat – perhaps the ancient cemetery of Mansura. Buyers of Graf portraits included many well-known figures – among them the Viennese founder of psycho-analysis, Sigmund Freud, who owned two from the group. While the few earlier finds of della Valle and Salt were painted in the encaustic (wax) technique, however, the Graf paintings were almost entirely in tempera and were artistically stiff. But a further batch of

(below left) Encaustic portrait of a wide-eyed boy, still bound in with the elegantly wrapped mummy – X-rays of which reveal the corpse to have been in an advanced state of decay. The work dates from the time of Trajan, AD 98–117, and was one of the prizes of Petrie's 1888 season.

(below) Portrait of a jewel-bedecked lady of the early 2nd century AD, again in encaustic, this time from Petrie's later season at Hawara in 1910–11.

As Petrie realized, these colossi had marked the entrance to one of the most famous monuments of antiquity – an enormous mortuary temple of 3,000 rooms known to the Classical authors Herodotus, Diodorus, Strabo and Pliny as the Labyrinth, since reduced to a mound of stone splinters. Excavation revealed that the temple had occupied 'an area about 1000 feet long, and 800 feet broad' – a vast space wherein, Petrie calculated, 'could be erected … all of the temples on the east bank of Thebes, and one of the largest on the west'.

1888
The Labyrinth

'A short work of a few days at Biahmu [in the Faiyum] resolved the question about the so-called pyramids there. So soon as we began to turn over the soil we found chips of sandstone colossi; the second day the gigantic nose of a colossus was found, as broad as a man's body; then pieces of carved thrones, and a fragment of inscription of [Ammenemes] III. It was evident that the two great piles of stone had been the pedestals of colossal seated statues, carved in hard quartzite sandstone, and brilliantly polished… The total height of the colossi was about sixty feet from the ground'

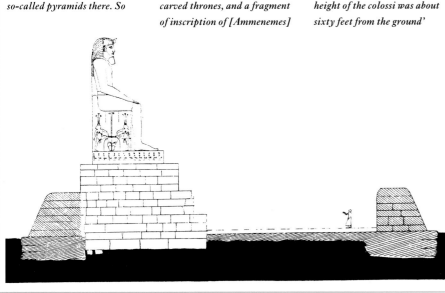

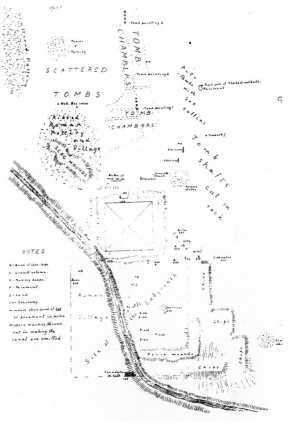

1888
A Colossal Head of Ammenemes III from Bubastis

One of Gaston Maspero's greatest admirers was the English author Amelia B. Edwards who, having first travelled up the Nile in the 1870s, fell in love with Egypt and determined to devote her life to the investigation and preservation of its antiquities. As a result of her energetic efforts, both in England and abroad, the Egypt Exploration Fund (EEF) was established in 1882, with the particular aim of exploring the Delta and digging sites of potential biblical interest.

One masterpiece from these early EEF excavations is this colossal and powerfully carved black granite head (British Museum EA 1063), originally with lifelike, inlaid eyes. It is now recognized as a portrait of a Middle Kingdom king, Ammenemes III, builder of the Labyrinth; at the time of discovery, however, it was thought to be of Hyksos date, by analogy with the peculiar sphinxes and other statues first discovered by Mariette at Tanis and elsewhere (•p. 53). The British Museum head was dug up by the EEF's principal excavator, Édouard Naville, at Bubastis (Tell Basta) in 1888, where the complete statue had been usurped, with its pair (now in Cairo, CG 383+540), by Osorkon II of the 22nd Dynasty.

the aesthetically more pleasing encaustic portraits was on its way – and now, for the first time, something would be learnt about their ancient context.

The year was 1888, and the young Flinders Petrie (•p. 67) had just arrived to begin work at the Faiyum site of Hawara:

> 'So soon as I went there I observed a cemetery on the north of the pyramid [of Ammenemes III]; on digging in it I soon saw that it was all Roman ... and I was going to give it up as not worth working, when one day a mummy was found, with a painted portrait on a wooden panel placed over its face. This was a beautifully drawn head of a girl, in soft grey tints, entirely classical in its style and mode, without any Egyptian influence. More men were put on to this region, and in two days another portrait-mummy was found; in two days more, a third, and then for nine days not one; an anxious waiting, suddenly rewarded by finding three ... Altogether sixty were found in clearing this cemetery, some much decayed and worthless, others as fresh as the day they were painted.'

Petrie would return to the site a few years later, reaping a similarly rich harvest.

Despite the numbers of portraits recovered, only a tiny proportion – 1 to 2 per cent – of the Roman burials from the site had been provided with them.

Petrie believed that these paintings had occasionally been commissioned during life and framed for display, though this conclusion is now questioned, as is his idea that the mummies with portraits in place were 'kept above ground for many years in rooms, probably connected with the house'. Most of the portraits have now been detached from their mummies. Yet they provide still a wealth of information about the clothing, adornment and physical characteristics of Egypt's wealthier inhabitants during Roman times.

(left) Gaudy mummy portrait of a young girl, from the 1888–89 season, still in place in the heavily gilded and gem-inlaid plaster mummy carapace, modelled in high relief with traditional Egyptian funerary scenes. The work dates from around the time of the Roman emperor Hadrian, AD 117–38.

(right) An elegant, Romano-Egyptian lady of the mid-2nd century AD.

(left) Painted and gilded stucco mummy-case of the early 1st century AD decorated, again, in a combination of Classical and traditional Egyptian styles. The subject of the appealing portrait is identified by a label in Greek below the broad collar: 'Artemidorus – farewell!'.

1888
The Palace of Amenophis III

The ruins of this once-magnificent palace complex erected by Amenophis III on the west bank at Thebes for the celebration of his *sed*-festivals were first recognized by Georges Daressy, Maspero's French assistant in the Bulaq Museum, in 1888. Daressy's tentative soundings – one of his first pieces of archaeological work – uncovered a number of rooms and several important sections of painted wall decoration, as well as an elaborate throne dais.

The modern name of the site, el-Malqata, translates as 'the place where things are picked up' – reflecting the vast quantities of brilliant blue faience, glass, blue painted pottery and other luxury artifacts with which the surface of this vast site was for years thickly strewn. Malqata has been investigated to particularly good effect by several expeditions since Daressy's day, including the

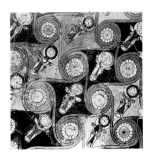

Metropolitan Museum of Art and, most recently, by a team from Waseda University, Tokyo. But much in the way of excavation – and more especially conservation – remains to be done.

1888
Artists' Sketches from the Valley of the Kings

The year 1888 was a good one for Daressy. Following his discoveries at Malqata, he set to work exploring the nearby royal burial ground famously known as the Valley of the Kings. Here, within the long-open tombs of Ramesses VI (KV9) and Ramesses IX (KV6), the young Egyptologist chanced upon a rich assemblage of votive stelae and figured ostraca – chips of limestone with humorous caricatures, casual doodles or preliminary sketches for larger and more formal projects – the largest collection ever found.

Some 300 pieces were recovered, most of them from KV9, where two artists' names predominate: those of Amenhotep and Nebnufer,

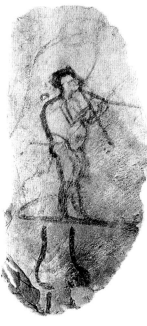

both draughtsmen from Deir el-Medina. Above we see a sketch of a pot-bellied, hunch-backed, double-pipe playing dwarf (CG 25040), perhaps a frequent visitor to the work on the tombs; below are two wrestling men (CG 25132).

1889
The Kahun Papyri

'This is a communication to the lord, life! prosperity! health! about having attention paid to your royal slave, Wadjhau, in making him learn to write without being allowed to run away.'
P. KAHUN VIII.1

Flinders Petrie's excavations at the site of el-Lahun in 1889 uncovered one of the great rarities of Egyptian archaeology – a virtually unaltered town of the 12th to 13th dynasties, still with much of its ancient furnishings in place. Once thought to have been built to house the workforce employed in constructing the nearby pyramid and temple of Sesostris II, the settlement, 'Kahun', is now recognized as a much larger, independent foundation. It consisted of 11 large and probably 500 small dwellings (of which 250 have

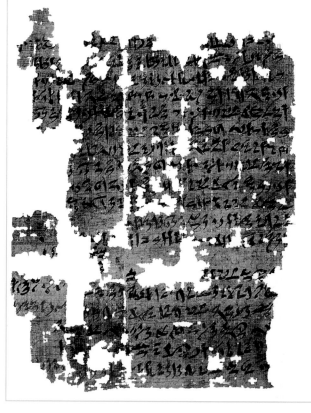

been uncovered), once housing upwards of 5,000 people. Among the surprises Petrie discovered in the ruins of this town were fragments of Minoan Kamares pottery from Crete (and imitations of it), attesting to significant Aegean trade. But Petrie's greatest find was an extraordinary quantity of contemporary documents on papyrus, including wills (notably those of Wah and Meryintef), medical texts and the only 'veterinary' papyrus to survive from Egypt, as well as a hymn of praise in honour of Sesostris III, and various letters, memoranda and accounts (Petrie Museum, UC 32036 et seq.). Further papyri, thought to be strays from the same site, were acquired by Ludwig Borchardt (·p. 136) at around the same time; these texts, comprising some 200 'frames', are now in Berlin (10001–450). 'As only five papyri of this early date were known before now', Petrie wrote of the Kahun texts in 1892, 'this is a wide addition to our sources'.

1891

MUMMIES OF THE PRIESTS OF AMUN: BAB EL-GASUS

Discovery/excavation
1891
by
Eugène Grébaut

Site
Thebes (Deir el-Bahri,
tomb DB B)

Period
Third Intermediate Period, 21st
Dynasty, 1070–945 BC

'At Luxor they have given a dinner to Monsieur Grébaut to celebrate the finding of the hundred-and-sixty-mummy tomb.'
CHARLES EDWIN WILBOUR

The discovery of the great cache of royal mummies at Deir el-Bahri in 1881 (•p. 64) would turn out to be the first of a series of group burials brought to light over the course of the next two decades. The location of the royal mummies' tomb had been divulged to the authorities by Muhammad Abd el-Rassul; and it was this same Abd el-Rassul who, in 1891, now an employee of the Service des Antiquités, alerted Eugène Grébaut, Maspero's successor as Director of the Service, to the sepulchre known as Bab el-Gasus – 'Gate of the Priests'.

This new tomb was also located at Deir el-Bahri, to the north of the lower court of Hatshepsut's temple, in an area which had not previously been dug. Clearing away the surface rubble, Grébaut found a series of regularly laid limestone slabs covering a layer of mud-bricks and a second layer of stone slabs giving access to a vertical and almost circular shaft some 14 m (46 ft) deep. This shaft was filled with densely packed limestone chippings, retained at the bottom by a mud-brick wall.

Grébaut and his assistant, Georges Daressy, made a hole in this intact wall-blocking to insert a candle and peer through, having no idea of what they might find or how big this new tomb might be. As their eyes focused, they must have been truly astonished: for the space was packed from floor to ceiling with busily decorated, yellow-varnished

(below) Unwrapping one of the mummies from the Bab el-Gasus cache: a painting from the end of the 19th century, by Paul Philippoteaux. Daniel Marie Fouquet, a French physician, leads the examination, a plump Gaston Maspero standing to his right. The audience comprises several well-known Egyptologists of the day, and their wives.

4000 BC
3000 BC
2000 BC
1000 BC
0
AD 700

81

coffins, and a mass of other funerary offerings besides. And the tomb turned out to be enormous – a neatly-cut corridor just under 2 m (6½ ft) wide and high, yet over 90 m (295 ft) long), with an unfinished extension running some 50 m (164 ft) to the west to a burial chamber and single storeroom beneath the lower court of the Hatshepsut temple . It was a layout strikingly similar to that of the tomb which had been employed for the first cache of royal mummies of 1881.

The nature of the find gradually became apparent. Grébaut and Daressy had chanced upon the undisturbed and almost perfectly preserved burial-place of the 21st-Dynasty Amun priesthood. And its yield was enormous: 153 sets of anthropoid coffins (two-thirds of which comprised outer and inner containers and a coffin board), 110 shabti-boxes (each with up to 400 faience figurines), 77 Osiris statues (the majority containing rolled funerary papyri), 8 wooden stelae, a similar number of painted wooden images of the mourner-deities Isis and Nephthys, and 4 sets of canopic containers. Nothing to compare with such numbers had ever before been found.

Clearance of the corridor began on 5 February 1891 and was completed on 13 February, with two processions of coffins and funerary equipment leaving the site each day under armed guard for the relative security of the Government steamer. The tomb-contents reached the Giza Museum safe and sound at the beginning of March.

Bab el-Gasus was an amazing survival from antiquity; the tragedy is that (as so often in the history of Egyptian archaeology) the find was never fully published – and probably now never can be. Several renumberings of the objects and the subsequent dispersal of much that was discovered – initially to a select few foreign museums on the occasion of the coronation feast of Khedive Abbas II Hilmy, but latterly elsewhere, sometimes via the museum shop – have greatly complicated attempts at untangling the finer points of the tomb's archaeology. The indications, none the less, are that the Bab el-Gasus mummies were (re)deposited on a single occasion, in a tomb quarried with this specific purpose in mind, during the reign of the 21st-Dynasty pharaoh Psusennes II – around 950 BC. The dead had evidently been swept up from their original places of burial, like the royal mummies before them (•pp. 64, 103), in the massive reorganization of the Theban necropolis which took place at the end of the New Kingdom.

(below left) Ground plan and section of the Bab el-Gasus tomb – showing the resemblance in form to the family vault of Pinudjem II (DB320) employed as a cache for the New Kingdom royal dead at the start of the Third Intermediate Period.

(below right) Lid of the outer coffin of a 21st-Dynasty lady, Taahuty – from the Theban priests' cache. It was presented to the British Museum in 1893 by the Egyptian Government, unable to cope with the vast quantities of burial furniture yielded by this single, amazing find.

WHAT WAS FOUND IN THE AMUN PRIESTS' CACHE

OBJECTS FOUND	QUANTITY	COMMENTS
baskets	32	15 containing provisions, 6 with floral garlands
bed	1	
boxes	6	5 containing pottery, 1 containing detached beards and hands from coffins
canopic jars	16	
coffins	153	101 double, 52 single
fans	2	
sandals	5 pairs	
shabti-boxes	110	
statues	79	77 Osiris figures (most containing a papyrus), 1 Isis, 1 Nephthys
vessels	5	
wooden stelae	8	

From Grébaut to Jacques de Morgan: 1892

'A day or two later came [Lord Milner's] news "Grébaut is out! and a mining engineer put in who is absolutely unknown, M. Jacques de Morgan, French, of course." Really he was the son of Jack Morgan, a Welsh mining engineer, and brother of a Parisian dealer in antiquities. He knew nothing whatever about Egypt but, as a capable business man, made the most reputable head that the French could find.'
W. M. FLINDERS PETRIE

With the resignation of the unpopular Grébaut, 'great satisfaction was felt and expressed by everyone'; and, despite the lukewarm reception accorded his replacement by Petrie (upon whose toes the new man was later brilliantly to tread), Jacques de Morgan (•p. 90) was generally welcomed and proved an exceptionally energetic head. His time as Director of the Antiquities Service was to be a profitable and exciting one, with spectacular discoveries made at Dahshur (•p. 88), Naqada (•p. 100) and, with the finding of the great Old Kingdom tombs of Kagemni and Mereruka (•p. 86), at Saqqara also.

As befitted his practical background, de Morgan's way was organized and systematic; he initiated the first published catalogue of Egypt's standing monuments and inscriptions, and began accurately to map the principal monuments in the field for the first time since Lepsius. Although neither of these ambitious projects would be followed up by his immediate successors, de Morgan had at least pointed the way for the future.

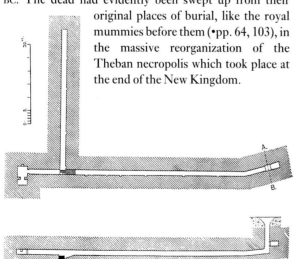

PAINTINGS FROM AKHENATEN'S PALACE AT EL-AMARNA

1893 The Tombs of Kagemni and Mereruka • 1893 The Min Colossi
1893 or before The Soldiers of Mesehti • 1893 The Abusir Papyri

Discovery/excavation
1891–92
by
W. M. Flinders Petrie

Site
el-Amarna (King's House;
Great Palace)

Period
New Kingdom,
18th Dynasty, reign of
Akhenaten, 1353–1335 BC

Amenophis IV-Akhenaten – the so-called 'heretic' pharaoh – built an entirely new capital city, Akhetaten, which was completely abandoned soon after his death. The site, in Middle Egypt, is today known as el-Amarna and has given its name both to the period and its art; it was first planned and superficially explored by John Gardner Wilkinson and his successors, most importantly the Prussians under Karl Richard Lepsius in 1843 and 1845. The discovery of the Amarna royal tomb, by locals, followed in the early 1880s, and, most famously, the Amarna Letters (•p. 72) in 1887.

The first archaeologist to excavate at the site on any scale was Flinders Petrie (assisted by the young Howard Carter: •p. 160) in 1891–92, attracted as much by the prospect of an untouched, single-period site as by the hope of further diplomatic correspondence. Interestingly, little of the peculiar magic which now surrounds the Amarna Period was then in evidence; before Petrie, this era and its distinctive art style were but little known – the Louvre had its statue of the king (•p. 24), and Wilbour had purchased his wonderful plaque (•p. 61), but the famous bust of Nefertiti (•p. 134) still lay buried in the desert sands, while Tutankhamun (•p. 160), a son of this ancient city, continued to slumber unsuspected in his richly provisioned tomb in the Theban Valley of the Kings.

Petrie's season of work at el-Amarna was short, sharp and to the point, and, though somewhat rough and ready by modern standards, it produced more information in a single season than many a more recent excavator has uncovered in a decade. Petrie's aim in excavation, always, was rapidly to characterize his site for the benefit of Egyptology and future diggers before moving on elsewhere, and this, at el-Amarna, he achieved admirably. The site was swiftly surveyed, and the key areas – the Great Temple, the Great Palace, the King's House, the Records Office, and much more besides – skilfully identified and investigated.

The little princesses

Petrie's el-Amarna season yielded several unexpected treasures – including potsherds which the excavator immediately (and to the great satisfaction of Aegean scholars)

4000 BC

3000 BC

2000 BC

1000 BC

0

AD 700

(left) An aerial view (taken in 1932) showing the central part of Akhenaten's remarkable new capital city at el-Amarna; the ground plan of the Small Temple of the Aten and, beyond that, the King's House, are clearly visible.

83

recognized as Mycenaean imports – but none more significant than the paintings. Most exquisite was part of a wall scene in glue tempera, showing two (of five or six) princesses with their parents, Akhenaten and his principal consort, Nefertiti – described by the Egyptologist Norman de Garis Davies as 'surely one of the very prettiest relics that the wide pre-Christian world has bequeathed to us' (in the Ashmolean Museum, Oxford, 1893.1-41).

This masterpiece, dated to the middle years of Akhenaten's reign, was revealed during the clearance of the so-called King's House (no. 13, Pendlebury P.42.1), a building located next to the Small Temple at el-Amarna. It was 'bewitched' from what remained of the original wall by its gifted excavator – who commemorated his success in its rescue in characteristic, understated fashion, with 'a couple of pages and a film from a Brownie camera in the memoir of the season's work'.

The painted pavements

During this same season, Petrie uncovered a series of painted floors and wall-footings, including two pavements in the columned rooms (E and F) and main hall of the Great Palace. These, by virtue of their spontaneity, are equally spectacular works of art. Although a glimpse of such paintings had been offered by Georges Daressy's brief work at the palace at Malqata in 1888 (•p. 79), and though further painted floors would later be brought to light at Memphis and, more recently, at Qantir (•p. 224), where there is evidence of gilding – the el-Amarna paintings were on an altogether unexpected scale. In room E of

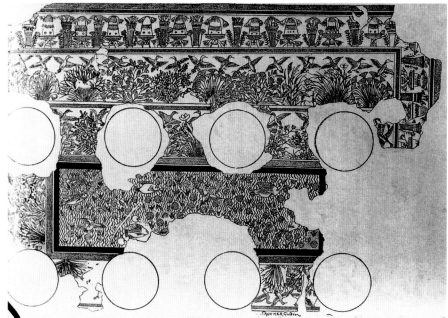

the Great Palace almost 80 sq. m (860 sq. ft) of the Great Pavement were uncovered, and in excellent condition. Following Petrie's careful clearance of the paintings and their stabilization with thin tapioca-water, a structure (financed by the short-lived English Society for the Preservation of the Monuments of Ancient Egypt) was built to protect them. They were to arouse gasps of admiration from all who were lucky enough to see them in situ.

Today, the overall design of the principal floor paintings is preserved in the watercolour copies which Petrie

(above) Petrie's careful drawing of a portion of the painted floor from Akhenaten's palace, with brilliantly painted registers of ducks and plants around a central, rectangular basin. The circles mark the original positions of stone column bases.

(left) Akhenaten's youngest daughters: the surviving portions (now in the Ashmolean Museum, Oxford) of an extraordinary scene depicting Akhenaten, Nefertiti and their children, discovered by Flinders Petrie still in position on one of the walls of the King's House.

(right) A photograph of the Great Pavement as protected beneath Petrie's shed. In order to keep out wind-blown sand, none of the windows was made to open – much to the discomfort of tourists in the stuffy, el-Amarna heat.

made and in part reproduced in his report on the season's work, *Tell el Amarna*, in 1894. Interestingly, an area near one of the removed limestone column bases showed that the Great Pavement in room E had been repainted, to a different design, at least once during its life. In the latest version calves gambol through leafy papyrus thickets, disturbing beautifully rendered pintail-ducks which spread their wings to fly to safety – all ranged around a central pool teeming with a variety of fish and abundant lotus. The design of the pavements in room F and the main hall was essentially similar, and all three rooms were interconnected with pathways depicting bound captives – suggesting to some that the complex formed part of the audience chamber of pharaoh, who would symbolically trample his enemies underfoot as he walked.

The wanton destruction of these paintings in 1912, that of Room E in particular, represented a tragic loss to Egypt's cultural heritage. As Petrie recalled:

> '*the department [of Antiquities] provided no path for [visitors], and the fields were trampled; so one night a man went and hacked [the pavement] all to pieces to prevent visitors coming... I was never even informed and allowed to pick up the pieces.*'

Those fragments which survived the attack were salvaged by the authorities, and partially (if not entirely accurately) restored and put on display in Cairo. These – together with Petrie's copies and the remains of further painted pavements later unearthed both by Alexandre Barsanti for the Cairo Museum and by the Egypt Exploration Society in 1934–35 – today convey at least some impression of the magnificence once presented by the original whole.

(centre & right) Salvaged fragments of the exquisitely painted flooring from el-Amarna, now in the Cairo Museum. 'Those who trod [it] discovered nature as it was created by the Aten, that nature which the god illuminated each day with his beneficent rays'.

85

1893
The Tombs of Kagemni and Mereruka

Two of Egypt's most famous tombs, the adjoining mastabas of Kagemni and Mereruka, were found by Grébaut's newly appointed successor, de Morgan, in July 1893 at Saqqara, to the north of the pyramid of Teti, first king of the 6th Dynasty. They marked the edge of a street of tombs later cleared by de Morgan's own successor, Victor Loret, and described by the Belgian art historian Jean Capart.

Full documentation of Kagemni's tomb (*below*) and its marvellous reliefs was begun by Friedrich Wilhelm von Bissing and his then assistant, the young Arthur Weigall. It was not until further clearance by the local Antiquities Service inspector, Cecil Firth, however, that the full extent of the monument was revealed. The tomb of Mereruka (whose burial chambers Firth also brought to light in 1921–22; *right*) was not adequately recorded until

1938, with the splendid publication of Prentice Duell, made possible by the generous support of the American oil magnate John D. Rockefeller Jr. The gap between discovery and publication – if the excavator puts pen to paper at all and is able to find a publisher – is frequently a long one.

Both tombs date from the time of Teti himself – that of Mereruka (a chief justice and vizier) from later in the reign, that of Kagemni (who shared similar titles) somewhat earlier. The tombs of the two men are remarkable not only for the quality of their reliefs – which are stupendous – but also for their increased size: that of Mereruka comprises some 33 corridors and chambers, with correspondingly more space available for lavish decoration and informative inscriptions.

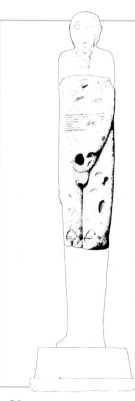

1893
The Min Colossi

While digging beneath the foundations of the Ptolemaic temple of Koptos (Qift) in 1893, Flinders Petrie found – and with characteristic flair immediately recognized the potential significance of – three crude and fragmentary colossal statues (Cairo JE 30770; Oxford, Ashmolean Museum, 1894.105c-e). From their original, ithyphallic form they could be identified as representations of Min – the ancient god of fertility – originally standing over 4 m (13 ft) in height.

The period of these statues has been much discussed, with dates as diverse as the Predynastic and First Intermediate Period proposed by a variety of scholars. The current view is that the figures are earlier – *c.* 3300–3100 BC – rather than later in date, and represent crucial evidence not only for the formative era of Egyptian sculpture but (from surface decoration in the form of exotic *lambis*-shells) for early trade links with the Red Sea.

Interestingly, a late, headless version of what may be one of these images was discovered by Adolphe Reinach at the same site in 1910–11.

Could this represent evidence for continuity in the practice of carving 'Min icons' at the site from the very dawn of Egyptian history?

Or had the colossi perhaps been rediscovered and re-erected at Koptos prior to Greco-Roman times to inspire the production of such related ex-votos? These and other questions raised by Petrie's Koptos discovery still await a definitive answer.

1893 or before
The Soldiers of Mesehti

Wooden tomb models depicting various aspects of everyday life are frequently found in burials of the earlier Egyptian dynasties, the practice reaching a peak in the Middle Kingdom during the 12th Dynasty (•p. 156). Few of the models which survive, however, can compare with the two extraordinary squads of soldiers – one Egyptian, one Nubian – interred with Mesehti, a local prince, at Asyut at the turn of the First Intermediate Period. The small soldiers of each troop are depicted with great vivacity and individuality – with details of clothes and weaponry accurately depicted down to the spotted hides of their shields.

The tomb was found by locals in 1893 or before, with the soldier-models eventually going to Bulaq, while Mesehti's statue and stick were acquired

respectively by two collectors William Joseph Myers (•p. 92) and William Macgregor (both pieces now at Eton College, ECM 1592, 2168). A few weapons and tools are also in the Petrie Museum at University College London.

Though archaeological information on the find is almost wholly lacking, similar tombs found intact at the same site and reported by Émile Chassinat and Charles Palanque in 1903 give at least an impression of how Mesehti's burial would have appeared when opened.

1893
The Abusir Papyri

Texts written in hieratic, the cursive script based on hieroglyphs, are not common, and texts from the Old Kingdom have tended to be among the rarest finds of all. The gradual filtering on to the antiquities market after 1893 of several fragments of 5th-Dynasty date was therefore greeted with enormous interest.

Ludwig Borchardt (•p. 136) of the Deutsche Orient-Gesellschaft was determined to track down the source of these papyri – to match his previous success with the collection of stray texts from Kahun (•p. 80). After three years of search he struck lucky: a few meagre scraps were brought to light at Abusir, and one, by a miracle, joined with a text purchased on the market, confirming the group's original findspot.

Subsequent excavations showed that the Abusir archive dated mainly from the reign of the 5th-Dynasty pharaoh Djedkare-Isesi, who chose to build his pyramid at south Saqqara rather than Abusir. This move necessitated the regulation of his predecessors' mortuary cults – and the generation of much paperwork.

Timetables of priestly duties, inventories, accounts and records of construction work and repair – all were represented in the archive and have told us much about the economic history of the Old Kingdom pyramid cults and the financial system underpinning the provision of offerings to the Egyptian god-kings.

THE ABUSIR PAPYRI:
What is where now?

DISCOVERY	ACQUIRED/EXCAVATED BY	PRESENT LOCATION
1893	Giza Museum	Cairo Museum
1893	Édouard Naville; sold after his death to Ludwig Borchardt	British Museum
1893	Urbain Bouriant; passed to French Institute, Cairo, and Gaston Maspero	Cairo Museum; Louvre
1893	W. M. F. Petrie	Petrie Museum, University College London
1903, 1904, 1907	Ludwig Borchardt, for Deutsche Orient-Gesellschaft	Cairo Museum; Berlin Museum

JEWELS OF EGYPTIAN PRINCESSES: DE MORGAN AT DAHSHUR

1894–95 A Cache of Statues of Sesostris I from el-Lisht

Discovery/excavation
1894–95
by
Jacques de Morgan

Site
Dahshur (pyramid complexes
of Ammenemes II, Sesostris III
and Ammenemes III)

Period
Middle Kingdom, 12th–13th
Dynasties, reigns of
Ammenemes II-Hor,
1929–c. 1745 BC

'During the winter of 1893–4 M. de Morgan paid a visit to the stony plateau on the west bank of the Nile, where stand the famous pyramids of Dahshur. The whole district is full of tombs, and all scholars have admitted this fact; yet, strangely enough, no systematic excavations have hitherto been made throughout it ... M. de Morgan turned his attention to the southern end, and the results of his labours have fully justified his decision ....'
ILLUSTRATED LONDON NEWS

Jacques de Morgan's excavations at Dahshur would secure his place in history as one of the greatest archaeologists – judged by results and the swiftness of publication – of 19th-century Egyptology. In three spells of work at the site between 1894 and 1895 he uncovered several rich tombs and the largest, most spectacular find of Middle Kingdom jewelry ever seen – objects noteworthy not only for their intrinsic value but also for their craftsmanship and form which, together with the jewels later found by Petrie at el-Lahun (•p. 138), stand without equal.

The owners of the Dahshur treasures (for the most part now in Cairo, CG 30857 et seq.) were, in chronological order: two princesses, It and Itweret, daughters of Ammenemes II; a queen, Khnemet, wife of Sesostris II; Sithathor, a daughter of Sesostris II and for some an elder sister of the Sithathoriunet discovered by Petrie at el-Lahun; queen Meret, the wife of Sesostris III; King Hor of the 13th-Dynasty; and a possible daughter of this king, the princess Nubheteptikhered. As their condition revealed, the majority of the jewels recovered had been worn in life.

(below) Plan showing the layout of the lower 'galerie des princesses' at Dahshur: 'T' and 'T1' mark the positions of the first and second caches.

(opposite) Jewels from Dahshur: (above) the broad collar and other jewels of princess Itweret, daughter of Ammenemes II, from her intact burial; (left) inlaid gold 'motto clasps' (the one in the centre is inverted), and other jewels from the second treasure, of Meret, wife of Sesostris II; (right) inlaid gold pectoral ornament of Ammenemes III, from the treasure of Queen Meret.

(left) Digging for gold: an imaginative reconstruction of Jacques de Morgan's subterranean treasure hunt.

The first and second treasures

De Morgan uncovered the first of his rich series of burials in 1894 in the northwest corner of the enclosure of the pyramid of Sesostris III. A shaft leading vertically downwards to the east of four small, stone superstructures, now identified as small pyramids, gave access to two galleries. Among the plundered burials of the lower of the two were the remains of an interment belonging to princess Sithathor. The mummy itself was long gone, carried off no doubt by thieves for the sake of its adornments, and the coffin lay empty. The wooden canopic chest with its four alabaster lidded jars for the viscera remained, however, and it was in a pit next to this chest that de Morgan found a decayed wooden box inscribed in silver hieroglyphs with the princess's name. Inside was a collection of her jewels – including a fabulous pectoral of Sesostris II and scarab of Sesostris III.

Pressing on further down this same corridor the next day, de Morgan, now knowing where to look, found a similar 'treasure': another coffin, again empty, and a further pit containing a second collection of jewels – all that remained of the burial of Queen Meret, wife of Sesostris III. This treasure included two splendid pectoral ornaments (of Sesostris III and Ammenemes III respectively), and a range of scarabs, rings, pendants and other exquisite jewels. De Morgan could hardly believe his luck.

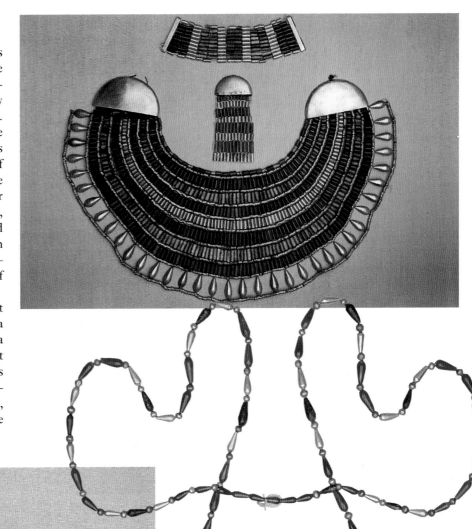

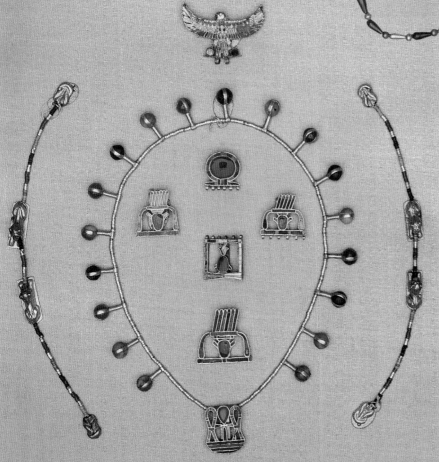

Triumphs of the second season

'Like Princess Ita's mummy, Princess Khnumet's head rested on a round circle of beaten earth. At the neck was a collar formed of gold beads and various signs in gold, encrusted with stones of carnelian, emerald and lapis lazuli. The two ends of this jewel were formed by falcon-heads of solid gold, encrusted with lapis lazuli and carnelian.

Each of the arms was ornamented with three bracelets … Two, placed near the wrists, were supplied with closures carrying the ankh sign inlaid with lapis lazuli.

The funeral furnishings of this mummy were very resplendent ….'

THE DAHSHUR JEWELRY

LOCATION	OWNER	IDENTITY	JEWELS
pyramid enclosure of Ammenemes II	It	daughter of Ammenemes II	(on body) collar, bracelets, bead apron, swallow amulet, beads, dagger
	Itweret	daughter of Ammenemes II	(on body) collar, bracelets, girdle, beads, dagger
	Khnemet	queen of Sesostris II	(on body) collars, bracelets, anklets, bead apron; (in box) diadems, circlets, clasps, pendants, beads
pyramid enclosure of Sesostris III	Sithathor	daughter of Sesostris II	(in box: 'first treasure') pectoral of Sesostris II, scarab of Sesostris III bracelet and other clasps, amulets and pendants, girdle, anklets, beads
	Meret	queen of Sesostris III	(in box: 'second treasure') pectorals of Sesostris III and Ammenemes III, scarabs of Ammenemes III and Meret, rings, pendants and amulets, bracelets girdles, anklets, beads
pyramid enclosure of Ammenemes III	Hor	king (13th Dynasty)	(on body) diadem, collar, gilded wood bracelets, beads, dagger, flail
	Nubhetepti-khered	daughter of Hor?	(on body) diadem, collar, bracelet, pendants, beads, dagger, flail

(right) The moment of triumph: de Morgan lifts the exquisite gold crown of Khnemet, wife of Sesostris II, from the queen's mummified corpse in this famous recreation first published in the pages of the *Illustrated London News*.

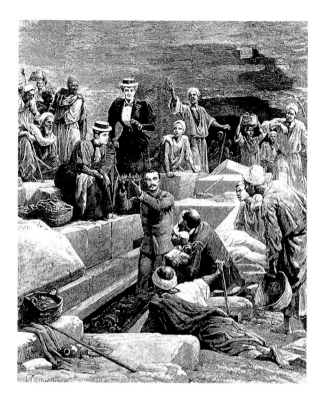

JACQUES JEAN MARIE DE MORGAN (1857-1924)

- Born Blésois, Huisseau-sur-Cosson, Loir-et-Cher, 3 June 1857
- Studies at School of Mines, Paris, working as a prospector in several parts of the world
- Director-General of the Service des Antiquités, 1892–97
- Excavates at Saqqara (•p. 86); Kom Ombo, 1893; Dahshur, 1894–95, discovering quantities of exquisite Middle Kingdom gold jewelry; Naqada, 1897 (•p. 100); and elsewhere
- From 1897 on, transfers his archaeological efforts to Susa, Persia
- Dies Marseilles, 12 June 1924

De Morgan's luck was set to continue, with the results of his second season at Dahshur in many ways more spectacular than the first. Shifting his attention to the enclosure wall west of the 12th-Dynasty pyramid of Ammenemes II, further burials of a range of Middle Kingdom royalty were uncovered. Unlike the tombs of the previous season, which had been plundered and their jewels missed only by chance in the dark and confusion of the robbery, four of this season's burials were intact. And of these four, three – those of the princesses It and Itweret and that of the elderly queen Khnemet – produced further and even more startling examples of the jeweller's art. Most exquisite of all were Khnemet's diadems, their recovery famously (if somewhat imaginatively) depicted in an *Illustrated London News* engraving of the time, hidden beneath a perfume chest together with 'a heap of jewels, collars [and] buckles … that had fallen there without any arrangement' along the tomb's eastern wall.

King Hor

De Morgan's third season at Dahshur, in the spring of 1895, focused on the area within the enclosure wall north of the 'Black Pyramid' of Ammenemes III, and yielded the burial of an unknown king – Hor. The most famous image from this disturbed shaft-tomb is a wooden *ka*-figure, 1.75 m (5¾ ft) high, extremely well-carved and with exceptionally lifelike, inlaid eyes of bronze, rock crystal and quartz. This was discovered in an inscribed wooden shrine at the entrance to the narrow burial chamber, turned on its back and accompanied by staves and other minor grave goods. Next to it lay another long box, containing further broken funerary items; while behind lay an inscribed, rectangular wooden coffin containing the king's plundered mummy, which was surmounted by a gilded wooden headpiece and embellished with a range of fragmentary objects, again of gilded wood. Beyond the wooden coffin, in a niche and wholly undisturbed, lay the king's wooden canopic chest. Alabaster and pottery vessels, a circular offering table, two stelae found elsewhere in the tomb, and a second, smaller and poorly preserved *ka*-image of gilded wood found in the approaches, completed the assemblage.

Who was this Hor? His age at death was some time ago estimated at 45 years or more. De Morgan argued that he was the son (or younger brother) and co-regent of Ammenemes III, who had died before he could exercise power in his own right; while Maspero, and others more recently, have preferred to see him as the little-known king, Auibre of the 13th Dynasty, successor but one to Sebekhotep I. According to these last scholars, the use of a seal bearing the prenomen of Ammenemes III to close Hor's canopic box was prompted by the burial's deposition within the 12th-Dynasty king's funerary environs.

Princess Nubheteptikhered

'… soon we found ourselves in the presence of an intact funerary chamber in which the various objects still occupied the place in which they had been deposited 4500 years ago.'

The shaft containing de Morgan's fifth and final burial, that of the princess Nubheteptikhered, was found close by that of Hor on 19 April, undisturbed but somewhat decayed through damp. Access, as previously, was by means of a vertical shaft opening into a corridor and a stone-lined burial chamber closed off with limestone blocks. The wooden coffin itself, its lid curved and embellished with gold foil bands, lay within a sarcophagus integrated into the structure of the tomb. Lifting the lid of this coffin revealed the body of a 44–45-year-old woman, once covered with gilded stucco, lying on her back with her head turned to the left. The skeleton remained articulated,

(left) The *ka*-image of King Hor, eternal repository of his double or vital force, finely carved in wood and with the eyes inlaid. The surface was originally embellished with painted gesso, gilded in places, which fell to dust at the time of its discovery.

(right) The impressive coffins (top and bottom) of King Hor and Princess Nubheteptikhered, and (centre, left and right) their associated canopic chests. Constructed from fine quality imported wood, the beauty of the grain was highlighted by bands of hieroglyphic text in applied gold foil.

with various items of jewelry still in place. Next to the sarcophagus lay the boxed canopic jars and the usual range of funerary goods: stone and pottery vessels, food offerings, and two wooden boxes containing a selection of ritual objects.

Despite this array of grave goods and the fact that we know her name, Nubheteptikhered's identity remains uncertain. The best that can be ventured, on the basis of similarities between this interment and that of Hor, is that king and princess were contemporaries, and for some father and daughter.

1894–95
A Cache of Statues of Sesostris I from el-Lisht

El-Lisht in the Faiyum was the cemetery of Itjtawy, the new capital of Egypt founded by Ammenemes I at the start of the 12th Dynasty. The site was first explored by the French Archaeological Institute in Cairo in 1894–95, and to particularly good effect. Many finds of sculpture have been made in Egypt, but among the finest is the cache of 10 well-preserved limestone seated statues of the founder's son, Sesostris I (Cairo CG 411–20),

which the French discovered deliberately buried near the northeast angle of the south pyramid's outer enclosure wall. These sculptures, which were unfinished, had been carved in dangerous times: Sesostris I is perhaps best known today from the hieratic 'Teaching' of his father, Ammenemes I, in which the dead king appears before his son to describe his assassination and warn him:

'Beware of subjects who are nobodies,
Of whose plotting one is not aware.
Trust not a brother, know not a friend,

Make no intimates – it is worthless!
When you lie down, guard your heart yourself,
For no man has adherents on the day of woe!'

THE FINEST FAIENCE: THE TUNA EL-GEBEL FIND

Discovery/excavation
1895
by
Egyptian locals

Site
Tuna el-Gebel

Period
New Kingdom to Roman periods, 18th Dynasty and after, c. 1550 BC–AD 300

4000 BC

3000 BC

2000 BC

1000 BC

0

AD 700

'Among the important pottery [sic] finds of past years few have yielded a richer harvest to the collector than a necropolis north of Assiout [Asyut], known as Tunah ....'
HENRY WALLIS

One of the most characteristic materials employed by the ancient Egyptians was faience, the brightly coloured frit in use from the earliest times for vessels, inlays and a variety of ornaments; and one of the finest assemblages of Egyptian faience anywhere in the world is the little-known collection put together by William Joseph Myers and bequeathed to his old school, Eton College, in 1899. What distinguishes the Myers collection from other assemblages of pretty Egyptian objects is the fact that many of the key pieces demonstrably originate from a single site – Tuna el-Gebel, the cemetery of Hermopolis Magna (modern el-Ashmunein) in Middle Egypt (•p. 194).

That Tuna el-Gebel was the scene of a great discovery of Egyptian faience during the mid-1890s is recorded by Henry Wallis, a contemporary of Myers and one of the earliest students of Egyptian glazed wares; and it is confirmed by the large number of faience objects with a Tuna provenance which began to enter the major Egyptian collections at this time, many of them via the German dealer Reinhardt. The local people, clearly, had stumbled on a rich and undisturbed area of the cemetery-site, which they were working carefully and with great profit.

Among the locals' booty Wallis noted 'vessels of all kinds, figures of the gods, elegant objects of personal adornment, and all the trappings and paraphernalia of the mummy. The art also covered a considerable period of time, ranging from the XVIIIth Dynasty, over the Ramesside times, to the Roman conquest'. Masterpiece after masterpiece of Egyptian faience is attested from the site – while of the tombs' more mundane contents nothing whatsoever is known, or at least can be recognized today.

William Joseph Myers, an officer in the King's Royal Rifles. On his death in 1899, Myers's fine if little-known collection of Egyptian art – put together with the help of Émile Brugsch and others and incorporating much from the 'Tuna find' – passed to his old school, Eton College, Windsor.

A winged image of the goddess Nut, fashioned in blue faience. Together with a winged scarab and polychrome representations of the four sons of Horus (opposite below) it was once attached as amuletic protection to the outer wrappings of a late New Kingdom mummy from Tuna el-Gebel.

Tuna el-Gebel, as the 1895 finds would seem to show, was a principal centre for high-quality faience manufacture, particularly during the Third Intermediate Period. Among the site's most typical products are delicate chalices, modelled in the form of either the blue or the white lotus and with naturalistic relief decoration or narrative scenes, together with rings, spacer-beads and amulets of the most delicate, openwork and technically challenging design.

As Henry Wallis wrote, and with little exaggeration:

'The sum total of the faïence excavated at Tunah was numerically large, and, regarded from an artistic point of view, of the first quality. It is perhaps not too much to assert that if the whole had been kept together, and all else of Egypt's pottery had perished, she could with it alone have gone into competition with the rest of the world, whether of ancient or modern times, and, if the judges were ceramicists, with fair chances of taking first honours.'

(right) A superlative example of the fine quality faience found at Tuna el-Gebel (and presumably produced nearby): a 22nd-Dynasty chalice modelled in the form of a blue lotus and with scenes in relief showing the king smiting enemies.

(left) Front and back of a delicate spacer-bead, with designs showing the victory of the god Horus over his enemies (top) and the triumphant rebirth of the creator sun god (below). The sophisticated openwork technique is characteristic of the Third Intermediate Period at Tuna.

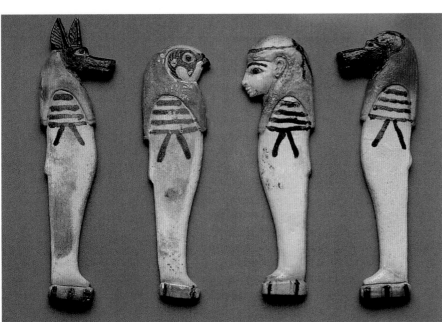

1895
PREDYNASTIC GRAVES AT NAQADA

1896 The Israel Stela • 1896 The Tomb of Hatiay
1896 The Ramesseum Papyri

Discovery/excavation
1895
by
W. M. Flinders Petrie
and J. E. Quibell

Site
Naqada

Period
Predynastic Period,
before c. 3000 BC

'Nearly 2,000 graves were excavated, scattered in three or four cemeteries, which extended over four or five miles …. The remains point to a regular ceremonial system, and among them are jars with wavy handles, containing scented fat, of which the by no means unpleasant odour is still discernible. There are also flint saws with finely serrated edges, and knives, daggers, and needles …. Mr. Petrie has succeeded in convincing a somewhat sceptical practical potter that the vases, which are of singularly beautiful form and outline, were made wholly by hand ….'
THE TIMES

Petrie's unprecedented discoveries at the ancient cemetery of 'Naqada' (actually situated between Tukh and Ballas) in 1895 were originally identified by the great man as the remains of a 'New Race' which had invaded Egypt following the collapse of the Old Kingdom. Petrie gradually discarded this hypothesis in favour of recognizing, rightly, the first evidence for Egypt's Predynastic inhabitants. In this he was following a suggestion first put forward by his *bête noire* (one of many), the then Director of the Antiquities Service, Jacques de Morgan, who, two years later at Abydos, not only uncovered similar graves but immediately recognized their true significance.

The general character of the Naqada graves was constant – a rectangular pit dug 1–1.2 m (3-4 ft) deep in the ground, with a roof of woven branches covered over with a low mound of earth. Occasionally, as with the burials of the more prosperous dead in the 57-grave cemetery T, the tomb was much larger (up to 4 by 2.75 m or 13 by 9 ft) and brick lined. The body, placed in the foetal position on a reed mat with the head generally orientated to the west, was surrounded by a greater or lesser number of grave goods which included pottery, stone vessels, beads and bracelets, flint knives, slate palettes and the occasional clay or ivory figurine. Many of the bodies had well-preserved skin and hair, similar to artificially prepared mummies. Interestingly, a small number of graves revealed evidence of 'secondary burial' – that is, interment of the corpse after decomposition and disarticulation – and possibly of human sacrifice also.

The precise dating of the individual graves (and other related finds made at Ballas and at Abadiya and Hu in 1898–99) within the larger framework of the later Egyptian prehistoric period was not at all apparent. But once the true, Predynastic nature of this material had been grasped, Petrie's creative mind went into overdrive, and it was not long before, in a flash of sheer genius, he saw the means to resolve the problem: typological classification.

Within the cemetery there was a clear archaeological break between the graves of the earlier prehistoric period and those of the later, and a stylistic development was apparent within the pottery of the two phases. By arranging the pottery and other grave goods in a numbered, theoretical, developmental sequence – 30 initially being the oldest, 80 the most recent, far-sightedly leaving room for manoeuvre at either end – Petrie was able to provide an internal, relative 'date' for each individual grave. These relative dates could then be related to the subsequent, Early Dynastic developments of these pottery forms to fix the Predynastic phases more precisely.

Petrie's analysis took six years of intense study before, in 1901, the results could be announced to the world. The foundation it laid was essentially a sound one, and would prove of immense value to those working in the Predynastic sphere for decades to come.

(left) A 'black-topped' jar, characteristic of the wares found in profusion at Naqada.

(below left & right) Fragmentary steatopygous figure of red-painted clay, and a more slender 'female figure in hard white clay … shewing the … decoration which was tatued [sic] or painted on the body'.

Petrie on Predynastic pottery

An insight into Petrie's unique, almost instinctive understanding of matters practical and scientific may be gained from the following analysis of the characteristic 'black-topped' pottery recovered in quantity from Naqada and other Predynastic sites:

'The prehistoric pottery of the earlier period is all of a soft body, faced with red haematite. As the pots were usually baked mouth downward, the brim was covered with the ashes; and these not being burnt through, reduced the red peroxide of iron to the black magnetic sesqui-oxide, such as is familiar to us in the black scale on sheet steel. The interior of the pot is likewise black, owing to the reducing gases from the ashes below; rarely the heat after the combustion has lasted long enough for the oxygen to pass through the pottery, and so redden the inside. Open dishes were also haematite-faced inside, and the iron is reduced to a brilliant mirror-like coat of black all over. The reason of the polish being smoother on the black than on the red part is that carbonyl gas – which is the result of imperfect combustion – is a solvent of magnetic oxide of iron, and so dissolves and re-composes the surface facing. On once understanding the chemistry of this, it is needless to discuss the old idea that smoke blackened this pottery.'

1896
The Israel Stela

'I had the ground cut away below, blocking up the stele on stones, so that one could crawl in … [Wilhelm Spiegelberg] lay there copying for an afternoon, and came out saying, "there are names of various Syrian towns, and one which I do not know, Isirar." "Why, that is Israel," said I. "So it is, and won't the reverends be pleased," was his reply'
W.M. FLINDERS PETRIE

'Israel is laid waste! Her seed exists no more!' This epic phrase is found upon the so-called Israel Stela (Cairo CG 34025), a black granite monument weighing almost five tonnes which was uncovered by Flinders Petrie in 1896 in the mortuary temple of Merenptah at Thebes. As the only reference to the tribe of Israel in any Egyptian text (among a listing of pharaoh's conquests in Year 5 of the reign), it aroused a storm of interest among biblical scholars. The document exists in another version at Karnak, in the court of the cachette.

Merenptah's inscription was carved on the reverse of a stela originally prepared for Amenophis III of the 18th Dynasty a century and more earlier; this previous king's funerary monument and associated structures at Kom el-Heitan had been the source for much of the building material employed by Merenptah in the construction of his own mortuary temple. Excavations at this later site by Horst Jaritz and the Swiss Institute of Archaeology in Cairo have, over recent years, brought to light an increasing number of fabulous limestone reliefs of Amenophis III, but also others of Hatshepsut, Tuthmosis III, Tuthmosis IV and Amenophis IV-Akhenaten, used as fill in the second pylon and elsewhere.

(below) The seven successive stages Petrie was eventually able to establish in the development of Predynastic pottery. The numbers on the right are the 'sequence dates' he applied to them.

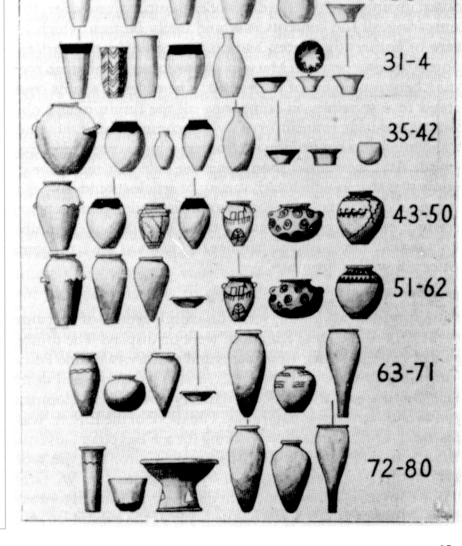

1896
The Tomb of Hatiay

The beautiful wooden coffin of the lady Henutwedjebu (*right*, Washington University, St Louis) was for many years one of the best-kept secrets of American Egyptology, its existence known to only a handful of specialists. It comes from the intact tomb of Hatiay, her husband, discovered by Georges Daressy at Sheikh Abd el-Qurna in 1896.

A contemporary of the 'heretic' pharaoh Akhenaten, Hatiay was a scribe and overseer of the double granary in the temple of the Aten – though the exclusivity of worship demanded by this god at el-Amarna itself is not adhered to either in the religious formulae on the burial equipment

or in the names and titles of Hatiay's family.

A decorated chapel once presumably stood at ground level, above Hatiay's crude funerary cavern (meant to remain unseen) in which the family's coffins and a few but choice items of burial equipment (*left*) had been deposited.

1896
The Ramesseum Papyri

By 1894, the great Flinders Petrie had become disillusioned with the Egypt Exploration Fund and left them to their devices, setting up a new and independent organization – the Egyptian Research Account (ERA), later transformed into the British School of Archaeology in Egypt. In 1896 the ERA, under British Egyptologist James E. Quibell, was digging beneath the brick magazines at the rear of the 19th-Dynasty Theban mortuary temple of Ramesses II (the Ramesseum – famous today for the fragmented colossus which inspired Shelley's celebrated poem, 'Ozymandias'). He discovered a much earlier tomb shaft (no. 5) which, on clearance, gave access to a series of small chambers. Excavation of these yielded nothing of note, but, at the base of the shaft itself, a small gessoed wooden box was revealed. This box proved to be 'about one-third full of papyri' and 'a lot of small objects' – including the wooden figure of a woman with Bes-mask and snake wands and a twisted, copper-alloy cobra wand. The assemblage was soon recognized as the professional equipment of a man of magic and medicine of the mid-13th Dynasty.

The poor condition of the documentary material hampered the study of this find for many years, until it was passed for treatment before the Second World War to the gifted German papyrus conservator Hugo Ibscher. Ibscher's success

with this unpromising haul was extraordinary, and the harvest for Egyptian studies immense – a rich and varied collection of documents (see table), literary, liturgical, magical, medical, and documentary, now divided between Berlin (A=10499, D=10495) and the British Museum (EA 10610, 10752–72).

While the Ramesseum papyri were the intellectual gain of the 1896 dig, the artistic prize was this exceptionally fine and well-preserved upper torso from a painted statue in indurated limestone, now recognized as Meryetamun, a daughter of Ramesses II who functioned as great royal wife after the death of Queen

Nefertari. A colossal statue of this same queen was recently discovered at Akhmim (•p. 219).

THE RAMESSEUM PAPYRI

DESIGNATION	NATURE OF CONTENTS
A	Tale of the Eloquent Peasant; Story of Sinuhe
B	Ramesseum Dramatic Papyrus; accounts and plan
C	Dispatches from Semna fortress; magical text
D	Ramesseum Onomasticon
E	Funerary liturgy; accounts
I	Discourses of Sasobek; accounts
II	Various moral pronouncements
III	Magico-medical text
IV	Magico-medical text; accounts
V	Magical text
VI	Hymn to Sobek
VII	Magical text; mathematical text?
VIII-XI	Magical texts
XII	Invocations to demons
XIII	Magical text; embalming diary?
XIV-XVII	Magical texts
XVIII	Dispatches from Quban fortress

1897–99
HIERAKONPOLIS: CITY OF THE FALCON-GOD

Before 1897 The Wife of Nakhtmin
1897 The Tomb of Neithhotep

Discovery/excavation
1897–99
by
James E. Quibell
and F. W. Green

Site
Kom el-Ahmar (Hierakonpolis)

Period
Predynastic–Old Kingdom,
Naqada II–6th Dynasty and
later, after c. 3000 BC

'The distinctive merit of these recent researches is that they appear to fill a large intermediate space between the aboriginal and the historical period, and extend our knowledge far back into what were the mists of a recordless antiquity.'
THE TIMES

The excavations carried out at Hierakonpolis ('City of the Falcon-god') on behalf of Petrie's Egyptian Research Account by James Edward Quibell and Frederick William Green over two seasons between 1897 and 1899 were, for protodynastic archaeology, among the most important ever undertaken. Yet, despite the exceptional glamour of the finds, the work has rarely received the popular recognition it deserves.

The site of Hierakonpolis is today known by its Arabic name, Kom el-Ahmar, 'The Red Mound'. In pre-classical times it was the town of Nekhen, home to the early falcon-god Nekheny (distinguished by his tall, double-plumed headdress); and as the ancient texts suggested – and as Quibell and Green's discoveries would demonstrate – Nekhen had been a key centre during the formative years of dynastic rule.

The site generally, and the cemetery in particular, had been thoroughly dug over before work began, not only by the ubiquitous *sebakhin* but also by the enterprising antiquities dealers of Luxor. After a disappointing spell examining what remained of the graves, Quibell and Green turned their attention to Kom el-Ahmar proper. Here, in the low-lying cultivation, beneath the mound covered in red potsherds which gave the site its modern name, lay the remains of the town and, in its southern corner, the temple of Nekhen itself, partially stripped away in the 1860s for materials to build a factory in nearby Esna.

The golden-headed falcon and other sculptures

Within the temple area proper the excavations revealed traces of a circular sand mound with retaining wall – evidently the earliest phase of the temple structure, which had provided the hieroglyph used to write the name of the city. To everyone's surprise, the finds here came thick and fast. Clearing a small, brick-lined pit at the north end of the temple site, within the third of a series of five chambers of a lateral chapel probably belonging to the Old Kingdom temple, 'there came into view a hawk of thin copper plate, with head

JAMES EDWARD QUIBELL
(1867–1935)

'Quibell … was leisurely, kindly, not exciting himself too much, interested in his work but not overpoweringly so … Quibell besides was young enough to retain the schoolboy delight in driving an older man [Petrie] to exasperation …'
MARGARET MURRAY

- Born Newport, Shropshire, 11 November 1867
- Graduate of Christ Church, Oxford; assisted Petrie (•p. 67) and the Egyptian Research Account at Koptos (1893: •p. 86), Naqada and Ballas (1894: •p. 94), the Ramesseum (1896: •p. 96), Hierakonpolis (1897)
- Inspector in Chief of Antiquities for the Delta and Middle Egypt, 1899–1904, the opposite number of Howard Carter (•p. 160); Chief Inspector in Luxor, 1904–05; appointed Chief Inspector for Saqqara, 1905 (his excavations including the reclearance of the tomb of Hesyre: •p. 55)
- Keeper, Cairo Museum, 1914–23; Secretary-General, 1923–25, when he retires
- Assists Cecil Firth in his excavations at Saqqara, 1925–31; director at the Step Pyramid, 1931–35
- Dies Hertford, 5 June 1935

4000 BC
3000 BC
2000 BC
1000 BC
0
AD 700

(below) The decayed but still-impressive enclosure of the 2nd-Dynasty king Khasekhem(wy) at Hierakonpolis, 'City of the Falcon-god'. One of Egypt's oldest mud-brick buildings, it stands in places to its massive, original height.

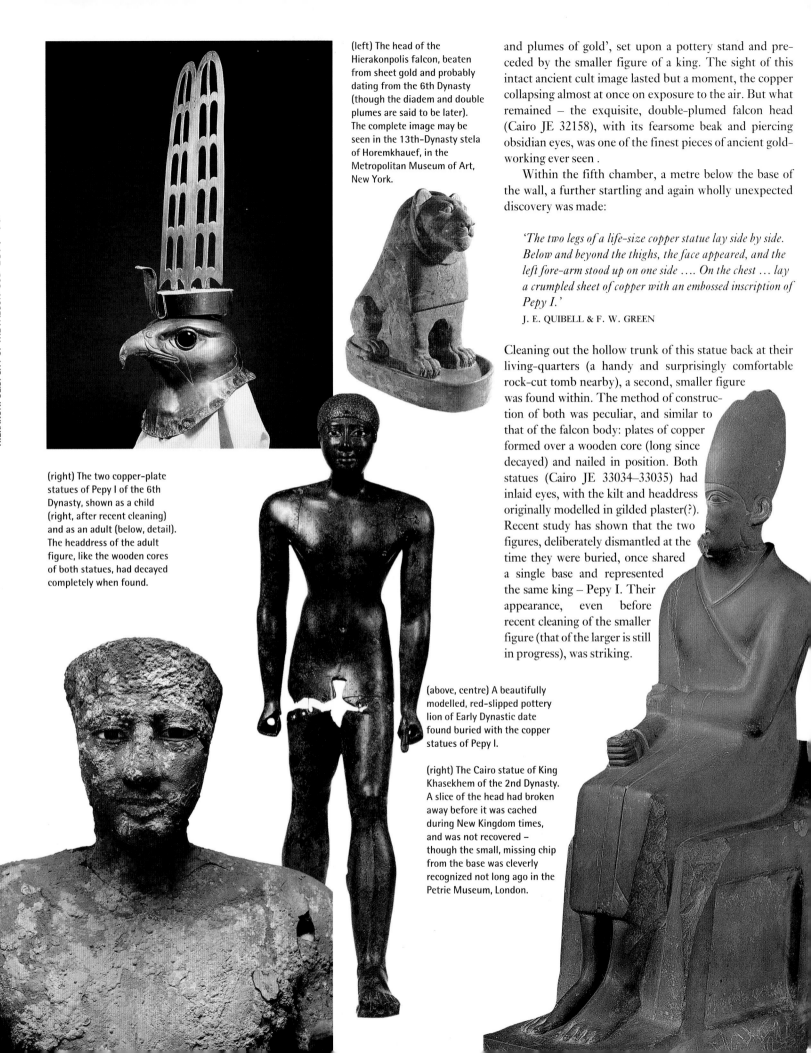

(left) The head of the Hierakonpolis falcon, beaten from sheet gold and probably dating from the 6th Dynasty (though the diadem and double plumes are said to be later). The complete image may be seen in the 13th-Dynasty stela of Horemkhauef, in the Metropolitan Museum of Art, New York.

(right) The two copper-plate statues of Pepy I of the 6th Dynasty, shown as a child (right, after recent cleaning) and as an adult (below, detail). The headdress of the adult figure, like the wooden cores of both statues, had decayed completely when found.

(above, centre) A beautifully modelled, red-slipped pottery lion of Early Dynastic date found buried with the copper statues of Pepy I.

(right) The Cairo statue of King Khasekhem of the 2nd Dynasty. A slice of the head had broken away before it was cached during New Kingdom times, and was not recovered – though the small, missing chip from the base was cleverly recognized not long ago in the Petrie Museum, London.

and plumes of gold', set upon a pottery stand and preceded by the smaller figure of a king. The sight of this intact ancient cult image lasted but a moment, the copper collapsing almost at once on exposure to the air. But what remained – the exquisite, double-plumed falcon head (Cairo JE 32158), with its fearsome beak and piercing obsidian eyes, was one of the finest pieces of ancient gold-working ever seen .

Within the fifth chamber, a metre below the base of the wall, a further startling and again wholly unexpected discovery was made:

'The two legs of a life-size copper statue lay side by side. Below and beyond the thighs, the face appeared, and the left fore-arm stood up on one side …. On the chest … lay a crumpled sheet of copper with an embossed inscription of Pepy I.'
J. E. QUIBELL & F. W. GREEN

Cleaning out the hollow trunk of this statue back at their living-quarters (a handy and surprisingly comfortable rock-cut tomb nearby), a second, smaller figure was found within. The method of construction of both was peculiar, and similar to that of the falcon body: plates of copper formed over a wooden core (long since decayed) and nailed in position. Both statues (Cairo JE 33034–33035) had inlaid eyes, with the kilt and headdress originally modelled in gilded plaster(?). Recent study has shown that the two figures, deliberately dismantled at the time they were buried, once shared a single base and represented the same king – Pepy I. Their appearance, even before recent cleaning of the smaller figure (that of the larger is still in progress), was striking.

The 'Main Deposit'

A third cache of material – the so-called 'Main Deposit' – was discovered beneath the walls of a structure located to the east of the temple area and to the south of the chambers containing the falcon and other statues. Much of this huge deposit had rotted away and was beyond recovery; but what could be salvaged included a mass of ivories, faience baboons, ibex, fish, falcons, a hippopotamus and other creatures, and a whole range of other objects besides – including a second, fragmentary statue of Khasekhem (Oxford, Ashmolean E517), in limestone (recording precisely the same number of kills as its companion), and two important commemorative maceheads (Oxford Ashmolean E3631–3632). With the possible exception of a (stray?) 18th-Dynasty scarab, all the finds from the Main Deposit may be dated to the Early Dynastic period or before, and were probably discarded objects ritually deposited in sacred ground – a cache of indescribable value for archaeologists today.

The Narmer Palette

Spectacular though all these discoveries were, from a historical point of view the most significant of the Hierakonpolis finds was an extremely large (64-cm (25-in) high) ceremonial greywacke palette (Cairo JE 32169), the precise findspot of which is today uncertain – either close to or within the Main Deposit. This extraordinary object was a larger version of the palettes used in everyday life and found by the hundred at Naqada (•p. 94) and

(right) King Narmer, wearing the white crown of Upper Egypt, smites a northern foe; one of the faces of the famous Narmer Palette.

And this was not all. Buried with the copper statues were two further items: a superb pottery lion with a shiny red slip (Oxford, Ashmolean 1896-1908 E 189), and the statue of a seated king (Cairo JE 32161). Carved in green stone and inscribed with the name of the Horus Khasekhem ('The powerful one appears'), last ruler of the 2nd Dynasty, this rare, early example of royal statuary was already broken when buried and lacked a large section of its head. Its base carries a record of 'kills': 47,209 Lower Egyptian rebels – a destruction which may have prompted the king to adopt the unifying name Horus-Seth Khasekhemwy ('The two powerful ones appear') in allusion to the two respective deities of north and south. This name also occurs at Hierakonpolis, on a granite block, with the additional epithet 'the two lords are at peace'.

Before 1897 The Wife of Nakhtmin

Despite its damage, this image of an unknown lady (Cairo CG 779b), wearing a heavy, braided wig and clutching in her left hand a bead necklace with counterpoise, is generally considered one of the most sensual works ever produced by an Egyptian sculptor. She is the wife of the military officer Nakhtmin (who is thought to have been a son of Tutankhamun's successor, the aged god's father Ay).

Carved in superb, indurated limestone and originally forming part of a dyad (of which the head

of Nakhtmin himself is also preserved: CG 779a), it comes without doubt from the couple's lost tomb – most probably at Sheikh Abd el-Qurna, Thebes. The fragments were acquired by the Giza Museum in 1897.

1897
The Tomb of Neithhotep

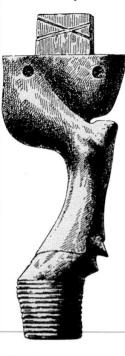

Taking up at Naqada where Petrie had left off in 1897, and at the same time as the French Coptic-scholar Émile Amélineau was pursuing his disastrous campaign of excavation among the Early Dynastic tombs at Abydos (•p. 109), Jacques de Morgan (•p. 90) set out to explore the remains of an early mastaba (*right*) which would open the eyes of the scholarly world for the first time to the architectural sophistication of Archaic Egypt.

De Morgan's work at this tomb revealed many inscribed objects from the period of Egypt's north–south unification in around 3000 BC, including several mentions of a king Hor-Aha – perhaps identical with the Menes of legend – and a queen, Neithhotep, presumably his wife. Further work at de Morgan's mastaba by John Garstang in 1904 suggested that the tomb belonged to the lady rather than to her king; Hor-Aha himself, as Amélineau's excavations showed, had been interred at Abydos. More recent theories assign de Morgan's tomb to a local worthy of the district. Of particular satisfaction to Petrie was the fact that the wavy-line decoration of the tomb's pottery jars corresponded to the latest manifestation of the vessel type in his theoretical sequence dating structure (•p. 94), confirming the basic reliability of the scheme.

(below) The body of this small, lapis lazuli statuette of a woman with clasped hands was discovered by Quibell in 1898 in the temple; the missing head, by a miracle, would be recovered by Harold Jones in 1906, digging at the same site under the direction of John Garstang.

themselves as artistic and historical documents from the earliest beginnings of the Egyptian state can hardly be exaggerated.

elsewhere, used to grind malachite for embellishing the eyes or face; unlike these earlier palettes, however, this example was decorated on both faces in relief in a highly developed Egyptian style. The scenes clearly commemorate the victories of a very early king labelled in hieroglyphic script 'Narmer'. This ruler is shown on the palette's upper surface wearing the red crown of Lower Egypt and on the lower surface wearing the white crown of Upper Egypt. Narmer evidently laid claim to both the north and south of the country – a fact which has led many Egyptologists in the past to venture an identification with the legendary Menes, the first unifier of the country in around 3000 BC.

The Hierakonpolis finds are still being studied, and, with work at the site itself continuing and the cleaning of the ivories again in progress a hundred years after their initial discovery, important new information is still being brought to light. The precise nature of Quibell and Green's discoveries has naturally been much discussed. But there seems little doubt that the excavators were correct in seeing the finds as obsolete dedications and temple equipment, buried intentionally during or some time before the New Kingdom. Whatever the precise circumstances of the ancient deposition may be, the importance of the finds

THE 'MAIN DEPOSIT'

statues, statuettes	basalt, limestone, faience, ivory
baboon figures	limestone, faience
dog(?) figure	limestone
falcon figure	limestone
frog figures	calcite, steatite
hippopotamus	faience
lion	limestone
scorpion figures	rock crystal, haematite, faience, pottery
model bedstead(?)	limestone, breccia
palettes	schist
mace heads	rock crystal, porphyry, serpentine, calcite, limestone, faience
knives	copper, flint
hammerstones(?)	flint
vessels and stands	quartz(?), porphyry, granite, gneiss, serpentine, calcite, steatite, limestone, faience, pottery
spoon	ivory
hetep-signs	gold foil
scarab	faience?
beads	faience
animal bones	
sheet metal	copper
indeterminate	quartz, calcite, ivory

1890s and before Aramaic Papyri from Elephantine
1898 Bab el-Hosan: 'The Tomb of the Horse'

Discovery/excavation
1898–99
by
Victor Loret

Site
Thebes (Valley of the Kings,
tombs KV34, 35, 36 & others)

Period
New Kingdom, 18th–20th
Dynasties, 1504–1070 BC

'[Émile] Brugsch said to an Arab that De Morgan was but a small devil but Loret is twenty devils.'
W. M. FLINDERS PETRIE

By 1896, the energetic Jacques de Morgan was beginning to feel restless, and the lure of excavating at the site of Susa in Persia was to prove irresistible: he resigned his position in 1897, abandoning Egypt for good (though his elder brother, Henri de Morgan, would return for a spot of excavating at Predynastic sites between Esna and Edfu in 1907-8).

Jacques de Morgan's successor as Director of the Antiquities Service was, inevitably, another Frenchman – Victor Loret, close to de Morgan in age but, in the unsettling effect his character had upon those he came into contact with, closer still to the disastrous Grébaut. The best the irascible Petrie could hope for was to 'gain his respectful hatred in place of his official arrogance'. Loret's time as Director was to be an unhappy one for all concerned, though it would hold its fair share of archaeological surprises.

'Soon after [Loret's] appointment [Émile] Brugsch Bey, the Curator of the Museum, came to me saying, "Yesterday I had occasion to see the new Director on a matter of business and accordingly knocked at the door of his room. When I entered he said: 'In future, Monsieur, I must ask you to send a note or card to me first of all when you wish to see me'. I replied, 'Monsieur le Directeur, my shadow shall never darken your threshold again.'" And it never did'
ARCHIBALD HENRY SAYCE

Little real work had been done in the Valley of the Kings since the battering-ram discoveries of Belzoni (•p. 18), and what digging there was – carried out by a motley

VICTOR CLÉMENT GEORGES PHILIPPE LORET (1859–1946)

- Born Paris, 1 September 1859
- Studies with Maspero at the École des Hautes Études and the Collège de France
- Member, French Archaeological Institute, Cairo, 1881, working among the royal and private tombs at Thebes; Director, 1886
- Reader, University of Lyons, 1886–1929, founding the school of Egyptology there
- Director-General of the Egyptian Antiquities Service, 1897–99, excavating in the Valley of the Kings, with impressive results, and at Saqqara (•p. 86); founds the Antiquities Service journal, *Annales du Service*
- Dies Lyons, 3 February 1946

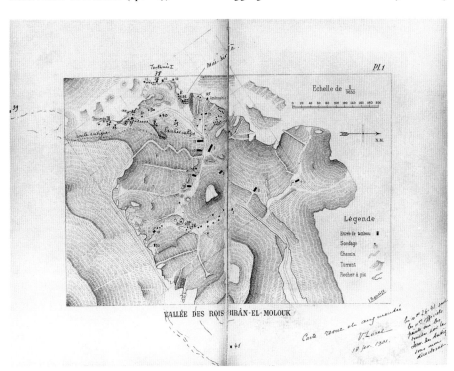

VALLÉE DES ROIS BIBÂN-EL-MOLOUK

(left) The map accompanying the published preliminary report on his work which Loret presented to Charles Edwin Wilbour – annotated by the excavator himself to take into account the results of the final season.

array of individuals, including Mariette – had produced little of note. Victor Loret, now the newly appointed Director, nevertheless felt that the site had potential, and initiated an ambitious programme of clearance – with staggering results. During the course of two seasons, Loret's workers (like Mariette, he did not maintain a permanent, personal presence at the excavations) would uncover an astonishing 17 new tombs; the Patagonian Samson was to be well and truly out-Belzonied.

The tomb of Tuthmosis III

Tuthmosis III is commonly referred to in the history books as 'the Napoleon of ancient Egypt', an epithet inspired not so much by his extraordinary imperial achievements as by what was previously thought (on the basis of a mis-measurement of the royal mummy – the feet were detached and the depth of the ankles was inadvertently omitted) to be his exceedingly small stature. As one of Egypt's most powerful kings, the discovery of his tomb by Victor Loret on 12 February 1898 was greeted with international acclaim. If it is relatively little-known today, this may be ascribed to its almost immediate eclipse – within a month – by even greater discoveries in the royal valley.

In fact, the tomb of Tuthmosis III (KV34), with its extraordinary elevated location, its superb cartouche-shaped burial chamber, and the elegant decoration of scenes from the Book of the Underworld (unrolled, papyrus-like, around the walls), represents one of the finest achievements of ancient Egyptian funerary architecture. Archaeologically, too, its significance was great: like Belzoni's best finds, it preserved a range of the original burial equipment – wooden statuettes of the king, fragments of wooden model boats and the odd bone and provision pot – though, as with almost all the Valley's burials, anything of metal or otherwise serviceable had been carried off in antiquity for recycling.

(right) An early 20th-century photograph showing the dramatic location of Tuthmosis III's tomb, hidden high and deep within the folds of the southern cliffs of the Valley of the Kings.

(below, left) Tuthmosis III's cartouche-shaped sarcophagus of fine, painted quartzite, in position within the king's tomb.

(below, right) The sarcophagus of Hapimen, a 26th-Dynasty high official whose agents evidently visited the tomb of Tuthmosis III to copy the king's monument many years after the mummy had been transferred for reburial, ultimately in the Deir el-Bahri cache.

In common, too, with Belzoni's tombs, the mummy of the royal owner had been removed for reburial elsewhere at the end of the New Kingdom; it had been recovered by Brugsch from the Deir el-Bahri royal cache in 1881 (•p. 64).

Following the tomb's abandonment by Tuthmosis III, KV34 had been employed for two intrusive private burials. Later still, during the 26th Dynasty, the tomb was visited again, this time by the tomb-architect of a Memphite high official called Hapimen. Commissioned to take a copy of the yellow-quartzite sarcophagus, the discerning architect perhaps also carried off the king's more manageable canopic chest for re-use at the same time. Hapimen's sarcophagus, subsequently looted, was in use for many years as a humble water-trough in the Cairo mosque of Ibn Tulun; it was collected and then surrendered by the French in 1801 (•p. 17) and is now among the sculptural treasures (EA 23) of the British Museum.

(left) Decorated face of a column in the burial chamber of Amenophis II's tomb: the goddess Hathor presents the sign for 'life' to the nose of pharaoh, newly received into the Underworld.

magnificent discovery in its own right, remarkable for its innovative architecture, the stark simplicity of its wall-paintings and its extensive, if badly shattered, funerary equipment. More extraordinary still – indeed a first in the excavation of the royal valley – was the fact that the king was found in place in his own sarcophagus, albeit contained in a replacement cartonnage coffin.

The tomb of Amenophis II

'The find is amongst the most interesting ever made in Egypt, as, although the jewelry, &c., were rifled from the tomb probably during the XX. Dynasty, the mummies of Amenophis and of seven other kings are intact....'
THE TIMES

Fresh from his triumphant discovery of the tomb of Tuthmosis III, on 9 March 1898 Loret found yet another royal tomb – that of Tuthmosis' son and successor, Amenophis II (KV35). This sepulchre was a

(above) The painted quartzite sarcophagus of Amenophis II. When Loret entered the tomb in 1898, the sarcophagus, of characteristic, early 18th-Dynasty cartouche form, still contained pharaoh's mummified body.

(left) The foot-end of Amenophis II's painted sarcophagus box, showing the goddess Isis kneeling upon the sign for 'gold' and flanked by two columns of hieroglyphic text.

What Loret found odd, however, as he began to take stock of his find, was the profusion of *other* corpses, scattered to left, right and centre. The first body he encountered, in the antechamber to the tomb, had been dramatically laid out on the battered hull of one of Amenophis II's wooden model boats. Three further mummies, stripped of their bandages, were neatly positioned in the more northerly of the side-rooms leading off the burial chamber; while, peering above the partially dismantled wall blocking the adjacent room, Loret discerned nine further mummiform shapes, this time coffined, arranged in two rows of six and three. These extra bodies, Loret assumed, must be burials of a later date – private interments like those in KV34 (above) which, as so often, had taken advantage of a convenient, pre-existing burial place. Then he took a closer look:

'The coffins and the mummies were a uniform grey colour. I leaned over the nearest coffin and blew on it so as to read the name. The grey tint was a layer of dust which flew away and allowed me to read the nomen and prenomen of Ramesses IV. Was I in a cache of

KV 35: WHO'S WHO IN THE SECOND ROYAL CACHE?

CAIRO NO.	NAME	WHERE FOUND	CAIRO NO.	NAME	WHERE FOUND
CG 61069	Amenophis II	burial chamber	CG 61079	Merenptah	2nd side room
–	anonymous remains	well-chamber	CG 61084	Ramesses IV	2nd side room
–	Sethnakht?	the body on the boat	CG 61085	Ramesses V	2nd side room
			CG 61086	Ramesses VI	2nd side room
CG 61070	'Elder woman' (Tiye?)	1st side room	CG 61081	Sethos II	2nd side room
CG 61072	'Younger woman'	1st side room	CG 61080	Siptah	2nd side room
CG 61071	anonymous prince	1st side room	CG 61073	Tuthmosis IV	2nd side room
CG 61074	Amenophis III	2nd side room	CG 61082	unknown woman D	2nd side room

royal coffins? I blew away the dust of the second coffin, and a cartouche revealed itself, illegible for an instant, painted in matte black on a shiny black ground. I went over to the other coffins – everywhere cartouches!'

(above) The mysterious 'body in the boat' in the tomb of Amenophis II – probably the cached body of King Sethnakht of the 20th Dynasty.

The tomb of Maiherpri

The discovery of a single royal tomb would have been reward enough for any excavator in the fickle Valley of the Kings; two, in the space of a month, was extraordinary. Yet a third – the tomb prepared by Tuthmosis III for the reburial of his grandfather, Tuthmosis I (KV38), would be made during the following season. And to this unparalleled total of 3 royal sepulchres, Loret was soon able to add or reclear a further 14 private tombs.

One of these, KV36, was of particular interest, since it had evidently been missed when the necropolis administration's salvage experts painstakingly searched the valley for tombs during the 21st Dynasty. The owner of this tomb – a highly-placed (half-) Nubian 'prince', Maiherpri (whose name translates as 'Lion on the prowl') – lay nested within two anthropoid coffins of wood in the tomb's single, small burial chamber. This, though superficially plundered of its more portable valuables at some stage during the New Kingdom, still preserved a varied selection of the owner's grave goods. These included a

Loret was astounded. Despite the fact that only a selection of Egypt's New Kingdom royal dead had been represented in it, the group of royal mummies brought to light at Deir el-Bahri in 1881 (•p. 64) had been regarded as an amazing one-off; few would have dared to wager that a second, equally imposing collection would turn up less than two decades later.

As with KV34, Loret cleared the tomb of Amenophis II with care; and, although he never published a full report on the discovery, what he has left to us is sufficient for a number of important conclusions to be drawn. The cached mummies had evidently been introduced into the tomb of Amenophis II from different locations at the turn of the 2nd millennium BC, perhaps on two separate occasions and probably at the time the burial of Amenophis II was 'restored' by the necropolis administration. A worthy, pious act, one might think – had it not involved the systematic stripping of anything and everything of value, to benefit the empty coffers of a government in decline.

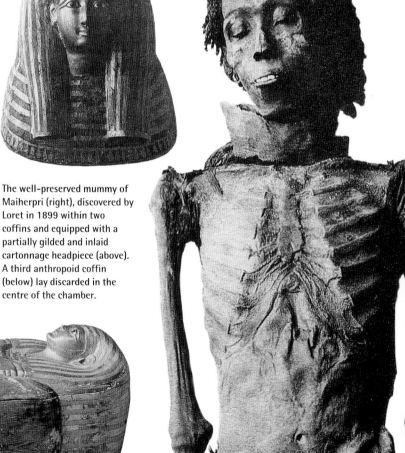

The well-preserved mummy of Maiherpri (right), discovered by Loret in 1899 within two coffins and equipped with a partially gilded and inlaid cartonnage headpiece (above). A third anthropoid coffin (below) lay discarded in the centre of the chamber.

rectangular wooden shrine, a third, 'spare' coffin (actually intended to nest within the other two, but by an unfortunate oversight made too large), a cartonnage mask covering the head of the mummy, a full set of canopic equipment, a germinating Osiris, papyrus, gaming equipment, various stone, glass, pottery and faience vessels, food provisions, and, intriguingly, a pair of dog collars. These latter perhaps indicate that Maiherpri was in some way linked with the royal animals found buried across the hill by Theodore Davis a decade or so later (•p. 117), not far from the tomb of Amenophis II. Prior to Davis's discovery of the tomb of Yuya and Tjuyu in 1905 (•p. 114), and Schiaparelli's find of the following year (•p. 126), Maiherpri's was the best preserved private burial so far revealed to science – and it was justly celebrated.

There was a curious sequel to Loret's discovery of Maiherpri in February 1902, involving the young Howard Carter, at that time searching for the lost tomb of Tuthmosis IV (•p. 113). Clearing the rock-face above KV36, Carter uncovered a small hollow in which he found concealed a yellow wooden box carrying Maiherpri's name and containing two intricately cut leather loincloths, a heavy sprinkling of coloured glass inlay fragments and gold foil discarded nearby. The box and one of the loincloths are now in Boston (MFA 03.1035-1036); the other garment found its way to the Chicago Natural History Museum. Here it was displayed for years, described – incorrectly – as an early example of a freemason's apron. A ridiculous idea – but its desirability had been strangely enhanced: said to have been stolen by an unscrupulous collector of such regalia, it has yet to be recovered.

ELEPHANTINE: THE PRINCIPAL JEWISH ARCHIVES

NAME OF ARCHIVE	NO. OF DOCS.	DATE	DESCRIPTION	PURCHASED/ EXCAVATED
Mibtahiah	11 legal docs.	471–10 BC	family archive	purchased
Ananiah	13 legal docs.	456–02 BC	family archive	purchased
Jedaniah	11 letters, 1 list	419–07 BC	communal archive	excavated

1890s and before
Aramaic Papyri from Elephantine

Aramaic was the *lingua franca* of the 5th-century BC Persian (Achaemenid) empire (of which Egypt formed a part), and texts written in the Aramaic script have been found at several sites along the Nile. The best-known archive is that from the island of Elephantine, which between 495 and 399 BC hosted a large Jewish garrison.

The existence of this Jewish community, with its own temple to Yahweh positioned alongside the shrine of the local ram-headed god Khnum, was first revealed in papyri acquired by Belzoni; other stray texts (ostraca) were subsequently acquired by Greville Chester in the 1870s, and, in the 1890s and early 1900s, by Charles Edwin Wilbour, W. Spiegelberg, A. H. Sayce, Lady William Cecil and Robert Mond. Formal excavation of the settlement began in 1904, providing a context for the extraordinary details of daily life revealed in the community's three principal archives.

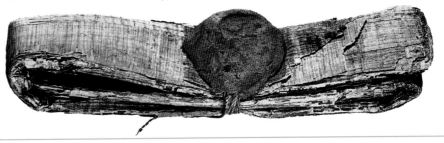

(left) One of two exquisite leather loincloths – each cut from a single hide – discovered by Howard Carter within a painted wooden box at the entrance to Maiherpri's tomb in 1902.

The return of Maspero, 1899

'Loret was now [1899] retired from Egypt. He was a man of limited vision; when I told him of a place being pillaged he remarked: 'C'est impossible! Il y a un règlement' ['That's impossible! It's against the rules']. He had by this time proved too unsuitable. He was given another post in France and the only man to save credit was Maspero, back again. He insisted on being Director of all the Museums at £1,500 a year and expenses, and had his way, for no one else was available ....'

W. M. FLINDERS PETRIE

VICTOR LORET'S EXCAVATIONS IN THE VALLEY OF THE KINGS

TOMB NO.	TOMB OWNER	SEASON FOUND	TOMB NO.	TOMB OWNER	SEASON FOUND
KV26	?	1898	KV36	Maiherpri	1899
KV27	?	1898	KV37	?	1899
KV28	?	1898	KV38	Tuthmosis I, second tomb	1899
KV29	?	1899			
KV30	?	1898	KV39?	?	1899
KV31	?	1898	KV40	?	1899
KV32	?	1898	KV41	?	1899
KV34	Tuthmosis III	1898	KV L		1898
KV35	Amenophis II	1898	KV M		1898

Maspero's second coming, after the ups and downs of the previous two decades, was greeted with approbation by Egyptians and Egyptologists alike. Lord Cromer had engineered the appointment: as he confided to A. H. Sayce, 'We must get rid of Loret … but if another Frenchman is appointed it must be Maspero. I want you, therefore, to write to him privately and persuade him to come, pointing out that if he will not accept the post we shall appoint [Henry George] Lyons'. Needless to say, the threat of a British Director was enough to settle the matter.

Maspero's influence on his return was greater than ever, and he continued to encourage foreign and also local involvement in excavations – some might say indiscriminately. His own passion would be the arrangement of the new Cairo Museum at Qasr el-Nil, beginning the immense task of publication in the pages of the monumental *Catalogue général*, and appointing to this project's staff many of the brightest scholars of the day – Georges Bénédite, Baron von Bissing, Ludwig Borchardt (•p. 136), Henri Gauthier, Percy Newberry, Pierre Lacau, George A. Reisner (•p. 132), and others. The demands of conservation, too, began to be addressed, most visibly through the continuing work of Georges Legrain (•p. 118) at Karnak, while in Nubia, threatened by the raising of the first Aswan dam, the new Director initiated the first campaign of 'rescue' archaeology and documentation the world had ever seen.

THE EARLY DIRECTORS OF THE EGYPTIAN ANTIQUITIES SERVICE (TO 1914)

Auguste Mariette: 1858–81
Gaston Maspero (1st term): 1881–86
Eugène Grébaut: 1886–92
Jacques de Morgan: 1892–97
Victor Loret: 1897–99
Gaston Maspero (2nd term): 1899–1914

EGYPT'S PRINCIPAL MUSEUMS

Bulaq Museum: 1863–91
Giza Museum: 1891–1902
Cairo Museum (Qasr el-Nil): 1902–present

As Sayce observed, 'Maspero had one weakness – it was the only one I know – and that was a craving for omniscience. He did not like new discoveries being made by his subordinates without his having any part in them'. It doubtless contributed to his success in the post. Naville provided a more fitting epitaph: 'the last representative of the heroic age of Egyptology'.

1898
Bab el-Hosan: 'The Tomb of the Horse'

Howard Carter (•p. 160) made his first discovery of an intact royal 'tomb' completely by accident while working for the Egypt Exploration Fund at Deir el-Bahri in November 1898: 'when riding home after some rain had fallen … the ground gave way under the horse's legs bringing both of us down. Afterwards, on looking into the small hole there formed, I saw traces of stone work'. Clearance of the feature (which had to wait until January 1900 and Carter's appointment as Inspector-General of Antiquities for Upper Egypt) proved a mammoth task.

Carter had anticipated a true burial, but what was eventually revealed was a large and undisturbed chamber containing a pristine painted sandstone statue (*right*), wrapped in linen, of a king wearing the red crown (Cairo JE 36195), and an empty, uninscribed coffin. A vertical shaft cut into the floor produced three wooden boats and some pots.

The nature of the deposit remains something of an enigma, though an association with the 11th-Dynasty king Nebhepetre Mentuhotep seems clear, and a link with one or other of this king's *sed*-festivals a distinct possibility.

It was opened in the presence of Lord Cromer, to great embarrassment – since there had been a general expectation of a more spectacular outcome. Carter determined, in the case of any future discoveries, to make doubly certain of what he had found before making any announcement. In the case of Tutankhamun, it was a strategy which would come back to haunt him.

THE OXYRHYNCHUS PAPYRI:
IN SEARCH OF THE CLASSICS

Discovery/excavation
1896–1906
by
Bernard P. Grenfell
and Arthur S. Hunt

Site
el-Bahnasa (Oxyrhynchus)

Period
Roman Period,
30 BC–AD 395

'[A] workman, angry at so poor a result, gave one of the [mummified] crocodiles a furious blow with his spade. It split open and proved to be wrapped in sheets of inscribed papyrus. As Hunt put it in one of his lectures, crocodile stock, previously at a discount, rose at once to a large premium.'

HAROLD IDRIS BELL

Despite earlier contacts (•p. 67), the culture and learning of the Greek world were first formally introduced into Egypt by Alexander the Great and his Ptolemaic successors. The Classical tradition took firm root, and by Roman times Egypt was famed as home to the greatest library in the ancient world, established by the Ptolemaic kings at Alexandria. Unfortunately the institution was damaged during Julius Caesar's siege of the city, drastically 'weeded' by Christians at the end of the 4th century AD, and its remnants finally consigned to the flames by the Arab invader Amr ibn el-As 250 years later. As a result, nothing of this magnificent collection has survived.

But sporadic finds of Classical papyri had been made outside Alexandria since the 18th century – a group of 40-50 texts, for example, appeared in Cairo in 1778, but, of these, only one found a buyer and the rest were burned for the sake of their aromatic smell. Increasing numbers of texts would be brought to light by the *sebakhin* during the 1870s; several, found at Meir, were acquired and exported with typical ingenuity by Wallis Budge (•p. 75) for his British Museum masters in 1888 and 1889, and proved to include a copy of Aristotle's *Constitution of Athens*, as well as important works by Herodas and Bacchylides.

Flinders Petrie seems to have been the first to find documents of the Classical period in context: at Hawara in 1888 – a roll of Homer's *Iliad*, Book II – and at Kom Medinet Ghurab in 1889 where, from cartonnage, he recovered fragments of the *Laches* and *Phaedo* of Plato (copied within a century of their author's death) and the lost *Antiope* of Euripides. The carbonized library discovered by Édouard Naville at Mendes in 1892 fared less well in that scholar's inexpert hands. With the subsequent appearance on the market of more texts – including, in 1894, a first roll containing the Revenue Laws of Ptolemy II Philadelphus – scholars at last awoke to the amazing potential of Egypt as a repository for the literature and history of the Greek and Roman world.

Such was the background to the first site-survey, organized in 1895 at Kom Aushim (Karanis) and Kom el-Asl (ancient Bacchias) by Bernard P. Grenfell, Arthur S. Hunt and D. G. Hogarth under the auspices of the Egypt Exploration Fund. It would prove to be the first of several fruitful seasons' papyrus-hunting. During the course of the next 18 years the EEF, under Grenfell and Hunt, recovered a mass (tens, if not hundreds of thousands) of documents and fragments, both literary and administrative, from three principal sites: el-Bahnasa – better known today by its Greek name, Oxyrhynchus; Umm el-Baragat (ancient Tebtunis), home to the crocodile cemetery referred to above, later dug by the Italians; and el-Hiba.

(below) The delicate task of extricating papyrus fragments from the ancient rubbish-mounds of Roman Oxyrhynchus was entrusted to specially trained Egyptian workers.

(above) Fragment of the Logia Iesou, or 'Sayings of Jesus', discovered at Oxyrhynchus in 1896–97 and received with immense interest by the public – some 30,000 copies of the initial publication were sold. Since the 1950s, it has been recognized that the Logia in fact form part of the uncanonical Gospel of Thomas.

4000 BC

3000 BC

2000 BC

1000 BC

0

AD 700

(left) A 2nd-century AD papyrus from Oxyrhynchus, listing the earliest directors of the famed library at Alexandria.

rubbish mounds yielded a rich store of papyri, while in three mounds the quantity of rolls found together was large enough to warrant the assumption that part of the archives had been thrown there at different periods.

The papyri range from the Roman conquest to early Arab times, each century being largely represented, and are for the most part written in Greek, with a sprinkling of Latin, Coptic, and Arabic. ... Mr. Grenfell's chief hope in digging the site of Oxyrhynchus – the prospect of finding early Christian documents – would seem to have been to some extent realized. Among the papyri discovered at the very beginning of the excavations was a leaf from a third century papyrus book, apparently containing a collection of Logia, or sayings of Christ. Some of those found in the fragment are not in the Gospels. The age, character, and value of these Logia are likely to be the subject of considerable speculation ...

The cream of the collection in point of size and condition, consisting of 150 large and complete rolls in many cases several feet long, has been retained by the Gizeh Museum, the rest of the collection, of which the bulk is, of course, in a very fragmentary condition, is on its way to England....'

Of these sites, it was Oxyrhynchus that aroused the greatest interest. 'One of the largest and most important finds of papyri in Egypt' was the verdict of *The Times* on Grenfell and Hunt's 1896–97 season here:

'The site ... had remained almost untouched by dealers and antiquity seekers, and offered to the excavators – what is in Upper Egypt now almost a thing of the past – a practically virgin field. Very few remains of buildings were discovered, the place having been long used as a quarry both for stones and bricks, but many of the ancient

(below) A serious Arthur Hunt and Bernard Grenfell photographed outside their office-tent at Oxyrhynchus. The greatest of friends, 'Together they published far more in quantity and with a higher degree of accuracy and acumen than either of them could have achieved alone'.

An impressive start, but some of the best finds were still to come: 'shortly before sunset [on 13 January 1906] we reached, at about 6 feet from the surface, a place where in the third century A.D. a basketful of broken literary papyrus rolls had been thrown away'. The texts included the *Paeans* of Pindar, a text of the anonymous 'Oxyrhynchus Historian', Euripides' *Hypsipyle*, Antiphon's *On Truth*, and several other previously lost works, as well as known texts of Plato, Thucydides and Isocrates.

The discovery of rare, illustrated fragments by Hunt's student, John Johnson, at Antinoe in 1913–14 would prove an appropriate climax to two decades of immensely productive salvage. With the outbreak of the First World War, the days of the dedicated papyrus-hunter, for the EEF at least, drew to a close, and the in-depth study and publication of the finds began in earnest.

NOTABLE LITERARY TEXTS
from the rubbish mounds of Oxyrhynchus

AUTHOR	TEXTS RECOVERED
Aeschylus	portions of several lost plays
Alcaeus	new fragments
anon.	4th-century BC history of Greece
Callimachus	fragments
Cercidas	Meliambi
Euripides	Hypsipyle
Pindar	Paeans, other lost poems
Sappho	new fragments
Sophocles	Ichneutae
anon.	Logia, or Sayings of Jesus
anon.	St John's Gospel

TOMBS OF EGYPT'S EARLIEST KINGS AT ABYDOS

1900 Six 18th-Dynasty Ladies • 1899 The 'Persian' Tombs
1900 The Pyramidion of Ammenemes III

Discovery/excavation
1897; 1899
by
Émile Amélineau;
W. M. Flinders Petrie

Site
Abydos (Umm el-Qaab)

Period
Early Dynastic Period, 1st–2nd
Dynasties, 2920–2649 BC

'The Egypt Exploration Fund has achieved a remarkable success at Abydos, where the work has been conducted by Professor Flinders Petrie and Mr. Mace. For the previous four years Abydos had been given over to M. Amélineau, who had had the luck, denied to his great predecessor Mariette, to light upon the tombs of the Kings of the first three dynasties. The objects found in these tombs, stelae of a rude style, stone bowls, flint knives, jars with clay sealings imprinted with short texts, roused the greatest interest among archaeologists, but the manner in which the excavations were made and recorded provoked from the same quarter a storm of hostile comment. M. Amélineau's control over his workmen was so imperfect that many of his finest objects were stolen and passed through dealers' hands, without any record of the details of their position, into various European collections.

In view of the great importance of the site, Professor Petrie determined to go over the ground again more thoroughly and scientifically and search the rubbish heaps of M. Amélineau's work. The result has brilliantly justified him.'
THE TIMES

Abydos had attracted the attentions of a multitude of diggers from the time of Napoleon on, and been exploited for its smaller finds – stelae and statuettes – with particular ruthlessness during the buccaneering days of the early 19th century. The exploitation continued under Mariette, who undertook the clearance of the Sethos I temple and much more besides (•p. 52). The site's abundant material wealth reflects its significance in Egyptian mythology: as the principal sacred centre of Osiris, lord of the underworld, it was the desire of every Egyptian to make pilgrimage there and mark the visit; and, during the Middle Kingdom in particular, Egyptian tombs were frequently furnished with model boats by which this pilgrimage might in perpetuity be achieved.

Petrie versus Amélineau

By chance, an ancient tourist attraction identified by later Egyptians as the tomb of Osiris – 'a vault built of unburned bricks, containing a granite cenotaph'– had been uncovered

(below) A 1st-Dynasty ivory label of King Den, from Amélineau's work at the Abydos royal tombs, dated to 'the first occasion of smiting the east'. The reverse carries an incised representation of a pair of sandals – presumably identifying the type of object to which the label was once attached.

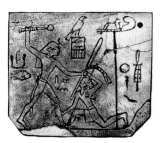

(left) Excavations in progress among the Abydos royal tombs: Petrie's work at the tomb of Den, looking east and showing the interior chambers and access stairway.

in 1897 during excavations carried out at that part of Abydos known as Umm el-Qaab, 'Mother of Pots', by a French Copticist, Émile Amélineau. It proved, in fact, to be the tomb of the 1st-Dynasty King Djer, and but the first of a series of similar sepulchres, the tombs of Egypt's earliest kings. A wonderful find, one might think – but marred by Petrie's claim that Amélineau was ill-suited to dig it.

Petrie's opportunity to demonstrate the Frenchman's incompetence came in 1899, and, as he records, the situation he encountered was appalling:

'The pottery jars were smashed, avowedly to prevent anyone else obtaining them. The stone vases, broken anciently by fanatics [were] stamped to chips ... the jars of ointment were burnt .... The most interesting remains of the wooden chamber of Zer [Djer] ... have entirely disappeared .... The ebony tablets of Narmer and Mena – the most priceless historical monuments – were all broken up ... and tossed aside in the rubbish.'

What Amélineau had been seeking, Petrie claimed, were pretty objects (most of which were later sold off at auction) – and what he had uncovered and could not carry

(above) Two small dolomite vessels from the royal tombs' clearance, their mouths covered with sheets of gold held in place by wire – typical of the exquisite quality of the grave goods of Egypt's earliest kings.

(above left) Flinders Petrie and his sister-in-law, Amy Urlin, behind the *ad hoc* ramparts of their Abydos camp – surrounded by ancient pottery and the impedimenta of excavation.

(below left) A mummified arm, with four exquisitely designed beaded bracelets clearly visible beneath the tattered wrappings. The limb had been ripped from one of the royal dead in antiquity, and was found hidden in a wall in the tomb of Djer.

(below right) The tomb of the 1st-Dynasty King Den as recently re-excavated.

away he had cold-bloodedly destroyed. If so, it was a miracle Petrie found anything worthy of salvage; but he did – and not only archaeological scraps.

From the Frenchman's debris heaps, Petrie was able to retrieve a mass of fragmentary documentation, and the list takes the archaeologist's breath away: food, drink, vessels of pottery and stone (including rock crystal), inscribed wood and ivory labels, weapons, furniture elements, gaming equipment, gold-mounted, precious stone vessels and the sceptre of the 2nd-Dynasty King Khasekhemwy.

Most exciting of all, the mummified arm of one of those buried in the tomb of Djer (perhaps his queen) was found hidden in a hole in the wall, presumably by an ancient robber who had subsequently failed to retrieve it. Miraculously, the arm, wrapped in linen bandages, was adorned still with four precious beaded bracelets (Cairo CG 52008-11), and was in due course proudly shipped off by Petrie to the museum at Giza. Sadly, as the excavator later records, 'Brugsch [the Curator] only cared for display; so from one bracelet he cut away the half that was of plaited gold wire, and he also threw away the arm and linen. A museum', too, the excavator wryly observed, 'is a dangerous place'.

THE ABYDOS ROYAL TOMBS

TOMB	OWNER	DATE
U-j	'Scorpion'	Protodynastic
B-10	Narmer	Protodynastic
B-19	Hor-Aha	1st Dynasty
O	Djer	1st Dynasty
Y	Merneith (queen)	1st Dynasty
Z	Djet (Wadj)	1st Dynasty
T	Den	1st Dynasty
X	Anedjib (Adjib)	1st Dynasty
U	Semerkhet (Mersekha)	1st Dynasty
Q	Qaa	1st Dynasty
P	Peribsen	2nd Dynasty
V	Khasekhem(wy)	2nd Dynasty

Cenotaphs or tombs?

The design of the substructures of the Abydos royal tombs clearly followed on from similar large Predynastic tombs encountered at Hierakonpolis and Naqada (•p. 100) – taking the form of brick-lined pits ranging in area from 100 sq. m (1,075 sq. ft) under Narmer to over 1,000 sq. m (10,765 sq. ft) for Khasekhemwy. Interiors were partitioned for the storage of the rich funerary equipment, and the burial chamber was lined with wood; on the surface, the grave was marked by little more than a mound of sand and a stela.

As monuments go, these were modest enough – so much so that, following Bryan Emery's impressive discoveries in in the Early Dynastic necropolis at Saqqara (•p. 182), the true status of the Abydos tombs was sub-jected to fresh scrutiny. Emery's contention was that the large and richly equipped tombs he had discovered were the true tombs of Egypt's first kings, and that the Umm el-Qaab monuments were merely cenotaphs. With the recognition by Cambridge Egyptologist Barry Kemp that each of the Petrie tombs was but one element in a larger architectural scheme, however, and was further comple-mented by monumental mortuary enclosures on the plain below (such as the Shunet el-Zebib, linked with Khasekhemwy of the 2nd Dynasty), Emery's theory today loses much of its original force.

1900
Six 18th-Dynasty Ladies

The site of Kom Medinet Ghurab at the entrance to the Faiyum is famous for its palace complex dating from the reign of the 18th-Dynasty king Amenophis III and after. Several notable sculptures in wood are reported from the site (•p. 123), and the year 1900 saw the discovery (by locals) of an unparalleled group of six exquisite statuettes – representing the harim ladies Maia, Mi, Nebetia, Tiy (*right*), Tuty and another, name unknown.

The group caught the eye and the imagination of Émile Chassinat, Director of the French Archaeological Institute in Cairo, who at once investigated and was able to establish that, besides the six little figures, the Ghurab find had included a circular ivory box of Syrian workmanship, a wooden cylinder box inscribed with the cartouches of Amenophis III and Tiye, and another box inscribed for Amenophis IV. If the source of these items was a tomb, then the fate of the coffins and mortal remains of these women is a mystery yet to be solved.

1899
The 'Persian' Tombs

Of the many exciting experiences the site of Saqqara has to offer, a visit to the so-called 'Persian tombs' (actually of 26th-Dynasty date) located to the south of the Unas pyramid ranks as one of the more memorable. The descent down the vertiginous 22-m (72-ft) deep shaft by means of a rickety iron spiral staircase gives access to the burial apartments of three tombs: those of the physician Psamtek, the admiral Tjanenhebu (one of whose faience *shabtis* is shown *right*), and the chamberlain

Padienaset. The group was discovered at the end of 1899 by Alexandre Barsanti. The tombs were intact – as usual with this type, the chambers had been deliberately flooded with sand following interment employing an ingeniously simple mechanism, making them notoriously difficult to dig – but the days of magnificent burial equipment were long-gone: the richest of the burials, Tjanenhebu's, boasted a mummy adorned with little more than a silver mummy mask, a bead net and a range of thin, sheet gold amulets (*left*) and jewels, together with a box filled with a few intrinsically worthless ritual objects. A number of other intact tombs of the type are attested in the arch-aeological record, the most recent discovery being that of Iufaa at Abusir in 1995 (•p. 236).

111

Sacrifice

Another interesting controversy surrounding the pre-2nd-Dynasty burials is the possibility of human sacrifice, suggested by the presence of subsidiary graves – in the case of Hor-Aha, a total of 36 arranged in three rows of 12. According to George A. Reisner (•p. 132), who studied the problem in detail, of 317 subsidiary graves associated with the tomb of Djer, it is likely that more than half were human sacrifices; of 174 graves associated with the tomb of Djet, as many as 113 were conceivably sacrificial; while in the case of Den, over 92 per cent of the tomb's subsidiary graves fall into this category. The remaining tombs show similar evidence for the practice, which has been confirmed by the latest German work.

(above) Store chambers within Abydos tomb U-j, newly discovered by the German Archaeological Institute, Cairo, showing one of the chambers still stocked with pottery storage vessels.

Recent work

'Dreyer contends … that Amélineau didn't deserve Petrie's criticism. "He worked alone with 500 workmen and very little money, and his reports were good", Dreyer tells us. Petrie, on the other hand, misinterpreted the site because he was unaware that Amélineau had dumped debris from one tomb into another.'
LYLA PINCH BROCK

Although Petrie worked several subsequent seasons at Abydos, and to good effect, nothing would match the brilliance of his rescue seasons at the Archaic royal tombs. It is ironic, therefore, that the great archaeologist has himself been out-Petried by the scholars of the German Archaeological Institute in Cairo, who have been looking again at the site since 1977, led by Günter Dreyer.

The workings of Amélineau which Petrie sieved in the late 1890s have been re-examined yet again by Dreyer and his team, with a success which has astounded everyone – not least in what Petrie himself had missed: ivory and bone labels, clay sealings, stone and pottery vessels, gaming items, and many more subsidiary burials (all of individuals under 25 years of age). In addition, an entirely new tomb, U-j, was discovered in 1988, and among its anciently ransacked contents was a decayed wooden shrine and an ivory *heqa*-sceptre of its royal, '0 Dynasty' owner, king 'Scorpion'.

Scorpion's name occurs on several hundred wavy-handled pots stockpiled here in two chambers, along with Canaanite vessels produced 'for export to Egypt only. This unique character, and their sheer quantity, points to well-established … trade relations' of a sophistication unexpected at this early date. But more than this: 'Labels … were etched with numerals of from one to four hieroglyphic signs'. That these labels can be read seems to show that writing began in Egypt earlier than previously recognized – a crucial discovery in itself.

1900
The Pyramidion of Ammenemes III

The sadly battered appearance of the Nile's numerous pyramids today – the current total stands at over 70 – bears little resemblance to their original gleaming splendour: the fine limestone casing stones have mostly gone, carted off for reuse or thrown into kilns to be burnt for lime, while the once-gilded pinnacles have for the most part disappeared without trace. The earliest such capstone – or pyramidion – is that discovered in fragments at the site of the 'Red Pyramid' of the 4th-Dynasty King Snefru at Dahshur, made of limestone; another, similar one was recently unearthed by Zahi Hawass at Giza. But the finest by far is that found on the east side of the 12th-Dynasty Dahshur pyramid of Ammenemes III.

The stone's beautifully cut faces offer a glimpse of the pyramid's ancient glory, while its texts preserve an insight into the eternal future to which the ruler aspired: 'May the face of the king be opened so that he might see the lord of the horizon [Horakhty] when he crosses the sky; may he cause the king to shine as a god, lord of eternity and indestructible'.

THEODORE DAVIS IN THE VALLEY OF THE KINGS: 'A NEW TOMB EVERY SEASON'

1902–04 John Garstang at Beni Hasan

Discovery/excavation
1902–14
by
Theodore M. Davis

Site
Thebes (Valley of the Kings, tombs KV20, 43, 45, 46–58, 60–61)

Period
New Kingdom, 18th–20th Dynasties, 1504–1070 BC

'His interest in archaeology was that of a hobbyist … at the first test, it was quick to go.'
JOSEPH LINDON SMITH

Theodore Monroe Davis, the American 'Maecenas' – the epithet was coined by Maspero, ever generous of spirit – had been a visitor to Egypt for several years before he took to digging as an amusing way of passing the time. The spur to excavate had come from Howard Carter (•p. 160), who had been taken on in 1899 by the Egyptian Government to serve as Inspector-General of Antiquities for Upper Egypt. Carter's enthusiasm had early been fired by the Valley of the Kings, and he wanted desperately to investigate its wadis in a thorough manner; but, since official funds were non-existent, he had to fish around for finance. Davis was the sponsor he landed.

Tuthmosis IV and Hatshepsut

Carter was initially looking for one particular tomb – that of Tuthmosis IV, bits and pieces from which had already turned up in the Valley. One of the first important items uncovered by Davis's money, however, on 26 February 1902, was a small box containing two leather loincloths belonging to the nobleman Maiherpri (•p. 105). Not until the following season, in 1903, did Tuthmosis IV finally give up his secret – KV43, a wonderfully cut and decorated sepulchre at the southern end of the site, still filled with the remains of a fine and extensive range of burial equipment. The king's mummy had been discovered five years before, in 1898, by Loret, removed to the Amenophis II cache (•p. 103); but propped up against the wall of one of the new tomb's side chambers was the mummy perhaps of his son, Webensenu, its stomach flapping open in a gruesome manner.

(left) The remote and magnificent western annexe of the Valley of the Kings. Theodore Davis's single-storey excavation house is just visible in the centre-left of the photograph, taken at the beginning of the 20th century.

(below) Antiquities Service inspector Arthur Weigall and his wife Corinna (left), standing before the entrance to the tomb of Ramesses IV with Theodore Davis and his dapper excavator, Edward R. Ayrton.

(above) The well-preserved sarcophagus of Tuthmosis IV, found by Howard Carter, working with Davis funding, in the spring of 1903. The curved head-end carries a representation of the goddess Nephthys, with the four sons of Horus on the visible side.

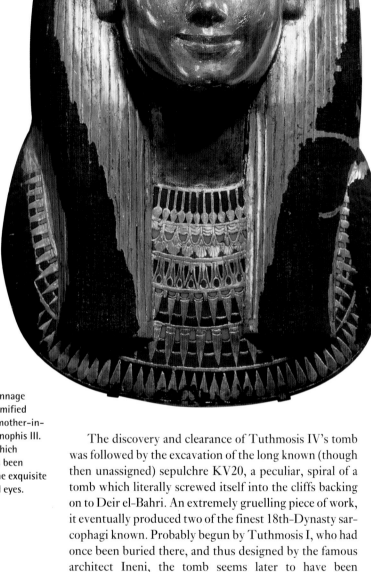

(above) Gilded cartonnage mask from the mummified body of lady Tjuyu, mother-in-law of pharaoh Amenophis III. The fine linen pall which covered the face has been removed to reveal the exquisite modelling and inlaid eyes.

(left) King Tuthmosis IV received into the next world by Osiris (right) and the goddess Hathor (left): detail of a scene in the antechamber of the king's tomb.

The discovery and clearance of Tuthmosis IV's tomb was followed by the excavation of the long known (though then unassigned) sepulchre KV20, a peculiar, spiral of a tomb which literally screwed itself into the cliffs backing on to Deir el-Bahri. An extremely gruelling piece of work, it eventually produced two of the finest 18th-Dynasty sarcophagi known. Probably begun by Tuthmosis I, who had once been buried there, and thus designed by the famous architect Ineni, the tomb seems later to have been extended by Hatshepsut as a double burial for herself and her kingly father.

Yuya and Tjuyu

Davis's first really big discovery in the Valley came in February 1905 with the finding of the small tomb of Yuya and Tjuyu (KV46), the parents of Queen Tiye, principal wife of pharaoh Amenophis III. Carter, to his immense chagrin, was now gone from the Valley, transferred to the north and replaced as Inspector by J. E. Quibell (•p. 97); while Quibell himself was in the process of handing over the reins to the recently recruited Arthur Weigall, a survivor of Petrie's harsh student regime at Abydos ('You lived on sardines, and when you had eaten the sardines you ate the tin').

Weigall, an extraordinarily evocative writer, describes the first sight of Davis's new find:

'Imagine entering a town house which had been closed for the summer; imagine the stuffy room, the stiff, silent appearance of the furniture, the feeling that some ghostly occupants of the vacant chairs have just been disturbed…'

The mummies of these ghostly occupants still lay within their coffins, surrounded by much of their burial finery, including furniture, caskets and a magnificent chariot to enable the military officer Yuya to continue his professional duties in the beyond. But, for all the apparent wealth, the tomb had clearly been disturbed in antiquity: the coffins had been opened, and the wonderfully preserved bodies rifled in a frantic search for jewels – perhaps (to judge from the evidence of seals) by those involved in quarrying the adjacent tomb KV3 for a son of Ramesses III some two centuries later.

(right) Massive coffin from the burial of Yuya in KV46 – the outer of three. Skilfully made of wood, the surface is painted in black resin and highlighted in gold leaf on a gesso ground.

(below) Yuya's cartonnage mask, with heavily gilded surface and inlaid eyes.

The exquisite, long-legged casket with vaulted lid from the tomb of Yuya and Tjuyu, richly inlaid with faience; the hieroglyphic inscriptions – the titulary of Amenophis III – are highlighted in gold.

E. R. Ayrton and 'the tomb of Queen Tiyi'

With Weigall's appointment as Chief Inspector of Antiquities for Upper Egypt in 1905, it was decided that Davis should employ his own archaeologist to supervise the day-to-day digging, since this was becoming a drag on the government official's time. The fortunate appointee was the youthful Edward Russell Ayrton, a well-respected English archaeologist trained under the British Museum Egyptologist H. R. Hall at Deir el-Bahri.

Ayrton's first season for Davis, 1905–06, produced a range of material of great archaeological interest, including the rubble-filled tomb of Siptah (KV47), the well-known 'animal tombs' (KV50–52), and the first evidence for the presence in the Valley of Tutankhamun: a small faience cup (Cairo JE 38330) 'found under a rock' not far from KV12, a mysterious tomb evidently intended for members of the royal family. Ayrton retired from the fray exhausted. The season to come, however, would be more demanding still.

The Valley's 55th numbered tomb – a single, well-cut chamber situated a few metres west of the long-known tomb of Ramesses IX (KV6) – was uncovered on 6 January 1907. The principal finds here were a large, dismantled shrine of gilded wood (fragments including Cairo JE 57175), which, from its texts, had been prepared for the burial of Queen Tiye by her son, Akhenaten, and a gloriously inlaid royal coffin (lid: Cairo JE 39627) from which the sheet-gold face and all identifying cartouches

filled up with mud and found to contain a few scraps of gold foil from a chariot harness – was all that remained of the burial of the still unaccounted-for Tutankhamun. And then, on 5 January 1908, Ayrton uncovered another small, single-chambered tomb, which was even more rewarding than Tomb 55. The lowermost of two strata in the washed-in fill of this tomb, KV56, produced the most spectacular group of 19th-Dynasty jewelry ever found in Egypt; it is known today, appropriately enough, as the 'Gold Tomb'.

had been removed. Archaeologically, the situation was complex in the extreme, and warranted the most careful documentation prior to excavation; in addition, the fragile state of most of the finds made it clear that their successful extraction would require an immense amount of patience. Davis understood neither of these requirements; little archaeological detail was ever published, and much of the material perished before it could be properly recorded. As a result, Tomb 55 remains one of the most argued-over finds in Egyptology.

Davis believed that he had discovered the tomb of Tiye herself, as indeed the shrine seemed to indicate; but the body in the coffin was that of a man (Cairo CG 61075). He could not reconcile the discrepancy, and did not try; Egyptologists since have attempted little else. No two agree; but the archaeology suggests that Tomb 55 originally held the bodies of both Tiye and Akhenaten, transferred from the Amarna royal tomb following the abandonment of el-Amarna as capital under Tutankhamun. The body found by Davis appears to be identified by a set of 'magical bricks' bearing the name of Akhenaten, recovered by Ayrton from the debris; while Akhenaten's mother appears, on equally good archaeological evidence, to have been removed from KV55 during the reign of Ramesses IX – perhaps to turn up, in the guise of the 'Elder Lady', in the Amenophis II cache in 1898.

(above) One of the altered canopic jar lids from the Tomb 55 burial.

The 'Gold Tomb'

The following season, 1907-08, saw Davis's team make further important discoveries, including KV54, a shallow pit containing refuse embalming materials and other items. Davis reckoned that this modest collection, together with the stray faience cup brought to light in 1905–06 and a subsequent discovery – tomb KV58,

THE 'GOLD TOMB'

OBJECT	NO.	MATERIAL	NAMES
circlet	1	gold	Sethos II, Tawosret
ear-pendants	2	gold	Sethos II
ear-pendants	2	electrum, carnelian, gold, faience	
earring	1	gold	Tawosret
earrings	2	electrum	
openwork ball beads/pendants	151	gold	
spacers	2	gold	
wedjat-eyes	4	electrum	
heart amulet	1	electrum	
shells	2	gold	
Taweret figures	6	gold	
Hathor heads	3	gold	
Heh-figure	1	gold	
flies	4	gold	
papyrus flowers	3	gold	
bracelets	2	silver or electrum	Sethos II, Tawosret
bracelets	4	gold	
bracelets	3	electrum	
finger-ring	1	gold	Sethos II
finger-ring	1	gold	Ramesses II
finger-ring	1	gold	Tawosret
finger-rings	2	gold, lapis	Tawosret
finger-rings	2	gold, faience	
finger-rings	2	gold	
plaques	13	gold	Sethos II
lion amulets	2	gold	
dog(?) amulet	1	gold	
Hathor-cow amulet	1	gold	
ibis amulet	1	carnelian	
Hathor-head amulets	2	carnelian	
Amun amulet	1	carnelian	
serpent-head amulet	1	carnelian	
bead inlay	1	carnelian	
hand overlays	2	silver	
miniature sandal	1	silver	
mirror-handle element	1	electrum	
jar	1	faience	Sethos II
jars	2	calcite	Ramesses II
jar	1	calcite	

THEODORE DAVIS: principal discoveries

TOMB	OWNER	EXCAVATOR	DATE
KV43	Tuthmosis IV	Carter	c. 18 January 1903
KV45	Userhet (overseer of the fields of Amun)	Carter	25 February 1902
KV46	Yuya and Tjuyu (parents of Queen Tiye)	Quibell	5 February 1905
KV47	Siptah	Ayrton	November 1905
KV48	Amenemopet (vizier)	Ayrton	1905–06
KV49	unknown (storeroom)	Ayrton	1905–06
KV50–52	unknown ('animal tombs')	Ayrton	1905–06
KV53	unknown	Ayrton	1905–06
KV54	(Tutankhamun embalming materials)	Ayrton	1907–08
KV55	Akhenaten; Tiye (cache)	Ayrton	January 1907
KV56	unknown (daughter of Sethos II and Tawosret)	Ayrton	5 January 1908
KV57	Horemheb	Ayrton	22 February 1908
KV58	unknown (chariot fittings)	Jones	10 January 1909
KV60	In (wet-nurse of Hatshepsut)	Carter	spring 1903
KV61	unknown (unused)	Jones	c. 6 January 1910

(above) The burial chamber of Horemheb, as it appeared when first found. Excavated by Edward Ayrton, it was Theodore Davis's last great discovery in the Valley of the Kings.

(opposite above) The Tomb 55 coffin as found, its lid pushed to one side to reveal the vulture-crowned mummy within.

(opposite below) Gold pendant earring of Sethos II from the 'Gold Tomb' – KV 56.

Horemheb

The discovery of the 'Gold Tomb' marked the pinnacle of Davis's excavating career; although he was to make further discoveries, nothing – short of Tutankhamun (•p. 160) – could hope to measure up, bullion-wise at least, to what had gone before.

Davis's last great find, made by Ayrton a few weeks after KV56, was the tomb of Horemheb, with its wonderful wall decorations, plentiful fragments of smashed burial equipment and the skeleton-remains of several burials. These last may indicate that the tomb had served as a hiding place for those royal mummies not represented in the Deir el-Bahri (•p. 64) and Amenophis II (•p. 103) caches.

Ayrton's successors in the direction of Davis's work proved to be far less fortunate: Ernest Harold Jones found virtually nothing and died in post; while Harry Burton, digging in the Valley on Davis's behalf a few months later, was even more unlucky, missing by the merest whisker in 1912 the still-hidden burial of Tutankhamun. But this was a king Davis had convinced himself was already found. Quite how mistaken he was in this belief would, of course, be demonstrated by Howard Carter and the Earl of Carnarvon in 1922, seven years after the American's death.

1902–04
John Garstang at Beni Hasan

'Number inscriptions already large. Some perishable … Much want help just now. Wire reply'
TELEGRAM, JOHN GARSTANG TO PERCY NEWBERRY

Many provincial, middle-ranking cemeteries of Middle Kingdom date have been dug in various parts of Egypt over the years; what makes Beni Hasan special is that the excavator bothered to record, photograph and publish in some detail what he had found.

The volume recounting the work of John Garstang at Beni Hasan between 1902 and 1904 appeared with exemplary speed in 1908, and its pages

convey still the excitement the excavator must have felt as he entered and searched an astonishing 888 tombs – to deal adequately with which he soon had to call upon outside help.

Over and above the mirrors, kohl pots, bows and arrows placed within the rectangular coffin or coffins, the excavations produced a number of musical instruments and sticks of household furniture. Most abundant of all, however, were the painted wooden models – granaries, butchery, bread- and beer-making scenes, and sail and rowing boats – so typical of the period. With these, crammed into the tombs' simple, rock cut burial chambers, the deceased hoped to maintain the élite lifestyle to which he aspired, or had been accustomed, in life.

THE KARNAK CACHETTE:
THE LARGEST FIND OF STATUES EVER MADE

1903 Glazed Tiles from Medinet Habu • 1903 The Face of Khufu

Discovery/excavation
1903
by
Georges Legrain

Site
Thebes (Karnak)

Period
Early Dynastic Period–
Greco-Roman Period,
after c. 3000 BC

'For a year and eight months we have been fishing for statues in the Temple of Karnak. We began about the end of November, 1903, and have continued uninterruptedly until now [February, 1905] …. Seven hundred stone monuments have already come out of the water, and we are not yet at the end ….'

GASTON MASPERO

The 'cachette' of statues brought to light at Karnak temple between 1903 and 1905 represents the largest find of statuary ever made in Egypt and perhaps anywhere in the world. The discovery belonged to the French architect Georges Legrain, working under the supervision of Gaston Maspero (•p. 64), Director of the Service des Antiquités, to restore and consolidate the complex of monuments following the disastrous collapse, on 3 October 1899, of 11 columns of the hypostyle hall. Maspero's line during the clearance had from the start been 'never to abandon any part until it had been thoroughly explored – walls, flooring, substructures – and until all the remains of earlier monuments that could be found there were brought out'. As a result of his thoroughness, many interesting objects and dismantled architectural features were salvaged, including the famous statue of Tutankhamun in the guise of the god Khonsu, a wonderful dyad of Tuthmosis IV and his mother, Tiaa, and a fine series of blocks from chapels first erected by Sesostris I of the 12th and Amenophis I of the 18th dynasties.

It was at the end of 1903 that Legrain's workmen, proceeding in Maspero's prescribed manner beneath the floor of court I before the 7th pylon of the Great Temple, began

GEORGES LEGRAIN
(1865-1917)

'This energetic and amusing French director of works for the Egyptian government ...'
JOSEPH LINDON SMITH

- Born Paris, 4 October 1865
- Studies art and architecture under Auguste Choisy (1841–1909) and others, followed by Egyptology under Paul Pierret (1836–1916) and Eugène Revillout (1843–1913) at the Louvre
- Member of the French Institute in Cairo, 1892-94, working at Aswan, Kom Ombo and el-Amarna
- Inspecteur-dessinateur, Service des Antiquités, from 1894, working at Kom Ombo, Gebel el-Silsila and Dahshur
- Begins work at Karnak, 1895, undertaking conservation work and uncovering the Karnak cachette in 1903; later appointed to the post of Chief Inspector of Antiquities in Luxor in succession to Arthur Weigall
- Dies Luxor, August 1917

(above left) A mud-soaked statue of Amenhotep son of Hapu is retrieved from its watery grave by Georges Legrain's workers.

(left) General view of the site – beneath the floor of the first court of the Great Temple of Amun

(below) This standard-bearing statuette named for Shoshenq, first prophet of Amun under Osorkon I of the 22nd Dynasty, is an earlier New Kingdom sculpture reinscribed.

1903
Glazed Tiles from Medinet Habu

When the visitor raises his or her eyes at Medinet Habu or in the great hypostyle hall at Karnak, a glimpse of still-fresh colours offers a reminder of what was once the brilliance of Egypt's architecture. A similar insight is gained when the excavator brings to light rare evidence of the faience inlays with which certain palaces and other structures, particularly in the New Kingdom, were partially decorated.

The best known of such inlays are those originating from el-Amarna and from the later, Ramessid Delta sites of Tell el-Yahudiya and Qantir. A much finer and more complete series, however, is that turned up by *sebakhin* in 1903 at the 'short stay' palace of Ramesses III at Medinet Habu. These last, chance finds were efficiently rounded up by the inspector of the time, Howard Carter (•p. 160), and are now for the most part in the Cairo Museum (JE 36457). Their discovery prompted Harry Burton to examine the area more closely on behalf of Theodore Davis in 1913.

Burton was a far better photographer than excavator, however; his digging caused much damage to the mud-brick structure of the temple-

palace and produced little in the way of objects to compensate for the destruction.

Originally set in wooden 'cloisons', the technology of these tiles is masterly, involving inlays within inlays and repeated firings. The effect is stunning, with pharaoh's enemies – Kushites, Libyans, Syrians, Mesopotamians, Hittites and 'Sea Peoples' – vividly brought to life in all their colourful glory.

(below) Granite sphinx inscribed between the paws with a cartouche of Tuthmosis III. The sculpture was extricated from the cachette on 27 March 1905.

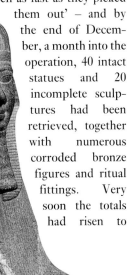

to uncover several fragments of a colossal calcite statue of King Sethos I. Their extraction was a messy business: the Nile was in flood, the water-table high, and the ground a sea of oozing mud. Below these fragments, however, several other statue-shapes could be discerned, and when these were themselves fished out, yet more sculptures were revealed below. 'They seemed to sprout among the men as fast as they picked them out' – and by the end of December, a month into the operation, 40 intact statues and 20 incomplete sculptures had been retrieved, together with numerous corroded bronze figures and ritual fittings. Very soon the totals had risen to an astonishing 751 statues and fragments in stone (including a *shabti*-figure of Amenophis III), some 17,000 bronzes, 'numerous wooden statuettes, impossible to preserve', a range of stelae, obelisks and offering tables, quantities of ram bones (the ram being the sacred animal of Amun, lord of Karnak), a few vessels in metal and stone, and a range of architectural elements. However, only the smallest proportion of the more important sculptures has ever been published; and, sadly, very few of the excavator's notes on the work appear to have come down to us.

The huge number and range of items rescued by Legrain from this watery grave (several of which inevitably fell into the hands of dealers or were otherwise dispersed) seems to have been deposited on a single occasion, during or immediately after the Ptolemaic period. Most were probably votive objects which had been deposited at Karnak by pious individuals who had visited the shrines of the Theban triad – Amun, Mut and Khonsu – during the preceding three thousand years. As a mix of sacred images and divine property, such objects could not be destroyed; burial within the sacred precincts was the only option open to a clergy anxious to avoid drowning in what must, by that time, have been a veritable sea of statues.

Legrain's work came to an end in mid-July 1905, because of the dangers posed by the water-table. But the deposit of sculptures was far from exhausted, and further statues and architectural fragments remain beneath the ground. One day, doubtless, they too will be retrieved to join their fellows on the surface as a further and most valuable source of information on the history, genealogy, art and iconography of ancient Egypt and her southern city.

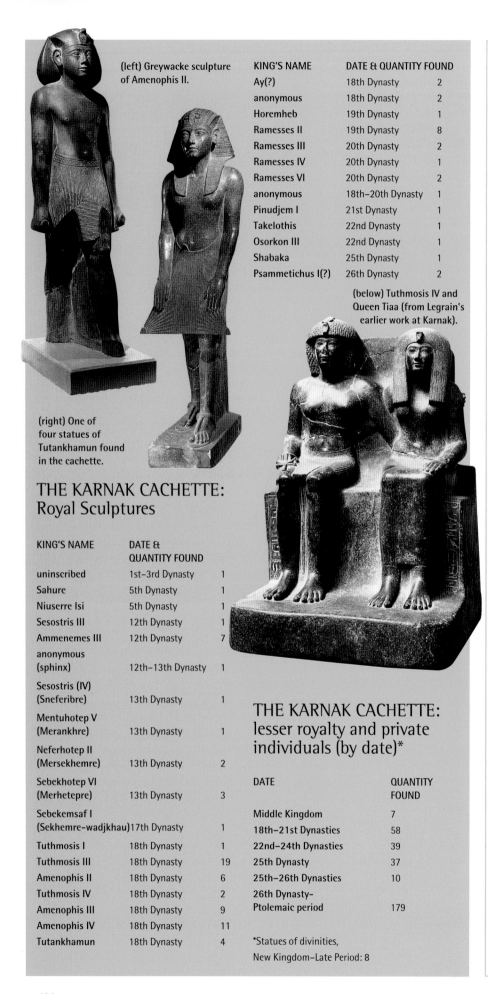

(left) Greywacke sculpture of Amenophis II.

(right) One of four statues of Tutankhamun found in the cachette.

(below) Tuthmosis IV and Queen Tiaa (from Legrain's earlier work at Karnak).

THE KARNAK CACHETTE: Royal Sculptures

KING'S NAME	DATE & QUANTITY FOUND	
uninscribed	1st–3rd Dynasty	1
Sahure	5th Dynasty	1
Niuserre Isi	5th Dynasty	1
Sesostris III	12th Dynasty	1
Ammenemes III	12th Dynasty	7
anonymous (sphinx)	12th–13th Dynasty	1
Sesostris (IV) (Sneferibre)	13th Dynasty	1
Mentuhotep V (Merankhre)	13th Dynasty	1
Neferhotep II (Mersekhemre)	13th Dynasty	2
Sebekhotep VI (Merhetepre)	13th Dynasty	3
Sebekemsaf I (Sekhemre-wadjkhau)	17th Dynasty	1
Tuthmosis I	18th Dynasty	1
Tuthmosis III	18th Dynasty	19
Amenophis II	18th Dynasty	6
Tuthmosis IV	18th Dynasty	2
Amenophis III	18th Dynasty	9
Amenophis IV	18th Dynasty	11
Tutankhamun	18th Dynasty	4

KING'S NAME	DATE & QUANTITY FOUND	
Ay(?)	18th Dynasty	2
anonymous	18th Dynasty	2
Horemheb	19th Dynasty	1
Ramesses II	19th Dynasty	8
Ramesses III	20th Dynasty	2
Ramesses IV	20th Dynasty	1
Ramesses VI	20th Dynasty	2
anonymous	18th–20th Dynasty	1
Pinudjem I	21st Dynasty	1
Takelothis	22nd Dynasty	1
Osorkon III	22nd Dynasty	1
Shabaka	25th Dynasty	1
Psammetichus I(?)	26th Dynasty	2

THE KARNAK CACHETTE: lesser royalty and private individuals (by date)*

DATE	QUANTITY FOUND
Middle Kingdom	7
18th–21st Dynasties	58
22nd–24th Dynasties	39
25th Dynasty	37
25th–26th Dynasties	10
26th Dynasty–Ptolemaic period	179

*Statues of divinities, New Kingdom–Late Period: 8

1903
The Face of Khufu

Egyptologists today know a good deal about the Great Pyramid of Khufu at Giza, including the name of the man plausibly charged with its construction – the vizier Hemiunu, overweight son of king Snefru, immortalized in the famous statue recovered from Giza mastaba G 4000 for Wilhelm Pelizaeus and now in Hildesheim (no. 1962). Yet named portraits of the actual owner of this famous monument, one of the Seven Wonders of the Ancient World, were for many years singularly lacking.

The portraits nowadays attributed to Khufu (Brooklyn 46.167, Berlin 14396, and, most recently, the Great Sphinx) carry no identifying texts – with the exception of this small (7-cm (2¾-in) high) ivory statuette now in Cairo (JE 36143). When it first came to light, during Flinders Petrie's clearance of the temple of Khentimentiu at Abydos in 1903, 'Unhappily the head was broken off and lost by the digger'. Fortunately, the excavator's policy of rewards would save the day: 'Petrie set the man [who had discovered the body] to sieve the tip-heap, promising him great reward if he found the missing piece, but nothing for the broken piece if he did not'. And by a miracle, as Petrie records, 'After three weeks of sifting, the head was recovered'.

Though in size only slightly larger than 'the tip of a little finger, it bore the most amazingly powerful portrait of the all-masterful king. When magnified, it might be supposed to be a life-size statue'.

While the 4th-Dynasty date of this minor masterpiece has not gone unquestioned (a 26th-Dynasty date having recently been proposed) it is still generally accepted.

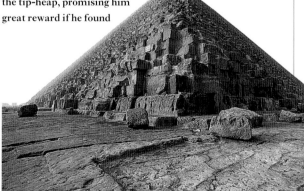

1904

IN 'THE PLACE OF BEAUTIES': NEFERTARI AND HER TOMB

1904–05 Two Portraits of Queen Tiye • 1905 The 'Proto-Sinaitic' Script
1904 The Gold Harsaphes from el-Ihnasya • 1905 The Brussels Relief of Queen Tiye
1905 The Treasure of Tukh el-Qaramus

Discovery/excavation
1904
by
Ernesto Schiaparelli

Site
Thebes (Valley of the
Queens, no. QV66)

Period
New Kingdom,
19th Dynasty, reign of
Ramesses II,
1290–1224 BC

(below) The Valley of the
Queens – a photograph taken
at the time of Schiaparelli's
excavations.

Ta set neferu – in popular (if misleading) translation 'the Place of Beauties' – was founded as a cemetery for the higher echelons of Egyptian society at the beginning of the 18th Dynasty on the west bank at Thebes. By later Ramessid times, many of Egypt's queens, princes and princesses were interred here. This cemetery, today better known as Biban el-Harim or the Valley of the Queens, was investigated and partially documented from 1826 on by Robert Hay and his successors – in particular J. Gardner Wilkinson, who in 1828 numbered (according his own system) the tombs then visible; Jean François Champollion (•p. 14), who visited the Valley in 1828-29; Ippolito Rosellini, who followed in 1834; and Karl Richard Lepsius whose Prussian Expedition arrived in 1845.

Extensive excavation did not commence until 1903, however, with the arrival on the scene of Ernesto Schiaparelli, Director of the Turin Museum. Schiaparelli's choice of sites was sensibly dictated by a wish to fill gaps in his institution's collection – in which aim he was exceedingly successful. He would quit the Valley a mere two years later, in 1905, considering it exhausted (a conclusion with which the recent team of French archaeologists led by Christian Leblanc is now able to concur). In those two years, however, Schiaparelli discovered much of interest (see table), including, in 1904, one of Egypt's most precious artistic gems – the tomb of Nefertari (Nofretiri), Ramesses II's principal wife and mother of at least six of her husband's numerous progeny.

The tomb of Nefertari is entered by a sloping staircase with central sarcophagus-slide leading down to a large, impressive doorway giving access to the tomb's first chamber with laterally placed side room. A second stairway similar to the first descends into the principal chamber of the tomb, which is embellished with four rock-cut pillars and three subsidiary store rooms, reminiscent of the layout in Ramesses II's own tomb.

ERNESTO SCHIAPARELLI
(1856–1928)

*'A great, learned and humble
Italian. Such was Schiaparelli.'*
A COLLEAGUE

- Born Occhieppo Inferiore,
  Biella, Italy, 12 July 1856
- Studies Egyptology at the
  University of Turin under
  Francesco Rossi (1827–1912)
  and in Paris under Maspero
  (•p. 64), 1877–80
- Director of Egyptian section
  of Florence Museum,
  1880–94; Director of Turin
  Museum , 1894–27,
  undertaking exceptionally
  productive excavations for the
  latter institution at Heliopolis,
  Giza, el-Ashmunein, Asyut,
  Qau el-Kebir, el-Hammamia,
  Thebes (Valley of the Queens,
  Deir el-Medina), 1903–20
- Dies Turin, 17 February 1928

4000 BC
3000 BC
2000 BC
1000 BC
0
AD 700

The tomb of Queen Nefertari. (above) General view of the burial chamber, following its recent restoration by the Getty Conservation Institute; the near left column has a representation of the leopard-skin clad *setem*-priest, master of ceremonies at the funeral. (left) A detail of the queen's face from the north wall of the antechamber.

(right) South wall of the antechamber, showing the access stairs leading down into the queen's sarcophagus chamber.

This sepulchre, one of the largest in the Queens' Valley, was a find of great architectural interest; but what struck the excavators even more (as it has all visitors since) is the sheer brilliance, in both colour and execution, of the painted-stucco relief decoration which covers every wall: scenes of Nefertari standing in the presence of and making offering to a range of deities, as well as extracts from ancient texts intended to guarantee the queen's safe and successful transition from this world to the next.

Nefertari's actual burial was, of course, destroyed in antiquity and the tomb, as others in the Valley, plundered and left effectively open and to its fate. Several scraps of the queen's equipment could be salvaged by Schiaparelli, however, among them fragments of a pink granite sarcophagus lid (the sarcophagus box evidently having been removed for reuse in antiquity) and pieces of the gilded wooden coffin, a mass of pottery fragments, remains of some 30 *shabti*-figures of resin-painted wood, the lid from a *shabti*-box, and the wooden *djed*-pillar from a magical brick found still in its wall recess. Similarly unearthed were the knob from a wooden chest (curiously inscribed with the name of King Ay of the 18th Dynasty), fragmented human remains (parts of legs), a rush sandal and pieces of rope and textile. In addition to these 'official' finds, several strays from Schiaparelli's work found their way into the hands of the antiquities merchants, to be

1904–05
Two Portraits
of Queen Tiye

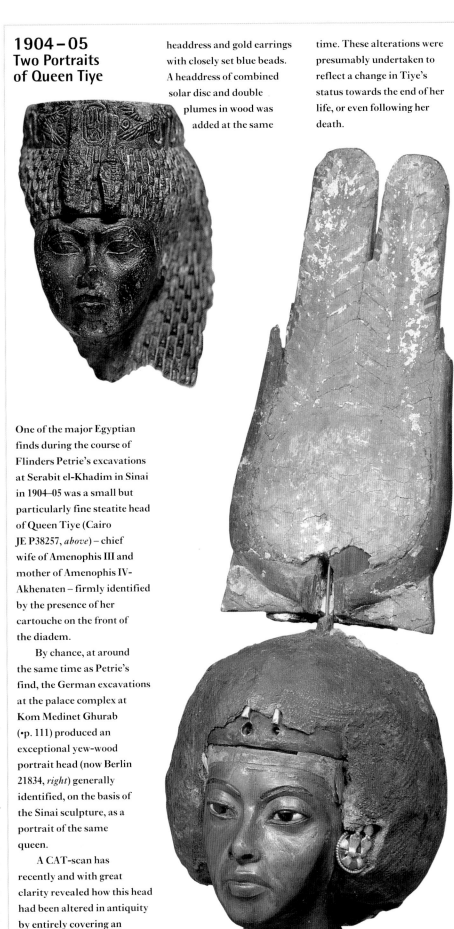

One of the major Egyptian finds during the course of Flinders Petrie's excavations at Serabit el-Khadim in Sinai in 1904–05 was a small but particularly fine steatite head of Queen Tiye (Cairo JE P38257, *above*) – chief wife of Amenophis III and mother of Amenophis IV-Akhenaten – firmly identified by the presence of her cartouche on the front of the diadem.

By chance, at around the same time as Petrie's find, the German excavations at the palace complex at Kom Medinet Ghurab (•p. 111) produced an exceptional yew-wood portrait head (now Berlin 21834, *right*) generally identified, on the basis of the Sinai sculpture, as a portrait of the same queen.

A CAT-scan has recently and with great clarity revealed how this head had been altered in antiquity by entirely covering an original, silver-sheet *khat*-headdress and gold earrings with closely set blue beads. A headdress of combined solar disc and double plumes in wood was added at the same time. These alterations were presumably undertaken to reflect a change in Tiye's status towards the end of her life, or even following her death.

1905
The 'Proto-Sinaitic' Script

Sinai has served both as military buffer zone and

trading conduit between Egypt and her eastern neighbours for millennia; during historic times, the area was also a source of both copper and turquoise.

During his excavations here, in 1904–05, Flinders Petrie discovered several texts written in an unknown script soon dubbed 'proto-Sinaitic'. Because of their obvious alphabetic nature, these caused much excitement among the scholarly

community. For Petrie, the inscriptions were written by contemporaries of the 18th Dynasty; for the great philologist Alan Gardiner, they were much older – 12th Dynasty. Did the alphabetic impulse travel from Egypt east, as Gardiner maintained, or vice versa? The debate – fuelled by John and Deborah Darnell's recent discovery of further texts in the Theban deserts – is set to continue.

1904
The Gold Harsaphes from el-Ihnasya

'During the course of clearing the hypostyle hall [of the temple at Ihnasya in 1904], at a depth of a few feet below the bottom of Dr. Naville's [previous] working, our men found a substructure of pavement; and as they dug the earth they saw a piece of gold showing in the ground…'.

This is how Flinders Petrie describes the chance discovery of a small but exquisite votive image of the local ram-headed god, Harsaphes (Herishef), delicately chased on the underside of the base with the cartouched prenomen, nomen and titles of the obscure, 23rd-Dynasty king Neferkare Peftjawybastet – a contemporary of the 25th-Dynasty Nubian king Piye who ruled from the city of Herakleopolis following the

collapse of central authority in Egypt at the end of the 9th century BC.

Whatever the political instability of the times, the Third Intermediate Period stands as one of the high points of Egyptian artistic and technological achievement, as this figure (now in the Boston Museum of Fine Arts, 1906.2408) and other finds from these times – particularly in faience (•p. 92) – clearly demonstrate.

1905
The Brussels Relief of Queen Tiye

This exquisite relief portrait of Queen Tiye, consort of pharaoh Amenophis III, was 'discovered' on the Paris art market in 1905 by the Belgian Egyptologist Jean Capart, badly defaced with Arabic graffiti.

It soon transpired that the relief had but recently been hacked from the wall of a known monument – the tomb of Userhet (TT47), overseer of the royal harim under Amenophis III, at

Thebes. A Henry Rhind tomb (•p. 46), it had been relocated by Howard Carter (•p. 160) in 1902.

Destruction of this sort was becoming increasingly common, but the sorry fate of Userhet's monument would go neither unnoticed nor unmourned. With the appointment of the English archaeologist Arthur Weigall as Chief Inspector of Upper Egypt in 1905, the safeguarding of the Theban private tombs was set as a priority; thanks to the liberality of a wealthy English industrialist,

Robert Mond, it became a reality.

Within a decade the process of numbering and initial conservation was in full swing, with the best tombs being cleared (both of rubble and squatters), listed in the *Topographical Catalogue of the Private Tombs of Thebes* (1913, with *Supplement*, 1924), and provided with iron doors. From now on, unwelcome intruders would be kept out, and the decorated walls in.

purchased by Albert M. Lythgoe for the Museum of Fine Arts in Boston. These included four *shabti*-figures and three fragments of jewelry. One more gold bracelet fragment, missed by Schiaparelli's workmen as well as by the thousands of tourists who have visited the tomb in the years since its discovery, came to light during work connected with the Getty Conservation Institute's restoration of the Nefertari wall paintings in February 1988.

The Getty's involvement in Nefertari's tomb was prompted by the immensely fragile state of the decorations, due in part to earthquake damage in antiquity, but more crucially to extensive, more recent salt efflorescence. Following the discovery of the tomb, the paintings had deteriorated badly, to such an extent that the tomb was closed in 1934. Thanks to the Getty's brilliant success in countering the work of nature and time, the tomb is once again open to an admiring public, as gloriously perfect now as it ever was in antiquity.

DISCOVERIES IN THE VALLEY OF THE QUEENS, 1903–1905

TOMB NO.	OWNER	STATUS
QV30	Nebiry	stablemaster
QV36	anonymous	king's daughter
QV43	Sethherkhepshef	son of Ramesses III
QV44	Khaemwaset	son of Ramesses III
QV46	Imhotep	vizier
QV47	Ahmose	king's daughter (17th Dyn.)
QV55	Amenherkhepshef	son of Ramesses III
QV66	Nefertari	great wife of Ramesses II
QV87	anonymous	–
QV88	Ahmose	king's son
QV89	anonymous	–
QV90	anonymous	–
QV91	anonymous	–

1905
The Treasure of Tukh el-Qaramus

'About the beginning of August 1905 a party of sebakhin … came upon a hoard of silver, including a large Greek crater and several fragmentary Egyptian censers: there was also a fine bronze head of a king, originally attached to some utensil …. A few days afterwards the workmen, proceeding gradually on their course, lighted upon a second hoard of treasure which altogether eclipsed the former discovery – a wonderful collection of gold bracelets and other ornaments, chiefly of Greek workmanship, silver vessels of various kinds and gold and silver coins.

CAMPBELL COWAN EDGAR

Vessels of precious (and not so precious) metal have always been rare in the archaeological record, owing to the fact that they were usually melted down for scrap and reuse at the end of their functional life. Nevertheless, several hoards of 'plate' have over the years turned up in Egypt, the great majority in the precincts of the Delta temples, where they were seemingly buried in times of unrest with the intention of retrieval at a later, safer date. One of the first to be reported was the so-called treasure of Tell

Timai (the ancient Greek Thmuis) – five silver vessels of the early 3rd century BC or thereabouts, which were secured by Émile Brugsch in 1871 for the Cairo Museum (CG 3581-85/53267, 53274-7). Several similar, if unprovenanced, hoards are also known, one acquired by the Metropolitan Museum of Art in 1917 (MMA 18.2.13-17).

The Tukh el-Qaramus treasure – totalling 'some 117 ozs.' – had been discovered by

sebakhin within the precincts of a temple first noted by Édouard Naville in 1887, in the remains of a group of doorless, mud-brick chambers. These were evidently the temple treasuries, and C. C. Edgar later cleared them in an attempt to shed further light on the find.

The excavation of chamber 2 produced a number of objects which supplemented the principal find: most notably, fragments of silver tubes from the censers recovered by the locals, a large silver sistrum or religious rattle, three silver dishes, a plate and two bowls, and a mass of silver coins – the majority of these stored in a pottery jar with the component parts of an amuletic necklace of gold and semiprecious stone.

A further week's excavation in other chambers within the building brought nothing further to light.

This oddly overlooked assemblage (about whose discovery 'no one will ever know the whole history') is conveniently dated by the coins – silver tetradrachms which may be assigned to the first half of the 3rd century BC. Like the similar Tell Timai treasure, it offers an interesting glimpse of the jeweller's and silversmith's craft during the early years of Greek rule.

THE TOMB OF KHA, ARCHITECT OF PHARAOH

1906 Hathor at Deir el-Bahri • 1906 Nubian Snow

Discovery/excavation
1906
by
Ernesto Schiaparelli

Site
Thebes (Deir el-Medina, tomb TT8)

Period
New Kingdom, 18th Dynasty, reign of Amenophis III, 1391–1353 BC

4000 BC
3000 BC
2000 BC
1000 BC
0
AD 700

'The mouth of the tomb was approached down a flight of steep, rough steps, still half-choked with débris. At the bottom of this the entrance of a passage running into the hillside was blocked by a wall of rough stones. After photographing and removing this, we found ourselves in a long, low tunnel, blocked by a second wall a few yards ahead. Both these walls were intact, and we realized that we were about to see what probably no living man had ever seen before ….'
ARTHUR WEIGALL

The year was 1906, and the Antiquities Service Inspector Arthur Weigall and Ernesto Schiaparelli (•p. 121), the excavator he was accompanying, were about to enter the burial of the architect Kha and his wife, Meryet, undisturbed since the early part of the 14th century BC. Schiaparelli and his 250 workers had been digging relentlessly, in shifts, for the better part of four weeks, with little to show for their efforts. Now came the reward.

Removing the first and then the second wall, Schiaparelli and Weigall found themselves in a roughly cut corridor of about standing height. To their left, lined up against the passage wall, was a selection of the deceaseds' burial furniture, including some baskets, a carrying-pole, a couple of amphorae, and a 'closet-stool' and bed of Kha, who had plainly been the last to be interred here. At the far end of the corridor stood a simple wooden door.

'The wood retained the light colour of fresh deal, and looked for all the world as though it had been set up but yesterday. A heavy wooden lock … held the door fast. A neat bronze handle on the side of the door was connected by a spring to a wooden knob set in the masonry door post; and this spring was carefully sealed with a small dab of stamped clay. The whole contrivance seemed so modern that Professor Schiaparelli called to his servant for the key, who quite seriously replied, "I don't know where it is, sir" .'

(above) Two-handled pottery storage jar – the body with *rishi* (feather) decoration, the linen-covered neck with various sacred emblems applied in brightly coloured paint. A hieratic docket records the owner's name – 'Kha'.

(above) The architect Kha, as depicted in a modest wooden funerary statue from the tomb.

(left) A simple wooden chest from the burial of Kha and Meryet, with naive painted scenes of the deceased and his wife seated before a loaded offering table, and poorly executed hieroglyphic inscriptions.

Without a key, the only means of gaining access to the single, vaulted chamber beyond was by carefully cutting the lock with a fret-saw; this done, the door swung open for the first time in more than three thousand years.

The burial was neat and orderly, the principal items covered with dust-sheets still strong to the touch, the floor carefully swept by the last to have left. A single papyrus-column lamp-stand of wood supported a copper-alloy saucer still containing the ashes produced by its ancient flame. 'One asked oneself in bewilderment whether the ashes here, seemingly not cold, had truly ceased to glow at a time when Rome and Greece were undreamt of, when Assyria did not exist, and when the Exodus of the Children of Israel was yet unaccomplished'.

The contents of the tomb were essentially those of any prosperous, 18th-Dynasty home, packed away in preparation for their re-use in the next life. A series of low tables (of wood and of rush construction) was piled high with offerings of vegetables, mashed carob and loaves in a bewildering range of sizes and shapes, while amphorae (some elaborately decorated) contained fine wines, grapes, salted meats (including duck), and flour, with conical-lidded baskets filled to the brim with yet more culinary necessities, including cumin and juniper berries. Next to the coffins were faded garlands, floor-coverings, a travelling mat with pockets for nightwear, and several additional items of

(below left) The burial chamber of Kha and Meryet's tomb, with linen-draped bed, stand, chair (with Kha's statue), stool and lamp – unseen and untouched for over three millennia.

(below right) Section of the well-preserved funerary papyrus from Kha's coffin: the deceased and his wife, hands raised in adoration, are received into the presence of Osiris, 'ruler of eternity', enthroned beneath a flower-bedecked canopy. A heaped table of offerings stands before.

furniture: Meryet's bed, made-up ready for use, the lady's wig, cosmetic and trinket boxes, her work-basket with needles, a razor, pins and a comb, as well as decorated storage chests packed with clothing. Upon a brightly painted and inscribed chair – itself a symbol of rank – had been placed a garlanded wooden figure of its owner, Kha, with other possessions ranged around: a single, folding, duck-headed stool, a tall cup-stand, washing ewer and stand and a bronze situla. Much of this material was inscribed with the owners' names; the calligraphy of the inscriptions was so poor, however, that, had any of the pieces from the tomb 'leaked' on to the antiquities market, they would have been instantly dismissed as fakes.

The mummy of Kha was contained in one rectangular and two nested anthropoid coffins, that of Meryet in a rectangular outer shrine containing a singular inner anthropoid coffin and a cartonnage mask. Within Kha's coffins was one of the earliest copies of the Book of the Dead on papyrus, 14 m (46 ft) in length and illustrated with high-quality coloured vignettes. A second funerary papyrus, of unexplained origin, is now in the Louvre in Paris (E 13988). The man's mummy was carefully and tightly wrapped, and, as X-rays reveal, equipped with several items of funerary jewelry (ear- and finger-rings, a *shebyu*-collar, *sa*-amulet and large pendant scarab). The mummy of Meryet was only loosely wrapped; X-rays of her body revealed the presence of funerary jewelry and a broad, floral collar.

As a time-capsule from the past, totally undisturbed since the last interment was made, Schiaparelli's find was quite unique.

Who was Kha?

The tools found in the tomb told of Kha's profession – architect to Pharaoh: a royal-cubit measure of gold-foil covered wood, evidently a gift from Amenophis II in recognition of Kha's efficiency, inscribed with the king's

(above) Brightly painted wooden box containing cosmetic vessels of alabaster, wood, faience and glass – the dressing table of Meryet.

names and titulary; a more utilitarian folding cubit of wood with its leather carrying-case; and a selection of wood-working implements. An empty wooden case intended to contain a hand-balance had also been included among the burial equipment, while what appears to be a leather manuscript, still tightly rolled, may well contain details of one or more of the architectural projects for which Kha had been responsible. We know that he was active during at least three and possibly four reigns – those of Tuthmosis III, Amenophis II, Tuthmosis IV and Amenophis III, when the ancient Thebes we know today first began to take shape.

The tomb chapel

Kha's decorated chapel, surmounted by a small pyramid, was known long before his burial apartments, having been brought to light by Bernardino Drovetti in the early years of the 19th century; and, by the strangest of chances, Kha's funerary stela had already made its way to Turin from here several decades before Schiaparelli's discovery of the tomb's burial chambers. Clearly the burial proper had escaped discovery in ancient and more recent times owing to the fact that it had been located within the hill *opposite* the tomb chapel, rather than beneath it.

Schiaparelli was a lucky excavator, and Kha was not the only intact tomb he uncovered during his relatively short time in Egypt. Digging at the cemetery of Gebelein in 1911, he encountered two more undisturbed burials – the 'Tomb of the Unknown', and that of the royal treasurer Ini, dating respectively to the Old and Middle Kingdoms. They, and Kha, provided Turin with the balance of materials Schiaparelli desired, and the museum's Egyptian collection is in consequence among the finest in the world today.

1906
Hathor at Deir el-Bahri

A sudden landslip at Deir el-Bahri on 7 February 1906, during the course of the Egypt Exploration Fund's diggings at the temple of Nebhepetre Mentuhotep, took everyone by surprise. To the amazement of all present, it revealed a small vaulted chapel built into the rock face by Tuthmosis III: 'a cow's head was outlined beneath in the gloom, and looked out curiously through the opening' from behind a forest of votive wooden phalluses. The paint of this sculpture was preserved in wonderful, fresh condition, and the odd fleck of gilt still glinted in the sun; that, and the delightful, placid expression of the sacred cow, drew a collective gasp of awe from all present.

The cow goddess Hathor was one of the principal deities of the Theban west bank, and Deir el-Bahri was her particular realm. This little shrine had been erected under the supervision of the well-known vizier Rekhmire (whose tomb and its inscriptions are famous to all students of Egyptology) as the ultimate destination of the sacred barque which crossed the river from Karnak during the Beautiful Festival of the Valley. Carefully disinterred by Naville and his team, the goddess and her shrine are now on display in Cairo (JE 38574-5).

1906
Nubian Snow

One aspect of Egyptian discovery not easily lending itself to popular discussion is philological research – with one charming exception:

'On Washington's birthday, 1906, [James Henry] Breasted had one of those experiences which delight the philologist. On the so-called Marriage Stela at Abu Simbel, he read that Ramses [Ramesses] II had prayed that when the Hittite princess and her party passed through the northern hills there might be no "rain or srq"... "This is, of course, the Egyptian transliteration for ... 'snow,' which is the earliest occurrence of the word as applied to Syria. It is curious to come to snowless Nubia to find such a word for the first time.'*

The study of ancient Egyptian language had advanced in leaps and bounds in the 80 years since Champollion's initial cracking of the hieroglyphic code (•p. 15), thanks to ground-breaking work from the German school and Adolf Erman, founder of the great German dictionary project which was to crystallize in the fundamental *Wörterbuch der ägyptischen Sprache* published in parts from 1926 on. Breasted (below, with his wife and son) studied under Erman during the early 1890s, and to good

effect. Besides benefiting from Erman's formidable scholarship, Breasted also absorbed his teacher's passion for great schemes: with his appointment as instructor in Chicago, he set himself the task of examining, copying and translating all the known historical texts from ancient Egypt (the achievement was published in his 5-volume *Ancient Records of Egypt* in 1906, following his great *History* of the previous year). In 1919, Breasted proposed to John D. Rockefeller Jr an ambitious plan resulting in the foundation of the Oriental Institute of the University of Chicago – which, in the field of texts and philology, brilliantly continues today where Champollion and Erman left off.

Discovery/excavation
1906
by
local Egyptians

Site
Tell Basta (Bubastis,
modern Zagazig)

Period
New Kingdom,
19th Dynasty,
c. 1307–1196 BC, or later

'One man turned up ... two vases in perfect preservation, one gold, the other silver, and also a quantity of silver jewellery, which he endeavoured to hide under the embankment with the aid of one of his comrades. They carried it away during the night, and sold it to a dealer ....'

GASTON MASPERO

Among the few dynastic temple treasures known from Egypt are the two hoards brought to light in 1906 at Tell Basta, ancient Bubastis, city of origin of the kings of the 22nd Dynasty. Famed today for its appealing patron deity, the cat goddess Bastet ('Bubastis' translates as 'The place of Bastet'), this had always been a city of some importance owing to its location on the principal route east from the capital, Memphis, and boasted a flourishing community. According to Herodotus, it possessed one of the most charming temples in the whole of Egypt – now sadly gone forever.

Indications of the first of the Bubastis treasures came to light on 22 September 1906, when a gold lotus cup bearing the cartouche of Queen Tawosret and three silver jugs inscribed for a king's butler and king's messenger, Atumemtaneb, were found. These were spirited away for profitable, if illicit, sale by the finders, who would later be imprisoned for the theft. Although the most important pieces were recovered by the authorities, a number of lesser items slipped the net to be acquired subsequently by the Berlin Museum and the Metropolitan Museum in New York. Excavations carried out on site a short time after successfully recovered a few additional scraps of the deposit, as the then Chief Inspector of Antiquities for the Delta, C. C. Edgar, reported:

(below) The better of the silver jugs from the first Tell Basta hoard, with solid cast gold handle in the form of an ibex, poised at the gold rim as if to drink from within. The body of the vessel was damaged by a workman's *touria* (pick) at the time of discovery.

'As soon as the [first] vases had been lodged in the Museum, I began a small excavation at Tell Basta. We knew whereabouts the treasure must have been found, though not the exact spot .... On the second day of the excavation we made a good find ... a little north of the temple .... The workmen here uncovered some small pieces of gold [which] turned out to be the scattered pieces of a necklace .... Besides these we found two small figures, one of gold and one of electrum ... and from the mouth of one of the workmen a flat piece of silver covered with gold leaf was extracted with some difficulty.'

(below) Detail of the repoussé decoration on a silver bowl of Atumemtaneb from the first Tell Basta treasure, now in the Metropolitan Museum of Art, New York: fishing and fowling in the marshes.

The second Tell Basta treasure was brought to light on 17 October 1906, several metres from the first and somewhat further from the temple site. Its precise relationship to the first hoard remains uncertain, though both were located some 20 m (65 ft) below known Roman levels on the site. 'It lay in one heap ... the lesser silver objects ... at the top; the gold was found below, amid the silver bowls ... [and] practically nothing was lost'. Here, too, the earliest pieces were Ramessid in date – two splendid articulated bracelets of Ramesses II, each modelled in relief on

DATABLE MATERIAL
from the Tell Basta treasures

MUSEUM NO.	TREASURE	DESCRIPTION	DATE
Cairo CG 53260	first	gold lotus cup	Tawosret
Berlin 19736	first	gold situla-like vessel	Tawosret
New York, MMA 07.228.212 (+07.228.196, .202, .233)	first	rim fragments(s) of silver strainer or bowl	Tawosret
Cairo CG 52575	second	pair of gold and lapis lazuli bracelets	Ramesses II
--	second	badly preserved fragment of silver	Ramesses II(?)

(below) 19th-Dynasty gold vessel from the first Tell Basta treasure, the body decorated in repoussé and with a heavily chased neck. The single ring handle turns through the body of a recumbent calf.

(above) Pair of gold and lapis double-goose bracelets inscribed with the name of Ramesses II, from the second Tell Basta Treasure.

the back with two double-headed geese with bodies of lapis lazuli.

Most scholars would today agree with William Kelly Simpson's assessment that the inscribed pieces date the two hoards – in contrast with Maspero's interpretation at the time: he believed that certain elements of the assemblages were early Islamic, 'part of the stock belonging to a goldsmith in a small town …'.

1907–11
Five Years' Explorations at Thebes

The fifth Earl of Carnarvon was a rich and somewhat unconventional English aristocrat who had first visited Egypt for the sake of his health following a serious motoring accident in Germany. A chance introduction to Gaston Maspero (•p. 64) prompted him to try his hand at digging as a way of surviving the otherwise interminable months of winter exile. By

1908 – having already distinguished himself by the discovery (in Carnarvon tomb no. 9) of two writing boards (Cairo JE 43216–7), one of which (*above*) recounted the story of the expulsion of the Hyksos by the 17th-Dynasty king Kamose (•p. 202) – he had taken on a professional to guide him in his work: Howard Carter. The pair worked well together, and at the site of Dra Abu'l-Naga, between 1907 and 1911, uncovered several other important burials, many of them untouched and yielding an enormous range of *bijoux*. One of the most significant (Carnarvon no. 37) was that containing the silver-alloy statuette of a boy, Amenemheb, of early 18th-Dynasty date and now in the Metropolitan Museum of Art in New York (MMA 26.7.1413). It was a fine piece; but, as the world now knows, for Carnarvon and Carter the future had far greater rewards in store (•p. 160).

destructively, layer by layer, on screen rather than on the operating table. Further, and even more dramatic, developments may be anticipated for the future in the field of DNA analysis.

1907
The Tomb of Two Brothers

'The whole of the funeral furniture and the larger coffins are as fine as anything known of this period ….'
FLINDERS PETRIE

The 'Tomb of Two Brothers' was discovered at Deir Rifa by a Qufti workman named Erfai, working under the supervision of the British Egyptologist Ernest Mackay. The entrance – in the courtyard of the tomb of the local prince Khnumaa (no. 2), their father – consisted of an open, sloping passage giving access to a rhomboidal chamber into which the tomb contents had been closely packed. The burials were undisturbed – despite the fact that the rock-cut chapel above had been decorated in black outline, presumably for re-employment several hundred years later during the reign of Ramesses III.

The contents of the burial were divided entire to Petrie's British School of Archaeology in Egypt, and passed to Manchester Museum where they have since been intensively studied, first by Margaret Murray, in 1908 (*above*), and more recently by a team led by Rosalie David.

Archaeologically, the assemblage is of no small significance owing to its condition and completeness; while the strikingly dissimilar physical characteristics of the two short-statured brothers have over the years aroused great interest among the scientific community.

Ground-breaking multi-disciplinary work carried out at Manchester has told us much about the occupants of the tomb – and has inevitably posed further questions still to be satisfactorily answered. Nakhtankh (21470) died aged around 60, having suffered from lung disease (pneumoconiosis) and heart disease and he may have been a eunuch; his skull shape was similar to that of the tomb-statue of Khnumnakht. The severely osteoarthritic Khnumnakht (21471) suffered from arrested growth, and was aged about 40 at the time of his death; his skull-type had similarities to that represented in the statue of Nakhtankh. In the preparation of the funerary equipment it seems there may have been some confusion.

Following the lead set by David, scientific research on mummies has continued apace with the development of tomography, or CAT-scanning. Using this technique fully wrapped corpses can be divested of their bandages, non-

THE TOMB OF TWO BROTHERS

NO.	NAME	DESCRIPTION
1	Nakhtankh	rectangular outer coffin, wood
2	Nakhtankh	anthropoid inner coffin, wood
3	Nakhtankh	mummy ('eunuchoid')
4	Nakhtankh	canopic chest, wood
5	Nakhtankh	canopic jars, pottery
6	Nakhtankh	large statuette of deceased, wood
7	Nakhtankh	small statuette of deceased, wood (found in 9)
8	Khnumnakht	rectangular outer coffin, wood
9	Khnumnakht	anthropoid inner coffin, wood
10	Khnumnakht	mummy
11	Khnumnakht	statuette of deceased, wood (found in 2)
12	Ir(?)	female offering bearer, wood
13	Iqi(?)	female offering bearer, wood
14	uninscribed	model sailing boat, wood
15	uninscribed	model rowing boat, wood
16	uninscribed	jar, pottery
17	uninscribed	dish, pottery

STATUES OF MENKAURE: REISNER AT GIZA

1908 Petrie's Qurna Burial

Discovery/excavation
1908–10
by
George A. Reisner

Site
Giza (pyramid of Menkaure)

Period
Old Kingdom, 4th Dynasty,
reign of Menkaure,
2490–2472 BC

4000 BC

3000 BC

2000 BC

1000 BC

0

AD 700

'Reisner's excavations at the two temples of Mycerinus [Menkaure]… had yielded sensational treasures … I relived with him the excitement of the opening of room after room filled with amazing sculpture in the round. Two alabaster portrait heads of the King, five complete statues, and the slate triad. He could hardly contain himself….'
JOSEPH LINDON SMITH

George A. Reisner, the American Petrie, began his scholarly career in ancient Near Eastern texts before being lured away by the charms of Egyptology as practised in Berlin by Adolf Erman and Kurt Sethe. Two productive years working on the *Catalogue général* of the Cairo Museum (amulets, boats and canopic jars) were followed by a spell as field director for a University of California expedition sponsored by Mrs Phoebe Hearst, mother of the American newspaper magnate William Randolph Hearst. At Deir el-Ballas and Naga el-Deir Reisner gained valuable experience as a dirt-archaeologist, before being appointed to the plum position of assistant professor of Egyptology at Harvard and director of the joint expedition sponsored by Harvard and the Boston Museum of Fine Arts at Giza.

Reisner's work at Giza was everything these institutions could have hoped for – carefully executed, scrupulously documented, and enormously fortunate in its finds. Its director was also impressively lacking in prejudice, eschewing the colonial arrogance which sometimes beset even the best excavations: the Egyptians worked with, not for him. As others have commented, such even-handedness reaped rich rewards, as demonstrated by the presentation to Reisner – completely out of the blue, by a *fellah* grateful for permission to carry off *sebakh* from the excavator's dumps at Deir el-Ballas – of the immensely important Hearst Medical Papyrus.

The Giza work would be notable not for its textual finds, but for its rich yield of Old Kingdom royal sculpture from Menkaure's pyramid and valley temples, important areas which Reisner had been extremely fortunate to be allocated. As he records:

GEORGE ANDREW REISNER
(1867–1942)

'… the finder of those Ethiopian heroes, Asphalta and Concreta!'
HERBERT E. WINLOCK

- Born Indianapolis, 5 November 1867
- AB, AM, Ph.D. Harvard; Travelling Fellow, 1893–96, studying Assyriology at Berlin, transferring to Egyptology under Kurt Sethe
- Temporary assistant, Berlin Museum, 1895–96
- Instructor in Semitics, Harvard University, 1896–97
- Director of Phoebe Apperson Hearst Egyptian Expedition and Hearst Lecturer, University of California, 1899–1905
- Assistant Professor, Semitic Archaeology, Harvard 1905–10
- Nubian Archaeological Survey, 1907–09; Director, Harvard-Boston Egyptian Expedition, and Assistant Professor of Egyptology, Harvard, 1910
- Curator of Egyptian Art, Museum of Fine Arts, Boston, 1910–42; Professor of Egyptology, Harvard University, 1914–42, digging widely both in Egypt and the Sudan
- Dies 1942, leaving his archaeological notes to the Boston Museum, and 'a collection of thirteen hundred detective stories' to Harvard

(right) The perfectly preserved pair-statue of Menkaure and an unnamed queen – the last and greatest of Reisner's magnificent Giza finds – as first revealed by the archaeologist on 18 January 1910.

(left) One of three complete and one fragmentary Menkaure triads uncovered by George Reisner in 1908: the king, wearing the crown of Upper Egypt, stands between Isis and the goddess of the 17th nome (or district) of Upper Egypt.

(below) Head from an alabaster statue of Menkaure (recognizable by his slightly bulbous nose). The king is shown wearing the *nemes*-headcloth – an unusual detail (which appears again at the very end of pharaonic rule) is the row of curls projecting from beneath the brow band.

SITES EXCAVATED by G. A. Reisner in Egypt

SITE	DATES EXCAVATED
el-Ahaiwa	1900*
Deir el-Ballas	1900-01*
Deir el-Bersha	1915**
Giza	1903-05,* 1905-10,** 1912-16,** 1923-37**
Kafr Ghattati	1924**
Koptos	1899-1900,* 1923**
Mesheikh	1912**
Mesaid	1910,** 1913**
Naga el-Deir	1901-04,* 1912,** 1923-24**
Naga el-Hai	1913**
Sheikh Farag	1913,** 1923-24**
Zawiyet el-Aryan	1910-11**

*For University of California, Berkeley
**For Museum of Fine Arts, Boston/Harvard University

'Previous to the excavation of the temples of Mycerinus [Menkaure], only thirteen statues and statuettes were known of kings of Dynasty IV.... In the temples of Mycerinus, the Harvard-Boston Expedition found seventeen statues equal in preservation ... and in addition fifteen statuettes presenting eight stages in the creation of a statue. ... This rich material made it necessary to revise the history of Egyptian art during its great creative period ....'

1908
Petrie's Qurna Burial

Flinders Petrie spent but little of his long life excavating at Thebes, but when he did it reaped dividends. His discovery at Dra Abu'l-Naga during the winter of 1908–09 of a shallow pit containing a woman and a young child proved an important and intriguing one. The principal coffin was of 17th-Dynasty, *rishi* ('feathered') design, painted and highlighted in gold, with the lid and base each carved from a single block of wood. The smaller, rectangular

coffin was accompanied by a dismantled wooden chair, two wooden stool frames, a wooden box and a rush basket, as well as a carrying pole with 16 pottery vessels suspended in nets. Both burials were intact and richly decked out with gold or electrum bangles, beads, earrings, girdle and collar. The two occupants may have been minor members of the Theban royal line, though no names survived. The group was divided to Petrie intact and presented to the museum in Edinburgh (1909.527) where it is currently undergoing renewed and detailed study.

(right) Colossal alabaster statue of Menkaure, now in Boston. It is thought that the exceptionally small head was the result of a last-minute change of design – from narrow white crown to broader *nemes* – which left insufficient material for the proper proportions to be maintained.

133

NEFERTITI, ICON OF ANCIENT EGYPT:
THE WORKSHOP OF THE SCULPTOR THUTMOSE

1913 The Tomb of Impy • Before 1914 The Gebel el-Araq Knife
1913 Statues of Amenhotep Son of Hapu and Paramessu from Karnak

Discovery/excavation
1912
by
Ludwig Borchardt

Site
el-Amarna

Period
New Kingdom,
18th Dynasty,
reign of Akhenaten,
1353–1335 BC

4000 BC
3000 BC
2000 BC
1000 BC
0
AD 700

(right) The head of Nefertiti – ancient Egypt's most beautiful woman. The surviving eye is a curved sheet of rock crystal held in place by the pigment delineating the pupil; as Egyptologist Rolf Krauss observes, traces of this pigment visible in early photographs suggest that the second eye had been present in antiquity and simply fell out.

(below) Scene from the tomb of Huya at el-Amarna, showing another master sculptor, Iuty, at work in his studio on a statue of princess Baketaten.

Following Petrie's ground-breaking season at el-Amarna in 1891–92 (•p. 83), work was continued at the site over a number of years by the epigrapher Norman de Garis Davies, who copied and published the decoration of the tombs of the principal nobles in his six-volume work *The Rock Tombs of El Amarna*. Thanks to Petrie and Davies, the Amarna 'look' – the distinctive hypernaturalistic style by which Akhenaten sought to articulate his revolution, hitherto represented by only a handful of works (•pp. 24, 61) – rapidly became established in the popular perception.

In 1907, the German archaeologists of the Deutsche Orient-Gesellschaft (the Berlin-based equivalent of the Egypt Exploration Fund/Society) under 'cocky little Ludwig Borchardt' took up again where Petrie had left off, this time in the city's outskirts. The results of their work would astonish the world.

Knowledge of but few artists has come down to us from ancient Egypt; and, since there was never any tradition of signing works, the names of these few have survived quite by chance. For the Amarna era we know of three by name: Iuty, 'overseer of sculptors of the great royal wife Tiye', who is shown in the tomb of Huya correcting in ink an unfinished statue of the king's daughter Baketaten; the chief sculptor Bek (son of Amenophis III's chief sculptor, Men, who was responsible for the extraordinary 'Colossi of Memnon' at Thebes), who claims in his famous quartzite stela in Berlin (1/63) to have been 'one whom his majesty himself instructed'; and, most famous of all, Thutmose, 'favourite of the good god, overseer of works and sculptor' to Akhenaten himself, whose existence is attested by a small ivory horse-blinker. It is this modest blinker which identifies the principal of the workshops discovered by Borchardt's team in house P 47.1-3 in the South Suburb of el-Amarna – where, on 6 December 1912, among the remains of a small, bricked-up room, the Deutsche Orient-Gesellschaft discovered the greatest collection of Amarna art Egyptology has yet seen.

The Thutmose gallery

The collection of works uncovered during excavation of the ruined, mud-brick villa of Thutmose remains one of the most important encountered anywhere in Egypt – a total of more than 20 prototype plaster casts (a similar example, rather worn, had been found by Petrie two decades before) taken, at various stages of production, from clay masters, together with a whole range of incomplete and finished sculptures, composite and otherwise, carved in a variety of

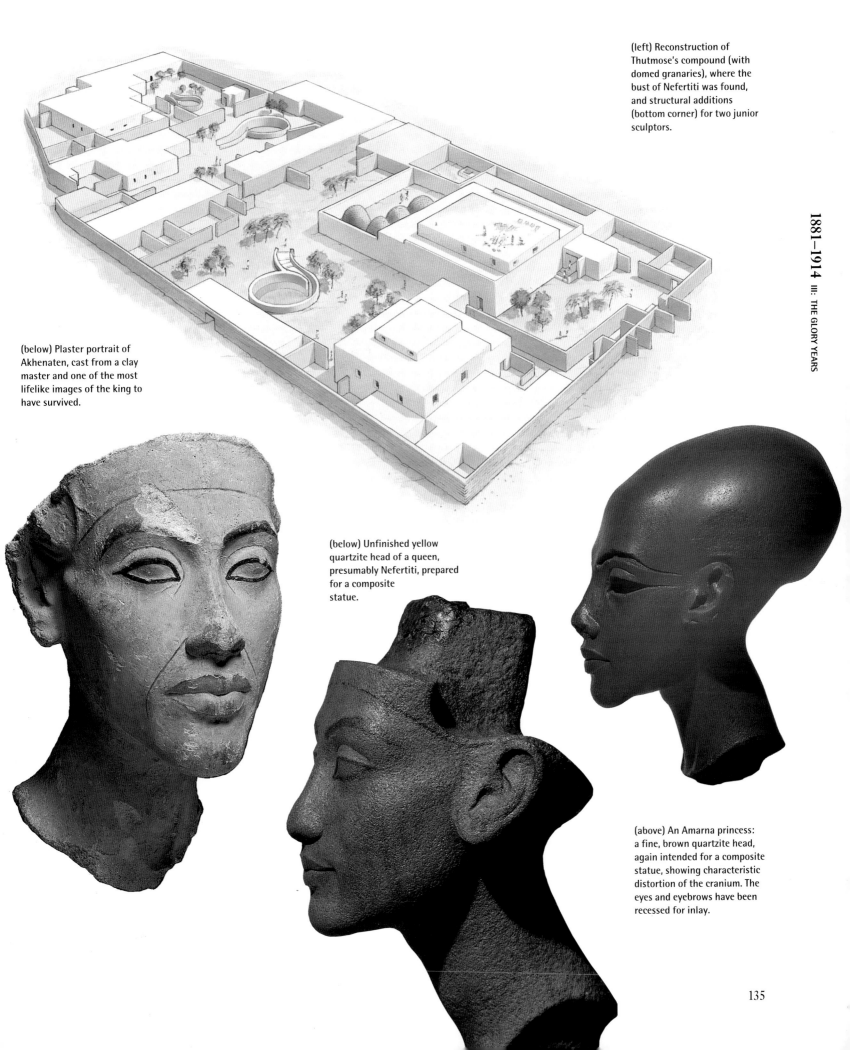

(left) Reconstruction of Thutmose's compound (with domed granaries), where the bust of Nefertiti was found, and structural additions (bottom corner) for two junior sculptors.

(below) Plaster portrait of Akhenaten, cast from a clay master and one of the most lifelike images of the king to have survived.

(below) Unfinished yellow quartzite head of a queen, presumably Nefertiti, prepared for a composite statue.

(above) An Amarna princess: a fine, brown quartzite head, again intended for a composite statue, showing characteristic distortion of the cranium. The eyes and eyebrows have been recessed for inlay.

135

- Born Berlin, 5 October 1863
- Trains as an architect, Technische Hochschule, 1883–87
- Egyptological assistant, Berlin 1883–87; studies Egyptology under Adolf Erman
- Initiates the *Catalogue général* of the Cairo Museum with Maspero
- Founds German Archaeological Institute, Cairo, 1907; Director to 1928
- Excavates Abu Ghurab and Abusir, 1898–1901 (•p. 87); el-Amarna, 1907–14
- Dies Paris, 12 August 1938; burial in Cairo

hard and soft stones. Most of the principal members of the court can with some likelihood be identified, including the pharaohs Amenophis III and Akhenaten, queens Nefertiti and Kiya, several of the royal daughters, and the high officials Amenhotep son of Hapu and the god's father Ay. There are also portraits representing other, predominantly private individuals whose role during the Amarna years must have been significant, but who, for the moment, remain unidentified.

The quality of all of these works is superb, but the unrivalled centrepiece of the Thutmose collection is ancient Egypt's most famous icon: the magnificent, painted bust of Nefertiti, shown wearing her characteristic, flat-topped crown. The portrait, modelled on a limestone core, is undoubtedly a work by the master himself and is perfect in every detail – though only one of its inlaid eyes is today preserved.

At the formal division of spoils a mere month after the discovery, the Nefertiti bust passed to Dr James Simon, the sponsor of the German excavations. In 1920 Simon made a formal gift of his collection to the state of Prussia; three years after that, the queen was unveiled to an astonished public – an event closely followed by outraged complaints from the Egyptian Government that the queen's portrait had left Egypt under irregular circumstances.

Accusations flew and solutions were proposed in an attempt to resolve this unhappy situation – but to no avail; in the years between the two world wars Western archaeological interests in Egypt inevitably suffered. The art-loving Führer, Adolf Hitler, faced with the possible repatriation of this, his favourite work of art from ancient Egypt, was destined to have the final say: 'What the German people have, they keep!'

1913
The Tomb of Impy

The burial chamber of Impy, a member of the Senedjemib family of architects and overseers of works at Giza, was found by George Reisner's Harvard-Boston team in 1913, untouched since the day the body was interred at the start of the 6th Dynasty. It contained more than 500 items in total, including Impy's rectangular coffin and pottery, copper vessels and ritual equipment, as well as this gold and faience broad collar. Impy's was the first of only two Giza tombs discovered intact by Reisner – the other being that of Hetepheres (•p. 168).

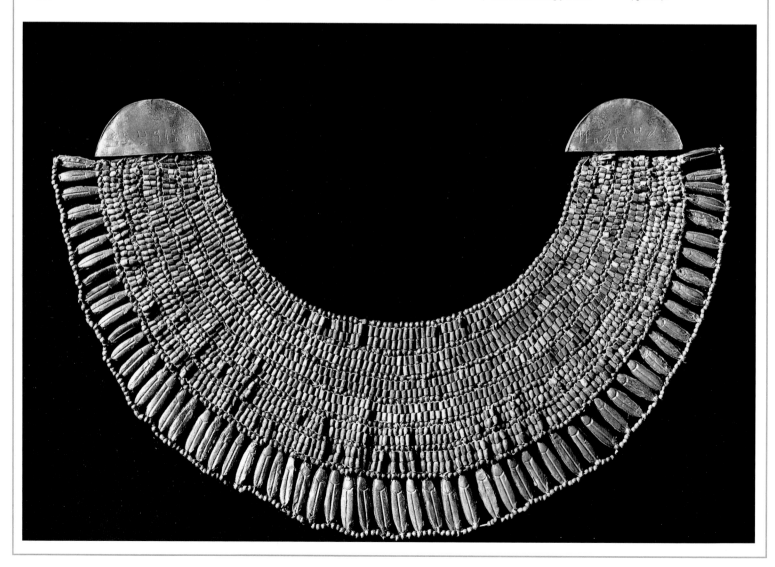

Before 1914
The Gebel el-Araq Knife

'… *of all the records of fighting and military expeditions [of the late Predynastic period] the most puzzling is surely the so-called Gebel el Araq knife*'
MICHAEL HOFFMAN

This famous object – a ripple-flaked flint knife-blade with elaborately carved hippopotamus-ivory handle – was acquired in Cairo for the Musée du Louvre (E 11517) in February 1914; it had apparently been dug out from a grave by Egyptian locals a short time before at the site of Gebel el-Araq, opposite Nag Hammadi. Dating from the late Predynastic period (*c.* 3000 BC), the interest of the piece lies in the subject matter of its grip. On its outer face (distinguished by an applied ivory boss) is a 'master of animals' motif in pure Mesopotamian style; while on the inner are two rows of men engaged in hand-to-hand combat, with a naval scene below. Many scholars still believe the iconography and subject matter reflect an invasion of Egypt by peoples from the east at this, the very dawn of Egyptian history.

1913
Statues of Amenhotep Son of Hapu and Paramessu from Karnak

While private stone sculptures are not at all uncommon in Egypt, examples of any scale and quality are rare, attesting to the power of the official represented and the high esteem in which he was held by the ruling king. The four statues uncovered by Georges Legrain near the western colossus of Horemheb at the base of the 10th pylon at Karnak on 25 October 1913 are among the finest and most important private statues ever found. Two (Cairo JE 44861-62) are images of Amenhotep son of Hapu, a high official of Amenophis III revered at the time as a great man and later as a god – a fact clearly reflected in the wear caused by thousands of pious hands reaching out to touch the sacred papyrus on the man's lap. The subject of the third and fourth of Legrain's statues (Cairo JE 44863-64) was the vizier Paramessu, the future king Ramesses I. These two men were responsible for many of the greatest building works carried out during the 18th Dynasty. Amenhotep son of Hapu's finest achievement as chief royal architect was the mortuary temple of Amenophis III with its famed statues today known as the 'Colossi of Memnon'; while Paramessu was associated with much of Horemheb's construction work at Karnak, including the pylon at the foot of which the four statues were found.

137

THE HIDDEN TREASURE
OF SITHATHORIUNET

1914 Middle Kingdom Wooden Sculptures from el-Lisht

Discovery/excavation
1914
by
Guy Brunton

Site
el-Lahun (Petrie tomb no. 8,
near the pyramid
of Sesostris II)

Period
Middle Kingdom,
12th Dynasty, reign of
Ammenemes III,
1844–1797 BC

'No one but my wife knows how we transferred the jewellery to London ....'
W. M. FLINDERS PETRIE

The pyramid of the 12th-Dynasty king Sesostris II at el-Lahun had first been investigated by the English Egyptologist Flinders Petrie in 1889–90, at which time he was able to enter the king's burial chamber. It was not until the end of 1913, however, that he returned to the site to explore the subsidiary tombs which work on other pyramids of the period had indicated were customarily to be found in the vicinity.

The burials within the first few shafts which Petrie was able, by careful scrutiny of the platform surrounding the pyramid, to locate and access had been robbed and destroyed in antiquity. A further shaft, open to the sky and smaller and less well-finished than the rest, seemed similarly lacking in potential. Then, descending this shaft, Petrie's Qufti helper observed a recess, filled with mud, which he began carefully to clear. Within a matter of moments there was a glint of gold; Petrie was informed, and his assistant, Guy Brunton, took over the work.

(above) Inlaid gold slide fastener for the gold, carnelian and faience beaded bracelet shown opposite (top, right), inscribed with the prenomen of King Ammenemes III of the 12th Dynasty.

(right) Early reconstructions, since superseded, of a variety of elements recovered by Guy Brunton among the el-Lahun treasure – including back-to-back lion heads from a girdle and amuletic claws from a pair of bracelets.

THE TOMB OF SITHATHORIUNET (PETRIE NO. 8)

ITEM NO.	OBJECTS FOUND	LOCATION
1	green felspar bead	shaft fill
2	red granite sarcophagus and lid	burial chamber
3	wooden coffin panels(?) (in recess)	
4	scraps of gold foil (in 2)	
5	limestone canopic chest with lid	
6	wooden canopic box (in 5)	
7	human-headed calcite canopic jars of Sithathoriunet (in 6)	
8	canopic jar contents (in 7)	
9	black granite fragment, inscribed (in the vicinity of 2)	
10	pottery	
11	wooden boxes (x5), containing treasure (see table)	recess
12	beads	offering chamber
13	calcite jar lid	
14	calcite and obsidian coffin eye	
15	copper scraps	
16	pottery dishes	
17	offerings of beef and fowl	
18	calcite 'magical' jar	

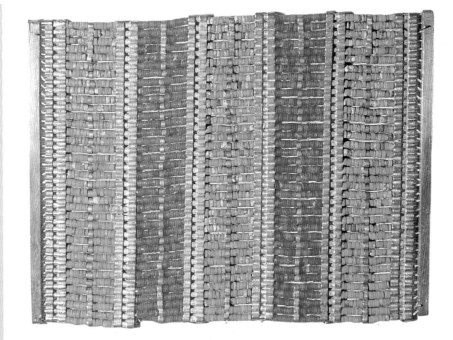

(right) Sithathoriunet's mirror. The oval reflector is of silver, now somewhat corroded, while the exquisitely modelled handle is a composite of obsidian, semiprecious stones and gold.

The meagre results of the season so far had done nothing to prepare for what lay in store – a spectacular hoard of Middle Kingdom jewelry and cosmetic vessels buried under 20 cm (8 in) of solidified, washed-in mud, a treasure originally contained in a series of five ebony caskets, since decayed by water:

(left) The first, and finest, of the two pectoral ornaments of Sithathoriunet, each incorporating the name of Ammenemes III. The style is remarkably similar to that of the jewels found with the lady's near-namesake, Sithathor, whose burial de Morgan discovered at Dahshur (●p. 88); possibly they originated in the same master-jeweller's workshop.

THE TREASURE OF SITHATHORIUNET

WINLOCK NO.	SIZE	BOX DESCRIPTION	CONTENTS
1	L 44.5 cm	ebony and ivory veneer, gold *djed*-pillar decoration	mirror, 2 wristlets, 2 anklets, 2 girdles, claw necklace, 3 lion armlets, 3 armlets with motto clasps, Sesostris II pectoral with bead necklace, 2 scarab rings, 2 large gold-handled razors, silver saucer, 2 small razors, two whetstones, mirror
2	L 35 cm	wood and ivory veneer, palace-façade design	8 calcite oil jars
3	L 14 cm?	wood, gold-foil edging? gold-headed studs? ivory inlay?	4 obsidian cosmetic jars
4?	L 38 cm+	undecorated wood?	diadem and wig/wig ornaments, 2 lapis lazuli scarabs, two armlets with motto clasps, smallest lion armlet, Ammenemes III pectoral with bead necklace
5	L 55 cm+	undecorated ebony?	wigs?

Division

Petrie's good fortune was set to continue. Maspero, as a magnificent gesture in this, his final year as head of the Antiquities Service, conceded to Petrie the greater part of the find, which he regarded as duplicating the Dahshur jewelry found by de Morgan in 1894–95 (•p. 88). But this, in its turn, posed further problems – not least the matter of how the excavator himself was to allocate it. Petrie's first thought was the British Museum, to whom 'I named in writing … £8,000 as the least value of what we had found'.

> 'The answer from the British Museum to my letter was that, if when they saw the things they thought they were worth it, they might be able to put their hands on a couple of thousand – a ludicrous treatment of the matter, which closed that door.'

A wonderful opportunity badly bungled – and one which will never arise again.

What was Britain's loss was nevertheless Egyptology's gain, for, in the end, the el-Lahun jewelry, one of the most spectacular hoards ever discovered in Egypt, went to the Metropolitan Museum of Art in New York. Now, thanks to expert study by Herbert Winlock and his team, and by scholars since, we know far more about the find, its original appearance and its small and slender owner than would ever have been thought possible.

'For a week, Brunton lived all day and every night in the tomb, gently extracting all the objects from the hard mud, without bending or scratching a single piece. Everything as it came up I washed in plain water with a camel-hair brush, so as not to alter the natural surface, and then photographed it.'

(right) Elaborate casket reconstructed from elements found with the el-Lahun treasure, together with a selection of its contents – including a reconstruction of the princess's mirror (see previous page), gold-handled copper razors, whetstones, a silver rouge dish and a series of obsidian cosmetic vessels elegantly mounted in gold.

140

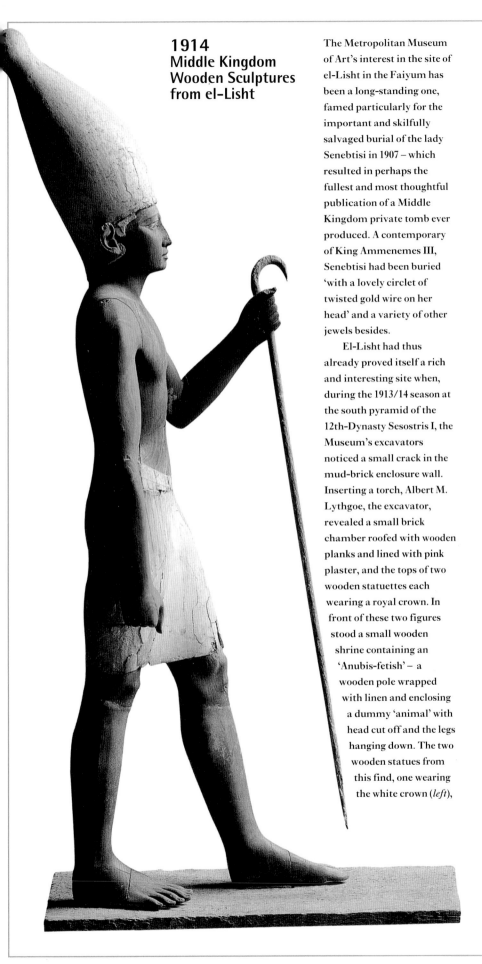

1914
Middle Kingdom
Wooden Sculptures
from el-Lisht

The Metropolitan Museum of Art's interest in the site of el-Lisht in the Faiyum has been a long-standing one, famed particularly for the important and skilfully salvaged burial of the lady Senebtisi in 1907 – which resulted in perhaps the fullest and most thoughtful publication of a Middle Kingdom private tomb ever produced. A contemporary of King Ammenemes III, Senebtisi had been buried 'with a lovely circlet of twisted gold wire on her head' and a variety of other jewels besides.

El-Lisht had thus already proved itself a rich and interesting site when, during the 1913/14 season at the south pyramid of the 12th-Dynasty Sesostris I, the Museum's excavators noticed a small crack in the mud-brick enclosure wall. Inserting a torch, Albert M. Lythgoe, the excavator, revealed a small brick chamber roofed with wooden planks and lined with pink plaster, and the tops of two wooden statuettes each wearing a royal crown. In front of these two figures stood a small wooden shrine containing an 'Anubis-fetish' – a wooden pole wrapped with linen and enclosing a dummy 'animal' with head cut off and the legs hanging down. The two wooden statues from this find, one wearing the white crown (*left*), now in Cairo (JE 44951), the other, wearing the red (*right*), ceded by the Egyptian government to New York (MMA 14.3.17), are quite exceptional, with 'the eyes, ears, and hands ... rendered with an exquisite and subtle attention to detail rarely found even in far larger statues'. Their precise function, and date, remain tantalizingly obscure.

141

SECTION IV
PHARAOHS AND MORTALS

'Maspero saw the museums of the world as one family, and in his divisions managed to see to it that each museum in Egypt was rewarded by a representative collection of fine objects …. But in 1914 the Egyptian government, through Lacau, announced a change….'
JOSEPH LINDON SMITH

In July 1914, a month before the outbreak of the First World War, Gaston Maspero retired for a second time and returned to France. His successor as Director-General of the Service des Antiquités was the white-bearded Pierre Lacau, whose nickname 'God the Father' was a telling one. Lacau's competence was undisputed: he was a brilliant scholar, an effective administrator, and a true friend to Egypt. But, like Grébaut and Loret before him, he could be stubborn and arrogant; and, while striving always to be courteous, diplomacy was not a strong suit.

Lacau's appointment marked the end of an era. Maspero had, it is true, been slipping a little in his later years, his behaviour and particularly his apportioning of finds becoming increasingly erratic; but he was an institution in his own right, had achieved an immense amount, and would be sadly missed – particularly by the diggers. Under Lacau's direction, the days of archaeological free-for-all gradually drew to a close. With the discovery of the virtually intact tomb of Tutankhamun in 1922, the stakes were raised dramatically: Howard Carter and the Egyptian authorities would clash not only over the ownership of the finds but the very rights of the excavator to work as he, not the Service, saw fit. All of this, set against a backdrop of re-emergent Egyptian nationalism, would result in the door of equitable division being banged shut for good.

Although many teams continued with their work, those of the Egypt Exploration Society (as the Fund was renamed in 1919), Petrie's British School of Archaeology in Egypt and the Metropolitan Museum of Art – expeditions more dependent than most on the old division system to sustain their work – turned their attention south to the Sudan or north to Syria-Palestine, or dropped out altogether. Only with the gradual acceptance that Egyptologists were digging for information, not things, would excavation in Egypt again achieve the levels of the glorious past.

The eerie gaze of Akhenaten: a detail of one of the series of colossal statues discovered at Karnak (●p. 172).

1915
THE TOMB OF DJEHUTYNAKHT AT DEIR EL-BERSHA

1915 Ptolemaic Egypt and the Zenon Archive

Discovery/excavation
1915
by
H. Lyman Story

Site
Deir el-Bersha (Wadi Deir el-
Nakhla, Tomb 10a)

Period
Middle Kingdom, 11th
Dynasty, perhaps reign of
Nebhepetre Mentuhotep,
2061–2010 BC

'The outstanding object in this tomb was the great outer coffin of Djehuti-Nekht [Djehutynakht] himself, the inner surfaces of which had been beautifully decorated by the hand of a master painter. Despite some damage caused by water when the ship which brought the coffin to Boston suffered a fire at sea, this is without doubt the finest painted coffin ever found.'
DOWS DUNHAM

Deir el-Bersha was the principal cemetery of Middle Kingdom Hermopolis, and here, in a series of decorated, rock-cut tombs (much destroyed by earthquake and later quarrying), the nomarchs of the 15th Upper Egyptian (Hare) district were laid to rest. The site has long been famous for the scene depicting the transport of a colossal statue discovered by Charles Brine before 1818 on a wall in the tomb of Djehutyhotep – a relief which, 75 years later, in an act of revenge for Eugène Grébaut's confiscation, without compensation, of what was left of the Amarna-letters' hoard (•p. 72), was lamentably attacked by the local inhabitants. The damage at least had the positive result of highlighting the vulnerability of el-Bersha's important records, and prompted the first organized expedition to the site. This was led by Percy Newberry for the Egypt Exploration Fund in 1891–93, one of the first expeditions on which Howard Carter (•p. 160) would cut his teeth as an archaeological draftsman. A few years later other Egyptologists, including Georges Daressy (in November and December 1897) and Ahmed Kamal (in 1900 and subsequent seasons), undertook excavation here, bringing to light several intact burials and much interesting funerary material belonging to the nomarchs and their officials.

In 1915, the American George A. Reisner (•p. 132), with Kamal's support, decided to try his own luck at the site. Work began on 17 March (continuing until 30 May) under the direction not of an archaeologist but of the Boston Museum registrar, H. Lyman Story – a man, it is said, more interested in arranging delivery from the US of the correct brand of cigars than in the work of detailed recording. Before long two rubble-filled shafts had been located in the courtyard of the otherwise destroyed tomb 10 (though thankfully without the dynamite Story had advocated to speed up the work of clearance). The first of these shafts was to prove extremely interesting.

The excavation of shaft 10a seemed at first to offer little hope of anything exciting, as an increasing quantity of fragments of rope, odd beads and broken boats and statuettes was extracted from the debris; but, 10.5 m (34 ft) down, beyond the partially walled-up entrance to the burial chamber, the excavator's luck changed. What met his eyes was a scene of utter confusion: dismantled coffins, wooden funerary models, a human head and torso, and fragments of jewelry and broken vessels – the remains, it transpired, of a double burial of the 'hereditary prince and controller of the two thrones', Djehutynakht, an 11th-Dynasty governor, and his wife who, confusingly, shared the same name. The tomb had been plundered, clearly, but what the robbers had left more than compensated for what they might have taken away. The prize turned out to be Djehutynakht's outer coffin, or rather its elaborately detailed interior decoration, which is of unparalleled

(above) Elaborately treated head from the mummy of Djehutynakht, with layers of linen moulded to the skull and eyebrows painted in black. Beneath the wrappings, as CAT-scans reveal, the tissues are well preserved.

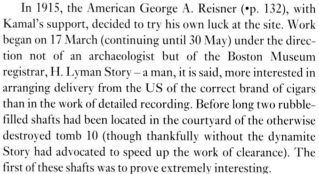

(left) Contemporary photograph showing the disturbed condition of the tomb's south corner, with the model-offering bearers (right) in position.

1915
Ptolemaic Egypt and the Zenon Archive

'Above all, [the Zenon documents] form a wonderful picture of life in Egypt in the very prime of the Alexandrian age. Every rank of society is represented among the correspondents, from the chief minister of the king down to the native swineherd writing from prison …. Moreover, though the correspondence is so varied in character, the fact that all the documents relate in some way to Zenon and his circle gives them coherence.'
CAMPBELL COWAN EDGAR

The Zenon archive has been described as 'the largest and best-preserved single archive of papyrus documents in history'. It comprises many thousands of documents – the

papers, written in Greek, of the manager of Ptolemy II's finance minister, Apollonius, spanning the period *c.* 260–240 BC.

The archive was discovered not in formal excavation but by Egyptian farmers at the site of ancient Philadelphia (Darb el-Gerza) in the Faiyum in 1915 and is now divided between several museum collections. The final haul includes letters, petitions, accounts and a few literary texts, offering a taste not only of life among the rich and poor in this provincial city but, through the ready pen of Apollonius, life also at the court of Ptolemy in Alexandria and as far afield as Caunus in Asia Minor, whence Zenon hailed.

'In one letter a garrulous and unknown correspondent reports to Zenon that he has called in an expert to "cure" some dice… the expert thinks poorly of them, and … refers to his practice at the court, where he has "cured" dice for Alexander the Etesian – a man who had once been king of Macedon for forty-five days (hence his nickname) and now some twenty years later he appears as a pensioner playing knuckle-bone at the court of Ptolemy Philadelphus.'
STEPHEN GLANVILLE

(above) Detail of the interior left side of Djehutynakht's elaborately decorated outer coffin, with representations of the offerings made for the eternal provision of the deceased.

(below) Procession of offering-bearers as recently reconstructed – a model of exceptional quality representing a priest(?) and three individualistically modelled female servants carrying provisions in perpetuity for the next world.

(right) The coffin's owner – Djehutynakht – seated holding his staff and wearing a broad collar, bracelets and kilt.

quality and ranks among the masterpieces of ancient Egyptian painting.

What we can reconstruct of Story's clearance of this chamber suggests that the wife had died before her husband, her burial being plundered at the time his coffins were later introduced – a feature often noted in multi-phase burials in Egypt. The likelihood is that the same band of undertaker-robbers returned after a decent interval to investigate the coffins of Djehutynakht himself. They knowledgably located the end of his coffins by removing a single abutting stone from the blocking of the burial chamber and neatly broke through and gained access to the man's mortal remains. Djehutynakht's mummified body was slid out before being ripped to pieces in the search for jewels; perched atop the outer coffin, his detached head, with its features modelled in linen and highlighted in paint, watched eerily as the plunderers stripped and perhaps set fire to his torso before retreating with their loot.

DJEHUTYNAKHT'S TOMB: THE CONTENTS

ITEM	HUSBAND	WIFE	UNCERTAIN
coffins	2	3	
mummy masks	1	1	
mummies	1	1	
jewelry, amulets			various
canopic chests	1	1	
canopic jar lid			1
model boats			55+
large oars			2
agricultural and domestic scenes			33+
offering bearers			12+
model food offerings			various
sticks and staves			250+
bows and model arrows			various
boxes			2
small tables			4
hes-vases (wood; faience calcite – mounted in sets of 4 on wood boards)			various
length of linen cloth			1
uncertain (vegetable matter)			1

THE JEWELS OF TELL EL-MUQDAM

Discovery/excavation
1915
by
C. C. Edgar

Site
Tell el-Muqdam
(Leontopolis)

Period
Third Intermediate Period,
22nd Dynasty, reign of
Osorkon III, 883–855 BC

Tell el-Muqdam marks the site of ancient Leontopolis, capital of the 11th Lower Egyptian nome (district) during the Ptolemaic period and a site of moderate importance throughout Egyptian history. Documented finds from here are few (though these include much of the collection put together by Dr Fouquet of Cairo and famously auctioned after his death in 1914); but occasionally they are impressive – none more so than in the case of one of the two small, vaulted tombs excavated in 1915 at the west end of the site by the local inspector following a tip-off from locals.

The existence of the waterlogged tomb had been known for some time, and seemed to offer few prospects; as C. C. Edgar, the Antiquities Service inspector, records:

> *'The north chamber, which contained a limestone coffin, had been plundered and the coffin smashed. The coffin in the south chamber, fortunately, was of red granite and had a very solid lid, so heavy that the local workmen were unable to shift it. Eventually we had to send a reis from the Museum to lift and remove it.'*

It had come as a pleasant surprise to the diggers to discover that the blocks of the south burial chamber were carved in sunk relief – though little could be done to study the decoration owing to the high water-table. It was even more gratifying to be able to fish out from within the mess of mud and fragments of decomposed corpse floating around within the sarcophagus itself several important items of jewelry, including a fine silver pectoral. For, thanks to the weight of the granite sarcophagus lid – a reused block – the southern tomb had entirely escaped the unwelcome attentions of robbers.

As the quality of the jewelry indicated, this was no ordinary burial. The heart scarab identifies the owner as a queen named Kama, presumably the mother of Osorkon III, Kamama, who had been buried in the temple-precincts of the home town to which, in death, she had clearly chosen to return.

(below) Gilded silver pectoral ornament from the burial of Queen Kama: the god Khnum (in massive lapis lazuli inlay) flanked by the goddesses Hathor (behind) and Maat (before).

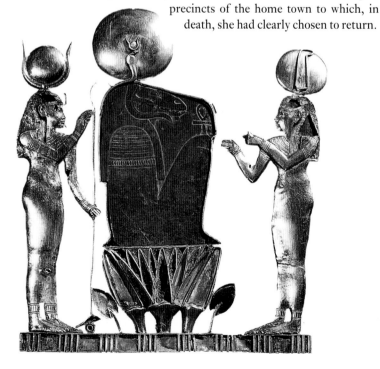

THE TREASURE OF QUEEN KAMA

CAIRO JE NO.	DESCRIPTION
45337	pectoral of gilded silver, lapis lazuli inlay
45338	human-headed scorpion amulet of gold, agate inlay
45339	gold circlet surmounted by inlaid uraeus
45340–41	pair of inlaid gold bracelets
45342–43	two fragmentary inlaid gold bracelets
45344	large scarab of lapis lazuli
45345	lapis lazuli *djed*-pillar amulet
45346	lapis lazuli disc
45347	large scarab of Egyptian blue
45348	lapis lazuli frog
45349	inlaid gold disc
45350	steatite scarab with name of Queen 'Kama' and extracts from Book of the Dead Chapter 26
45351	crude Taweret amulet in lapis lazuli
45352	small agate box
45353	single-handled vase of alabaster
45354	three handled vase of alabaster
45355–56	two two-handled vases of alabaster
45357	alabaster canopic jar, with human-headed lid
45358	alabaster canopic jar, with cynocephalus-headed lid
45359	alabaster canopic jar, lacking lid
45360	alabaster canopic jar inscribed for the lady Pypu, lacking lid
45361	bronze uraeus with traces of gilding
45362	faience *shabti* with remains of inscription

4000 BC
3000 BC
2000 BC
1000 BC
0
AD 700

NUBIAN TOMBS OF THE 25TH DYNASTY: NURI AND EL-KURRU

1916 The Carnarvon Gold Amun

Discovery/excavation
1916–20
by
George A. Reisner

Sites
Nuri and el-Kurru

Period
25th Dynasty, reigns of
Kashta–Tantamani,
770–657+ BC

The American archaeologist George A. Reisner's excavating career stretched from Giza in the north (•pp. 132, 136) to the very limits of Egyptian influence in the south, beyond the 6th cataract, where he carried out excavations at several important sites. These included Meroe (•p. 35) and the region known as Napata – comprising Gebel Barkal (where he began work in 1915), and the cemeteries of Nuri and el-Kurru, where the Kushite kings of Egypt's 25th Dynasty were interred.

Nuri

'Of the many interesting objects which have come to us from Nuri, perhaps the series of [shabti] figures are the most revealing. They were found in almost every tomb, were almost all inscribed, and it is from them primarily that we have learned the names of these people. In some tombs they were found in great profusion: those of King Taharqa alone numbered over a thousand [1,070], all of hard stone, and ranging in size from eight to thirty-two inches ...'
DOWS DUNHAM

Reisner's excavations at Nuri were spread over several seasons beginning in 1916, and witnessed the discovery of the tombs of some 20 kings and 53 royal women ranging in date from 690 to 337 BC. The names of only a few of these rulers are known to history, the most significant being Taharqa, the powerful Nubian pharaoh under whose rule Egypt had flourished following an extended period of political stagnation following the collapse of the New Kingdom.

Despite its remoteness, the burial practices revealed in the course of Reisner's work at Nuri were almost wholly Egyptian. Not only were the kings buried in pyramids – albeit smaller than the giants of earlier periods – but their burials employed the full range of funerary equipment. This included sarcophagi and/or

(below) Excavations in progress before the pyramid-tomb of Taharqa at Nuri (Nu1): a classic shot of local diggers and basket-boys supervised by western archaeologist (in the white suit).

SITES EXCAVATED BY G. A. REISNER IN THE SUDAN

SITE	DATES EXCAVATED
Archaeological survey	1906–11
Begrawiya (Meroe)	1920–23
Gebel Barkal	1916, 1918–20
Kerma	1913–16
Kumma	1924
el-Kurru	1918–19, 1920
Mirgissa	1931–32
Nuri	1916–18, 1920
Semna	1924, 1927–28
Shalfak	1931
Uronarti	1924, 1928–30
All for Museum of Fine Arts, Boston/Harvard University	

nested anthropoid coffins, precious metal face masks, scarabs and other amulets and regalia, as well as vessels of gold, stone and pottery, food provisions and other commodities, stored within the three rock-cut chambers which characteristically underlay the pyramid proper. Within the small funerary chapels erected on the eastern face of these pyramids, stelae and offering tables were placed.

As at el-Kurru (below), the tombs had been robbed, but in a very rough and ready manner and, to the excavator's delight, very selectively. One of the most productive tombs cleared was that of Aspelta, a successor of Taharqa, which, thanks to an ancient roof collapse, preserved much of what had been removed from its companion burials.

(above) With the pyramids of Nuri in the background, two of Reisner's Sudanese workers sort the extraordinary quantities of *shabtis* recovered from Taharqa's tomb (Nu1) in 1917.

El-Kurru

'A few miles down stream from [Gebel] Barkal lies the early Kushite cemetery of El Kurru, a sadly ruined site ... but one of great interest, for here our Expedition found the tombs of all but one of the Kings of the Egyptian 25th Dynasty, those rulers of Kush who turned the tables on declining Egypt and conquered their erstwhile overlord ... [The work] threw a

(above) Mummy ornament of sheet gold, representing a winged Isis; from pyramid 10 at Nuri.

(left) A selection of Taharqa's *shabtis*, showing the range in sizes and materials. The quality of these sculptures was as impressive as the quantity found.

THE ROYAL TOMBS OF THE 25TH DYNASTY

KING	DATES	LOCATION
Kashta	770–750	el-Kurru (?)
Piye (Piankhi)	750–712	el-Kurru (Ku 17)
Shabaka	712–698	el-Kurru
Shebitku	698–690	el-Kurru
Taharqa	690–664	Nuri (Nu 1)
Tantamani	664–657+	el-Kurru

flood of light on a hitherto little known period of ancient history, and yielded some of the most beautiful of the small objects that we have in the [Boston] Museum'
DOWS DUNHAM

Reisner's work at Nuri had left him rather puzzled: for, given the scale and extent of the cemetery there he had quite reasonably hoped to discover the tombs of those Kushite kings who had actually held sway in Egypt during the 25th Dynasty. He had, in fact, found the tomb of only one of the six – that of Taharqa. Where were the others? For his next season (1918-19), Reisner transferred his men to an unpromising looking site across the river – el-Kurru, marked by a single ruined pyramid. He entertained little hope of finding his quarry, but his scepticism was happily to be misplaced (see table).

The cemetery at el-Kurru proved to have been founded around or even before the turn of the 2nd millennium BC, and its use can be divided into two principal phases. The first, pure Kushite phase lasted for a century or so, with tombs developing from a modest gravel tumulus to a rectangular stone mastaba above a simple burial pit – all heavily plundered. Tombs of the later phase, beginning around 750 BC, had stone superstructures in the form of rather attenuated pyramids, with stair access to one or two rock-cut burial chambers below. The excavation of this later phase of tombs revealed further evidence for the employment of Egyptian-style funerary practices, including evisceration (attested by the presence

1916
The Carnarvon Gold Amun

The collection of Egyptian antiquities assembled by the fifth Earl of Carnarvon under the guidance of his associate and friend Howard Carter contained more than its share of masterpieces, among them this spectacular, solid gold image of the god Amun. Carter acquired the figure, measuring 18 cm (7 in) high in its present, damaged state, in 1917, from a dealer in Cairo. He was informed that the piece had been dug up by *sebakhin* the previous year in the area north of the Great Temple of Amun at Karnak – a provenance which is plausible but cannot be tested. Although Carter believed that the image dated from the 18th Dynasty – specifically the reign of Tuthmosis III – art historian Cyril Aldred has convincingly demonstrated, on grounds of style, that the figure is a product of the 22nd Dynasty.

That it represents one of the most important divine images in precious metal ever to have been brought to light in Egypt is undisputed. Presumably, by its scale, a rich ex-voto rather than a cult statue in its own right (•p. 155), the figure is now rightly prized as one of the treasures of Egyptian art at the Metropolitan Museum in New York (MMA 26.7.1412).

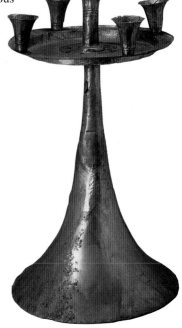

of canopic equipment) and, more importantly, *shabti*-figures – an indication that human sacrifice, hitherto widely practised in the area, was now a thing of the past. The characteristically Nubian custom of burial on a bed, however, rather than burial within a coffin, was, for most non-royals, set to continue.

Though the cemetery at el-Kurru, which included the burials of the influential Kushite queens, had been ransacked in antiquity, there was, as Reisner's work would reveal, still a great deal left for the dedicated archaeologist to find, including much precious metalwork and jewelry.

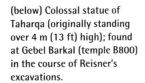

(below) Colossal statue of Taharqa (originally standing over 4 m (13 ft) high); found at Gebel Barkal (temple B800) in the course of Reisner's excavations.

(right) Bronze trumpet-shaped libation stand from the tomb of King Piye (Piankhi) of the 25th Dynasty, el-Kurru (KU17).

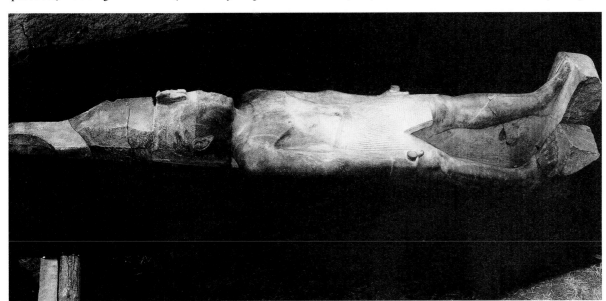

1916

'THE TREASURE OF THREE EGYPTIAN PRINCESSES'

1919 The Tomb of Petosiris at Tuna el-Gebel

Discovery/excavation
1916
by
Egyptian locals

Site
Thebes (Qabbanat el-Qurud)

Period
New Kingdom,
18th Dynasty, reign of
Tuthmosis III,
1479–1425 BC

4000 BC

3000 BC

2000 BC

1000 BC

0

AD 700

'When we saw the tomb [in 1928] we were guided by old Mohammed Hammad, one of the robbers who had found it, and according to him the passageway [leading to the burial chamber] had been blocked at both ends ... According to old Mohammed's story, the objects were all in the chamber, arranged in an orderly way on a layer of chip which covered the floor, and were buried only by the rock which had subsequently fallen from the roof or been washed in by the floods. ... [T]he coffins were still recognizable, lying side by side with their heads against the southern wall, but were totally rotted by damp.
... [S]uch a burial could well have followed [the ladies'] simultaneous deaths from an epidemic. Or, ... they may all have been the victims of an execution for some palace conspiracy.'

HERBERT E. WINLOCK

The tomb of the 'Three Princesses' – actually three minor wives of Tuthmosis III – first came to the notice of the inhabitants of Qurna at the end of July 1916, following one of the violent rainstorms which occasionally strike the area. At one particular spot, high in the cliffs of the Cemetery of the Apes (Qabbanet el-Qurud), water still pouring down the rock face was seen to disappear without trace at the cliff's base – as it turned out, into a forgotten tomb. This was immediately emptied by its fortunate finders. 'Before the middle of August it was pretty generally known throughout Kurneh and Luxor that an extraordinary treasure had been found'.

Much of the assemblage ended up in the Metropolitan Museum of Art in New York after passing through the hands of Howard Carter and Lord Carnarvon, at a goodly profit, and to Herbert Winlock fell the task of making sense of it all. The quantity and quality of the material was, at that time, unparalleled for the 18th Dynasty: queenly diadems and headdresses, earrings, broad collars, necklaces, amulets, bracelets, finger rings, finger- and toe- stalls, metal sandals, mirrors, canopic jars – and a host of vessels of precious metal, glass and stone. Inevitably, perhaps, the treasure had been 'padded' by the dealers before it could be studied, both with genuine objects of inappropriate date and with a number of complete fakes; some of these were noted at the time of Winlock's publication, but others have cleverly been recognized since by American Egyptologists Christine Lilyquist and Peter F. Dorman, among them several of the more spectacular metal vessels.

The ancient owners of this assemblage were identified by the principal

(above) A selection of necklace elements acquired by the Metropolitan Museum of Art through Lord Carnarvon and Howard Carter. The treasure had been 'padded' by local dealers, with several items (including the fifth string of plaques seen here) turning out, on later inspection, to be wholly modern fabrications.

(left above) A silver canister with stopper, inscribed in three columns of hieroglyphic text for Queen Menwi; her companions Merti and Menhet each possessed a similar container, the precise function of which is unknown.

(left below) A queenly headdress from the tomb, as formerly displayed in the Metropolitan Museum of Art New York. The central crown is of gold, once inlaid, from which are suspended some 800 interlinking rosettes still preserving much of their original inlay of carnelian, turquoise and glass.

150

THE TREASURE OF 'THREE PRINCESSES':
The principal finds

NO.	DESCRIPTION	INSCRIPTION
JEWELRY OF DAILY LIFE		
1	inlaid gold headdress	
2	gold gazelle-head headdress	
3	gold earrings (5 pairs)	
4	broad collar of gold, falcon-head terminals	Tuthmosis III
5	broad collar of gold, double-lotus terminals	Tuthmosis III
6	broad collar of gold, single-lotus terminals	
7	miscellaneous beads, amulets, pendants, gold etc. (some fake)	
8	string of faience disc beads	
9	bracelets decorated with cats, gold etc. (3 pairs)	
10	bracelets with bead inlay, gold etc. (3 pairs)	Tuthmosis III
11	miscellaneous bracelets, gold etc. (some fake)	including Hatshepsut, Tuthmosis III
12	scarab rings, gold etc. (8)	including Hatshepsut, Tuthmosis III
13	beaded belts, gold etc. (3)	
FUNERARY JEWELRY		
14	heart scarab collars, gold etc. (3)	Menwi, Menhet, Merti
15	*seweret*-bead bangles, gold etc. (3)	
16	bead bangles, gold etc. (2)	
17	bifurcated amulets, gold (3)	
18	broad collars with falcon-head terminals, sheet gold (3)	
19	vulture pectorals, sheet gold (3)	
20	finger- and toe-stalls (54)	
21	sandals, sheet gold (3 pairs)	
22	canopic jars, human headed lids (3 sets)	Menwi, Menhet, Merti
COSMETIC OBJECTS		
23	mirrors, gold and silver (2)	one, Tuthmosis III
24	cosmetic vessels, various stones, some with gold rims (12 or more)	Tuthmosis III
25	cosmetic jars, various stones (approx. 30)	Tuthmosis III
DRINKING VESSELS		
26	drinking vessels, gold (fake) (15)	Tuthmosis III
27	handled vessels, gold (?) (6)	
28	drinking vessels, silver (2)	
29	canisters, silver (3)	Menwi, Menhet, Merti
30	drinking vessels, glass (2)	one, Tuthmosis III
31	drinking vessel, calcite	Tuthmosis III
32	drinking vessels, felspar (2)	
33	amphorae/wine jugs, calcite (7 or more)	

(above) The reconstructed elements of a broad falcon collar from the 'Three Princesses' burial. The terminals and pendant-beads are of thin sheet gold, inlaid with semiprecious stones and glass.

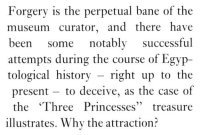

(below) A single bracelet from one of the three pairs of this design represented in Carnarvon and Carter's haul, with beads of gold and semiprecious stone. The clasp is surmounted by miniature reclining cats in gold and carnelian, with two further examples perhaps originally of faience now missing.

finds as wives of Tuthmosis III: 'The names of these three women,' Winlock noted, 'were Menhet, Menwi, and Merti, written with the syllabic writing commonly used for foreign words'. Perhaps, he suggests, 'since such names have a distinctly alien flavour ... the last suggests the later Hebrew or Aramaic name Martha ... they were the daughters of Syrian chieftains ...'. This view is still generally accepted.

The tomb of Menhet, Menwi and Merti had clearly escaped detection by the merest hair's breadth in antiquity: for, close by the entrance, Howard Carter in 1916 and Winlock and his team in 1928 noted several graffiti mentioning the presence in the near vicinity of the royal scribe Djehutymose and his son, Butehamun. The names of these individuals are well known to us today, charged as they were by the Theban high priests of the 21st Dynasty, with the task of seeking out old, rich tombs scattered around the Theban area for salvage and reburial. The rarity in modern times of intact Theban burials is primarily due to these two men. As Winlock notes, 'It is clear that the inspectors knew that there was a tomb somewhere near by'; fortunately for us, the weather that day must have stayed fine, and the ancient scribes missed it.

On forgery

Forgery is the perpetual bane of the museum curator, and there have been some notably successful attempts during the course of Egyptological history – right up to the present – to deceive, as the case of the 'Three Princesses'' treasure illustrates. Why the attraction?

151

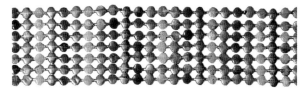

(top) Another reconstructed broad collar from the burial, with inlaid pendant beads, counterpoise and lotiform terminals inscribed with the king's prenomen; and a belt of beads modelled after acacia seeds (above).

'The love of money has always been a marked characteristic of the Egyptian, and here the ingenuity of the descendant of the old craftsman asserts itself. There is no doubt that he has, from time to time, been assisted by various Europeans, but he is producing replicas of antiquities, scarabs, figures, models, so cleverly cut and made that it puzzles many of the best experts to say whether they are false or real. Some of these imitations are sold for very high prices. If the discovery of a fraud is made in time, part of the money will sometimes be refunded.

'The Egyptian forger would not consider that he had done anything particularly dishonest in deceiving a man in that kind of way. His only regret would be that the fraud had been discovered, and he would muse upon the unfairness of Fate, for here he had been with a fortune within his grasp, only to lose it.'
T. G. WAKELING

1919
The Tomb of Petosiris at Tuna el-Gebel

'... a much-travelled and highly cultured man [who] apparently employed a Greek designer for the scenes of everyday life on the exterior portions of his funerary monument.'
CYRIL ALDRED

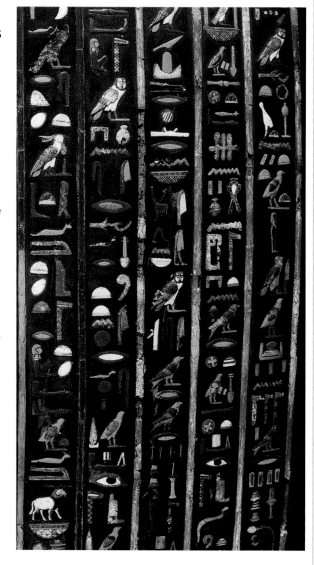

The idiosyncratic, temple-like family tomb of Petosiris, high priest of the god Thoth at Hermopolis, dates from the very end of the Egyptian dynastic period, around 340 BC, less than a decade before the arrival of Alexander the Great. Decorated in a peculiar mix of traditional and more adventurous foreign styles, it was first discovered at the end of November 1919 by an el-Ashmunein local, and was subsequently dug by the French antiquities inspector Gustave Lefebvre. The burial apartments, partially cut into the bedrock, were brought to light the following year.

The owner's mummy had been carried off by robbers, but his wooden coffins remained; the finest and best preserved of these (*below*) is now in Cairo (JE 46592), distinguished by its five columns of exquisite, glass-inlaid hieroglyphic text (*above*) taken from Chapter 42 of the Book of the Dead and among the best work of its kind to have survived. The fragmentary front panel of a very similar coffin from the group is now in Turin.

Further work was carried out at Tuna el-Gebel over the following decades (1931–52), by Sami Gabra and the University of Cairo, most famously and to good result among the catacombs of the ibis, Thoth's sacred creature. Excavations would be continued behind the tomb of Petosiris to reveal 'a complete town ... [with] houses ... all attached to tombs ... their purpose ... to shelter the families of the deceased when they visited ... during the various religious feasts ... which sometimes lasted for two or three days'. As with the monument of Petosoris, the structures show an extraordinary mix of Egyptian and Classical styles.

THE BURIALS OF ASHAYET
AND 'LITTLE MAYET'

Discovery/excavation
1920
by
Herbert E. Winlock

Site
Thebes (Deir el-Bahri)

Period
Middle Kingdom,
11th Dynasty, reign of
Nebhepetre Mentuhotep,
2061–2010 BC

The 11th-Dynasty temple of king Nebhepetre Mentuhotep at Deir el-Bahri, by the side of Hatshepsut's later and more famous monument, had first been excavated by Édouard Naville for the Egypt Exploration Fund, revealing a series of six shrines, associated, Naville believed, with six robbed pits. Herbert Winlock, the Metropolitan Museum's excavator, was not convinced and decided to have another look. He found that only four of Naville's pits were connected with the six shrines, and that behind lay two additional shafts Naville had missed. And, against all odds, the burials within were still present.

The first of these (no. 17) contained 'a great wooden coffin' belonging to the lady Kemsit, 'tipped on edge … and underneath this we could see a cover of the sculptured limestone sarcophagus of "Ashayet"'. Both the limestone slab-sided sarcophagus and the inner, rectangular wooden coffin proved magnificent creations. Ashayet's body, in a mummiform cartonnage, was still inside the coffin, and with her 'her statuette, archaically stiff, with gold bracelets and a red skirt held up by white suspenders'.

(below left) Deir el-Bahri and the ruins of Nebhepetre Mentuhotep's mortuary temple – site of Winlock's find.

(below) Wooden funerary statuette of Ashayet, which had been placed within her wooden coffin beside the mummiform cartonnage containing her body.

(below) An interior detail of Ashayet's sarcophagus, showing the beautifully preserved paint. The monument was constructed of separate limestone slabs joined at the corners with bands of copper.

Within the massive sarcophagus of Winlock's second pit (no. 18) was found 'a little white coffin, absolutely intact, bearing the name of Mayet – "the Cat"'. Inside this was yet another coffin, and then the mummy itself beneath a pile of folded linen, lying upon its side 'with the eyes of her plaster mask gazing through the eyes painted on her coffins …. Carefully the linen was cut away, and one after another five charming necklaces appeared … [just] as little Mayet wore [them] four thousand years ago.'.

A mass of finds, a mass of information. Yet precisely who this small child was 'must' – for the moment at least – be left to our imaginations'.

LETTERS FROM A HECTORING FATHER: THE HEQANAKHT PAPERS

Before 1921 The Yellow Jasper Face from the Carnarvon Collection
1922 or before Flesh of the Gods: A Silver Cult Image of Horus the Elder

Discovery/excavation
1920
by
Herbert E. Winlock

Site
Thebes (Deir el-Bahri, tomb of
Meseh in the court of TT315)

Period
Middle Kingdom, 12th
Dynasty, reign of Sesostris I,
1971–1926 BC

'... the private letters of a garrulous old farmer-priest, which have taken us right up the back stairs of a household of four thousand years ago and let us eavesdrop on domestic squabbles of the days of Abraham.'
HERBERT WINLOCK

The Heqanakht papers – a small archive of papyrus documents now in the Metropolitan Museum of Art in New York (MMA 22.3.516–523a–e) – were discovered during the 1920–21 season by Herbert E. Winlock and the Metropolitan's Egyptian Expedition at Deir el-Bahri. The findspot was a passage within the undisturbed burial of Meseh, a dependant of the vizier Ipi in the court of whose own tomb (TT315) that of Meseh had been dug. The documents had been used, along with other rubbish, to even up the floor and form a sliding ramp for the coffin. To judge from the intact seal on the document now numbered III, it is possible that it and others were never delivered; as a result, some have suspected foul play, the inspiration for Agatha Christie's ancient Egyptian thriller, *Death Comes as the End.*

(right) Heqanakht addresses
his estate manager Merisu, in
the first document from the
archive (verso) '... you must
turn the housemaid Senen out
of my house .... It is you who
are responsible for letting her
mistreat my new(?) wife!'

The first scholar to work on the letters was the philologist Battiscombe Gunn, and the full archive was ably published by T. G. H. James several years later; a 'stray' from the archive turned up in private hands shortly after. Gunn, James and others concluded that Heqanakht, the absentee farmer-landlord and writer of the correspondence, had acted as *ka*-servant on Ipi's behalf during the reign of Nebhepetre Mentuhotep of the 11th Dynasty. Hans Goedicke and Dorothea Arnold have since proposed that the archive is to be dated somewhat later. Goedicke suggests the reign of the 12th-Dynasty king Ammenemes I, while Arnold prefers a date early in the reign of his son, Sesostris I, when he was still co-regent with his father.

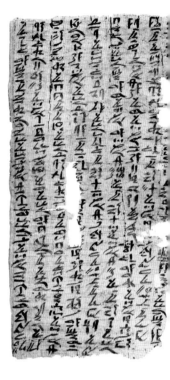

Before 1921 The Yellow Jasper Face from the Carnarvon Collection

The first published mention we have of this broken, 12-cm (4¾-in) high yellow jasper face from the collection of the fifth Earl of Carnarvon (now in New York, MMA 26.7.1396) is in the catalogue of the Burlington Fine Arts Club exhibition of 1921, where it is described as coming 'From a composite statue of Queen Nofretete [Nefertiti]'. The attribution is based in part on the use of yellow stone – yellow being the traditional colour for indicating female flesh – and presumably upon Lord Carnarvon and Howard Carter's (informed?) understanding that el-Amarna was the original findspot of the piece before it reached the Egyptian antiquities market. In 1959, the fragment was re-identified as the lower part of a portrait of Tiye, the consort of Amenophis III and Akhenaten's mother; more recently, Dorothea Arnold has suggested an attribution to Akhenaten's secondary wife, Kiya. Whatever the truth (which will perhaps only be settled when – and if – the missing portions are one day brought to light), the fragment stands without peer, a rare example of Egyptian composite sculpture carved with extraordinary sensitivity in one of the most precious and intractable materials known to ancient man.

The documents provide a unique, if tantalizing, glimpse into ancient Egyptian daily life in the heartland of the country and – if Arnold is correct – at a crossroads in its history, shortly after the establishment of the new capital of Itjtawy near el-Lisht (from where Heqanakht may have been writing). Heqanakht's letters reflect the everyday concerns of a man of his class – his relationships with, and the make-up and various responsibilities of his household, and far more besides.

The essence of the archive's principal character was ably summed up by the discoverer, Herbert Winlock:

> '[Heqanakht] relished … the opportunity of reminding [his family] that they were "eating his bread" and that "everything was his and the whole household dependent on him". He was a fussy and hectoring old fellow whose letters were prodigally strewn with "Mind this," "Be very careful and be very active," and "I shall hold thee responsible for it". "Do not fail to answer about everything I have written thee about," he insists, "for see, this is a year for a man to work for his master"; or again, "this is not a year for a man to be negligent towards his master, or his father, or his brother".'

We can recognize the type: for all their temporal and cultural distance, the Egyptians were living, breathing people, flawed as well as saintly, very much like ourselves.

> 'It is a son who speaks to his mother, namely, the mortuary priest Heqanakht to his mother Ipi and to Hetepet: How are you both? Are you alive, prospering, and healthy? In the favour of Montu, lord of the Theban nome!
>
> And to the entire household: How are you? Are you alive, prospering, and healthy? Don't worry about me, for I am healthy and alive.
>
> Now [stop complaining]. Whereas the whole land has died off, you haven't hungered; for when I came south to where you are, I fixed your food allowance in good measure. Isn't the Nile inundation very low? Since our food allowance has been fixed for us according to the nature of the Nile inundation, bear patiently, each of you, for I have succeeded so far among you in keeping you alive.
>
> Lest you be angry about this, look here, the entire household is just like my children, and I'm responsible for everything so that it should be said, "To be half alive is better than dying outright". Now it is only real hunger that should be termed hunger since they have started eating people here, and none are given such rations anywhere else …
>
> Communication by the mortuary priest Heqanakht to Merisu and to Hety's son Nakht, who is subordinate: Only as long as my people keep on working shall you give them these rations. Take great care! Hoe every field of mine, keep sieving the seed grain, and hack with your noses in the work …!'
>
> P. HEQANAKHT II

1922 or before
Flesh of the Gods: A Silver Cult Image of Horus the Elder

'Solid silver seated figure of Horus …. Sheathed with gold – some of which is missing. ?Cleaning. … Condition of silver where exposed good …'
HOWARD CARTER

Howard Carter first encountered this fabulous image of a falcon-headed god on 6 April 1922 in the hands of the dealer Nicolas Tano in Cairo. It was then still in its grey, lumpy, uncleaned state but Carter was sufficiently astute to realize that the piece would not only clean, but clean well, as he noted in his diary. Had he not been distracted in the coming months with the discovery of the tomb of Tutankhamun, the figure would doubtless have found its way into the Carnarvon collection. Instead it passed into other hands, and remained in its corroded condition until the late 1970s when its true splendour was revealed by careful cleaning.

Doubtless a representation of Horus the elder, the figure would originally have sported a separately fashioned double-crown. The body itself is of solid silver, and, as surviving fragments show, was originally sheathed in gold to reflect the ritual composition of the god's bones and flesh. It weighs in at an extraordinary 16.5 kg (36 lb 6 oz) and stands some 42 cm (16 ½ in) high. The eyes are of rock crystal, and the surviving wig inlays are of lapis lazuli – a further allusion to the divine status of the piece. The statue (now in the Miho Museum, Shigaraki, Japan) is the largest and most precious metal figure to have survived from ancient Egypt, and may be identified, with some confidence, as an exceptionally rare temple image used in the actual celebration of the god's cult.

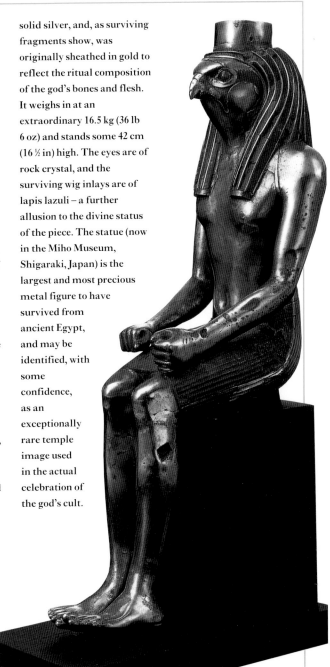

THE HEQANAKHT DOCUMENTS

JAMES NO.	CONTENT
I	letter, Heqanakht to his 'manager' Merisu
II	letter, Heqanakht to his mother Ipi and to a relative Hetepet; Heqanakht to Merisu and Nakht son of Hety
III	letter, Heqanakht to the overseer of the Delta, Herunufer
IV	letter, Sitnebsekhtu the daughter to Sitnebsekhtu the mother
V	five separate accounts and list of woods and wooden objects
VI	account
VII	two separate accounts
VIIIa	account
VIIIb	letter?
[IX]	account

THE MODELS OF MEKETRE: ANCIENT EGYPT IN MINIATURE

1920 The Golden Uraeus of Sesostris II from el-Lahun

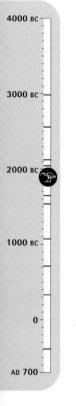

4000 BC

3000 BC

2000 BC

1000 BC

0

AD 700

Discovery/excavation
1920
by
Harry Burton;
Herbert E. Winlock

Site
Thebes (Deir el-Bahri, beneath portico of TT280)

Period
Middle Kingdom,
12th Dynasty,
reign of Ammenemes I,
1991–1962 BC

(below) 'The beam [illuminated] a little world of four thousand years ago... '– Meketre's wonderful models photographed as they lay in their rock-cut hiding place.

'The site is weirdly impressive. The great buttressed cliffs of tawny limestone practically enclose a deep circus a quarter of a mile in diameter. In the bottom are the almost obliterated traces of the avenue leading up to the supposed site of the mortuary temple of the last king of the Eleventh Dynasty. High above, around the rim of the circus where the cliffs start vertically upward, are the black mouths of the tombs of the courtiers ...'
HERBERT WINLOCK

The spectacularly sited tomb of the rich and powerful royal chancellor and high steward Meketre had first been dug by Georges Daressy in 1895, and was worked again by the English industrialist and enthusiastic amateur Robert Mond seven years later. Much remained to be done, however – even the tomb-owner's name was at that stage a mystery – and the Metropolitan Museum of Art Egyptian Expedition, with a few weeks to spare at the end of the 1919–20 season, decided to examine the area more closely. Their aim was 'to re-clear the corridors and pits of the tomb so that we could draw the plan which our predecessors had neglected to make. Scientific virtue rarely gets such striking or such unexpected rewards as it did on this occasion'.

The tomb itself had been heavily robbed and broken up in antiquity, though extensive fragments of the burial proper were brought to light – 22 pieces of the man's coffin, inscribed with extracts from the Pyramid Texts and (probably) Coffin Texts – while the chapel's painted relief fragments are among the finest known from the period. But the archaeologists had secretly hoped for more from the work, and were in a dismal mood back in their dig headquarters when a note was brought from the photographer Harry Burton, still finishing up on site, asking them to come quickly. Reluctantly, they complied, and were suitably unimpressed when Burton pointed out the reason for the summons. As Winlock records, 'There was nothing for us to see but a ragged hole in the rock … but when one by one we lay flat on the ground and shot a beam of light into that crack one of the most startling sights it is ever a digger's luck to see flashed before us':

'The beam [illuminated] a little world of four thousand years ago, and I was gazing down into the midst of a myriad of brightly painted little men going this way and that. A tall, slender girl gazed across at me perfectly composed; a gang of little men with sticks in their upraised hands drove spotted oxen; rowers tugged at their oars on a fleet of boats, while

HERBERT EUSTIS WINLOCK (1884–1950)

'Extraordinarily articulate, and a brilliant archaeologist, Winlock was highly respected for his scientific ability and adored for his sunny disposition, sparkling wit and high sense of humour [which was] almost always benevolent, even when he was going after a stuffy and jealous colleague.'
THOMAS HOVING

- Born Washington DC, 1 February 1884
- Educated Harvard, A.B. 1906, with honorary degrees subsequently conferred by Yale, Princeton, Michigan and Harvard, 1933–38
- Archaeologist with the Metropolitan Museum of Art Egyptian Expedition almost continuously from 1906–31, working at el-Lisht, Kharga Oasis, Thebes and elsewhere with impressive results; Director of the Egyptian Expedition, 1928–32
- Curator of Egyptian Art, Metropolitan Museum of Art, 1929–39; Director of the Museum, 1932–39, Director Emeritus, 1939–50
- Dies Venice, Florida, 26 January 1950

(below) Meketre seated within his pavilion reviews the estate cattle: the largest and most lifelike of the tomb owner's many funerary models.

1920
The Golden Uraeus of Sesostris II from el-Lahun

'[The Qufti worker Hosni Ibrahim] once told me that he often visits the Cairo Museum just to admire the uraeus in its glass case, and to recall that day [in 1920] … when he first held it in his hands. It is memories such as this which lend glory to the lives of these men, and inspire them with hope whenever they tackle a new site.'

ZAKARIA GONEIM

'There had been some doubt, for various reasons, whether [Sesostris] II was actually buried in the Lahun pyramid or not [but] there can now be no question on the matter. In 1920 it was decided to make a thorough clearance, or rather turning over, of the débris in the pyramid rooms and passages. A start was made with the rock-cut offering chamber leading out of the sepulchre on the south. There only some 6 ins. of dust and rubbish covered the floor, and within half-an-hour the uraeus from the king's crown was brought to light …. It is of solid gold, inlaid with the usual stones' – lapis lazuli, turquoise, carnelian. 'At the back two loops are sunk into the hollow of the tail: these are for attaching it to the crown ….' Prior to Tutankhamun, this magnificent jewel (Cairo JE 52702) was 'the only [known] piece of regalia actually worn by an Egyptian king'.

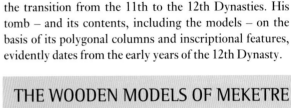

(above) Fishing for the hereafter: two canoes drag a trawl net between them to ensure for their owner a constant supply of fresh fish in the next world.

the transition from the 11th to the 12th Dynasties. His tomb – and its contents, including the models – on the basis of its polygonal columns and inscriptional features, evidently dates from the early years of the 12th Dynasty.

one ship seemed foundering right in front of me with its bow balanced precariously in the air. And all of this busy coming and going was in uncanny silence, as though the distance back over the forty centuries I looked across was too great for even an echo to reach my ears.'

(above) Offering-bearers stock the tomb of Meketre with provisions – a similar composition to that found in the tomb of Djehutynakht at el-Bersha (•p. 145).

The find was stupendous. Winlock's Egyptian workmen had uncovered a small and totally untouched chamber – a Middle Kingdom equivalent of the Old Kingdom *serdab*, or statue room – crammed with a pristine collection of exquisitely detailed, painted wooden funerary models intended to recreate for their owner in the next world, in its every detail, the life he had cherished in this. Such models had been found before, and would be found again, in great numbers; but in quality or completeness nothing before or since has ever come close to the wonder of Meketre's little hoard.

Winlock concluded that the owner had died during the reign of Nebhepetre Mentuhotep. Recent study of the tomb and its models, however, suggests that Meketre's 50–60 years of life in fact spanned several reigns, from Nebhepetre Mentuhotep through to Ammenemes I, and

THE WOODEN MODELS OF MEKETRE

DESIGNATION	DESCRIPTION	LOCATIONS
A	residence of Meketre	Cairo JE 46721
B	residence of Meketre	New York MMA 20.3.13
C	inspection of cattle	Cairo JE 46724
D	cattle stable	New York MMA 20.3.9
E	butcher shop	New York MMA 20.3.10
F	granary	New York MMA 20.3.11
G	brewery and bakery	New York MMA 20.3.12
H	weaving shop	Cairo JE 46723
J	carpenter shop	Cairo JE 46722
K	female offering bearer with drink	Cairo JE 46725
L	female offering bearer with food	New York MMA 20.3.7
M	group of four offering bearers	New York MMA 20.3.8
N	travelling boat with sail	Cairo JE 46720
O	travelling boat with oars	New York MMA 20.3.1
P	travelling boat with sail	Cairo JE 46719
Q	travelling boat with oars	New York MMA 20.3.2
R	kitchen tender with sail	Cairo JE 46718
S	kitchen tender with oars	New York MMA 20.3.3
T	yacht with sail	New York MMA 20.3.4
U	yacht with paddles	Cairo JE 46716
V	yacht with sail	Cairo JE 46717
W	yacht with paddles	New York MMA 20.3.5
X	sporting boat	New York MMA 20.3.6
Y	fishing canoes with trawl	Cairo JE 46715

1920 Statues of Meryrehashtef

Discovery/excavation
1920
by
Herbert E. Winlock

Site
Thebes (Deir el-Bahri, beneath
portico of TT280)

Period
Middle Kingdom, 12th
Dynasty, reign of
Ammenemes I, 1991–1962 BC

'The supposedly exhausted corridors of the tomb of [Meketre] had yielded a veritable treasure [of tomb models] which justified our clearing its causeway and courtyard more thoroughly than we had at first intended .... But again ... luck was with us for, right on the edge of our predecessors' excavations at the top of the causeway, we found ... the little untouched tomb of a servitor of the great man, named Wah.'
HERBERT WINLOCK

The discovery of the tomb of Wah illustrates that, in Egyptian archaeology, it is wise never to take anything for granted: the area in which the burial was found was well dug over, and had already yielded unanticipated treasures. Little else of interest ought reasonably to have been expected – but there were indeed further surprises in store, on 24 March 1920, as the excavator Herbert Winlock, in his inimitable style, describes:

'During the week that we were moving the models [of Meketre: •p. 156] we brought the gang up from the palace [of Malqata, where other works had been in progress] and, thus reinforced, the workmen were turned into the parts of the courtyard which had every appearance of having been dug before.... In a place where the rock begins to descend sharply, [a member of Meketre's household] Wah had had a little slope cut leading into a tunnel about twenty-six feet long, and five and a half feet high and wide. The entrance, when we discovered it, was still securely blocked with mud bricks and when we had photographed them and taken them down we could see his coffin standing at the back undisturbed.

(below) X-rays of Wah's mummy, taken in 1935, reveal his hidden funerary treasures.

Everything was exactly as the priests had left it four thousand years ago. Just inside the doorway lay a few wisps of burnt straw – ashes as impalpable as those of a cigarette – which had dropped from a torch burnt at the time of the funeral. Carelessly thrown to one side was a pall of white linen with which the coffin had been covered when it was brought up the hill, and passing under the coffin itself lay the three linen tapes with which it had been tied, unknotted and dropped to either side. Just as it had fallen at the foot of the coffin lay the knob of wood with which the lid had been lowered and which the undertakers sawed off, once the lid was pegged in place. On the side of the coffin near the head were painted the eyes through which the dead man could look out on to the world and in front of this "window" had been deposited twelve conical loaves of bread, the right fore leg of a beef, cut off as the dead man's share of the funeral banquet, and a jug of beer. The beer jug was of exactly the same shape as those in the model brewery of Meket-Re' and had been stoppered, as those were represented as being, with a ball of clay. But the beer had worked, shot the stopper off in one direction and rolled the jug over the opposite way, and where it had spilled on the floor there was a hard dried crust.'

The mummy of Wah

Wah's rectangular wooden coffin proved to contain a well-preserved mummy lying on its left side so as to see out through the coffin's magical painted eyes, with a wooden headrest placed beneath the head, a resin disk on

(below) Stages in the unwrapping of the body: top, as found, with gilt-faced cartonnage peeking shyly out through the bandages; middle, the bulk of the padding and bandages removed; bottom, the shrivelled corpse.

(MMA 20.3.203) was displayed as found, in its plump, fully wrapped condition, with the charming gilt-faced cartonnage headpiece peeping out from the top: Wah had not been a person of great rank, and the feeling had been that unwrapping the body would probably yield little of interest. This again was a mistaken assumption. X-rays of the mummy taken 15 years after its arrival revealed that Wah's 'neck, his chest, and his wrists were loaded with the jewelry fashionable in Thebes about 2000 B.C.'.

The subsequent unwrapping process was painstakingly documented so that the mummy could later be reconstituted. It revealed not only Wah's magnificent collection of jewelry, but that their owner was a relatively young man, estimated to have been in his 30s at the time of his death. Yet for all of this – the abundance of silver, more prized than gold at this early date, clearly attests to his wealth – the mummification process itself was relatively unsophisticated.

the floor and a copper mirror in front of the face. At the feet of the mummy were a pair of wooden model sandals and a wooden statuette of the deceased wrapped in linen. On top of this assemblage, some 38 sheets of fringed, folded linen had been packed in, containing three staves – the uppermost sheet having been finally 'sealed' with a smearing of resin.

The bulk of this extraordinary find was divided to the Metropolitan Museum of Art, where it was eventually studied in detail. For several years the mummy

(above) Five necklaces as found within the wrappings of the mummy, of gold, silver, a variety of semiprecious stones, glazed steatite and faience.

(above) Wah's superb silver scarab, inscribed on its back with the names and titles of Wah and his master, Meketre, and decorated on the flattened base with an incised scroll pattern and amuletic hieroglyphs.

1920
Statues of Meryrehashtef

'... we were at Sedment by December 17 [1920]. It was an awful upland of desert ... [but] the prize of the season [was] a small rock chamber of a chapel [with] a pit in the corner of the courtyard. About ten feet down in this were three wooden figures of the owner Mery-Ra-ha-shetef at different ages, the youth, the landowner, and the elder; the youth [British Museum EA 55722] is the most detailed and spirited statuette of the Old Kingdom'
FLINDERS PETRIE

UNWRAPPING THE MUMMY OF WAH

NO.	DESCRIPTION	NOTES
1	shawl, wrapped kilt-like around the outside	docket: 'Linen of the temple protecting Nytankhsekhmet, true of voice'
2	12 bandages spiralling up and down, each up to 12 m (40 ft) in length and 15 cm (6 in) wide	
3	sheets and large pieces of linen, folded to pad out the mummy to a cylindrical shape	
4	layer of bandages thickly coated with resin	
5	20 more sheets and pads	cartonnage mask fully revealed
6	10 more sheets and pads	
7	second layer of bandages thickly coated with resin	
8	12 more sheets and pads	beneath: first layer of jewelry – 4 bead necklaces (gold, silver, semiprecious stones, faience)
9	6 more bandages and pads	beneath: second layer of jewelry – string of beads on chest; 4 large scarabs (2 silver, 1 lapis lazuli, 1 faience) over crossed arms
10	6 large bandages, and a dozen pads and sheets	
11	third layer of resin-coated bandages; arms and legs wrapped separately	this layer: jewelry – faience broad collar; matching bracelets and anklets; house lizard; cricket
12	quantities of bandages and sheets	jewelry: *seweret*-bead of carnelian on left palm

- mummy: arms crossed over the chest
- unplaced on mummy: dead mouse 'dropped on the mummy's knees and hidden under the next bandages'
- total amount of linen employed in mummy wrappings: 375 sq. m (4,000 sq. ft); 845 sq. m (9,100 sq. ft) in total from the tomb
- 60+ sheets with ink dockets – hieroglyphic sign or owner's name (11 of Wah himself); names often torn out in antiquity; six dated linens – reigns of Nebhepetre Mentuhotep and Ammenemes I

THE TOMB OF TUTANKHAMUN

Discovery/excavation
1922
by
Howard Carter

Site
Thebes (Valley of the Kings, tomb KV62)

Period
New Kingdom, 18th Dynasty, reign of Tutankhamun, 1333–1323 BC

4000 BC
3000 BC
2000 BC
1000 BC
0
AD 700

(above) One of the seals employed to close the tomb following the interment of the king. Tutankhamun's prenomen is enclosed in the cartouche positioned above the jackal and nine prisoners motif.

'We are working in untouched stuff so one never knows what may come – I hope a hundred times something good ....'
HOWARD CARTER

Hints at the existence of Tutankhamun's burial in the Valley of the Kings had been uncovered by Theodore Davis (•p. 115) in 1905 and 1908, in the form of a small faience cup inscribed with the king's name and, from pit KV54, in an assemblage of embalming refuse and other material. With the discovery of the small, single-chambered KV58, which produced a small cache of gold foil fragments inscribed with the names of Tutankhamun and Ay, Davis believed he had the tomb itself, from which these materials had strayed.

Howard Carter and his sponsor, the fifth Earl of Carnarvon, held just as strongly that Davis was mistaken in his view, and that the tomb of Tutankhamun still remained to be found. It had not escaped their notice that neither of the caches of royal mummies (•pp. 64, 103) had produced the king's body, which, they reasoned, might indicate that the tomb had survived intact. To their colleagues, though, Carnarvon and Carter were chasing a fantasy.

Their fantasy would none the less resolve itself into fact on 4 November 1922, with the discovery of a rock-cut step below the entrance to the tomb of Ramesses VI (KV9). This step proved to be the first of a series leading down to the walled-up entrance to a tomb, plastered over and stamped with large oval seals of six types, five inscribed with the prenomen of Tutankhamun – 'Nebkheprure'. After several years of fruitless digging, at the start of what had been intended as their final season in the Valley of the Kings, it was little short of a miracle.

Exploring the tomb

'At last have made wonderful discovery in Valley; a magnificent tomb with seals intact; re-covered same for your arrival; congratulations.'
HOWARD CARTER

HOWARD CARTER
(1874–1939)

- Born Kensington, 9 May 1874, son of the animal painter Samuel John Carter
- Educated at home owing to 'delicate health'
- Staff artist with the Egypt Exploration Fund, 1891–99, working at Beni Hasan and el-Bersha, 1892–93, and Deir el-Bahri, 1893–99; digs with Flinders Petrie at el-Amarna, 1891–92 (•p. 83)
- Chief Inspector of Antiquities, Upper Egypt, 1899–1904, undertaking much work in the Valley of the Kings; Chief Inspector of Antiquities, Lower Egypt, 1904–05, resigning following a *fracas* with a party of French tourists at Saqqara
- Artist/dealer/dragoman, Luxor, 1905–08
- Archaeologist to Lord Carnarvon, 1908–23, digging at Thebes (Dra Abu'l-Naga, Deir el-Bahri, Valley of the Kings) and other lesser sites
- Discovery and clearance of the tomb of Tutankhamun, 1922–32
- Dies Kensington, 2 March 1939

(left) Lord Carnarvon and his daughter, Lady Evelyn Herbert, photographed at Luxor station with Howard Carter (far left) and the governor of Qena province.

(above) The entrance to Tutankhamun's tomb, showing the steps leading down to the first sealed doorway.

(left) One of the pair of large and impressive wooden guardian statues which stood flanking the sealed entrance to the burial chamber. Carved from wood, painted with black resin and highlighted in gold leaf, the statues reproduce precisely the king's height and appearance in life.

TUTANKHAMUN'S TREASURES: What was found and where

OBJECT CLASS	A	B	C	D	E	F
archery equipment		•	•	•	•	•
baskets			•			
beds			•			•
bier				•		
boat models					•	
boomerangs and throwsticks			•			
botanical specimens			•	•	•	
boxes and chests	•		•		•	•
canopic equipment					•	
chairs and stools			•			
chariot equipment				•	•	•
clothing			•	•	•	
coffins (king)				•		
coffins (others)					•	
cosmetic objects		•	•		•	
cuirass						•
divine figures			•	•	•	
fans				•	•	
foodstuffs			•			
gaming equipment		•	•			
gold mask				•		
granary model					•	
hassocks			•			
jewelry, beads, amulets	•	•	•	•	•	
labels		•	•	•		
lamps and torches			•	•		
mummies				•		
musical instruments			•	•		
pall and framework				•		
portable pavilion			•			•
regalia			•	•	•	
ritual couches			•			
ritual objects			•	•	•	•
royal figures		?	•	•	•	
sarcophagus				•		
sealings	•	•	•	•	•	
shabtis and related objects			•	•		•
shields				•		
shrines			•	•	•	
sticks and staves			•	•	•	
swords and daggers				•		•
tools			•		•	•
vessels	•	•	•	•	•	•
wine jars	•	•		•		
writing equipment			•		•	

A Entrance staircase
B Corridor
C Antechamber
D Burial Chamber
E Treasury
F Annexe

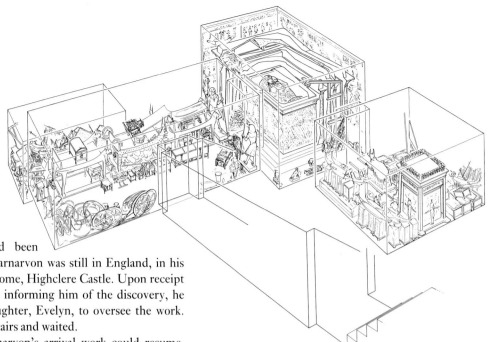

The discovery had been made while Lord Carnarvon was still in England, in his stately Hampshire home, Highclere Castle. Upon receipt of Carter's telegram informing him of the discovery, he set sail with his daughter, Evelyn, to oversee the work. Carter filled in the stairs and waited.

With Lord Carnarvon's arrival work could resume, and within a relatively short time the tomb doorway again stood revealed. It was now that Carter noticed, for the first time, a resealed hole in the top left-hand corner, indicating that the tomb had been entered, most probably by robbers. Not knowing quite what to expect, the excavators set to dismantling the sealed doorway and emptying the rubble-filled corridor behind. Ominously, mixed in with the dust and limestone chippings of the fill were several smashed and broken fragments. Would the entire tomb prove to be in this condition?

By 4 o'clock in the afternoon of 26 November 1922, the corridor stood empty, with a second plastered and sealed doorway revealed at the far end – this again reclosed at the top left. Making a small hole, Carter inserted a candle to test for foul gases, and then peered in:

> *'At first I could see nothing, the hot air escaping from the chamber causing the candle flame to flicker, but presently, as my eyes grew accustomed to the light, details of the room within emerged slowly from the mist, strange animals, statues, and gold – everywhere the glint of gold.'*

It was the greatest find archaeology has ever seen.

(above) Cut-away view showing the physical layout of the tomb – steps, entrance corridor, Antechamber, Annexe, Burial Chamber and Treasury – and distribution of the myriad treasures buried with Tutankhamun.

(left) Row of caskets neatly arranged at the entrance to the Treasury. According to dockets on the lids, before their rifling by tomb robbers they had contained a collection of royal jewelry.

(right) Opening the nest of four sealed funerary shrines. These proved to conceal a superb quartzite sarcophagus, three anthropoid coffins – the innermost of solid gold – and the masked mummy of the king, untouched since the day of the burial.

The tomb and its history

KV62, as the tomb is now officially numbered, consisted of but six elements: the entrance stairway; the rubble-filled corridor; the Antechamber, with its animal-headed couches, chariots and life-size guardian figures; the Annexe, a store chamber originally intended for the king's wine jars and food provisions; the decorated Burial Chamber, with its four massive gilded wooden shrines surrounding a quartzite sarcophagus and three coffins (the innermost of solid gold) holding the king's mummified corpse; and the Treasury, primarily intended for the royal canopic equipment. As tombs went, it was exceptionally small and oddly arranged, and it soon became apparent that it was most probably a private affair subsequently adapted for royal use. Work on cutting Tutankhamun's 'official' place of burial, perhaps situated in the West Valley, had evidently progressed but a little way at the time of his unexpected death, and other arrangements had therefore to be made in a hurry.

There was burial furniture everywhere, crammed into corners and piled to the very ceilings, in the richest display of material ever recovered from an Egyptian tomb – and this after it had been robbed *twice* in antiquity!

The first robbery had occurred within a very short time of the king's funeral, and was very likely committed by those who had assisted in stocking the burial. The thefts were discovered, and the entrance corridor filled with rubble as a deterrent to future illicit access – in vain. A second robbery took place shortly after, but this time the intruders were far less fortunate: they were evidently caught in the act, with some of their loot found by Carter still wrapped in a headscarf ready for carrying off. The robbers' fate will have been gruesome – mutilation and impalement on a sharpened stake.

This brutal deterrent clearly did the trick: there would be no further attempts to enter the sepulchre. With the oblivion to which the heretic Amarna pharaohs were consigned during the succeeding Ramessid period, and the erection on the site of the tomb some years later of a series of store chambers and workmen's shelters, the burial of Tutankhamun was completely forgotten.

(left) Tutankhamun's breathtakingly beautiful gold portrait mask, found still in place on the royal mummy.

(above) Pharaoh's alabaster canopic chest: the four human-headed stoppers concealed hollows with four miniature gold coffins for the dead king's embalmed viscera.

(below) Two exquisite inlaid gold pectorals from the tomb – the upper usurped from Akhenaten, the lower with a cryptic spelling of Tutankhamun's name.

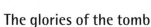

The glories of the tomb

The discovery of Tutankhamun's tomb was to shed new and wholly unexpected light on the richness and sophistication of the Egyptian court during the later years of the 14th century BC. Though royal burial equipment and palace furnishings had previously been found in the Valley (•pp. 18, 101, 113), such items were rare and, by their generally broken state, unreadable save to a few informed scholars. Now, thanks to Carnarvon and Carter's magnificent find, the world at large could see with its own eyes what the archaeologists meant by that phrase 'the glory of ancient Egypt'.

Tutankhamun's tomb contained a mix of items: those, like the shrines, sarcophagus, coffins and mask, required for the funerary ritual and the young king's continued survival into the beyond; but more personal items, also, which had been familiar to pharaoh in life. It is these last which so eloquently humanize the boy: his jewelry and the royal regalia; a mass of clothing and textiles; a range of boxes, chests, thrones, chairs, stools and beds from the royal apartments; the king's chariots and weaponry (including a perfectly preserved dagger of newly discovered iron); a mass of fans, sticks and staves (one 'A reed which His Majesty cut with his own hand'); precious oils and cosmetics; games and gameboxes; musical instruments (most famously the silver and copper trumpets, eerily sounded in a BBC broadcast in 1939); pharaoh's writing equipment (but curiously no papyri); a precious, carefully coffined lock of his beloved grandmother Tiye's hair; and all the pots, pans, baskets and provisions that would be needed to sustain the king on his final journey. Nothing to compare with this glittering haul had ever been encountered before.

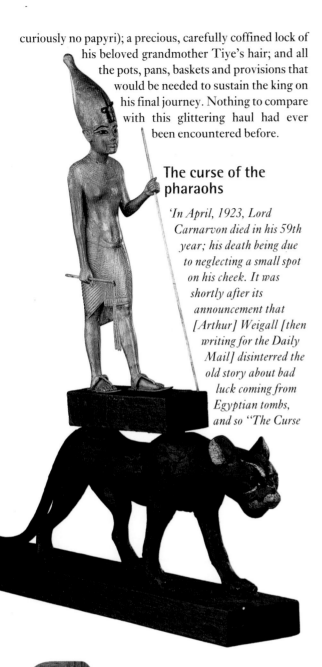

The curse of the pharaohs

'In April, 1923, Lord Carnarvon died in his 59th year; his death being due to neglecting a small spot on his cheek. It was shortly after its announcement that [Arthur] Weigall [then writing for the Daily Mail] disinterred the old story about bad luck coming from Egyptian tombs, and so "The Curse of Tut'ankhamûn" came into being.

When my wife and I protested to Weigall, he said: "But see how the public will lap it up."

And it has; every death of any person even remotely connected with the tomb has been put down to "the curse." Carter died in 1939, aged 66, [Harry] Burton in 1940, and [The Times reporter, Arthur] Merton from a motor accident in 1942, and in each the "curse" has been mentioned or implied.

It is very certain that when [Alfred] Lucas, [Douglas] Derry or I [Antiquities Service inspector at the time of the discovery] pass away, the same silly story will be exhumed.'
REX ENGELBACH

The fifth Earl of Carnarvon, sponsor of Carter's work in the Valley of the Kings, died as the result of an infected mosquito bite on 5 April 1923. Such a fate, as Silvio Curto has pointed out, 'was not unusual in Egypt; Schiaparelli's first assistant in the Valley of the Queens and elsewhere, Francesco Ballerini, had died in the same way'. But the press, anxious to maintain public interest in the Tutankhamun story, preferred to ascribe it to a curse (•p. 231), the inevitable result of disturbing pharaoh's eternal rest, by which all manner of calamities would be explained in the years to come.

The Valley since Tutankhamun

For some decades following Carter's momentous discovery, the Valley of the Kings dropped from Egyptological view, a victim of its own success: with the discovery of Tutankhamun, it was assumed, there was nothing left to find. Nowadays we know better. Since the 1960s, with

(above) Large, finely carved wooden *shabti* from the tomb, shown wearing the *nemes*-headdress and clutching the crook and flail, symbols of the king's earthly rule.

(left) Gilded wooden statue of pharaoh, mounted on the back of a leopard.

(below) Tutankhamun's second coffin, of gilded wood richly inlaid with glass and semiprecious stones. It had originally been made for an earlier king.

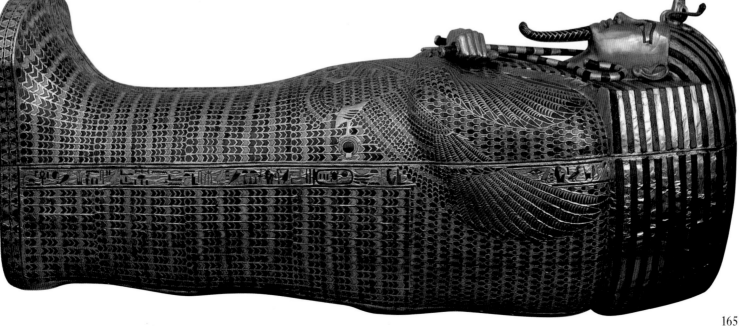

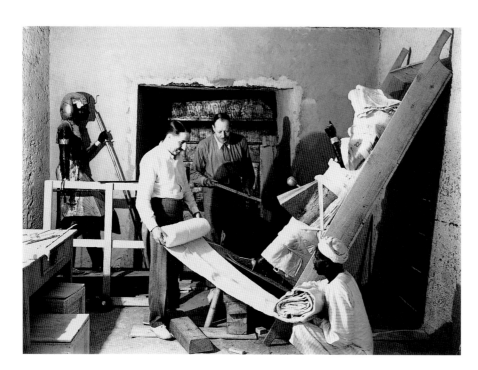

(above) Howard Carter, his assistant 'Pecky' Callender and an Egyptian worker carefully pack the two guardian statues with layers of cotton wadding in preparation for their safe removal from the tomb.

the change of emphasis from treasure to knowledge and the appearance of that unassailable compendium of information, *The Royal Necropoleis of Thebes* by Elizabeth Thomas, interest in the Valley of the Kings has burgeoned.

Several expeditions are today active in the field, clearing again the long-known tombs in a search for missed data, and excavating anew in those areas of the royal wadis ignored by Theodore Davis and the winning team of Carter and Carnarvon. The results have been impressive – and occasionally surprising: two new and intact princely sarcophagi (of Amenherkhepshef and Mentuherkhepshef, offspring of Ramesses III and VI respectively) in the long-known tomb of Bay (KV 13), discovered by Hartwig Altenmüller and a team from the University of Hamburg in the early 1990s; and the ongoing revelation of architectural megalomania currently being revealed by Kent Weeks and the Theban Mapping Project within KV5 (•p. 220), a tomb prepared for the sons of Ramesses II. The Valley of the Kings is a place with much still remaining to be done – and, it may be ventured, much still to be found.

Politics after Tutankhamun

'... M. Lacau, in the sixty-five years you French have directed the Service, what opportunities have you given us?'
AHMED KAMAL

(right) Examining the royal mummy: Professor Douglas Derry makes the first, tentative incision in the bandages, watched by Carter and officials of the Antiquities Service. The quantity of superb jewels found concealed within the wrappings would astonish the excavators.

The urbane and generally popular Gaston Maspero had retired from his second term as Director-General of the Service des Antiquités in 1914, to be succeeded by another Frenchman, Pierre Lacau. Lacau's appointment amounted to far more than a simple change of face: believing firmly that Maspero had been lax in his dealings with foreign excavators, and too generous in his divisions, he determined that the system must be reformed.

In these times of emergent nationalism, however, matters were soon to run out of control. Following the discovery of Tutankhamun there had been an unseemly tussle over ownership of the tomb and its treasures, and the political temperature was raised to dangerous levels. Nor were matters helped by Ludwig Borchardt's decision at this time to reveal the existence of the fabulous Nefertiti bust (•p. 134). Whose country was this? the Egyptians began to ask. Why should foreigners have any rights whatsoever over Egypt's heritage? Casualties of the backlash included a new, $10 million Cairo Museum, which John D. Rockefeller Jr had offered to 'finance; the project was rejected as yet another means of asserting Western control.

As difficulties increased over the coming years, foreign expeditions, many dependent on a supply of objects, often as a means of raising finance, went into decline. Some, unable to adapt to the times, withdrew altogether – Flinders Petrie's British School of Archaeology quit Egypt for good in 1927 to dig in Palestine; and in 1936, when the new regulations for division were finally introduced, the Metropolitan Museum of Art and the Egypt Exploration Society for a time followed suit.

Others, however, pressed on, and to good effect – including the newly re-admitted Germans under Günther Roeder at el-Ashmunein (•p. 194) and the French under the direction of Pierre Montet at Tanis (•p. 189). More significantly, although there had been Egyptian Egyptologists in the past (such as Ahmed Kamal), the period would see the emergence of the first, fully fledged Egyptian excavators – the most prominent being Selim Hassan (•p. 178), trained in the field by the great Austrian Egyptologist Hermann Junker. Hassan's endeavours at Giza, like those of his mentor, not only achieved impressive results, but would be published in full, in several large and abundantly illustrated volumes which remain of great value to scholarship today.

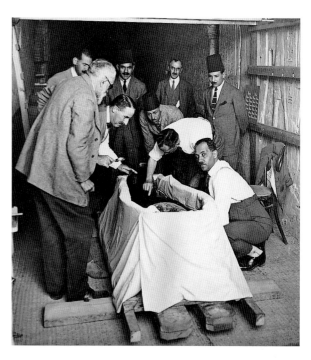

THE SLAIN SOLDIERS OF AN EGYPTIAN KING

Discovery/excavation
1923
by
Herbert E. Winlock

Site
Thebes (Deir el-Bahri,
cemetery 500, tomb 507)

Period
Middle Kingdom, 12th
Dynasty, probably reign of
Ammenemes I, 1991–1962 BC

'... the place had been completely plundered ages ago, and had been left strewn with torn linen rags among which had been callously thrown a ghastly heap of robbed and mutilated bodies. There seemed very little likelihood that the thieves had left anything for us ....'
HERBERT WINLOCK

Mass burials of mummies have been frequently found in Egypt, especially at Thebes, and tend to attract little interest. One such cache uncovered by the Metropolitan Museum team within tomb 507, next to the tomb of Chancellor Khety (TT311) in the cliffs to the north of the Hatshepsut causeway, initially aroused the usual, lukewarm enthusiasm – until it became obvious that not only were these mummies of much earlier date than usual, but of one particular class within Egyptian society.

Because of its unappealing contents, clearance of the tomb, first discovered in the spring of 1923, was deferred until March 1927. The work yielded around 60 bodies but fragments of no more than two or three early Middle Kingdom coffins of ordinary quality. The diggers' belief that this was no more than a late catacomb seemed to be confirmed: 'In the hot sun [the bodies] were extraordinarily unpleasant ... and they had all the look of the dried-up corpses of Copts .... Still, there was something not quite Coptic about the bandages'. The remains were therefore searched more carefully, and some 62 linen dockets recovered. To the excavators' amazement these, like the coffins, were revealed as early Middle Kingdom in date. The find suddenly took on a new interest.

A closer look at the bodies themselves revealed these thinly wrapped corpses

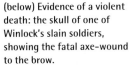

(below) Evidence of a violent death: the skull of one of Winlock's slain soldiers, showing the fatal axe-wound to the brow.

'to be [the bodies of] remarkably vigorous men, every one in the prime of life ... [with] not ... a single shaven head among the lot. On the contrary, every one of these men had a thick mop of hair, bobbed off square at the nape of the neck as on the contemporary statuettes of soldiers from Assiut [Asyut, •p. 87].'

Were these, then, the actual bodies of such soldiers? The proof was soon to come. 'We ... had methodically measured the first nine bodies when the tenth was put on the table and Brewster ... noticed an arrow-tip sticking out of its chest'. By the end of the post-mortem, a dozen or more arrow wounds had been identified, with others probably missed, together with in excess of 28 head wounds caused by sling-shot or similar missiles falling from above or by the mace used to finish off the wounded. Six of the bodies had been defiled by predatory birds.

Winlock's conclusion was that these were soldiers of Nebhepetre Mentuhotep, fourth king of the 11th Dynasty, who had reunited the country by defeating the Herakleopolitan line then ruling at the same time in the north; more recent opinion is that they are probably somewhat later in date. The cause for which they had fought and lost their lives will probably remain unknown, but that they had been accorded the privilege of burial in the royal precincts was a clear mark of the honour with which their bravery was acknowledged by the ruling king.

(above) Another head, the facial features well preserved, with broken nose and depressed fracture of the skull over the right eye.

4000 BC

3000 BC

2000 BC

1000 BC

0

AD 700

THE MYSTERY TOMB OF QUEEN HETEPHERES

1924–33 Statues and Tiles at the Step Pyramid of Djoser

Discovery/excavation
1925
by
Alan Rowe;
George A. Reisner

Site
Giza (near pyramid of Khufu,
tomb G7000x)

Period
Old Kingdom, 4th Dynasty,
reign of Khufu, 2551–2528 BC

'This intact tomb … presented for the first time in the history of Egyptian excavation an opportunity of studying the burial of a great personage of an early period, 1500 years older than the royal tombs of the New Kingdom. Looking in from a small opening, [we] had seen a beautiful alabaster sarcophagus with its lid in place. Partly on the sarcophagus and partly fallen behind it lay about twenty gold-cased poles and beams of a large canopy. On the western edge of the sarcophagus were spread several sheets of gold inlaid with faience, and on the floor there was a confused mass of gold-cased furniture.'

GEORGE A. REISNER

On 2 February 1925, the photographer to George A. Reisner's Harvard–Boston expedition at the Giza pyramids was setting up his tripod when one of the legs dislodged not a loose piece of bedrock but a portion of plaster. Examining the area more closely, it became clear that the plaster had been laid to conceal the entrance to a tomb shaft.

The clearance of this shaft was carried out in Reisner's absence (Reisner himself was still in the United States) by his British assistant, Alan Rowe. At a depth of around 30 m (100 ft), the shaft gave access to a single chamber, walled-off with limestone blocks which had clearly not been disturbed since antiquity.

Significant intact burials at Giza, which has seen more than its fair share of antiquarian interest, are rare; Reisner by 1925 had discovered only one – the tomb of Impy (•p. 136) –

(above) Setting the scene for Reisner's wonderful discovery: the great pyramid of Khufu, Hetepheres' son, with the pyramid of Khufu's successor, Khephren, behind.

(left) The entrance to the burial shaft of Hetepheres, with block and tackle in position to facilitate access by the archaeological team and the removal of the queen's fragile and fragmented treasures.

1924–33
Statues and Tiles at the Step Pyramid of Djoser

DJOSER'S SERDAB

The Step Pyramid complex of Djoser, second king of the 3rd Dynasty (2630–2611 BC), is famed today as the world's earliest large-scale monument in stone (translating in this material several reed and wood prototypes). Though constructed at the dawn of dynastic history, the purity of its architectural form is sublime: for tourists of the New Kingdom who left their graffiti here three thousand years and more ago, it was 'as though heaven were within it, [the sun god] Re rising in it'. The site has now, in part, been restored to some semblance of this original glory by the French architect Jean-Philippe Lauer, who arrived on the scene following Cecil Firth's work at the site in 1924–26 (and is there still).

Visitors to the Step Pyramid today are usually invited by their guide to peer through one of two cylindrical apertures drilled into the *serdab* (enclosed statue room) on the north side of the Djoser complex and observe the face of the pyramid's original owner. What they are looking at is in fact a modern copy of the king's plastered, painted and Clark-Gable moustached *ka*-statue, a full-sized sculpture of limestone in which the life-force of the deceased king could reside, observe the world beyond the grave, and receive offerings of incense.

The original (*left*) was removed to the Cairo Museum (JE 49158) shortly after its

discovery by Dows Dunham (who had been seconded to Firth's work by Reisner's Giza camp) in the season 1924–25.

Djoser's statue presents a number of interesting features, including an archaic form of *nemes*-headcloth with pointed lappets covering his striated wig, and evidence of inlaid eyes, long ago pricked out. The inscription on the front of the base, carved in raised relief, identifies the subject: 'Netjerykhet' – the name by which Djoser is acknowledged throughout his mortuary structure. The pharaoh's almost leonine profile offers a striking image of kingly power at this long-distant time.

A second statue also found at the site is of greater significance still, though it consists of little more than the inscribed base. This carries the name not only of Netjerykhet-Djoser, but also, in the most elegant of hieroglyphs, the name and titles of that all-round wise man and architect of Djoser's monument, Imhotep – one of the most influential, and mysterious, personages of the early ancient world (•p. 206).

OTHER DISCOVERIES

'From 1924 to 1931, the English archaeologist Firth … threw fresh light on the constructions surrounding the Pyramid; the "Northern Building" … the "Southern Building" … the "Heb-sed" court … and the "T" temple … the entrance colonnade … the South Tomb … and the fortified enclosure-wall. In 1928, the same explorer actually discovered under the Pyramid a new chamber adorned with blue tiles [below], and three steles of King Zoser [Djoser] …. After him, Quibell and Lauer explored the deeper underground galleries of the Pyramid, of which Firth had only caught a glimpse. They discovered there in 1933 two alabaster sarcophagi … and a store of about 30,000 hard stone vases.'

ÉTIENNE DRIOTON

and that was 12 years previously. The excavators therefore felt some satisfaction at finding a second. Their satisfaction increased when an inlaid inscription on a carrying-chair announced who the owner of this new tomb actually was: Queen Hetepheres, wife of King Snefru and mother of Khufu, builder of the largest pyramid at Giza – the greatest construction in stone the world has ever seen. An added source of pleasure for Reisner was that the discovery eclipsed, if only momentarily, the triumphs of Carnarvon and Carter at the tomb of Tutankhamun (•p. 160) – two men the 'sea-green incorruptible' Reisner loathed as arrogant and colonial, and had done everything in his power to discredit as unprincipled treasure-seekers and adventurers.

The excavation of Hetepheres' packed burial chamber was mostly carried out by the unsung Dows Dunham, and proved long and difficult – not to say downright dangerous, since Dunham himself, had he not been wearing a pith helmet, would probably have been killed during an early stage of the clearance when a piece of rock unexpectedly fell from the ceiling of the chamber. Clearance was complicated by the restricted space, in which no more than two excavators were able to manoeuvre at any one time, and by the enormous heat generated by the electric light. Conditions were relieved somewhat by a carefully arranged ventilation fan, bringing down the temperature to a more bearable 27–29ºC (80-85ºF). Immense care had, of course, to be exercised in the instal-lation of this fan, since the organic components of the burial furniture had decayed almost completely – so much as a vigorous sneeze would have blown away the entire find:

'I remember once, quite early in the work, while Reisner and I were together in the tomb, I made some remark that he found amusing, and he let out one of his hearty laughs. Instantly, there was a slight rustling noise as a fragment of sheet gold at the back of the chamber slid down to a lower position as a result of the vibration of air set up by the noise.'
DOWS DUNHAM

The great fragility of Hetepheres' burial equipment was from the start a matter of serious concern, but the generous amounts of gold foil with which many of the objects had been embellished preserved to a large degree their general form. And this state of affairs, aided by careful note-taking and meticulous scale drawings (amounting to 1,701 manuscript pages) and excellent photography (a total of 1,057 shots), would eventually permit the principal finds to be reconstructed on new wood, and their superb design and quality to be recovered – to supplement and explain the abundant evidence from reliefs and tomb paintings which has survived for funerary materials of this sort. The whole enterprise represented nothing less than 'a miracle of patience'.

(left) The excavation of Hetepheres' tomb almost completed: a youthful Dows Dunham records the position and contents of the queen's disintegrated bracelet casket at the southern end of the chamber.

The moment of truth

The opening of the queen's sarcophagus, well on in the second season of work at the tomb, was keenly anticipated – but proved the most extraordinary anticlimax, as Dows Dunham records:

'On March 3, 1927, a distinguished company [of 8 or so people] assembled one hundred feet underground …. At a nod from Reisner, the jacks that had been placed for the purpose began to turn. Slowly a crack appeared between the lid and the box. Little by little it widened until we could see into the upper part of the box; nothing was visible. As the lid rose higher we could see further into the interior and finally to the bottom of the box …'

The artist Lindon Smith, who was present, takes up the story:

'When it was sufficiently raised for me to peer inside, I saw to my dismay that the queen was not there – the sarcophagus was empty! Turning to Reisner, I said in a voice louder than I had intended, "George, she's a dud!"
Whereupon the Minister of Public Works asked, "What is a dud?"
Reisner rose from his box and said, "Gentlemen, I regret Queen Hetepheres is not receiving." And added, "Mrs. Reisner will serve refreshments at the camp."'

The mystery of the canopic chest – and new answers

Following this disappointment, the excavators turned their attention to the queen's canopic chest, which they had located hidden within a sealed niche. This, paradoxically, was *not* empty, but turned out to contain four packets of viscera, three still floating in a solution of natron, the salt used in the embalming process. How to account for this peculiar state of affairs?

Desperate to tie all the facts together, Reisner came up with an ingenious explanation. He concluded that Hetepheres' original tomb, perhaps at Dahshur, had been violated shortly after the burial had been made, and that her body had been carried off and destroyed. This appalling fact, Reisner believed, if not the robbery itself, had been concealed from Khufu, and what remained of

(above) Hetepheres' gilded bracelet box, reconstructed in new wood. The bracelets themselves are of silver inlaid with carnelian, lapis lazuli and turquoise.

(left) Gold vessel from the queen's funerary treasure, beaten from a single sheet of metal and beautifully burnished. It was found in a small box containing razors and two companion pieces, also in gold.

his mother's burial, minus the corpse, was transferred to Giza.

Reisner's colourful hypothesis has rightly been questioned, most compellingly by Mark Lehner in 1985. Lehner has suggested an alternative and much simpler explanation – that Reisner's tomb was not the secondary but the original burial place of the queen-mother, intended to align with a projected satellite pyramid, GI-x, which was never built; and that the queen's body was removed at a later stage, at Khufu's instigation, for reburial within a new satellite pyramid, GI-a or GI-b – where it was presumably destroyed in antiquity. For whatever reason, the queen's original burial equipment – including her viscera – had been abandoned within G7000x. And here it would lie, forgotten and undisturbed, for a further five thousand years.

HETEPHERES: the principal finds

alabaster sarcophagus (JE 51899)

alabaster canopic chest (JE 52452)

wooden bed-canopy, gold covered (JE 57711)

wooden curtain box, gold covered and inlaid (JE 72030)

wooden bed, gold covered and inlaid (JE 53261)

wooden armchairs (2), gold covered, one inlaid (JE 53263, Temp. reg. 22.2.60, various)

wooden carrying-chair, gold covered and inlaid (JE 52372)

wooden chests (approx. 8), containing linen, pottery, stone vessels, mud seals, flints, and a variety of miscellaneous debris

wooden box, gold covered and inlaid (Temp. reg. 22.2.60, various), containing:

    beadwork (garment?)
    wooden box with calcite ointment jars, etc. (JE 52373)
    copper ewer and basin
    stone (2) and pottery (2) vessels
    wooden headrest, gold and silver covered (JE 53262)
    wooden box, gold covered, with silver bracelets
      (JE 53265-81; MFA 47.1699)
    gold and silver dishes, gold and copper razors and other cosmetic
      objects; ivory bracelets

tubular leather case with sticks (2), gold and silver covered (JE 89619)

stone and pottery vessels (various)

basket

copper tools (various)

•Most objects in Cairo (JE; Temp. reg.); minor pieces (and facsimiles of major items) in Museum of Fine Arts, Boston (MFA)

AN AMARNA KING AND HIS QUEEN: THE KARNAK COLOSSI

1926 Scarabs from Deir el-Bahri

Discovery/excavation
1925
by
Henri Chevrier

Site
Thebes (Karnak)

Period
New Kingdom, 18th Dynasty,
reign of Amenophis IV-
Akhenaten, 1353–1335 BC

The cutting of a drainage ditch to the east of the enclosure wall of the Great Temple of Amun at Karnak in 1925, under the supervision of the French Inspector Henri Chevrier, was to have unexpected results. The work turned up two statues from a fallen colonnade of sandstone images in extreme Amarna style, confirming the existence, within Amun's domain, of a temple complex erected by Amenophis IV-Akhenaten to the god Aten during the early years of his reign. Although a fragment from this same colonnade had previously been brought to light by Georges Legrain in the Karnak Cachette (•p. 118), in 1904 (CG 42089), its significance had passed unrecognized.

Excavations carried out by Chevrier between 1925 and 1932 would uncover a startling total of 25 of these Amarna colossi (of an original 28, to judge from the number of surviving bases), and a part of the foundation of the building to which they had originally belonged – the *Gem-pa-aten* temple, a structure much better known now from the *talatat* and from excavations carried out since by American Egyptologist Donald B. Redford (•p. 209).

Amenophis IV-Akhenaten (left) and his consort, Nefertiti (right), as represented in two of the series of colossal images discovered by Henri Chevrier at Karnak. Designed to be viewed from below, the images appear peculiarly elongated when seen face on.

The Karnak colossi are extraordinary, powerful creations, originally seen as representations of the king alone – the 'neutered' form of at least one of the images inspiring an extensive literature on the heretic's supposedly flawed sexuality. Despite such theories – 'which, on the whole contribute less to scholarship than they reveal of their authors' particular bent' – British Egyptologist J. R. Harris is surely correct in seeing the statues as images both of Amenophis IV and of his influential consort, Nefertiti, shown in their respective guises as the deities Shu and Tefenet. Nefertiti's pivotal role during Akhenaten's reign, and her functioning as co-regent and possible successor to the king, are aspects of the Amarna 'revolution' only now being appreciated by a wider Egyptological audience.

(left) Work in progress: several fragmentary colossi litter the ground at the site of Chevrier's spectacular find, East Karnak.

1926
Scarabs from Deir el-Bahri

The Metropolitan Museum of Art's excavations at Deir el-Bahri, in the vicinity of the mortuary temples of Nebhepetre Mentuhotep of the 11th Dynasty and Hatshepsut of the 18th, are justly celebrated. The Museum's work was so productive that it is the subject of a book in its own right: Herbert Winlock's *Excavations at Deir el Bahri, 1911–1931*. Highlights of these excavations include the remains of several major sculptures of Hatshepsut herself, deliberately smashed in antiquity; the discovery of the regal though unused second tomb (TT353) of the queen's favourite, Senenmut, architect of her temple; and numerous intact burials belonging to greater and lesser individuals of earlier and later date.

A more modest class of find, though not lacking in either aesthetic appeal or historical significance, is the amuletic scarab beetle, whose regenerative connotations provide a particularly appropriate metaphor for the rebirth of the deceased in the next world. Amulets of this creature are occasionally encountered in foundation deposits placed at the beginning, and at various stages, of work on a building project.

Many foundation deposits are known from ancient Egypt – including several (positioned in a rather haphazard manner, reflecting the developing nature of the plan) at Hatshepsut's mortuary temple at Deir el-Bahri (*below*).

The three deposits uncovered during 1926 differed from those already known both in the number and precision of the scarab amulets they contained. In deposit G there were some 192; in H, 11; and in I, 96 – making 299 in total, all of green-glazed steatite and of the highest quality. The relative abundance of Hatshepsut scarabs in the three hoards clearly reflects the queen's responsibility for the construction of the mortuary temple, with scarabs of her nephew and ward Tuthmosis III (some of which carry the early form of his name Menkheperenre) conveniently dating its founding to the early part of that king's reign.

FOUNDATION DEPOSITS G, H, I	
QUANTITY	DESCRIPTION
2	Tuthmosis I
31	Tuthmosis III
153	Hatshepsut
18	Nefrure
18	Amun
77	motto/design

THE LIBRARY OF KENHERKHEPSHEF, SCRIBE AND SCHOLAR

Discovery/excavation
1928
by
Bernard Bruyère

Site
Thebes (Deir el-Medina, in the vicinity of tomb 1165)

Period
New Kingdom, 19th Dynasty, before and after the reign of Merenptah, 1224–1214 BC

4000 BC
3000 BC
2000 BC
1000 BC
0
AD 700

Despite the discovery by locals of the intact family tomb of the workman Sennudjem in 1886 (•p. 69), the potential of Deir el-Medina as a rare microcosm of ancient Egyptian life and death during a relatively restricted period (18th–20th Dynasties) went unrealized for some years. The excavations of Ernesto Schiaparelli (•p. 121) of the Egyptian Museum in Turin (who dug sporadically between 1905 and 1909 in the northern part of the village and in the necropolis – bringing to light the tomb of the architect Kha: •p. 126), the restoration work of Émile Baraize in the Ptolemaic temple, and the village and tomb excavations carried out close-by by the German scholar Georg Möller in 1913 would set the scene; but it was only with the intensive series of excavations carried out since 1917 by the Institut français d'archéologie orientale (IFAO) in Cairo that the nature and rich potential of the site and its many, many inscriptions came to be fully appreciated.

The director of the French work during much of this long campaign was Bernard Bruyère (1922–40 and 1945–51). Under his supervision all areas of the site were explored, most notably the village itself and, on its outskirts, the so-called 'Grand puits', or Great Pit – in fact, a huge, walk-down well – which contained more than 5,000 limestone ostraca. The study of these texts has shed important and indeed unique light on the lives of the individual villagers and the history of the settlement – births, deaths, marriages, divorces, disputes, strikes, religion, law and order. Bruyère also uncovered a number of well-provisioned burials, including the essentially intact tombs of the lady Madja and the workman Sennufer. Digging has now for the most part ceased, but the processing, study and publication of the IFAO's findings continues to this day.

One of the most intriguing finds of the Deir el-Medina seasons was the library of Kenherkhepshef. The tale of the archive's discovery is of the usual, convoluted variety. Alan Gardiner, who first studied the exceptional group of literary, magico-medical and other hieratic papyri in the library of the late Sir Alfred Chester Beatty, believed that they, like the Ramesseum papyri (•p. 96), must, because of their content, have formed the professional outfit of a magician and medical practitioner. This view we now know to have been mistaken. As with the Harris Papyrus acquired 75 years before (•p. 45), it is clear that the Chester Beatty texts (now divided essentially between London and Dublin) were 'strays' from a much larger and less specialized documentary cache, excavated by the French in 1928 between two tomb chapels close to shaft no. 1165 at Deir el-Medina. The Chester Beatty and IFAO texts are manifestly parts of a single whole; and what transpires is that the owner was no magico-medical wise man but a worker involved in the quarrying and decoration of Pharaoh's tomb – the scribe Kenherkhepshef.

My heart flutters hastily,
When I think of my love of you;
It lets me not act sensibly,
It leaps from its place.
It lets me not put on a dress,
Nor wrap my scarf around me;
I put no paint upon my eyes,
Nor am I anointed.
'Don't wait, go there', says [my
heart] to me,
As often as I think of him;
My heart, don't act so stupidly,
Why do you play the fool?
Sit still, the brother comes to you,
And many eyes as well.
Let not the people say of me:
'A woman fallen through love!'
Be steady when you think of him,
My heart, do not flutter.
WOMAN IN LOVE: AN EXTRACT
FROM PAPYRUS CHESTER BEATTY I

(below) The well-preserved settlement of Deir el-Medina, occupied by workers employed in the quarrying and decoration of the New Kingdom royal tombs in the Valley of the Kings and the Valley of the Queens. This was Kenherkhepshef's home, and the findspot of his extraordinary library.

THE LIBRARY OF KENHERKHEPSHEF

DESIGNATION	DESCRIPTION
P. Chester Beatty I	Contendings of Horus and Seth; love songs; hymns; hymn in praise of Ramesses V; cattle-sale document
P. Chester Beatty II	Story of the Blinding and Subsequent Vindication of Truth
P. Chester Beatty III	dream book; Battle of Kadesh; letter to the vizir Panehsy
P. Chester Beatty IV	monotheistic hymns; student's miscellany
P. Chester Beatty V	Hymn to the Nile; short texts in letter form; magical texts
P. Chester Beatty VI	medical prescriptions; magical text
P. Chester Beatty VII	magical spells against scorpions; spells against fever etc.
P. Chester Beatty VIII	magico-religious texts
P. Chester Beatty IX	Ritual of Amenophis I; portion of a magical text; book of invocations; book of protection
P. Chester Beatty X	extracts from a book of aphrodisiacs
P. Chester Beatty XI	Story of Isis and Re; magical texts; accounts; hymn to Amun; spells for safety upon the river etc.
P. Chester Beatty XII	extracts from a magical text with mythological allusions
P. Chester Beatty XIII	magical text
P. Chester Beatty XIV	religious text
P. Chester Beatty XV	magico-medical text
P. Chester Beatty XVI	magical text; accounts
P. Chester Beatty XVII	extracts from the satirical letter of Hori
P. Chester Beatty XVIII	extracts from a miscellany; medical text
P. Chester Beatty XIX	extract from the Satire on the Trades
P. Deir el-Medina I	Teaching of Ani; magical texts
P. Deir el-Medina II	portion of P. Naunakht II–III
P. Deir el-Medina III–XVI	letters
P. Deir el-Medina XVII	list of bronze utensils
P. Naunakhte I?, II–III, IV?	will documents
P. Geneva 15274?	incantation against scorpion stings; memoranda

Kenherkhepshef is well known to Egyptologists from many documents, official and ephemeral, which have survived from Deir el-Medina. He first appears in Year 33 of Ramesses II, becomes scribe of the tomb in Year 40 and retains that office until the end of the reign of Sethos II – a period of over 40 years. A less than popular official, there are signs that he not only became lax in the execution of his office but corrupt and receptive to bribes. His heart was not in his work, it seems, but in his books – and, in later years, increasingly with his new, 12-year-old wife.

The breadth and depth of interests reflected in Kenherkhepshef's library is surprising, but perhaps not unrepresentative of the reading matter of an educated Egyptian of pharaonic times. The scholar's genes were sadly not passed on. Although after his death his books seem initially to have been kept safe by the family, it is clear that the precious rolls gradually fell into use as convenient jotting-pads or as a ready source of scrap paper.

Worse was to come. In a curious pendant to the discovery of the Kenherkhepshef library, one of the series of Late Ramessid Letters (•p. 24), written at the very end of the New Kingdom by the scribe Djehutymose to his son, the scribe of the tomb Butehamun (British Museum EA 10326), contains the following aside:

'Now as for the documents onto which the sky rained in the house of the scribe Horsheri, my (grandfather), you brought them out, and we found that (they) had not become erased. I said to you: "I will unbind them again". You brought them down below, and we deposited (them) in the tomb of Amennakht, my (great-grand) father.'

(below) A page from one of the texts in Kenherkhepshef's collection, Papyrus Chester Beatty III: extracts from the 'dream book', including the memorable 'If a man sees himself ... shaving his lower parts, BAD; it means mourning...'.

Not only does the findspot of the Kenherkhepshef papyri correspond closely with Djehutymose's description of the place in which he stored the soaked texts, but at least one of the Chester Beatty texts – P. Chester Beatty I – displays clear evidence of water damage. The library had, it seems, become a liability, not so much 'deposited' in the necropolis for safekeeping as perhaps unceremoniously dumped by the scholar's philistine heirs.

1930 A Crock of Gold from el-Amarna
1929–30 Mersuankh and his Statues

Discovery/excavation
1929
by
Herbert E. Winlock

Site
Thebes (Deir el-Bahri
tomb DB358)

Period
New Kingdom, 18th Dynasty
and later, c. 1550–945 BC

'By the middle of January [1929] we had finished our search for statue fragments [of queen Hatshepsut] in the [Deir el-Bahri] quarry and our workmen were gradually clearing the deep deposits of rubbish lying on the hillside of Hat-shepsut's temple ... On it we had noticed two chip heaps, weathered during centuries and almost hidden by drifted sand and by fallen rock ... [It] was ... possible that what we had here were heaps of chip from the tunneling of some undiscovered tomb or tombs in the shale strata, and it was on this that we pinned our hopes ...

On February 23rd – six weeks after we had started the work on the hill – the Reis Gilani reported that the men had found a rough hole in the rock under their feet ...'

HERBERT E. WINLOCK

(below left) Outer anthropoid coffin of Queen Meryetamun, a masterpiece of the wood-carver's art which, before its 'restoration' by Pinudjem I's officials, had been richly decorated with gold and embellished with colourful inlays of glass.

The tomb uncovered by Winlock's men below the temple of Hatshepsut at Deir el-Bahri at the start of 1929 was found to contain two separate burials: an intrusive interment at the entrance belonging to the lady Nany, a 'king's daughter' of the 21st Dynasty; and, in the innermost recesses of the sepulchre, the burial of an early 18th-Dynasty queen by the name of Meryetamun. 'The silence, the dark, and the realization of the ages that [this last] coffin had laid there ... all combined in creating an eerie effect; and whatever one may expect, that does not happen so very often in digging'.

While the first of these burials proved, on closer scrutiny, to be of only moderate interest – one of many of this date and type recovered at Thebes over the years – the latter was quite unique, both artistically and archaeologically. Meryetamun proved to have been buried within two coffins, the outer of which was not only of the highest quality but of immense scale – towering over 3 m (10 ft) when stood on its feet, reminiscent of the gigantic coffins of the queens Ahhotep and Ahmose-Nofretiri from the Deir el-Bahri royal cache (•p. 64). Meryetamun's inner coffin was of much smaller proportions, and within lay her neatly wrapped mummy – 'festooned with garlands still fresh enough to

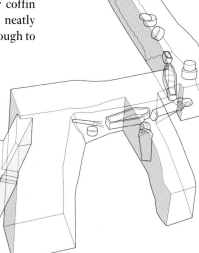

(left) Hieratic docket on Meryetamun's mummy, recording an official inspection in Year 19 of Pinudjem I – at which time the burial was 'restored'.

1930
A Crock of Gold
from el-Amarna

'The vase was lying less than a foot below the surface. A chip had been made in the lid ... by the tethering stake of a local worthy. His feelings on hearing what he had missed are recorded, but inconvenient to print.'
HENRI FRANKFORT AND
J. D. S. PENDLEBURY

The excavations carried out by the Egypt Exploration Society at el-Amarna between 1921 and 1936 carried on from where Petrie and the Deutsche Orient-Gesellschaft (•pp. 83, 134) had left off, and uncovered much evidence for the history both of the site and of this important period in Egyptian history. The EES excavations were resumed under the direction of Barry Kemp in 1977, and the digging continues, in closer detail than ever before.

The work carried out at el-Amarna in the 1920s and 1930s was very relaxed in feel. It nevertheless yielded its fair share of exciting finds, and, on one occasion, the glint of gold. In 1930 the team of John Pendlebury discovered a hoard of precious metal buried beneath the floor of a house (T 36.63) in the North Suburb of the city, contained

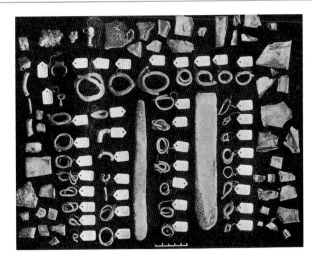

in a large globular pot, 24 cm (9½ in) high, with a smaller bowl inverted over the top to form a lid. 'With a certain amount of unwillingness to perform what they knew by experience to be a fruitless and troublesome task, the workmen prized off the lid and shook the earth inside to loosen it. A bar of gold dropped out. Then came twenty-two bars of gold, much silver, and a figurine of a Hittite god in silver with a gold cap' – followed by an audible silence.

Much about the find remains obscure. Most likely, the hoard was a metalworker's collection of scrap (though the excavators thought it was 'part of a thief's loot'), the ends of several bars showing evidence of having been cut, presumably as and when a specific quantity of metal was required. The material was divided in Cairo, and most of those pieces apportioned to the EES passed on to the Bank of England for melting down; they 'gave us £200 for it, which was credited to the funds for digging at Amarna the following season'. Such drastic methods of fund-raising, thankfully, are very much a thing of the past.

THE CROCK OF GOLD FROM EL-AMARNA HOUSE T 36.63

DESCRIPTION	QUANTITY
Hittite silver amulet	1
rough-cast gold bars	23
rough-cast silver bars	2
silver 'rings'	27
fluted silver 'rings'	10
crescent-shaped silver earring	1
drop-shaped silver earring	1
silver vessel fragments	several
silver sheet fragments	several

(opposite page) Cut-away drawing of the tomb, with Meryetamun's coffin as found in the innermost chamber beyond the 'well'. The burial of the 21st-Dynasty princess Nany, introduced later, was subsequently displaced from its outer coffin.

show the colours of their flowers'. Everything about this burial was neat, ordered and seemingly untouched. Yet there was something not quite right: the funerary furniture was sparse and poor – consisting of little more than a few sealed baskets of debris; while beneath the well-preserved, painted surfaces of the queen's coffins it was evident that the bulk of the glass inlays had been prised out; further inspection revealed that the paint in fact replaced original surfaces of gold foil and leaf.

The puzzle was resolved by a fine ink inscription written in hieratic across the front of Meryetamun's shroud: 'Year 19, 3rd month of *akhet*-season, day 28. On this day the inspection of the king's wife Meryetamun': the queen's burial had been set in order in antiquity. For Winlock, the condition of Meryetamun's burial reflected a pious act of restoration on the part of priests who had stumbled upon her robbed tomb, perhaps by chance, but we now know better. For it is apparent that the burial of Meryetamun had been divested of all its valuables – impressions of the queen's precious jewelry were found on the mummified body – not before but *during* this inspection. As further dockets were to reveal, the 'Year 19' of the 'restorers'' text was of the high priest of Amun and would-be 'king' Pinudjem I, during whose 'reign' such defilement was the official order of the day – with the accruing riches of the Theban dead doubtless helping to sustain both his dubious regime and his kingly aspirations.

1929–30
Mersuankh and his Statues

The Giza necropolis has, over the years, attracted the attention of many Egyptologists, most famously the American George A. Reisner (•p. 132), the Austrian Hermann Junker, the Egyptian Abdel-Moneim Abu Bakr, and, most recently, the well-known excavator Zahi Hawass (•p. 229). The excavations of Selim Hassan, a Junker student, were similarly productive. Extending over a period of ten years between 1929 and 1939, they resulted in the uncovering of a great number of tombs prepared for Old Kingdom officials of both higher and lower rank. Not a few of Hassan's discoveries were of well-preserved statues of the tomb owners and their servants; Junker's best known find was perhaps the group image of the dwarf Seneb and his family (Cairo JE 51280).

Like his teacher, Hassan published what he found, in 10 volumes which appeared between 1929 and 1960. One find will serve to characterize the results – the small tomb belonging to the 'overseer of young men of the Palace', Mersuankh, a dependant of the great, late-5th Dynasty official, Rawer. Mersuankh's tomb, was distinguished by the range of

naive painted limestone sculptural types – single, double and pair and family statues, as well as servants – in an excellent state of preservation, recovered still in place in the structure's two *serdabs* and discarded in the tomb's robbed burial shafts (see table).

THE STATUES OF MERSUANKH

FINDSPOT	MATERIAL	TYPE
serdab 1	limestone	triple statuette of Mersuankh
serdab 1	limestone	female brewer statuette
serdab 2	limestone	double statuette of Mersuankh
serdab 2	limestone	double statuette of Mersuankh and his wife
serdab 2	limestone	triple statuette of Mersuankh and his two daughters
shaft 145	limestone	statuette of a man, probably Mersuankh
shaft 151	limestone	three fragments of a double statuette of Mersuankh and Hathorwer
unknown	pink granite	fragmentary statuette of Mersuankh

EMERY AT BALLANA AND QUSTUL: THE TOMBS OF THE X-GROUP

1931 Tutankhamun's Colossi • 1932 The Statues of Heqaib

Discovery/excavation
1931-34
by
Walter Bryan Emery

Sites
Ballana & Qustul

Period
X-group, 3rd–6th centuries AD

'In 1931 members of the Archaeological Survey of Nubia, directed by Mr. W. B. Emery, decided to examine in detail the series of large mounds, which had been generally regarded as natural, which lay on both sides of the Nile near the villages of Ballâna and Qustul in Nubia. These proved to be tumuli which covered tombs of the Byzantine Period, and resembled those previously excavated at Gammai, at Firka, at Wawi and on the island of Sai, all south of Wadi Halfa, in the Sudan.'
REX ENGELBACH

When, in 1929, it was decided to raise the level of the first Aswan dam for a second time (the structure had been completed in 1904, and the first raising of its height had taken place a decade later), a three-season survey of the threatened area, similar to ones undertaken by Weigall in 1905 and Reisner in 1907–09, was initiated by the Egyptian government. Director of the 150-strong team of Egyptian workmen was the young Walter Bryan Emery, assisted by L. P. Kirwan; the Italian archaeologist Ugo Monneret de Villard undertook a separate survey of the Christian sites which were threatened by the flooding.

One of the first places at which Emery and his diggers stopped off was a small village, Ballana, distinguished from a hundred similar settlements by a series of mounds varying in height between 2 and 12 m (6½ and 40 ft). As with a further set of tumuli across the river, at Qustul, these mounds proved, on excavation, to cover the burials of the kings and nobility of the imaginatively named 'X-group' peoples of the 3rd–6th centuries AD.

(far left) Unusual bronze face lamp from Tomb 3 at Qustul, with silver-set garnet eyes. The hole for filling the lamp with oil is in the forehead, that for the burning wick below the chin.

1931 Tutankhamun's Colossi

By the time the Chicago Oriental Institute team had encountered two superb statues of painted quartzite (Cairo JE 59869+60134, *right*; Chicago OI 14088) in 1931, their subject – Tutankhamun – had been raised to the status of Egypt's most famous son (•p. 160). The site at which the statues were found – the mortuary temple prepared for Ay and taken over by his successor, Horemheb – and the presence of this latter's palimpsest cartouche on the belt, remind us of why the boy-king had been lost to the world for so long: as a son of the hated Akhenaten, the youthful pharaoh was relegated to the status of non-person and his works usurped by others. Had not Carnarvon and Carter uncovered his tomb in 1922, Tutankhamun would languish still as a minor footnote in the pages of Egyptian history.

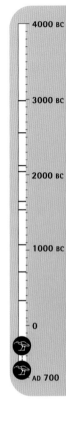

4000 BC

3000 BC

2000 BC

1000 BC

0

AD 700

(above) One of the large tumuli encountered by Emery at Ballana, covering the burial of a local king.

(right) A naive, lion-shaped bronze censer excavated by Emery from tomb 80 at Ballana. Originally suspended on chains, the burning incense escaped through the nostrils and mouth when it was swung

(far right) Bronze lamp with a Christian cross, still mounted on its original pricket base. From tomb 95 at Ballana; c. 3rd century AD.

'... one royal burial [at Ballana] ... by good fortune had remained intact. This chamber had been built on a higher level than the other tombs, and so had escaped the robbers' attention. It was the burial of a queen. The body had been partially destroyed by water, but the silver and jewelled treasures which clothed it – crown, earrings, necklaces, bracelets, rings, anklets, and toe rings – were in good preservation, and formed the largest complete find of jewellery yet made at Ballana ...'
ILLUSTRATED LONDON NEWS

The tombs of the Ballana and Qustul royal dead are closely similar, each being equipped with a long ramp leading to a large pit in which the burial chambers were constructed in mud- or fired-brick. This structure was then covered over with a mound, the size depending on the importance of the owner. There were several burial apartments, closed by a nailed and sealed wooden door and finally blocked off with a mud- brick wall: the burial chamber proper, in which the king or queen was laid out in leather clothing, bedecked with jewels (predominantly of silver); and various storage chambers, in which the grave-goods were placed – food and wine, ivory-embellished caskets, gaming equipment, shields and weapons, silver, bronze and ceramic vessels and other ornaments (some inscribed in Greek or Meroitic), and textiles (including silk).

Although some of the metalware bore clear Christian motifs, these had probably been obtained by trade or in war; long after the old religion had died out in Egypt proper, the X-group people continued to worship Isis, Horus, Bes and other gods of the Egyptian pantheon. The finer points of Egyptian theology had probably now been lost, however, to judge from the obvious enthusiasm for human and animal sacrifice – male and female servants, strangled by means of knotted cords; richly caparisoned horses despatched by blows from an axe; camels; cattle; dogs; donkeys; and even a humble tortoise – all offered to accompany the spirits of the dead rulers into the life beyond.

(left) Stand for an oil lamp in bronze, modelled in the form of Eros holding a vine branch. Dating from around the 2nd century AD, it was discovered by Emery in tomb 114 at Ballana.

(below) Crown of silver set with carnelians and surmounted by three horned solar discs with double plumes. It was found in place on the head of a queen in the burial chamber of Ballana tomb 47.

1932
The Statues of Heqaib

During more than half a century, Labib Habachi was one of Egypt's most active scholars, his archaeological career beginning with his appointment as Inspector in the Service des Antiquités at Aswan in 1930. And it was here, two years later, on the island of Elephantine, that an important discovery of pre-Middle Kingdom sculpture was made, associated with a series of shrines dedicated to a 6th-Dynasty governor of the district named Heqaib.

Heqaib is well known from his autobiography inscribed on the façade of his Qubbet el-Hawa tomb, where he records, for posterity, the successes of his life. Foremost among these was his achievement in bringing to an end Nubian incursions into his fief from the south – and it was perhaps on account of his brave deeds

that the man was deified shortly after his death. Heqaib's cult attracted particular attention under the 12th and 13th Dynasties.

With the resumption of excavation on the site in 1946, the total number of statues found rose to almost 40, both complete and fragmentary, together with some 50 altars, small shrines, stelae and offering tables – materials of great intrinsic value and importance which shed light both on the local history of the Aswan district and the genealogy of its rulers at this time.

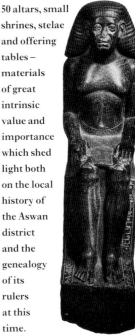

(right) Love charm in barbaric Greek, written on a sheet of gold foil – from tomb 2 at Ballana.

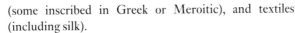

GREAT TOMBS OF EARLY EGYPT: EMERY AT SAQQARA

1930s The Jewels of the High Priest Herihor

Discovery/excavation
1935–39
by
Walter Bryan Emery

Site
Saqqara

Period
Early Dynastic Period, 1st
Dynasty, 2920–2770 BC

4000 BC
3000 BC
2000 BC
1000 BC
0
AD 700

WALTER BRYAN EMERY
(1903–1971)

- Born Liverpool, 2 July 1903
- Educated St Francis Xavier's College, Liverpool. Subsequently trains as a marine engineer before going on to study Egyptology at Liverpool University under Percy Newberry and Thomas Eric Peet, 1921–23; MA Liverpool 1939
- Assists on the Egypt Exploration Society's excavations at el-Amarna, 1923–24; Director, University of Liverpool excavations at Luxor and Armant, financed by Robert Mond, 1924–28, at the latter site stumbling upon the Bucheum; Director, Archaeological Survey of Nubia, 1929–35, where he discovers and excavates the burial mounds at Ballana and Qustul (•p. 179); Director of Excavation at North Saqqara, 1935–39
- Following a period of war-work and diplomatic service, appointed Edwards Professor of Egyptology, University College London, 1951–70; Field-Director for the Egypt Exploration Society in Nubia 1957–63, resuming work at Saqqara in 1964 (•p. 206)
- Dies Cairo, 11 March 1971

Walter Bryan Emery had won his archaeological spurs in 1925/26 with the discovery of the Bucheum at Armant, south of modern Luxor – the Late Period burial place of the sacred Buchis bulls. In 1929 he was appointed as Director of the Archaeological Survey of Nubia (•p. 179), and by 1935 was Antiquities Service inspector at Saqqara. This would mark the start of a lifetime's fruitful involvement with that rich and extensive site, falling into two overlapping phases: his discovery and excavation of the Early Dynastic necropolis; and his work in the catacombs of the sacred animal cemetery (•p. 206).

The exploration of the Early Dynastic necropolis represented a continuation of work begun in 1930 by Emery's predecessor, Cecil M. Firth, brought to an early close by Firth's death the following year. Taking up where Firth left off, Emery began to clear the tomb now known as mastaba 3035 and found, to his surprise, that the niched or 'palace-façade' superstructure was not solid but compartmentalized – similar to the tomb of Queen Neithhotep discovered by de Morgan at Naqada in 1897 (•p. 100) and closer still (in that the burial chamber proper was placed below ground) to another early tomb,

mastaba 'Giza V', discovered some years before by Flinders Petrie. As the work of excavating mastaba 3035 progressed, Emery uncovered chamber after chamber, until an astonishing 45 interior rooms had been laid bare. What is even more astounding is that *not one* of these chambers had previously been disturbed – and within them had been stored an immense funerary assemblage of metal, stone and pottery vessels, and other items, including the oldest surviving papyrus roll, perfectly made but sadly uninscribed. The owner, it appeared, was the seal-bearer Hemaka, who had lived under King Den of the 1st Dynasty.

The following seasons, 1936–39, would prove equally productive. Another mastaba tomb, 3471, dating from the reign of an earlier 1st-Dynasty king, Djer, yielded a haul particularly rich in copperware; while excavation of the superstructure of tomb 3504, though robbed, and on more than one occasion, would produce some 1,500 stone and 2,500 pottery vessels of excellent quality and design.

It immediately struck Emery how much more impressive were the superstructures of these mastabas – and in many ways how much richer their content – in comparison with the tombs excavated by Amélineau and later by Petrie at Umm el-Qaab, Abydos (•p. 109); the presence of subsidiary burials (which to Emery suggested human sacrifice) seemed striking also. The idea began to form that Petrie might perhaps have been misled in his analysis of the Abydos tombs – that Abydos was not, after all, the burial place of Egypt's Early Dynastic kings, and that Petrie's 'tombs' were in fact no more than commemorative cenotaphs. The actual place of burial of a united Egypt's first kings, Emery reasoned, would more likely have been at Saqqara, close to the new administrative capital, Memphis. Could it be that the Saqqara tombs he was now digging represented not the mastabas of high officials, as he had first thought, but the tombs of the kings themselves?

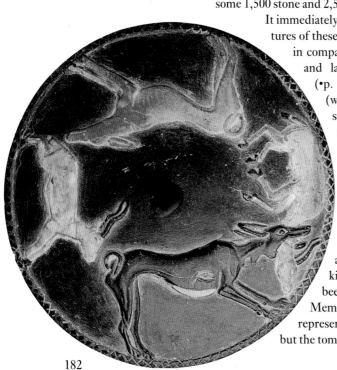

It was an interesting possibility, and one that attracted an increasing number of adherents – until it was pointed out that the Abydos tombs in reality formed but one part of a larger complex, and thus that the disparity in size between them and the supposedly more impressive Saqqara monuments was more apparent than real. Emery's tombs, for all their richness, it now seems clear were prepared not for the kings themselves but for the realm's wealthiest, most pampered and powerful officials and administrators – men upon whose organizational abilities and communication skills (writing) depended the sure and rapid development of the early Egyptian state.

(above) Bulls' heads modelled in clay and fitted with genuine horns, arranged in front of the elaborate brickwork of mastaba 3504.

(opposite above left) Ivory label of King Djer, found in the tomb of Hemaka (mastaba 3035).

(opposite below left) Black steatite 'gaming disc' from the tomb of Hemaka, with a spectacular scene of dogs at hunt inlaid in contrasting cream stone.

(opposite right) Emery's axonometric reconstruction of the impressive mud-brick tomb 3504, which he sought to identify as that of King Wadj of the 1st Dynasty.

(left) Excavations in progress: the stone 'portcullis' of mastaba 3500 (which dates from the reign of the 1st-Dynasty king Qaa) still in position at the east end of the substructure.

(right) The well-preserved palace-façade of mastaba 3506 (west face). Erected during the reign of another 1st-Dynasty king, Den, no evidence was found to suggest the name of the ancient owner.

1930s
The Jewels of the High Priest Herihor

John Romer once suggested that, if it ever came to light, the tomb of Herihor, high priest of Amun and arch-tomb-looter during the closing years of the New Kingdom, might well 'make Tutankhamun look like Woolworths'. If the items currently on loan to the Roemer-Pelizaeus Museum in Hildesheim are anything to go by, Herihor's burial may already have been discovered in the Theban hills, and indeed yielded gold – though not, it seems, on a scale to compete with the boy pharaoh. The jewels consist of three bracelets – two of simple, penannular form, and a third (*below*) with a fragmentary inlay of unshaped turquoise (bearing an image of the ithyphallic god Min) and an inscription recording the owner's name: 'The high priest of Amun-Re, king of the gods, Herihor, [true] of voice'.

Associated with the bracelets is a relief-decorated chalice, of similar date, and not improbably from the same find.

183

THE TOMB OF THE PARENTS OF SENENMUT, HATSHEPSUT'S FAVOURITE

Discovery/excavation
1936
by
Ambrose Lansing
& William C. Hayes

Site
Thebes (Sheikh Abd el-Qurna)

Period
New Kingdom, 18th Dynasty,
reign of Hatshepsut,
1473–1458 BC

As will by now be apparent, the Egyptian Department of the Metropolitan Museum of Art in New York has always demonstrated a discerning eye in its choice of excavation site. The results of the work at Sheikh Abd el-Qurna during the seasons 1930–31 and 1935–36, however, were exceptional even by their high standards. The area chosen to clear was the rubble-filled slope below the entrance to the long-known Qurna tomb of the great steward of Amun, Senenmut (TT71). Though born of humble parents, this official rose to become one of the most powerful men in the land, owing his influence to his position as Queen Hatshepsut's favourite, and, indeed (if we are to believe the interpretation of at least one scurrilous graffito of the time), her physical intimate also.

As the Metropolitan team were to discover, several members of Senenmut's immediate family and perhaps of his retinue also were interred in the vicinity of this tomb before he decided to prepare a more extravagant burial-place for himself – TT353, discovered by Herbert Winlock and the Metropolitan Museum team in 1927 beneath the temple of Hatshepsut at Deir el-Bahri. Neither of these tombs seems to have been employed, however, and the fate of the man's physical remains is a mystery.

For the Museum's 1935 season, work was concentrated on the earlier tomb of Senenmut and on that part of the lower slope immediately to the east of it. Several modest but interesting interments of the period were soon uncovered, including that of the lutanist Hormose and another burial sometimes identified (though on rather slender grounds) as that of Senenmut's sister, Ahhotep. The carefully wrapped body of a small mare was also uncovered, buried in an enormous rectangular coffin of reused wood, together with the first Egyptian saddle ever found. This burial was a find of rare importance, since the horse was a relative newcomer to Egypt – an import from the east introduced by the Hyksos and an immensely valuable animal even in the 18th Dynasty. For the excavators 'it is not much of an assumption to consider this a pet horse, nor much more hazardous to assume that it was Sen-Mut's favorite mount' – though purists will maintain that firm evidence for the riding of horses other than by grooms is difficult to come by at this early date. A second 'pet', again sometimes associated with Senenmut on the basis of its discovery here, was a cynocephalus baboon, found buried in a similar wooden box-coffin to the south. Bandaged with care, the creature was accompanied by a saucer of raisins for its sustenance in the afterlife.

Ramose and Hatnufer

By Christmas it was clear that the 1935/36 season was shaping-up to be a good one – and there were further surprises in store. At the end of the season the burial of a man, Amenhotep, came to light, perhaps a younger brother of Senenmut. But before that, digging higher up the slope of the hill beneath the collapsed artificial terrace in front of Senenmut's tomb, the Metropolitan Museum's workers encountered a further assemblage of objects, hidden in the rubble: a rectangular wooden tambourine, part of a

WILLIAM C. HAYES
(1903-1963)

'… a big-boned handsome man, with an easy and genial manner that was as genuine as the shyness and reserve that lay beneath it.'
DOWS DUNHAM &
HENRY G. FISCHER

• Born Hempstead, Long Island, 21 March 1903
• Educated Princeton, MA 1926, going on to study medieval and Byzantine art before joining the Metropolitan Museum of Art's Egyptian Expedition to Deir el-Bahri, 1927-36; Assistant Curator of Egyptian Art, from 1936; Curator 1952-63
• Dies New York, 10 July 1963

(left) The steward Senenmut, favoured official – and possible lover – of Queen Hatshepsut, shown holding his ward Neferure; a statue of black granite pulled out from the Karnak Cachette in 1904 (•p. 118).

(right) Low wooden chair from the Theban burial of Ramose and Hatnufer, Senenmut's father and mother – a symbol of the elevated social status they enjoyed, at least in death, thanks to their energetic son.

headrest and the sections of a dismantled wooden chair. The presence of the chair, a symbol of rank and wealth, seemed to indicate that here was a find of above-average interest. And beneath the deposit, as it was gradually freed from its rubble packing, there came into view the plastered blocking of an intact tomb. Everyone held his breath:

> 'The removal of the blocking ... laid bare a tiny, rectangular doorway flanked by rough jambs of cut limestone, and, behind it, one small, rock-cut chamber, 1.3 meters in height, 2.5 meters deep, and 2.9 meters wide. ... [Within,] practically no free space remained.'

As Ambrose Lansing and William C. Hayes record, 'the eye was immediately confronted by an uninscribed, white Canopic chest, shrine-shaped and mounted on sledge runners ... and, beside and behind it, a mass of coffins, boxes, baskets and jars'.

The inevitable question was posed: who did this tomb belong to? The answer was close to hand: 'by raising one corner of the pall over the foot end of the black coffin, ... we were able to read ... the name ... of the "House-mistress Hat-nufer" ... [and] the name "Ra'-mose"'. Lansing and Hayes had found the undisturbed tomb of the parents and other members of Senenmut's immediate family, buried in style by their *arriviste* son close to his own intended place of interment. The condition of this new tomb's contents proved excellent, unaffected either by damp or by the otherwise ubiquitous white ant (though the burial equipment had been nibbled at by mice).

Five days after the initial discovery, the tomb had been fully and carefully cleared. As soon became apparent, most if not all of the funerary equipment was to be

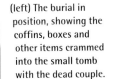

(left) The burial in position, showing the coffins, boxes and other items crammed into the small tomb with the dead couple.

(below) The burial chamber of Ramose and Hatnufer as first encountered by the archaeologists– 'a mass of coffins, boxes, baskets and jars'.

ascribed to Hatnufer (known to her family and friends as 'Tjutju'), the wilful mother of Senenmut on whom, we may guess, she doted. The father, Ramose, had died some years before his wife and before his son's elevation, and was originally accorded a much more modest burial. He and the other poorly embalmed individuals in the tomb had evidently been transferred from this earlier place of interment to share with Hatnufer, early in Hatshepsut's rule, the benefits of their newly elevated son's influence and success.

185

THE TOD TREASURE: TRIBUTE FROM EAST AND WEST

1937 The Unas Causeway: A Gallery of Egyptian Art

Discovery/excavation
1936
by
Fernand Bisson de la Roque

Site
el-Tod (Temple of Montu)

Period
probably Middle Kingdom,
12th Dynasty, reign of
Ammenemes II, 1929–1892 BC

The site of el-Tod (ancient Djerty), on the east bank of the Nile opposite Armant (Hermonthis), was for many centuries one of the principal sanctuaries of the falcon-headed god Montu. Work here was first undertaken in 1933, by a French team under the direction of Fernand Bisson de la Roque; and three years later, digging beneath the 5th-century AD mud-brick church, the excavators came upon what they believed to be a temple of Sesostris I. Here, in the stone foundations, had been concealed the 'Tod treasure'.

Bisson de la Roque recalled the date and time of the discovery precisely: 8 February, 1936, at 4 o'clock in the afternoon. A cache of Saite (26th-Dynasty) bronze figures of Osiris had just been brought to light, a common and unremarkable find; and then, deeper in the same foundation sand underlying the temple, an intriguing clunk signalled the first of four cast copper chests hit by the workmen's tools. Digging stopped for the archaeologists to investigate. These coffers, to judge from the large copper nails sprinkled around, had themselves originally been contained in caskets of wood, which had rotted away to nothing during the course of countless Nile inundations.

The four caskets were cleaned and found to be of two sizes: 45.5 cm (18 in) and 30 cm (12 in) in length. As the working day was drawing to a close, they were removed to the dig house, the men remarking excitedly upon their weight. One was opened that same evening, the remaining three over the course of the next few days, by running a chisel down the corroded grooves in which the lids ran and then banging off the ancient sealing rivet. As the lids were gradually eased back, the contents came into view.

The two larger coffers were packed with lapis lazuli in both raw and worked states, the two smaller with ingots and other items of gold (6.98 kg (15 lb) in total) and intact and crushed silver vessels, silver ingots and other items (these weighing some 8.87 kg (19.5 lb) in total). Interestingly, the best pieces – those in a worked state or those which were intact – had in antiquity been placed carefully on the top, so that they would be seen first when the coffers were opened.

Careful cleaning of the boxes themselves revealed on each of the lids and front end-panels an extended cartouche containing the names and titles of Ammenemes II of the 12th Dynasty – identifying, so the archaeologists assumed, the king by whom the treasure had been deposited, perhaps in his

(below) Caskets, vessels, ingots and other items, now in the Louvre and originally forming part of the treasure found at el-Tod in 1936 by Fernand Bisson de la Roque.

1937
The Unas Causeway:
A Gallery
of Egyptian Art

The discovery of the Unas causeway, linking the mortuary temple of the king's pyramid with his valley temple, was an event of some importance in Egyptian architectural studies. The survival rate of such riverside pyramid elements has generally been poor, representing as they did to later generations eminently convenient quarries for the supply of prepared fine stone. From what survived of the 5th-Dynasty pyramid causeways at Abusir and of the 6th-Dynasty causeway of Pepy II at Saqqara, the plan of such structures was already apparent; it was clear also that they could be embellished with fine scenes in delicate, raised relief, but little of this decoration had survived to draw much in the way of conclusions as to nature and content. From a study of the far more substantial remains now brought to light by Selim Hassan at Unas, it was obvious that 'some of these scenes [were] of great interest and artistic merit'.

The interior surfaces of the Unas causeway – a covered passageway 690 m (2,264 ft) long, 2.6 m (8½ ft) wide and 3.15 m (10 ft) high –

were originally decorated for their entire length with scenes illuminated by natural light from a narrow opening which ran down the centre of the roof. Many of the blocks had gone, but much remained. Progressing from the land of the living in the east to the realms of the dead

in the west, the subject matter of the reliefs can be seen gradually to have developed from such mundane matters as the transportation from Aswan of columns and other architectural elements, through scenes depicting hunting (including giraffe),

agriculture, warfare and the marketplace to vignettes from the *heb-sed* or ritual of royal rejuvenation.

'*... one of the most curious, and at the same time, absolutely unique representations, is that of some wretched, famine-stricken men and women. The curious scene, which was found in a trial sondage over the lower ... part of the causeway, is puzzling. The persons represented seem to be foreigners, but nothing remains to afford us a clue as to their identity or the cause of their wretched plight. Most of the figures are nude, but a few wear narrow girdles, and they are mostly arranged in groups; they are emaciated in the extreme.*'

As Hassan observed, 'These figures present a stark and fearful realism; they display expressions of mental and physical suffering and utter despair, such as had never before appeared in the art of the Old Kingdom.... The excellence of the work ... makes us regret all the more the loss of the rest of the scene, and the inscriptions which would have told us the story of these unhappy creatures'. What they and similar fragments recently discovered at the causeway of Sahure in fact bring to life are the all too frequent realities of ancient Egyptian existence. To see these images is to experience the horrors of famine described in such monuments as the Sehel rock inscription, which purports to document an earlier tragedy lasting for seven trying years in the time of the 3rd-Dynasty king Djoser.

father Sesostris II's memory. Here before them, evidently, lay a unique deposit of foreign tribute, the cement of ancient diplomatic ties, hailing from as far afield as Afghanistan in the east (the source of the lapis lazuli) and the Mediterranean world to the west (the apparent origin of the silver vessels).

The treasure was in due course generously divided between Cairo and the Louvre in Paris. Because of its early dating and the fact that for several of the pieces contained in the treasure exceptionally close Minoan parallels could be cited, it seemed a godsend to students of Aegean chronology in particular. In a study of the find by Barry Kemp and Robert Merrillees, however, it is suggested that the collection is stylistically later than the Middle Kingdom, and that the cache was found not in a sealed, 12th-Dynasty context but in a substantially later phase of the temple construction employing antiquated containers. However, whether such arguments outweigh the evidence of the inscriptions not only of the caskets but also of their contents, remains to be seen.

(below) Two of the flimsy silver bowls and a handled cup from the Tod treasure. The designs are thought by many scholars to show strong Minoan influence.

(bottom) The temple of Sesostris I at el-Tod, the site where the treasure was found.

THE CASKETS AND THEIR CONTENTS

Contents of the two large bronze coffers (empty weight 37.5 kg)

pieces of lapis lazuli: raw state and workshop scraps (various)

cylinder and button seals: lapis lazuli, some with cuneiform inscriptions (various)

inlays: lapis lazuli (various)

bracelet: gold, silver, lapis lazuli

beads and pendants: lapis lazuli and carnelian (various)

pieces of quartz: amethyst and obsidian (various)

Contents of the two smaller bronze coffers (empty weight 13.9 kg)

rectangular ingots: gold (10), numbered in hieratic, total weight 6.5 kg

rectangular ingot fragment: gold

melted pieces: gold (8)

cup: gold

ear(?) pendants: gold (2)

oval ingots: silver (12), max. weight 134.66 g

chains: silver (25), each consisting of 4–5 rings, max. weight 108 g

bar ingots bent into rings: silver (4), max. weight 268.10 g

handled vessel with lid: silver

cups (with and without handles): silver (153; 143 folded, 10 intact; one with Middle Kingdom hieratic inscription for 'the messenger Nenit'

lion (1-deben weight?): silver

pendants, finger-rings: silver (various) – including a silver pendant of Minoan style with spider motif alien to Egypt

1939–46
ROYAL TOMBS AT TANIS:
TREASURES OF THE THIRD INTERMEDIATE PERIOD

Discovery/excavation
1939–46
by
Pierre Montet; A. Lézine

Site
Tanis ('temple of Anta')

Period
Third Intermediate Period,
21st–22nd Dynasties,
1040–783 BC

'We removed the earth and saw a larger slab, like a lintel stone, in front of two small, flat stones, like the doors of a wardrobe. I took a quick look and tested it with Ibrahim's cane. It sounded empty, like an underground chamber which is not entirely filled ... I write this note and I shall then go down to the site, as it seems to be an important moment ....'
PIERRE MONTET

The discovery in the Delta city of Tanis of a series of rich kingly tombs of the 21st and 22nd Dynasties by the French Egyptologist Pierre Montet ought to have captured the imagination of the world. But it did not: Europe was on the brink of war, and in no mood for the fripperies of Egyptology. Only recently, with an increased interest in the Third Intermediate Period prompting major exhibitions in Paris, Edinburgh and elsewhere, has Montet's brilliant find been accorded the attention it so richly deserves.

Montet was a fortunate excavator. An Egyptologist by training, in 1921 he nevertheless left the Nile Valley to dig until 1924 at Byblos, in the Lebanon. Here he uncovered a temple and a rich, royal necropolis dating from the first half of the 2nd millennium BC. Many of the objects excavated (as well as a good number of pieces inadvertently discarded by the excavators and subsequently recovered by locals) underlined the close contacts which had existed in antiquity between Egypt and her Western Asiatic neighbours; it was this particular avenue of research which Montet wished to pursue. Since Tanis at that time was (mistakenly) equated with Avaris (p. 224), capital of the Asiatic Hyksos invaders and the biblical 'Ramses', it seemed, on his return to Egyptian archaeology, a good place to start.

The burial-complex of Osorkon II (Tomb I)

'"Do you see a cartouche on the walls, can you read a name?"
Stupefied, I could see little.
"Osorkon! It's the tomb of Osorkon", I cried out at last ...'
GEORGES GOYON

PIERRE MONTET
(1885–1966)

- Born Villefranche-sur-Saône, 27 June 1885
- Student of Victor Loret, University of Lyons; Institut français d'archéologie orientale, Cairo, 1910–14
- Excavates at Byblos, Lebanon, 1921–24, discovering the richly provisioned tombs of local rulers contemporary with the Egyptian Middle Kingdom
- 1929–39 excavates at Tanis, pursuing his interest in interconnections in the ancient Near East, finding the royal necropolis of the 21st and 22nd dynasties, and at Abu Rawash (1st-Dynasty necropolis)
- Subsequently Professor of Egyptology, University of Strasbourg
- Dies Paris, 18 June 1966

4000 BC
3000 BC
2000 BC
1000 BC
0
AD 700

(right) Tanis: the excavated walls of the royal burial chambers, originally buried deep underground. The superstructures of the tombs had been wholly destroyed in antiquity.

(above) The component parts of this early Montet find spell out the name of King Ramesses II – disc (*Ra*), child (*mes*) and plant (*su*) – the whole under the protection of the falcon-god Hauron.

189

(left) The first entry into the tomb of Psusennes I, 18 March 1939: Pierre Montet descends into the beyond, while Georges Goyon, his assistant, steadies the ladder.

(right) The mummy of Psusennes I, its gold headpiece still in position, laid out (somewhat incongruously) for examination by Pierre Montet in the French dig-house.

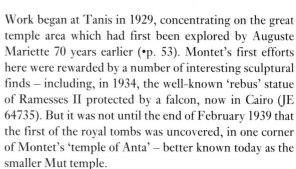

Work began at Tanis in 1929, concentrating on the great temple area which had first been explored by Auguste Mariette 70 years earlier (•p. 53). Montet's first efforts here were rewarded by a number of interesting sculptural finds – including, in 1934, the well-known 'rebus' statue of Ramesses II protected by a falcon, now in Cairo (JE 64735). But it was not until the end of February 1939 that the first of the royal tombs was uncovered, in one corner of Montet's 'temple of Anta' – better known today as the smaller Mut temple.

Montet himself perceived no trace of any Third Intermediate Period superstructures here, but as subsequent work has revealed, the area above the tombs seems to have been remodelled during the reign of Shoshenq III into a giant, mud-brick mastaba. This had subsequently been swept away, and the royal tombs, by this time forgotten, were found directly beneath the remains of several mud-brick Ptolemaic workshops and artists' studios. The presence of the first of the royal sepulchres thus came as a complete surprise.

'Montet, seeing his dreams realized, seemed paralysed by emotion':

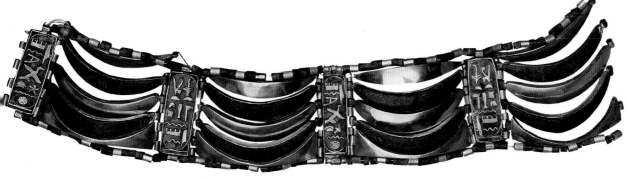

(left) A bracelet of elegant design, one of three arm-ornaments sharing similar decorative features dedicated by Smendes, high priest of Amun at Thebes, for the burial of Psusennes I. The four finger rings are from the same treasure.

(below) The lid of the extraordinary silver coffin prepared for King Heqakheperre Shoshenq (II), the head modelled after the falcon-god Horus, lord of kingship; found in Tomb III, room 5.

'I had the earth and stones blocking the entrance removed, and went down into a square chamber with walls covered with figures and hieroglyphics; this led into another chamber with a large sarcophagus emerging from the earth which filled three quarters of two rooms. The cartouche is that of Osorkon [II]. [G.] Goyon then [J.-L.] Fouge[rousse] came in, and then the overseer. Everyone is overjoyed. I had Hassanein's team come with all the carts so that we could clear this remarkable structure as quickly as possible ….'

The French excavators had in fact entered not via the original entrance shaft, but through the roof. In their method of construction, the tomb's underground apartments proved to be a development towards that of the 'Persian tombs' of Saite times (•p. 111): the burial chambers had been built of limestone and red granite blocks (reused from earlier Ramessid structures nearby) at the bottom of a huge excavated pit which was then filled – with subsequent access achieved by means of subsidiary shafts some 4 m (13 ft) deep.

As anticipated, the tomb had been much disturbed in antiquity, but its regal nature was apparent none the less.

(left & right) Two inlaid gold bracelets, bearing the cartouches of Psusennes I but recovered from the burial of Amenemope.

(opposite left) The gold mask of Psusennes I. While superficially similar to the fabulous headpiece found by Howard Carter on the mummy of Tutankhamun, it compares poorly both in materials and execution.

The limestone walls of its suite of four rooms were decorated with painted reliefs from the Book of the Dead and the Book of the Night. In the first chamber (I-1) was what remained of a reburial of pharaoh Shoshenq III; the second (I-2) contained an empty and uninscribed granite sarcophagus; chamber I-3 boasted a fine old granite sarcophagus which had been usurped by Takelot II, together with a few scraps of burial equipment inscribed for this same king and for Osorkon I. Chamber I-4, however, contained the still rich burials of Osorkon II – owner of the complex – and a princely son of this king by the name of Hornakht.

The burial-complex of Psusennes I (Tomb III)

It was becoming clear to Montet that he was now playing for high stakes: he had stumbled inadvertently (but in hindsight perhaps not unexpectedly) upon a veritable necropolis of Third Intermediate Period kings, and there were probably more burials to be found. A sweep of the area was initiated – and a further burial complex duly discovered, even more extraordinary than the first.

Montet's recorded reaction to the excitement of his entry into this second tomb, on 17 March 1939, again through the roof, may have lacked originality – 'a day of marvels worthy of the Thousand and one nights' – but it was appropriate enough. Dropping gingerly into another small, decorated chamber in what this time would prove to be the tomb of king Psusennes I, Montet found himself surrounded by veritable heaps of burial equip-

A CHRONOLOGY OF MONTET'S (and Lézine's) work at Tanis

DATE	DESCRIPTION
1929	start of excavations at Tanis
27 February 1939	entry into burial chamber of Osorkon II (I-4)
18 March 1939	entry into tomb of Psusennes I and discovery of Shoshenq II (and Siamun and Psusennes II (III-5))
21 March 1939	opening of silver coffin of Shoshenq II (in presence of King Farouk)
6 April 1939	transport of Shoshenq II treasures to Cairo Museum
15 January 1940	examination of burial of Hornakht (in I-4)
15 February 1940	opening of burial chamber of Psusennes I (III-1)
28 February 1940	opening of sarcophagus of Psusennes I (in presence of King Farouk)
1 March 1940	opening of silver coffin of Psusennes I
3-7 March 1940	removal of jewelry of Psusennes I
7 March 1940	transport of Psusennes I treasures to Cairo Museum
16 April 1940	entry into burial chamber of Amenemope (III-2)
17 April 1940	opening of sarcophagus of Amenemope (in presence of King Farouk)
3 May 1940	transport of Amenemope treasures to Cairo Museum
13 February 1946	discovery of burial chamber of Wendjebauendjedet (III-4)

THE TANIS ROYAL TOMBS

TOMB	ROOM	OWNER
I	1	anonymous
	2	empty
	3	Takelot II
	4	Osorkon II; Hornakht
II	1	empty
	2	anonymous
III	1	Psusennes I
	2	Amenemope
	3	empty sarcophagus of Ankhefenmut
	4	Wendjebauendjedet
	5	Shoshenq II; Siamun; Psusennes II
IV		original tomb of Amenemope
V		Shoshenq III
VI		unidentified
VII		unidentified

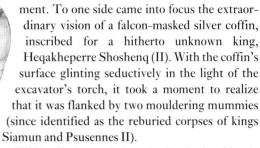

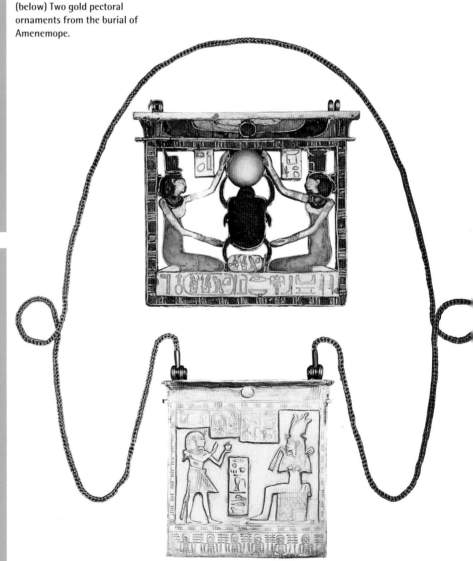

ment. To one side came into focus the extraordinary vision of a falcon-masked silver coffin, inscribed for a hitherto unknown king, Heqakheperre Shoshenq (II). With the coffin's surface glinting seductively in the light of the excavator's torch, it took a moment to realize that it was flanked by two mouldering mummies (since identified as the reburied corpses of kings Siamun and Psusennes II).

While all three of these bodies had evidently been disturbed in antiquity, two granite chambers beyond – concealed behind a decorated wall and protected by huge granite boulders riding on copper rollers – seemed to be untouched. That to the one side contained the rich and undisturbed burial of the tomb owner, Psusennes I, with canopic jars, *shabti*-figures and gold and silver vessels piled up before the sarcophagus (which turned out to have been usurped from the burial of Merenptah in the Valley of the Kings); while the chamber to the other side, originally prepared for Psusennes' mother, Queen Mutnodjmet, contained the rich burial of King Amenemope.

(above) A pair of simple funerary sandals from the mummy of Shoshenq II, fashioned in sheet gold.

(below) Two gold pectoral ornaments from the burial of Amenemope.

192

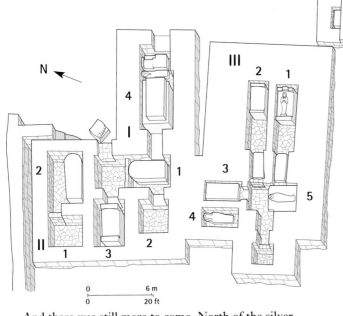

And there was still more to come. North of the silver coffin of Heqakheperre lay a further chamber, containing the empty coffin of a general called Ankhefenmut. Then, following the resumption of work on 13 February 1946 by Alexandre Lézine, the undisturbed burial of another military man, Wendjebauendjedet, was uncovered in a chamber lying alongside. It was scarcely less productive in jewels and burial equipment than that of Psusennes I.

The latest discoveries at Tanis have raised the total number of tombs in this royal burial complex to seven – though none of the more recent finds is in any way comparable to the riches turned up during Montet's time. Work on interpreting the site and its elements is continuing, but it is a regrettable fact that, owing to poor preservation of the organic materials and the haste with which the first burials were cleared (see table), many aspects of the necropolis and its history are – and are likely to remain – uncertain.

(above) The layout of the principal mausoleum at Tanis (see table opposite).

(right) Gilded and inlaid upper part of the wooden coffin of king Amenemope, Psusennes I's successor and the occupant of Tomb III, room 2.

(left) Gold pectoral ornament from the mummy of Shoshenq II, with lapis, felspar and glass inlays: the sun god Amun-Re-Horakhty, flanked by goddesses who spread their wings in a gesture of protection.

(above) Silver bowl with inlays and gold embellishments, from Wendjebauendjedet's burial (Tomb III, room 4). The finely chased hieroglyphic inscription records that it was a gift to the general from King Psusennes I.

1942 The Tomb of Prince Shoshenq • 1944 Ptahshepses' Belt
1945 The Nag Hammadi Codices

Discovery/excavation
1939
by
Günther Roeder

Site
el-Ashmunein

Period
New Kingdom, 18th Dynasty,
Amarna Period, 1353–1333 BC

4000 BC
3000 BC
2000 BC
1000 BC
0
AD 700

'In the season 1946-47 I first saw the reliefs, several hundred in all and none greater than twenty-one or twenty-two inches in length, though many were much smaller … That they must originally have been at El-Amarna is self-evident, but it is equally obvious that they could not possibly have been found there'
JOHN COONEY

El-Ashmunein – ancient Hermopolis Magna, cult-centre of the god Thoth – has been the focus of several archaeological expeditions, from the papyrological searches of the Italians and Germans – under Schiaparelli (•p. 121) and Evaristo Breccia, and Otto Rubensöhn respectively – in the early 1900s, to the more recent archaeological and architectural work of the British Museum under Jeffrey Spencer. The site is a difficult one, much destroyed since antiquity, but has provided its fair share of surprises. On one level, the Italians would find 'fragments of papyri decorated with human or animal figures and plant-like designs to be used as patterns for weavers' shops, as the subjects were those typically found on Coptic textiles' – pieces unique in the Egyptian archaeological record. Of quite another degree of importance, however, was the discovery made by the German Egyptologist Günther Roeder in the years leading up to the outbreak of the Second World War.

During excavations carried out on the west side of the so-called Sphinx Gate at el-Ashmunein, Roeder's men encountered some 1,500 blocks which had been employed as constructional material by Ramesses II. On closer inspection, it was noticed that these blocks were decorated with sunk reliefs in Amarna style, and here and there could be picked out the names of the Aten and of Akhenaten and his chief queen Nefertiti. Clearly, the blocks had been transported from across the river and the site of Akhenaten's abandoned capital city, el-Amarna – a city whose monuments the early Ramessid kings had begun to draw upon as a convenient quarry for prepared building materials.

GÜNTHER ROEDER
(1881–1966)

'Dr Reuder [sic] … had lunch with us. This person quarrelled with Daddy [Cecil Firth] … because the latter said that some cats were born without tails, and nearly "called him out" over a mud brick …'
DIANA FIRTH

- Born Schwiebus, Germany, 2 August 1881
- Educated at Jena and at Berlin under Adolf Erman; doctorate 1904
- First employed as an Egyptologist in the Berlin Museum; Egyptian Antiquities Service from 1907, working in Nubia copying the temples of Debod, Kalabsha and Dakka and cataloguing the shrines in the Cairo Museum
- Director of Pelizaeus-Museum, Hildesheim, 1915–45, directing work at Hermopolis for the museum between 1929 and 1939
- Dies Cairo, 6 November 1966

(below) Remains of a pylon from the small Amun temple at Hermopolis, begun by Ramesses II and decorated by Sethos II and Merenptah. The entire structure was built from reused limestone blocks of Amarna period date.

1942
The Tomb of Prince Shoshenq

This was a productive time for those with an interest in rich burials of the Third Intermediate Period, beginning with the discovery of the Tanis royal tombs (•p. 189) by Pierre Montet in 1939. And now, in early 1942, the Egyptian scholar Ahmad M. Badawi was to bring to light the rich burial of the crown prince Shoshenq, a son of Osorkon II and high priest of Ptah at Memphis.

The burial of Shoshenq was located among a group of élite tombs of 22nd-Dynasty date at a site known as Kom el-Fakri, some 250 m (820 ft) to the west of the fallen Ramesses II colossus (•p. 26), near the place where Badawi had previously uncovered the embalming houses of the Apis bulls.

On clearance, the tomb yielded a wonderful treasure of funerary jewelry (*right*), including gold finger-, toe- and penis-stalls, gold sidelock embellishments, a green stone heart scarab and an early 'Horus-on-

the-crocodiles' amulet (•p. 33) – as well as the prince's sarcophagus, canopic jars, *shabti*-figures (some 200 in total) and alabaster vessels.

(right) A selection of blocks from Roeder's find at Hermopolis: (top to bottom) Akhenaten with a branch of olives; the languid royal torso; a fishing scene.

These so-called Hermopolis blocks were photographed by Roeder and his team before the close of work in what, with the outbreak of war, was to be their final season at the site. A short time after the expedition's departure for Germany, however, the reliefs would find their way from the German magazines on to the Cairo antiquities market. And it was here that a selection of these and others (perhaps originating from unofficial excavations carried out on the eastern side of the Sphinx Gate), now prettily repainted in a range of pastel shades, were seen by Brooklyn Museum curator John D. Cooney shortly after the war ended.

The Hermopolis reliefs have in recent years been studied with impressive results by the German scholar Rainer Hanke, shedding important light on the history of the Amarna period. The most famous of their number is perhaps that which has established once and for all the status of the boy-pharaoh Tutankhamun as the son of a king. Now scattered around the world, the best among them – and they are exceptionally fine – have ended up in the Metropolitan Museum of Art in New York, in a generous bequest from the great American collector Norbert Schimmel.

1944
Ptahshepses' Belt

Excavations carried out by Abdel Salam M. Husein in the vicinity of the Unas valley temple in January 1944 resulted in the unexpected discovery of a grey schist sarcophagus (Cairo JE 87077) which, on opening, proved to contain the flooded and disintegrated body of an Old Kingdom prince, Ptahshepses, probably a son of Unas, last king of the 5th Dynasty. Careful excavation of this watery grave revealed that the otherwise undistinguished deceased was wearing a unique 'gold belt ..., with its pattern of small beads quite intact, and only slightly damaged by crushing at each side' (JE 87078). Conserved *in situ* with molten wax, it has since been brilliantly conserved by A. Y. Moustafa and is now on display in the Cairo Museum.

1945
The Nag Hammadi Codices

Egypt has long had a tradition of producing spectacularly important biblical texts. Among such finds may be numbered the Nag Hammadi codices, found by chance in December 1945 by two farmer brothers, Mohammed and Khalifa Ali, concealed in a jar at the base of a large boulder below the Gebel el-Tarif in northern Upper Egypt. Thinking that the vessel might contain gold, they smashed it open – and out fell a collection of grimy, leather-bound papyrus books.

The collection, now thankfully reassembled in Cairo, consists of 12 complete books and fragments of a 13th, which the Alis' mother had attempted to destroy in a sub-plot of murder and mayhem worthy of fiction.

Translated from the original Greek into Coptic and concealed for safe-keeping by a Christian Gnostic community in around AD 400, the archive represents the greatest ever single contribution to Gnostic studies. Each of the volumes comprises several tracts – 52 in total, of which 6 are duplicates. Since only 6 of these 46 texts were previously known, the Nag Hammadi find has expanded the corpus of Gnostic literature by an impressive 40 titles – of which 75 per cent are preserved intact.

Most probably the Nag Hammadi archive, like that discovered in 1952 at Gebel Abu Mena (the Bodmer Papyri, or Dishna Papers, after their findspot) belonged to the monastic order founded by St Pachomius, who was born at nearby el-Qasr (ancient Chenoboskion).

AFTER
1945

SECTION V
DIGGING FOR ANSWERS

'It is undeniable, I think, that excavation has of recent years absorbed too much of the activity of Egyptologists; the demands of Science have tended to be subordinated to the demands of the Museums, and the acquisition of antiquities has become the primary object, and the acquisition of knowledge concerning the Ancients a secondary consideration.'
ALAN H. GARDINER

The years after 1936 – with the tightening of the antiquities' laws, the advent of the Second World War, revolution in Egypt and the Suez crisis – proved difficult ones for foreign archaeologists. With the proposed erection of an enlarged, Russian-financed dam at the first cataract in 1960, however, came an opportunity for renewed international involvement in Egyptian exploration: UNESCO, with the agreement of the now independent Egyptian state, organized a fresh and co-ordinated campaign of survey and excavation of the areas under threat. Primarily a documentation and salvage operation, great new discoveries were few – and nor were they expected. More important than 'wonderful things' was the era of renewed international co-operation the campaign ushered in.

Today it is estimated that the Supreme Council of Antiquities (successor of the old Service des Antiquités and the former Egyptian Antiquities Organization) issues permits to more than 100 foreign missions a year, a third of them working in Thebes – to which may be added a similar number of Egyptian expeditions. Archaeology on the banks of the Nile has never been so active. But now, as Gardiner had wished, the quest is for information, not objects: the work is slower, more methodical, and increasingly specialist. It tends to be focused on sites which have already been dug over in the hope that more meaningful contexts for earlier finds might still be salvaged – or else on sites threatened by nature or man.

As a result of this necessary change of emphasis, the list of intrinsically spectacular finds from excavations has slowed, though it has not entirely ceased; while the number of discoveries made by chance has continued much as before.

A diver of Jean-Yves Empereur's underwater survey examines a colossal, queenly torso of Hellenistic date lying on the sea-bed, Alexandria harbour, before being raised in 1995.

THE TELL EL-MASKHUTA TREASURE

1950 The Treasure of Queen Takhut

Discovery/excavation
1947
by
Egyptian locals

Site
Tell el-Maskhuta

Period
Late Period, 27th Dynasty,
probably reign of Darius II,
424–404 BC

'In 1947 the Cairo art market was inundated with a seemingly inexhaustible supply of Greek coins known as Athena tetradrachms, a type of coin frequently found in Egypt and usually of no especial interest. But the quantity of these coins was exceptional and there were rumours of even greater quantities that were melted down. Evidence from various sources shows that the coins were found at Pithom in the eastern Delta together with silver vessels and agate ornaments now in Brooklyn ....'

JOHN D. COONEY

Tell el-Maskhuta was the first site excavated for the Egypt Exploration Fund by Édouard Naville in 1883, uncovering a series of mud-brick magazines which were immediately (if improbably) identified with those built by the Hebrews while in bondage in biblical Pithom. It was a site later investigated by Charles Trick Currelly in 1905 for Petrie's Egyptian Research Account, and work has been carried out here since, notably by American archaeologist J. S. Holladay Jr.

The discovery of a spectacular hoard of silver vessels and coins was made by local diggers sometime before or during 1947. No firm details of the context of the find are recorded (John Cooney's version of the story is that both coins and silver 'seem to have been found in a storeroom or underground chamber of a shrine dedicated to the foreign goddess Alat'), and even the precise make-up of the hoard is unclear. But certainly the original find was an impressive one. The service was large: the assemblage seems to have included a silver head vase, now in the British Museum (GR 1962,12-12, 1), two silver jugs and handles, and as many as 17 complete and broken silver bowls, four of which bear late 5th-century BC dedicatory texts in Aramaic (16 – and perhaps 17 – complete vessels or fragments are now in The Brooklyn Museum, 54.50.33-42, 55.183). Several unusual, gold-mounted agates (Brooklyn 54.50.1-31) are also mentioned in connection with the haul, which Cooney, on the basis of the texts and the strong Persian overtones in the decoration of the vessels, dates no earlier than the late 27th Dynasty – that is, around 410 BC, a few decades earlier than the analogous hoard found at Tukh el-Qaramus in 1905 (•p. 125).

(left) Fragmentary Greek head vase in silver – said to have formed part of the Tell el-Maskhuta treasure, recovered by locals from the ruins of a shrine dedicated to the goddess Alat.

THE LATER DIRECTORS OF THE EGYPTIAN ANTIQUITIES SERVICE (SINCE 1914)*		
Pierre Lacau: 1914–36	Abd el-Fattah Hilmy: 1959	Nur el-Din: 1988
Étienne Drioton: 1936–52	Mohammed Anwar Shoukry: 1960–64	Sayed Tawfik: 1989–90
Mustafa Amer: 1953–56	Mohammed Mahdi: 1964–66	Mohammed Ibrahim Bakr: 1990–93
Abbas Bayoumi: 1956–57	Gamal Mukhtar: 1967–77	Mohammed Abdel Halim
Moharram Kamal: 1957–59	Mohammed Abd el-Qader Mohammed: 1977–78	Nur el-Din: 1993–96
	Shehata Adam: 1978–81	Ali Hassan: 1996–97
	Fuad el-Oraby: 1981	Gaballa Ali Gaballa: 1997–
	Mohammed Abdel Halim	

*Some dates approximate

Shepenwepet; finger- and toe-stalls; and a pair of miniature sandals.

Further investigations at the site, by Shehata Adam and Rashid Nueir, followed in February 1951. The excavations revealed the mud-brick structure of Takhut's tomb, as well as fragments of her *shabti*-figures; while to the south of the tomb were discovered two large blocks inscribed with the name of the queen's husband – Psammetichus II of the 26th Dynasty.

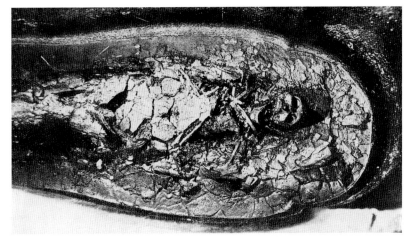

1950
The Treasure of Queen Takhut

In April, 1950 a peasant working close to ruins set aside for future archaeological excavation on the site of ancient Athribis (Tell Atrib) in the Delta inadvertently ran his plough into the side of a buried sarcophagus of white quartzite.

Investigation by the antiquities authorities rapidly established, from the presence of a column of hieroglyphic text enclosed in a cartouche, that the owner was a Late Period queen by the name of Takhut. It was an interesting find; what made it especially so was the fact that the burial had not been disturbed since ancient times.

When the lid was removed, it became apparent that the previous two-and-a-half thousand years had none the less taken their toll. The wooden coffin contained within had rotted away almost completely, and the mummy itself was in a similar decayed state (*above right*). A search among the debris, however, soon revealed a virtually complete array of queenly funerary jewels in a variety of precious metals (*right*) and stones (now in Cairo, JE 88963-89045). The haul included a small gold mask for sewing on to the shroud (*above*); a diadem; winged *ba*-birds; a fine jadeite heart scarab; a scarab of Psammetichus I; a fine chalcedony jewel engraved with an image of the god Bes; Hathor and lily amulets; a Bes image; several amethysts, one engraved with the name of

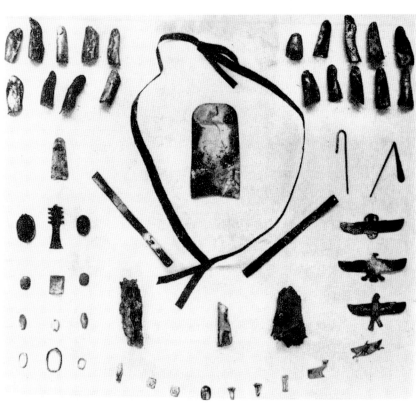

1952

THE LOST PYRAMID OF SEKHEMKHET

1954 The Stela of Kamose

MUHAMMAD ZAKARIA GONEIM (1911–1959)

'Most of the time he wears dark glasses as a protection against the fierce Egyptian sun …. When he removes them his eyes twinkle with fun and good humour.'
LEONARD COTTRELL

- Born Gharbiya in the Delta, 1911
- Diploma in Egyptology, University of Cairo, 1934
- Assistant to Selim Hassan, 1937, involved in the discovery of the Unas causeway reliefs (•p. 187); Inspector at Aswan, Edfu, 1939–43; Keeper of the Theban Necropolis, 1943; Chief Inspector, Upper Egypt, 1946-51, clearing the tombs of Kheruef (TT192) and Montuemhat (TT34); Keeper of the Saqqara Necropolis, 1951; appointed Director of Cairo Museum, 1958, but dies before taking up the appointment
- Suicide by drowning in the Nile, Cairo, 12 January 1959

Discovery/excavation
1952
by
Zakaria Goneim

Site
Saqqara

Period
Early Dynastic Period, 3rd Dynasty, reign of Sekhemkhet, 2611–2603 BC

4000 BC
3000 BC
2000 BC
1000 BC
0
AD 700

(below left) The great 'White Wall' of Goneim's pyramid complex is of characteristic 'palace façade' design and still well preserved to a height of almost 3 m (10 ft).

(below right) The southeast corner of the pyramid, showing the inwardly inclined interior courses of the structure's first 'step'; the man indicates scale. The similarity to the construction of Djoser's pyramid is apparent.

"'Where's the pyramid?" my professional colleagues would ask jocularly, and I had no answer; only an inner faith that somewhere beneath that vast expanse of sand I would eventually find what I was looking for.'
ZAKARIA GONEIM

Pyramids, it might be thought, are difficult things to lose, even by the exceptionally careless; but only when finished or intact. Where little more than the substructure of the monument had ever been completed, the concept of disappearance is easier to grasp.

The man who found Sekhemkhet's lost pyramid was the talented (if ill-fated) Egyptian excavator Zakaria Goneim, Keeper of the Saqqara Necropolis. The first portion of the monument to be brought to light was a section of the enclosure wall – Goneim's 'White Wall' – which bore a close resemblance to the enclosure wall of Djoser's pyramid complex (•p. 169). Encouragingly, one of its building blocks was later found to a carry a red ink graffito, 'Imhotep' (the name of Djoser's architect), indicating to Goneim what probably lay in store. The prize itself was revealed on 29 January 1952, at the very end of the first season: 'a series of independent walls leaning one on the other and inclining inwards at an angle of about 75 degrees, and *the stone courses were at right angles to the slope of the walls*'. As the construction showed, this was no ordinary pyramid, but a *step* pyramid.

The search for the entrance to Sekhemkhet's underground chambers began in January 1954. In Djoser's monument, the entrance was located on the north side, at some distance from the pyramid proper, beneath the king's mortuary temple. Clearing away the sand on this side of Sekhemkhet's pyramid, Goneim located a similar structure, but no sign of access to the underground apartments. He shifted his diggers further to the north, where he had previously noticed a large depression in the sand, and there the entrance was soon disclosed: 'a long, open, rock-cut trench enclosed at the top by massive supporting walls'.

Miraculously, the masonry blocking of the doorway was intact, though the right half had evidently been rebuilt in antiquity; when the pyramid was finally opened on 9 March 1954, therefore, the event was followed with great public interest.

The excavator, partially dismantling this wall, jumped down into a corridor filled with rubble a short distance ahead. As this debris was gradually cleared, hundreds of funerary vessels were recovered, in hard and soft stones and arranged in layers on the passage floor, similar to deposits already familiar from Djoser's pyramid (•p. 169). And then a magnificent surprise: the gleam of gold, and

(left) The splendid sheet-gold cosmetic box from the pyramid's entrance passage: the hinged lid and base are fashioned in the form of a bivalve shell.

(above) The sloping ramp today, which allowed Goneim to gain access to the underground portions of Sekhemkhet's unfinished pyramid structure.

view, completely blocked with a dry-stone masonry fill which turned out to be a massive 3 m (10 ft) thick. By 31 May 1954 Goneim and his *reis* were able to scramble through the hole they had made.

> *'When we had picked ourselves up and the lamp was raised, a wonderful sight greeted us. In the middle of a rough-cut chamber lay a magnificent sarcophagus of pale, golden, translucent alabaster. We moved towards it. My first thought was, "Is it intact?"'*
> ZAKARIA GONEIM

It was. Closed in a unique manner, by a vertically sliding calcite panel which had been plastered into position, it showed no evidence of disturbance. A decayed funerary wreath lay on top – 'success seemed to be in sight'.

All the evidence pointed to this being the burial of Sekhemkhet himself, undisturbed since the 3rd Dynasty. But another, nail-biting month was to pass before the surprising secret of the sarcophagus was revealed to a select

21 precious metal armlets, a hollow gold wand, a wonderful lidded-box in the shape of a bivalve shell, a pair of electrum tweezers and a needle, as well as a scatter of gold, carnelian and faience beads and gold spacers – the contents of a decayed wooden casket, untouched since the day of deposition. Other finds included a group of mud-sealed jars inscribed with the name of Sekhemkhet, copper vessels and copper and flint tools, and an ivory 'label' with a list of linens, inscribed with the 'Two Ladies' name of the pyramid owner: Djesertyankh.

Some 31 m (102 ft) from the entrance, on the west side of the corridor, a doorway led into a second corridor turning to the north, running back on itself and leading to a T-shaped gallery with two north–south extensions, containing 132 small magazines or store chambers – a layout paralleled in the pyramid at Zawiyet el-Aryan and elsewhere, including the much later tomb of the sons of Ramesses II, KV5, in the Valley of the Kings (•p. 220).

The alabaster sarcophagus

The excavation of the descending main corridor continued through May 1954, the work becoming more and more difficult, and beginning to look less and less promising – until the outline of a rock-cut doorway came into

(below) The superbly figured and cut alabaster sarcophagus, with its sliding end-panel raised: although remnants of ancient funerary bouquets lay undisturbed on top, the interior proved to be empty.

group of officials and Egyptologists – on 26 June 1954. A scaffold was erected above the sliding panel, and a rope attached for the workmen to heave on. Gradually, slowly, the 227-kg (500-lb) block began to shift, inch by inch. Two hours later it had moved sufficiently for Goneim to peer in: 'I went down on my knees .... The sarcophagus was empty'. Immense disappointment.

During Goneim's clearance of the entrance corridor there had been an accident in which one of the workmen suffocated to death. A veil of gloom had descended over the work. 'I was strangely uneasy', Goneim wrote. 'It is difficult to describe this feeling … a mixture of awe, curiosity, and uncertainty … I felt that the pyramid had a personality and that this personality was that of the king for whom it was built and which lingered still within it'. If so, it was an evil presence. Three years later, in 1959, at the height of his career, Goneim committed suicide.

Later work

Others would follow in the work, however, without ill-effect. Seeking to solve the mystery of Sekhemkhet's pyramid complex, Jean-Philippe Lauer (*below*) took up, in 1963, where Goneim had left off. Lauer's particular aim was to uncover Sekhemkhet's southern tomb – a feature which work at the Step Pyramid had indicated was probably to be found at the site of the 'lost' pyramid also. His excavations were able to demonstrate formally what Goneim had long supposed – that the Sekhemkhet complex had been almost doubled in size during the course of its construction, which meant that any southern tomb – if it existed as an original feature of the complex – would be found relatively close to the pyramid proper. And it was – between 1965 and 1967, on the south side, below a completely destroyed mastaba. Beneath its west end had been cut a huge, 3-m (10-ft) square shaft leading down to a corridor running from west to east. And this contained, at its far end, a rotted wooden coffin of early type containing the bones of a two-year old boy – presumably a royal prince, robbed shortly after the burial. Sekhemkhet himself has so far evaded discovery – though, as Lauer has observed, the underground portions of this pyramid complex have yet to be fully cleared.

Sekhemkhet's monument is but the largest of a series of 'mislaid' pyramids. Other lost structures continue to be found, and with increasing frequency – most recently those of the 6th-Dynasty queens Meritites and Ankhesenpepy II (discovered at Saqqara by French archaeologist Audran Labrousse in 1995 and 1998). Still more have been known for years under another guise, and only recently recognized for what in fact they are – such as the 'mastaba' tombs of Khuwit at Saqqara (a Zahi Hawass discovery), and of the queens located to the south of the Sesostris III pyramid at Dahshur. More, doubtless, will follow.

1954
The Stela of Kamose

'No Egyptological discovery of recent years has caused more excitement among scholars ...'
ALAN GARDINER

During the course of his early excavations in the Theban necropolis, the fifth Earl of Carnarvon 'found among the loose debris of pottery and fragmentary mummies on a ledge near the entrance to a plundered tomb in the Birâbi, not far from the mouth of the Deir el Bahari valley' a broken writing tablet of wood (•p. 130). This tablet turned out to preserve tantalizing extracts from a text of extraordinary historical significance, relating the expulsion from Egypt by the 17th-Dynasty king Kamose of the foreign, Hyksos rulers who had for a generation and more occupied northern Egypt. In 1919, the British philologist Battiscombe Gunn suggested that the Carnarvon text might well be a 'schoolboy copy' from a stela originally set up at Karnak – and this hunch was confirmed with the discovery at that site, by Henri Chevrier in 1932 and 1935, of fragments of a large stela which duplicated the first 15 lines of the Carnarvon tablet text. With the discovery of these scraps, the Egyptologists' appetite was well and truly whetted: if only other fragments from this text could turn up to shed further light on this crucially important event!

This hope was exceeded when, on 25 July 1954, the Egyptian scholar Labib Habachi uncovered at Karnak an intact *duplicate* of the fragmentary and incomplete first stela which continued the story from the point the Carnarvon tablet left off. The find – 'one of the most thrilling discoveries in the Temple of Karnak' – was made among 17 blocks undisturbed since they had been employed in antiquity as the foundation for a statue of Ramesses II.

Three of the blocks carried representations from one of the *heb-sed* ceremonies of Amenophis III, while four others came from one of the dismantled Karnak structures of Amenophis IV-Akhenaten (•p. 209). At the bottom of the pile lay the main prize: the limestone Kamose stela itself, 2.2 m (7 ft) high by 1.1 m (3 ½ ft) wide and some 28 cm (11 in) thick, placed face down on a bed of sand. And, as scholars had hoped, it proved to 'narrate a hitherto entirely unknown and important historical incident in the attempts to throw off Hyksos rule'.

KHUFU'S BOATS AT THE GREAT PYRAMID

1956 Nefruptah • 1957 A Head of King Userkaf

Discovery/excavation
1954
by
Kamal el-Mallakh

Site
Giza (south side of the
Great Pyramid)

Period
Old Kingdom, 4th Dynasty,
reign of Khufu,
2551–2528 BC

'Like a cat ... I closed my eyes. And then with my eyes closed, I smelt incense, a very holy, holy, holy smell. I smelt time ... I smelt centuries ... I smelt history. And then I was sure that the boat was there.'
KAMAL EL-MALLAKH

In 1954, Kamal el-Mallakh, then a young Antiquities Service inspector in the days before he went on to make name for himself in the world of journalism, was conducting routine clearance work along the southern boundary wall of the Great Pyramid at Giza when he came upon a thin line of pink mortar which attracted his attention. This mortar proved to delineate the edge of a pair of long, narrow pits, arranged end to end – that on the west covered over with 40 massive limestone slabs, that to the east with 41 such blocks. Examining those of the eastern pit more closely, el-Mallakh found a mason's mark – a cartouche containing the name of Djedefre, Khufu's successor on the Egyptian throne, by whose orders the stones – each weighing up to 16 tonnes – had presumably been set in place.

Only with difficulty did el-Mallakh manage to persuade his superiors in the Antiquities Service that his discovery was worthy of further investigation, the prevailing view being that he had found nothing more than a section of the pyramid's foundations, or a part of the paved courtyard. But on 26 May he made a hole in the 22nd block covering the eastern pit and inserted his torch. The beam illuminated what at first looked like a pile of lumber; then the tip of a large oar came into view – and el-Mallakh immediately realized that here, before him, was a full-size, dismantled boat from the very beginnings of Egyptian history. And another, presumably, lay close by.

The discovery of these boat-pits, with their contents intact, was to create an international storm of interest – and foment such jealousy within the Antiquities Service that el-Mallakh's immensely promising archaeological career never recovered.

(above) Kamal el-Mallakh who, as a young architect-archaeologist, first noticed the slab-covered boat pits. His dogged persistence in continuing with the exploration led to a discovery which astonished the world.

Excavation and reconstruction

Such boats and their emplacements had been found before – by de Morgan at Dahshur, of Middle Kingdom date – and would be found again – most recently the fleet of 12 found by David O'Connor at Abydos in 1991, dating from the Early Dynastic period; but the Giza finds were, and are likely to remain, in a class of their own.

The magnificent vessel now on display in the Giza boat museum bears little resemblance to the neatly arranged piles of dusty struts and sections

(left) King Khufu's boat photographed as it lay, dismantled, in the first of the pits discovered by Kamal el-Mallakh. The 1,224 individual pieces of cedar, acacia, sidder and other woods would take over ten years to reassemble.

4000 BC

3000 BC

2000 BC

1000 BC

0

AD 700

1956
Nefruptah

The intact burial of Nefruptah, believed to be a daughter of Ammenemes III of the 12th Dynasty, was uncovered by officials of the Egyptian Antiquities Service beneath a ruined mud-brick pyramid

in 1956, some 2 km (1 ¼ miles) to the southwest of this king's own funerary complex at Hawara. The wooden inner coffin and organic remains had decomposed, but from the mud-soaked lower layers of the black granite sarcophagus were extracted the component parts (since restored) of a rich collection of the owner's amuletic burial equipment – most dramatically a falcon collar (Cairo, JE 90100; *below*), as well as an apron, bracelet, anklets, flail (JE 90200; *left*) and other items of gold, carnelian and felspar.

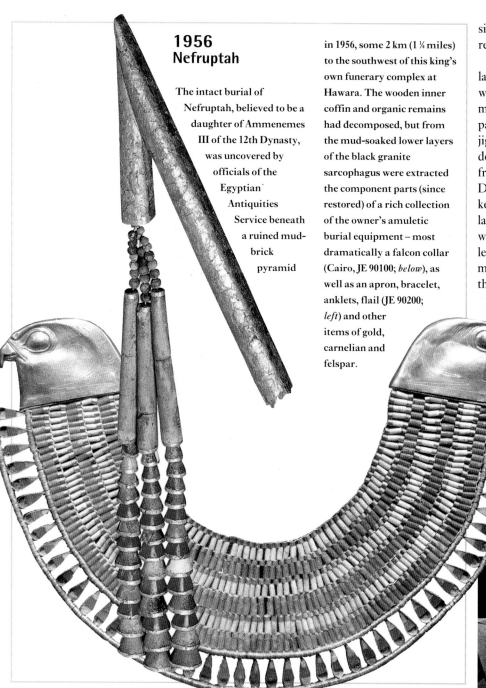

sidder and other woods ranged out before him in the Giza restoration shed.

Hag Ahmed was helped in his task by the fact that the layout of the pieces in the pit reflected the sequence in which the ship had been dismantled; and many of the elements carried notations indicating from which particular part of the boat they came. None the less, it was basically a jigsaw puzzle without a picture-key, and would take over a decade – and five dummy runs – to complete. What arose from the chaos, in 1968, was a royal barque of the 4th Dynasty, complete with cabin. Constructed without a keel, its timbers occasionally pegged but for the most part lashed together with metres and metres of rope (which would tighten when wet), it measured 43.4 m (142 ft) in length and 5.9 m (19 ft) in the beam, and had a displacement of some 45 tonnes. Despite its six pairs of oars – these were probably employed solely for steering – the boat itself would have been towed by smaller craft.

The second boat pit

The Khufu boat, as reconstructed, is one of the most impressive sights of Egyptian archaeology; yet, until it is properly housed in a climate-controlled environment, its long-term future will remain a cause for a concern. Within its pit, the conditions for preservation had been close to perfect, the planks containing a static 10 per cent moisture – unlike the extremes of both temperature and humidity the fragile timbers experience today. The vulnerability of the restored boat is high-

(right) Hag Ahmed Youssef Moustafa in his workshop. Because of the enormous size of Khufu's boat, much of the preliminary work of reconstruction was accomplished with the aid of reduced-scale models.

which el-Mallakh's torch first revealed in the eastern pit. The boat as we see it is the breathtaking achievement of one man – Hag Ahmed Youssef Moustafa, principal restorer within the Antiquities Service, then working under the overall supervision of Dr Zaki Iskander, the Department's chief scientist.

Thanks to the air-tight seal of the roofing slabs, the environment of the boat pit had remained constant and the condition of the contents – arranged in some 13 distinct layers – was generally sturdy. Following preliminary consolidation of overlying cloth and matting, by December 1955 the enormously delicate task of removal could begin. By late June 1957, the pit stood empty, and the following autumn Hag Ahmed could turn his practical attention to the reconstruction of the 651 elements (1,224 individual pieces) of burnished cedar, acacia,

1957
A Head of King Userkaf

This lightly moustached greywacke head of a king wearing the red crown of Lower Egypt (Cairo JE 90220) was discovered in the spring of 1957 at Abusir by a joint German-Swiss mission under the direction of Herbert Ricke. It is evidently a portrait of the 5th-Dynasty king Userkaf, in the remains of whose funerary temple it and other fragments were recovered. The quality of the piece is remarkable, and its similarity to the portraits of Menkaure (•p. 132) striking. Not impossibly, it originated from the same sculptural studio.

lighted by the sadly decayed condition of its still-dismantled pair. Recently re-investigated by a Japanese team from Waseda University in Tokyo, the hope (perhaps vain) is that this boat, too, may one day be restored to join its companion on the desert surface, alongside their owner's magnificent pyramid-tomb.

(below) Hag Ahmed's assistants check the lashing of the timbers in the final reconstruction.

(right) An imposing legacy: Khufu's majestic boat as drawn (top) and fully reconstructed in its museum at Giza.

205

THE SACRED ANIMAL
NECROPOLIS, SAQQARA

1964–65 A Statue Finds its Face

Discovery/excavation
1964–71
by
Walter Bryan Emery

Site
Saqqara

Period
Late Period, 26th Dynasty–
Ptolemaic period,
664–30 BC

4000 BC
3000 BC
2000 BC
1000 BC
0
AD 700

'Since December 1964 Professor Emery has been excavating in the archaic necropolis, not far from Zoser's [Djoser's] Step Pyramid, and the first two seasons' work revealed a great nexus of catacombs (mostly of Saite-Persian date) running under a First Dynasty necropolis. The galleries of these catacombs were packed with thousands upon thousands of mummified ibises, and the overwhelming suggestion was that these were the offerings of pilgrims coming in search of health to the shrine of the deified Imhotep, who had become identified with the Greek god of healing, Asklepios. From this it was argued that somewhere in the neighbourhood of these catacombs must lie the temple and that the temple would be sited in the neighbourhood of Imhotep's tomb ....'
ILLUSTRATED LONDON NEWS

The latter years of Bryan Emery's life at Saqqara (•p. 182) were dedicated to a single end, an obsession – the desire to crown a long and successful excavating career with the discovery of the tomb of Djoser's chief minister, Imhotep, architect of the Step Pyramid (•p. 169), in later times revered as a powerful sage and identified with Asklepios, the Greek god of healing. Cecil Firth, J. E. Quibell (•p. 97) and George A. Reisner (•p. 132) all believed that this burial would most naturally have been located in the Early Dynastic necropolis at North Saqqara, and it was here that Emery concentrated his search.

Significantly, it was an area densely strewn with potsherds dating not from the earliest dynasties but from the end of pharaonic history. Emery first tested the site in 1956, revealing the remains of a 3rd-Dynasty mastaba tomb and two purificatory sacrificial bulls; he also recovered the remains of mummies of the sacred ibis which had originally

(opposite above right) A wall of ibis mummies. The birds, embalmed and placed in sealed pottery jars, were purchased by pilgrims as offerings to the god and buried in their thousands in the underground catacombs which honeycomb North Saqqara.

(opposite below) Gilded bronze group of Isis suckling the infant Horus, from the principal Temple Terrace deposit. When found, the statuette was wrapped in fine linen which left exposed only the faces of the two divinities.

(above) A votive bronze image from Emery's excavations, depicting the sage Imhotep, architect of Djoser's Step Pyramid, who was worshipped as a god at Saqqara and elsewhere during the 1st millennium BC. Emery's great dream – unrealized – was to discover the man's tomb.

(left) A section of the extensive, subterranean galleries in the Sacred Animal Necropolis, with separate, rock-cut niches designed to contain a mummified and coffined baboon – sacred creature of Thoth, god of learning.

been deposited here and at various sites (including Tuna el-Gebel, where their brimming catacomb was discovered by Sami Gabra) by devout pilgrims during Ptolemaic times. Such jars, clearly, were the source of the mounds of late potsherds littering the surface: evidently there was a catacomb close by, which had contained many more burials of this sort. Could these embalmed animals, manifestations of the god Thoth, be in some way connected with Imhotep's later cult as wise man, healer and 'first chief one of the ibis'? Did they mark the location of Imhotep's hypothetical cult centre – the man's tomb?

Excavation to resolve these questions began in earnest a decade later, on 5 October 1964, following the interruption to Emery's digging schedule imposed by the Nubian rescue campaigns. The first support for his thesis, as he believed, came two months later. Clearing one of the burial shafts of the 3rd-Dynasty tomb no. 3510, Emery's workers unex-

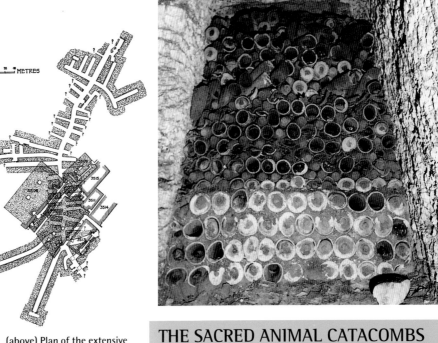

THE DEITIES OF THE PRINCIPAL TEMPLE TERRACE DEPOSIT

'… the most notable [of the Temple Terrace caches] was in a pit [lined with 10 re-used stelae: 5 hieroglyphic, 4 Carian, one uninscribed] below the stone paving of Shrine D. When first opened the pit was found to contain a large number of bronze statuettes arranged in an orderly manner … Below them were three wooden shrines and a wooden statue of Osiris embellished with coloured glass inlay and standing on a limestone base. More bronze statuettes were found packed in the wooden shrines, some of them wrapped in linen … which accounts for their extraordinary state of preservation, many of them being in mint condition … Apart from those of bronze, statuettes of deities in wood and stone were also recovered from the shrines.'

W. B EMERY

DEITY REPRESENTED	QUANTITY FOUND
Anubis	2
Apis	4
Bes	1
Harpokrates	32
Hathor	2
Horus	3
Imhotep	1
Isis	26
Khnum	1
Min	2
Mut	1
Onuris	1
Osiris	19
Ptah	4
Sekhmet	2
Thoth	1

(above) Plan of the extensive complex of ibis galleries discovered beneath mastaba 3510 in 1964.

THE SACRED ANIMAL CATACOMBS

ANIMAL-TYPE	DATE RANGE
cows (mothers of Apis)	Year 1 Psammuthis (393 BC)–Year 11 Cleopatra VII (41 BC)
baboons	4th–1st centuries BC
falcons	?4th–1st centuries BC

pectedly broke through into an underground complex of corridors and side-galleries reminiscent of Mariette's Serapeum (•p. 40) but far more extensive. It was the first of two catacombs stuffed with mummified ibises ('At a conservative estimate, well over 1½ million …'). Other galleried mass-burials would follow with the excavation of the Temple Terrace – the remains of one of the temple institutions which administered the animal cults – over the next years. These included the catacomb of the cow-mothers of the sacred Apis bull (the Iseum, for which Mariette himself had haphazardly searched in the 19th century), that of the baboons, and the burials of the sacred falcons. A further ibis gallery was uncovered closer to the dried-up lake of Abusir where the birds were presumably bred.

The extraordinary range of animals interred at Saqqara – ram-, cat-, dog- and even lion-burials have been recorded at various parts of the site – is without parallel, and many details relating to their rearing, killing and processing are still obscure.

Emery's excavations in the sacred animal galleries and at the Temple Terrace were to produce several important subsidiary finds – rich caches of

207

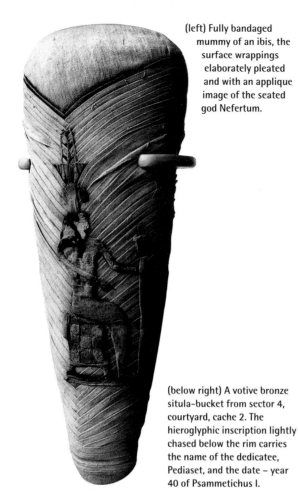

(left) Fully bandaged mummy of an ibis, the surface wrappings elaborately pleated and with an applique image of the seated god Nefertum.

(below right) A votive bronze situla-bucket from sector 4, courtyard, cache 2. The hieroglyphic inscription lightly chased below the rim carries the name of the dedicatee, Pediaset, and the date – year 40 of Psammetichus I.

stone sculpture and bronze votive images, of temple furniture, of anatomical *donaria*, and quantities of immensely important papyri – hieratic (18), demotic (761), Aramaic (194), Greek (32) and Arabic – literary and documentary, the study of which is still continuing, as well as ostraca (see below). Many of the objects represented *ex-voto* offerings, and some, to be sure, had plausible associations with the divine Imhotep. But the tomb of Imhotep the man was to prove elusive. Bryan Emery died during the seventh year of his search, in 1971, his life's work unfulfilled but his legacy for the study of the Saite and Ptolemaic periods a rich and impressive one.

The dream ostraca

'... the waste-paper basket of a troubled man'
JOHN RAY

The Saqqara 'dream ostraca' represent but one group of materials turned up by chance in the course of Emery's immensely productive Imhotep diggings. They comprise 65 demotic texts written on pottery and limestone which document the divinely inspired dreams of a scribe known as Hor of Sebennytos. Hor, a convert to the god Thoth, lived during the middle years of the 2nd century BC at Saqqara, close to the god's sanctuary at the entrance to the north ibis catacomb. Here he set up shop as a proto-

1964–65
A Statue Finds its Face

During the course of their work of clearance at Deir el-Bahri in 1907, the Egypt Exploration Fund brought to light an extremely fine torso in a beautiful, marble-like, white stone. The scale, modelling, material and extensive remains of paint marked the piece out as a sculpture of major importance; as a work of art, however, it had one fatal flaw: the face had been neatly cleaved off in antiquity, and was missing.

The hope has long been entertained (particularly by the torso's present owners, the Metropolitan Museum of Art: MMA 07.230.3) that the missing face would one day turn up.

When at last it did, in 1964–65, scholars were astounded – not only by the outstanding quality of the work, but by its virtually pristine state of preservation. The finders of Tuthmosis III's face were the Polish expedition under Jadwiga Lipinska, the findspot the king's temple. It is now in Cairo Museum (JE 90237).

therapist, to advise and comfort others using his god-given powers.

Hor's scribblings represent drafts for a petition he was preparing for submission to the king, Ptolemy VI Philometor – to counter an unspecified charge concerning the food of the ibises at Isiospolis. (He had perhaps been embezzling the divine bird seed.) They make fascinating reading, shedding much light on the character and thought processes of the man himself and, more significantly, on the political events he had not only lived through but, it seems, actually foretold. The high-point in his interpretative career had occurred in 168 BC when, following a dream, he was able to assure Pharaoh that the recent invasion of Egypt by Antiochus IV Epiphanes of Syria would come to naught. By this, Hor's prophetic stock had risen overnight.

THE AKHENATEN TEMPLE PROJECT: REBUILDING BY COMPUTER

1967 Amenophis III and Sebek: a Statue from Damansha
1960s A Hoard of Middle Kingdom Bronzes from the Faiyum

Discovery/excavation
since the 19th century;
analysis since 1965
by
Ray Winfield Smith &
Donald B. Redford

Site
Thebes (Karnak)

Period
New Kingdom,
18th Dynasty, Amarna Period,
1353–1333 BC

(below) Cutting out photographs of the blocks prior to matching with the aid of a computer. Size, pigmentation, image and inscription were all carefully recorded and shared characteristics quickly established.

'Through photography of the relief-carved faces of these blocks, and with the aid of a computer, we have matched thousands of stones and have seen superb works of art take form again after thousands of years ....'
RAY WINFIELD SMITH

Archaeological reconstruction is often spoken of as a jigsaw puzzle, though hardly ever has the metaphor been so aptly employed as when applied to the work of the Akhenaten Temple Project. The brainchild of the late Ray Winfield Smith, its director from 1965 to 1972, with the aid of nascent computer technology the ATP was able to reassemble on paper a highly important series of temple reliefs carved from Silsila sandstone and dating from the early period (pre-Year 5) of the reign of Amenophis IV-Akhenaten. These 34,752 reliefs had been completely dismantled after a mere two decades by Horemheb at the start of the 19th Dynasty, and perhaps even before.

The scattered fragments of this razed Atenist temple complex had first been encountered as re-used rubble fill at Karnak during the 19th century. Further *talatat* (as the characteristically small blocks were named – a three-hand-width unit taken from Islamic architecture) would be uncovered subsequently: at Karnak (mostly re-employed, partially defaced and stacked upside down as core-rubble within the 2nd and 9th pylons and the foundations of the hypostyle hall); at Luxor temple (within the Ramesses II pylons); and as far afield as Medamud to the north. Upon this extensive corpus of tantalizing fragments, Smith and subsequently Donald Redford endeavoured to impose some sense of order.

DONALD. B. REDFORD
(1934–)

- Born 2 September 1934
- B.A./M.A./Ph.D. Near Eastern Studies, University of Toronto
- Lecturer Brown University, 1959–61; Assistant/Associate Professor, University of Toronto, 1962–98; since 1998, Full Professor, Pennsylvania State University
- Director, excavations of University of Toronto and State University of New York, Binghampton, at the Temple of Osiris, Karnak, 1970–72; Director, Akhenaten Temple Project of the University of Pennsylvania, 1972–76; Director, East Karnak Excavations, 1975–91; Director, excavations at Mendes since 1991; Epigrapher, Theban Tomb Survey, since 1992

Computers

'None of us will ever forget the thrill when we achieved our first match of two Aten Temple blocks. ... Asmahan Shoucri ... cried out with an exclamation of delight. She had seen that photoprints of two blocks fitted to form part of a scene showing sunrays and a hieroglyph. Most auspiciously, the inscription said,
"The god's heart is pleased"...'

Although the ATP was not the first body to display an interest in reassembling the *talatat* – the French Egyptologists Maurice Pillet and Henri Chevrier, officials of the Antiquities Service working at Karnak, during the 1920s and 1930s (•p. 172), had harboured a similar dream – it was the first to achieve any notable success. This was due, in no small part, to the then novel application of computer technology, provided by IBM. The carved (and frequently polychrome)

4000 BC
3000 BC
2000 BC
1000 BC
0
AD 700

face of each block was photographed in black-and-white and in colour, to a uniform scale, and the characteristics of each scene sorted with computer assistance and analysed, eventually yielding paper-reconstructions of several long-dismantled scenes of Akhenaten's Karnak structures. These include reliefs from the temple 'Enduring in Monuments of the Aten for Eternity' (more conveniently referred to as *Rud-menu*), which was reconstructed from *talatat* found in the 9th pylon and at Luxor temple; and the 'Mansion of the *Benben*', a structure within the *Gem-pa-aten* temple complex, one of the first of Amenophis IV's Karnak building-works. A third structure was 'Exalted is the Monument of the Aten for Eternity' (the *Teni-menu*), which is known from another series of 9th pylon blocks. The precise physical form and ritual function of these monuments are still largely uncertain.

Excavations

The fact that only a relatively small proportion of the Karnak *talatat* could in fact be reconstructed (the French

(above) The rays of the solar disc, or Aten, present 'life' to the nose of Nefertiti: relief on a sandstone *talatat* block.

(left) Reconstructed elevation of the south colonnade of the Gem-pa-aten temple, with Chevrier's colossi (•p. 172).

(below) Ranks of neatly stacked sandstone blocks from Akhenaten's dismantled Karnak temples reused as fill in the structure of the 9th pylon.

have done further work since) was to inspire Redford and his team to undertake fresh excavations on the site of East Karnak from 1975 on – with some considerable success:

'We've been able to identify the line of the south wall of the temple and we know a good deal about the installation of that wall. It was in the form of a colonnade which ran around the first court of the temple. It bounded on the outside by a mud-brick temenos wall. The colonnade was lined on the inside by ... colossal statues ... [•p. 172].

We have been able to find the south-west corner, to trace the west wall of the temple and to find its entrance – which surprised us – and then proceed along until ... we found the north-west corner of the site and the north wall. So, now we have the lines of three walls ...

We have also been able to recover along the lines of the wall – and this was a surprise to us and we were very gratified – hundreds of fragments of talatat with relief on them. In many cases these fragments, even though they are very, very small, are enough to give us a clue as to the thematic nature of particular scenes at particular points along the walls of the temple.'

DONALD B. REDFORD

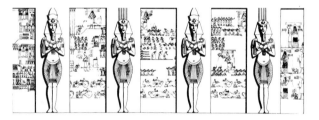

TEMPLE AND SHRINE NAMES OCCURRING IN THE KARNAK *TALATAT*

NAME	NO. OF OCCURRENCES NOTED
Gem-pa-aten ('Rediscovery of Aten') in the Per-aten ('House of Aten')	about 75
Hut-benben ('Mansion of the benben') in [the temple] Gem-pa-aten	about 48
Seh-en-pa-aten ('Booth of Aten') in [the temple] Gem-pa-aten	5
Rud-menu-en-aten-er-neheh ('Enduring in monuments of Aten for eternity')	36
Teni-menu-en-aten-er-neheh ('Exalted of monuments of Aten for eternity')	9
Weskhet-... ('Court ...')	2
Akh-... ('Glorious ...')	1
Per-aten ('House of Aten')	unspecified

1967
Amenophis III and Sebek: a Statue from Damansha

Prior to the discovery of the Luxor cache in 1989 (•p. 226), one of the finest known statues of Amenophis III (though usurped by Ramesses II) was this 7-tonne, alabaster dyad of the king supported by the god Sebek. It was recovered from the site of the god's previously unrecognized temple at Damansha, near Luxor (ancient Sumenu) by Hassan Bakry on 27 July 1967, during the cutting of the Sawahel Armant Canal. The statue had been placed at the bottom of a vertical, water-filled shaft believed to have been a tank for the keeping and breeding of Sebek's earthly manifestation – the crocodile.

Another fine sculpture – a block of dark granite surmounted by two carved crocodiles, dedicated by Nebnufer, a treasury official of Amenophis II – was recovered from another part of the same underground complex, as the excavator describes:

'The monument of Neb-nufer was found standing on a rectangular sandstone slab ..., with a pair of bronze wheels ... on each side of its lower surface ... This slab was placed above another sandstone slab ... with two grooves on its upper surface, coated with lead and bronze ...'.

'By means of the bronze wheels running in the grooves,' Bakry continues, 'the upper slab could be moved forwards in order to partly open the basin' – for food to tumble down into the snapping jaws of the divine monsters below.

1960s
A Hoard of Middle Kingdom Bronzes from the Faiyum

The precise circumstances surrounding the discovery of this, the most important group of Middle Kingdom bronzes ever brought to light, are unclear, but the findspot is reputed to have been the pyramid complex of Ammenemes III at Hawara in the Faiyum (•p. 77) and the date as recent as the mid- to late 1960s. The assemblage consisted of at least ten items (see table), datable, on stylistic and inscriptional grounds, to the reign of this same king. Three of the group represent Ammenemes III himself (one, *right*, at a scale of three-quarters life-size), with two fragmentary images of queens, four statuettes of high officials – two named, and one (Ortiz cat. 34) with an invocation to 'Sebek lord of Crocodilopolis' – as well as one small image of a crocodile.

The quality of these sculptures is extraordinarily high, both artistically and technically, the private portraits in particular displaying an individuality of expression seldom equalled in the art of the period. In contrast with the part-cast and part-sheet construction of the Hierakonpolis statues of Pepy I (•p. 98), the Faiyum group was produced wholly by casting, using the 'lost-wax' method; while one of the group (Ortiz no. 37) represents the earliest occurrence of copper-gold alloy (similar to Japanese *shakudo*) so far encountered.

In their original state, with lifelike eyes and lavish, contrasting inlays or overlays of gold and electrum, the assemblage must have been breathtaking; today, despite the corrosion and deliberate stripping of much of their precious metal embellishment prior to burial (perhaps during Hyksos times), the dramatic presence of the sculptures is undiminished.

THE FAIYUM BRONZES

COLLECTION	DESCRIPTION
George Ortiz, Geneva, cat. 36	bust of king wearing *nemes*
Munich ÄS 6982	standing king
George Ortiz, Geneva, cat. 37	kneeling king
George Ortiz, Geneva, cat. 35	standing queen
private colln., Geneva	queen's wig
George Ortiz, Geneva, cat. 33	standing official, Senwosret
George Ortiz, Geneva, cat. 34	standing official, Senebsuma
Louvre E27153	standing official
Munich ÄS 7105	standing official
Munich ÄS 6080	crocodile

211

Discovery/excavation
1974
by
Miroslav Verner

Site
Abusir (pyramid complex of Raneferef)

Period
Old Kingdom, 5th Dynasty, reign of Raneferef, 2419–2416 BC

'The Czech excavations ... have revealed a wealth of interesting material. The enormous Fifth Dynasty tomb of the vizier Ptahshepses has yielded new information on the dazzling career of this royal hairdresser ... while the excavation of a hitherto unknown pyramid complex of a Queen Khentkaus added a new dimension [to the history of the period. But the] expedition's most important discovery was the identification of an unfinished pyramid as the burial place of Raneferef ....'
MIROSLAV VERNER

MIROSLAV VERNER (1941-)

- Born 1941
- Studies Egyptology and Prehistoric Archaeology at Charles University, Prague, 1960–65; Ph.D. 1969, 1991
- Assistant Professor, Charles University, 1991; Professor, 1993
- Field Director, Czech Institute of Egyptology excavations at Abusir and Abusir South, 1976; Head of Czech Institute, 1978

A cluster of pyramids belonging to the rulers of the 5th Dynasty is aligned on a rough diagonal along the desert cliffs at Abusir, north of Saqqara. At one end of this diagonal, to the southwest of the mortuary complex of King Neferirkare, the existence of an unfinished pyramid had long been known, though the identity of its owner remained uncertain. A glimmer of light was shone on the problem by a fleeting reference in the Abusir Papyri (•p. 87) – fragment 45C – to an additional mortuary complex within striking distance of Neferirkare's tomb. The complex in question was assigned to Raneferef, an obscure successor-king of the 5th Dynasty who was most probably identical with Neferirkare's son.

Excavations had first been carried out at the site at the turn of the 19th century by the German Egyptologist Ludwig Borchardt (•p. 136), but with little result. Armed with the information of the Abusir texts, however, the Egyptologists of Charles University, Prague, under the direction of Miroslav Verner, determined to take another look. Verner's geophysical survey of the site revealed the presence of a large mortuary temple of mudbrick, originally with large, wood-columned hall, to the east of the pyramid base; and, just beyond the point where Borchardt had abandoned his digging, a limestone block with a quarrymark containing the cartouche of Raneferef confirmed the suspected identification.

The complex revealed

The excavators believe that Raneferef had died perhaps as young as 20, and before work on his pyramid had progressed much beyond the lower levels. After his death, the wall-

(below) The pyramid field of Abusir, the principal funerary monuments shown (left to right) being those of Raneferef, Neferirkare, Niuserre, Ptahshepses, Sahure and Shepseskare(?), and the sun temples of Userkaf and Niuserre.

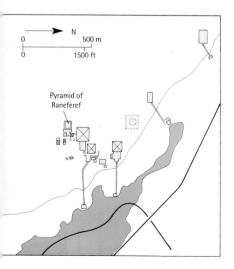

Pyramid of Raneferef

(left) 'The Mound' – the mastaba-like first layer of Raneferef's unfinished pyramid at Abusir, before excavation, as seen from the pyramid of Neferirkare.

1978
The Verses of
Cornelius Gallus

Greco-Roman papyri, as we have seen (•p. 107), are not uncommon survivals in the dry, preservative sands of the Egyptian desert. Of these, it must be said that few are of actual historical consequence, and only the tiniest fraction can today be directly connected with figures of note. One, long known, is a document in Leiden (G6) bearing what is supposed to be the signature of Ptolemy IX (107–88 BC) – one of the earliest autographs in the world; another is a letter thought to be in the hand of the Roman emperor Severus Alexander (AD 222–235), from the vast Oxyrhynchus archive.

A more recent find in a similar vein comes from the Nubian fortress site of Qasr Ibrim (ancient Primis; *right*), now being excavated by the Egypt Exploration Society – part of a papyrus roll bearing verses of the Roman Prefect

of Egypt, Cornelius Gallus, lover of the slave Lycoris and cultured friend of Strabo. Though held in high regard by Augustus, Gallus became (as Lemprière, the classical encyclopaedist delicately puts it) 'forgetful of the favours which he had received, and he pillaged the province, and then conspired against his benefactor … for which he was banished ….

This disgrace operated so powerfully upon him, that he killed himself in despair'.

Why should this important Roman's verses turn up at Qasr Ibrim? The publishers of the text 'exclude the pleasant speculation that', while in Egypt, 'Gallus sent a copy of his own works to the client prince whom he installed' there after 20 BC. But I wonder…

tops were levelled-off by a successor and faced with white limestone (much of it stripped away in the New Kingdom) to transform the structure into a mastaba-type tomb with flat top and square ground-plan; no doubt this led to its unofficial appellation at the time – 'the Mound'.

Fascinating as this new information is, it is the finds from the site which have caused the greatest stir. These include a range of fine, if fragmentary, sculptures of the king (including six portraits) in pink limestone, diorite, basalt, quartzite and wood, all from the mortuary temple's columned hall; wooden images of captives, from this same area; two wooden cult boats; and a large quantity of sealings of various types, gilded faience appliqués from boxes(?), tools, and vessels in a range of hard stones.

Most important of all, however, are the papyri – a second Abusir hoard which promises to shed even more light on the workings of the Egyptian state at this time. These documents (which are still being studied) comprise many large sections and over 2,000 smaller fragments, and include several unique royal decrees. They were found in the northwest part of the temple where, originally rolled

Fragmentary faience tile of exceptional quality, from the mortuary temple of the pyramid, with remains of two divine figures from adjacent scenes, highlighted with gold foil overlay.

213

and fastened around with leather thongs to be placed in wooden storage chests, they had been roughly tipped out in antiquity.

The Czech excavations indicate that Raneferef's mortuary institution began to fall into decline as early as the reign of Djedkare, and, by the time of Pepy II, had ceased to celebrate the king's memory. The anarchy of the First Intermediate Period will have witnessed the robbery of the tomb complex – a blow from which, it seems, despite a brief revival of the royal cult at the start of the Middle Kingdom, neither it nor the other mortuary establishments at Abusir was ever able fully to recover.

(right) The Czech excavations in progress, the pyramid of Neferirkare in the background.

(above) French papyrologist Paule Posener-Kriéger and Antiquities Inspector Usama el-Hamzawi with the newly discovered statuette of the pyramid owner (right). Delicately modelled in fine limestone, the piece still retains considerable traces of its original colour.

(far right) Among the most important finds from Verner's work have been extensive quantities of papyrus documents – here a section of a roll from the archives of Raneferef's mortuary temple.

NEW KINGDOM TOMBS AT SAQQARA

1978 A Treasure of Ramesses XI • 1982 The Face of Most Ancient Egypt
1981 The Colossal Statue of Meryetamun

Discovery/excavation
since 1975
by
Geoffrey T. Martin

Site
Saqqara

Period
New Kingdom, 18th–19th
Dynasties, 1550–1196 BC

'A visitor to the site before 1975 would have viewed a landscape uncluttered by monuments of any kind .... An observant visitor might have noticed rough rectangular depressions in the sand: the outlines of buried tomb courtyards.'
GEOFFREY MARTIN

One of the richest sources of antiquities for the early explorers was the New Kingdom necropolis at Saqqara, though the precise find-spots of many of the pieces, which subsequently found their way to a number of museums, remained uncertain. Geoffrey T. Martin decided to investigate the problem on the ground. What he was particularly looking for was the tomb of Maya – Tutankhamun's treasurer, and a prominent official in the administration of the Theban royal necropolis. Lepsius's map in hand (he had been the last to investigate the area), what Martin in fact found was the lost tomb of Horemheb – as it turned out a far greater prize – though Maya, obligingly, would follow a few seasons later.

Horemheb

'Shortly after the excavation opened it became clear that we had been fortunate enough to come down exactly on top of one of the most important tombs of the New Kingdom in the Memphite necropolis, that of Horemheb, commander-in-chief of Tutankhamun.'
GEOFFREY MARTIN

GEOFFREY THORNDIKE MARTIN (1934–)

- Born 28 May 1934
- Educated University College London (B.A. 1963); Corpus Christi College, Cambridge and Christ's College Cambridge (M.A. 1966; Ph.D. 1969; Litt.D. 1994)
- Lady Wallis Budge Research Fellow, Christ's College, Cambridge, 1966–70; Lecturer in Egyptology, UCL, 1970–78; Reader, 1978–87; Professor, 1987–88
- Excavated at Buhen, Sudan, 1963; Saqqara, since 1964; Valley of the Kings (with Nicholas Reeves), since 1998; epigraphic work/excavation in the royal wadi at el-Amarna, 1969, 1980

4000 BC
3000 BC
2000 BC
1000 BC
0
AD 700

soon became apparent as the outline of the surviving walls emerged from the sand, revealing their wonderfully carved relief scenes.

Although only a few of these reliefs had been left *in situ*, the decoration of the tomb could be partially completed by those blocks which, during the 19th century, had been removed to Leiden and London together with a large stela and a range of statues of the owner and his wife. Other blocks had been reused in the structure of the nearby Coptic monastery of Apa Jeremias – a liberty which the general would have been in no position to complain of: a number of the blocks *his* builders had used were themselves appropriated from earlier structures in the area, including the Step Pyramid.

The tomb reliefs tell us a great deal about the historical situation in Egypt at the close of the 18th Dynasty, particularly in Horemheb's specialist field – the military – with evidence of battles, plunder and captives during the reign of his ward, the young Tutankhamun. But about Horemheb himself, the man and his personal life, they reveal frustratingly little.

Four Old Kingdom burial shafts had been appropriated and adapted for the underground elements of the tomb. The excavators believe that the principal shaft had been employed for the interments of the anonymous first wife of Horemheb and for his better-known second wife, Mutnodjmet; Horemheb himself was clearly buried in the tomb he later prepared in the Valley of the Kings – KV57, uncovered by Theodore Davis in 1908 (•p. 117).

Excavation of a subsidiary shaft located in the outer courtyard yielded several items of Ramessid burial equipment, the most spectacular of which – a magnificent gold

The Memphite tomb of Horemheb, prepared before the great general and regent of Tutankhamun ascended the throne in his own right following the death of King Ay, was excavated over several seasons between 1975 and 1978 by the Egypt Exploration Society in collaboration with the Rijksmuseum van Oudheden, Leiden. The original magnificence of the structure – which measured almost 50 m (165 ft) in length and had a pylon once standing over 7 m (23 ft) high constructed of stone-clad mud-brick –

(previous page, left) Door-jamb at the entrance to Horemheb's tomb-chapel.

(previous page, right) Scribes record the living booty from Horemheb's conquests.

(top) The second courtyard of the tomb-superstructure, as reconstructed by Martin and the EES/Leiden team.

(left) Nubian captives, their individual features masterfully captured by the artist's chisel.

(left) The victorious Horemheb is rewarded by his king, the young Tutankhamun: gold collars of valour are set in place by the military officer's retainers.

(below) Asiatic and Libyan chieftains supplicate before the all-powerful Tutankhamun, while an Egyptian interpreter relays their grovelling words.

1978
A Treasure of Ramesses XI

'One evening, when everyone else had packed up and gone home, I suddenly noticed a particularly smooth block of stone [at the mouth of the shaft within tomb KV4 in the Valley of the Kings]. It shifted easily, and underneath I was amazed to see a complete statue of Ramesses XI; at his feet a heap of treasure gleaming in sunlight for the first time in three millennia ...'
JOHN ROMER

John Romer's clearance of the tomb of Ramesses XI (KV 4)

'treated' within KV4, it seems, was Hatshepsut – Romer was able to salvage several fragments of her regal wooden coffin from the debris of the tomb's deep shaft; while fragments from the burial of her step-son, Tuthmosis III, were also found.

Ramesses XI himself had never employed KV4 – political uncertainty evidently prompted him to seek burial in the north, in a tomb as yet undiscovered – and Romer's work yielded few finds from the reign. Among these, however, were three of an original four foundation deposits placed at the mouth of the burial-chamber shaft;

between 1978 and 1980 revealed many fragments relating to its reuse at the end of the New Kingdom as a workshop for the stripping of the royal dead by the government commission charged with dismantling the necropolis. Among the dead so

and within this assemblage of plaques and images was a beeswax figure of the king standing before the goddess Maat. A rare and beautiful sculptor's model – originally intended, we may guess, to be cast in metal – it is now displayed in Luxor Museum.

217

ear-pendant with central medallion showing a sphinx rampant – is perhaps to be associated with the burial of Bintanat, a daughter of Ramesses II who seems to have been interred here during the reign of her brother, Merenptah.

Other small finds of interest included Mycenaean potsherds, masses of broken 18th-Dynasty burial equipment, and a hieratic wine-jar docket dating to Horemheb's Year 13. This is the highest reign-year so far attested for this king, and for Martin and his colleagues it reflects the probable date of Mutnodjmet's interment.

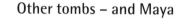

(right) Elaborate gold ear-pendant from the Horemheb excavations – believed to originate from a later, Ramessid burial at the site, that of the princess Bintanat.

(opposite, left) Detail of a limestone dyad of Maya and Meryet, removed from the tomb during the 19th century and now in the Rijksmuseum, Leiden.

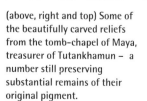

(above, right and top) Some of the beautifully carved reliefs from the tomb-chapel of Maya, treasurer of Tutankhamun – a number still preserving substantial remains of their original pigment.

Other tombs – and Maya

'My God, it's Maya!'
JACOBUS VAN DIJK

Following on from the discovery of Horemheb's funerary monument, the extension of the EES–Leiden work would uncover several further tombs. The first of these – belonging to another Ramessid princess, Tia – was located in 1975 and cleared in 1982; two others – constructed during the reign of Ramesses II for an overseer of builders named Paser and for one Raia, a chief of singers in the Memphite temple of Ptah – were found in 1981. But it was not until 1986, 11 years after the search had first begun, that Geoffrey Martin's original quarry – Maya – at last came into view.

'At the beginning of February 1986, in excavating one of the shafts in the courtyard of an army officer, Ramose … we found that we were able to enter the subterranean parts of a tomb adjacent on the north through a robbers' tunnel … [W]e … were not in a particular hurry, not expecting to find anything dramatic, and being concerned at that stage with the prosaic business of manoeuvring into position the cable for our generator … A second or two passed; my Dutch colleague and I held the light bulb above our heads and gazed down beyond the stairway. We were totally unprepared for the sight that met our eyes: a room, full of carved reliefs, painted a rich golden yellow!'

As the courtyard above was cleared, many more beautiful reliefs of Maya were recovered, the best still preserving extensive remains of the original paint. Within the extraordinary painted chambers themselves, the original burial equipment had been well pillaged in antiquity and, in the moist conditions prevailing, only a few scraps (if of superb quality) could be recovered by the excavators. Among other things, what these scraps tell us is that Maya died during the reign of Horemheb, and that he shared his tomb with his wife Meryet – the elegant woman depicted in the tomb's reliefs and in the wonderful Leiden pair-statue which first inspired Geoffrey Martin to embark on his quest.

1982
The Face of Most Ancient Egypt

The earliest phases of human activity in the Nile valley were encountered in 1901 at Thebes by the German Georg Schweinfurth. Further contributions to Egyptian prehistory were made by Gertrude Caton-Thompson, digging in the Northern Faiyum between 1924 and 1928, where she discovered two previously unidentified Neolithic cultures; and by Hermann Junker at the site of Merimda-Beni Salama in the western Delta, which he excavated for ten years between 1929 and 1938. The continuation of the Merimda excavations by the German Archaeological Institute in 1982 brought to light the earliest sculptural work known from Egypt. This crudely modelled but dynamic head (Cairo JE 97472) dates from the latter part of the 5th millennium BC. At just over 10 cm (4 in) in height, it seems originally to have been mounted on a stick, with its face perhaps embellished with tufts of hair.

1981
The Colossal Statue of Meryetamun

Two decades ago, Akhmim – situated across the Nile from modern Sohag and a settlement of some importance in antiquity – was the site of an extraordinary discovery. Building works in the suburbs to the northeast of the town revealed a number of sculpted stone fragments, including part of an immense, serpent-bedecked *modius* with double-feathered crown. For Egyptologists, the find came as something of a surprise in an area which had previously yielded little, but it hit no headlines. And then, in 1981, the statue to which the headdress belonged was uncovered nearby.

Carved in limestone and measuring more than 6.5 m (21 ft) tall, the new Akhmim statue was first encountered lying face down before the remains of a temple gateway dating back to the 19th Dynasty and before.

A spectacular find, described as one of the outstanding examples of 19th-Dynasty sculpture, this was no ordinary, kingly colossus: for, unusually, the subject was a queen, Meryetamun, principal consort of Ramesses II after the death of Nefertari, identified by a vertical column of hieroglyphic text on its dorsal pillar.

1987
A TOMB FOR THE SONS OF RAMESSES II

Discovery/excavation
1987
by
Kent R. Weeks

Site
Thebes (Valley of the Kings, tomb KV5)

Period
New Kingdom, 19th Dynasty, reign of Ramesses II, 1290–1224 BC

4000 BC
3000 BC
2000 BC
1000 BC
0
AD 700

"'Kent! Kent! It's fantastic! Oh, it's so wonderful! Come back here! Please!'
… Twenty minutes later, we crawled out of the tomb, sweating and filthy and smiling. As the magnitude of our discovery began to sink in, I thought to myself, "I think I know how we're going to be spending the next twenty years". I turned to shake hands and receive congratulatory hugs from our ecstatic workmen. Everyone smiled and laughed and kept repeating, "This is the biggest tomb in the valley! The biggest tomb in the valley!"'
KENT WEEKS

The most familiar sites often yield the most surprising results – and tomb KV5 in the Valley of the Kings is a good example of this phenomenon. The tomb had stood partially open since the early years of the 19th century at least, when, in 1825, the first three debris-filled chambers were examined by the British Egyptologist James Burton. Howard Carter seems to have taken a peek, too, in 1902, before the entrance was lost to sight a short time later. Relocated by American Egyptologist Kent R. Weeks in 1985/86, the extraordinary scale of the monument only became apparent when digging began in earnest in 1987. The number of rooms so far brought to light has risen from Burton's three to well over a hundred, many with walls decorated in relief, arranged in the somewhat disconcerting manner of 'an octopus, with a body surrounded by tentacles'.

The tomb is now known to have been intended as a mausoleum for the sons of Ramesses II – a far from exclusive club with the names of at least 52 members recorded – of whose burial equipment (sarcophagi, coffins, canopic chests and jars, *shabti*-figures, jewelry, chariots and pottery) a good many broken fragments have so far been

(opposite above) An image of Osiris, lord of the Underworld, carved in the rock face at the junction of the T-shaped corridor complex, as first encountered. The face was damaged in antiquity.

(opposite below) The excavator and his assistant carefully search the dust and rubble for fragmentary remains of wall plaster and ancient burial equipment.

(left) The extraordinary underground labyrinth revealed by Kent Weeks's excavations in KV5 – so far. The work of clearance is still ongoing, and further chambers may be anticipated.

(below) The walls of several chambers within KV5 were originally decorated in delicate relief in applied lime plaster. Since antiquity, however, these have been much destroyed and now present the excavators with an intriguing reconstruction challenge; a detail of Chamber 1, west wall, south half.

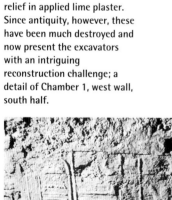

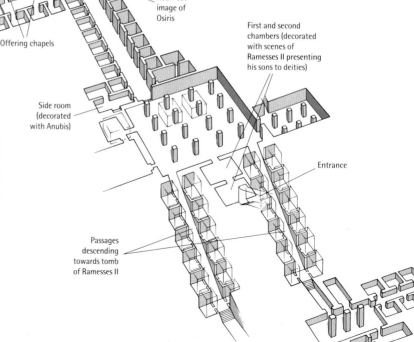

Rock-cut image of Osiris

Offering chapels

First and second chambers (decorated with scenes of Ramesses II presenting his sons to deities)

Side room (decorated with Anubis)

Entrance

Passages descending towards tomb of Ramesses II

recovered, as well as several bodies in varying states of preservation.

The final completion of this work – with the conservation difficulties the clearance of such an extensive underground complex inevitably throws up – promises to take many years yet, and the full publication longer still. If the chance of finding rich and undisturbed burials here must be considered slight – it is a tomb which suffered an attempted robbery during the reign of Ramesses III, and was systematically stripped by the necropolis administration at the end of the New Kingdom – there is little doubt that, architecturally at least, KV5 has a story of enormous interest yet to tell.

> 'the tomb probably contains more than 150 corridors and chambers, and we have cleared fewer than 7 percent of them.... But I am convinced that when we have finished, KV5 will be the best-documented and best-protected tomb in the Valley ... and its former occupants, the sons of Ramesses II, will have given us more information about their lives and their society than we have today ...'
> KENT WEEKS

AKHENATEN'S PRIME MINISTER, APEREL

Discovery/excavation
1987–97
by
Alain-Pierre Zivie

Site
Saqqara

Period
New Kingdom, 18th Dynasty,
reigns of Amenophis III
and Akhenaten,
1391–1335 BC

4000 BC

3000 BC

2000 BC

1000 BC

0

AD 700

'After 10 years of searching and digging, archaeologist Alain Zivie reached a sealed chamber more than 60 feet below the Egyptian sands.

He breached the wall and was almost overcome by the foul smell of an ancient tomb. From the light of a pocket torch, he was able to see a vault six feet across, rich in relics, jewellery, funeral figures and burial urns.

Professor Zivie stepped hesitantly forward to become the first man to enter the tomb in 3,300 years.

He knew then he had made an important discovery, but it is only now that the real significance is coming to light ...'
SUNDAY EXPRESS

During my first season of fieldwork in Egypt, with the Egypt Exploration Society at North Saqqara, I often wandered down to the base of the cliff below the Antiquities Service rest-house to peer into the barely accessible rock-cut chapels of Aperel and his contemporaries, wondering why we were not digging here, in this far more appealing collection of nooks and crannies, than in the less than

compelling remains of the destroyed, Late Period temple known as the Anubieion. Two years later, a French Egyptologist, independently inspired by the site, began work here. Not long after, he would reveal, hidden beneath a false staircase, the man's barely disturbed and richly provisioned burial chamber – one of the most important archaeological discoveries to be made in recent times.

The hidden chamber

Work on investigating the cliff face into which the tomb of Aperel (or Aperia, as his name is sometimes written) had been cut was undertaken in 1981 by Alain-Pierre Zivie and the Mission archéologique française du Bubastieion – named after the ancient temple of the cat-goddess Bastet, whose mummified creatures had been packed into the corridors and shafts of the earlier tombs situated below. Digging through the unhealthy debris of the tomb's

(below) The burial chamber as first encountered by Zivie's team – a delicate, chaotic mass of broken funerary furniture. Its successful clearance, over several seasons, has been a triumph of human patience and archaeological technique.

(below) The cliff face at Saqqara into which the tomb of Aperel (its entrance is visible immediately below the end wall of the Antiquities Service rest-house) and other New Kingdom worthies were cut.

later feline occupants was difficult and unpleasant, and it would be a dusty seven years before the burial chamber of Aperel was finally reached in the fourth and lowermost level of the tomb substructure, some 20 m (66 ft) below ground level.

It was an astonishing find: the burial chamber proved had been concealed beneath a false staircase – a far from unique subterfuge, perhaps, judging from the 'testing' to which many tomb staircases appear to have been subjected over the years. Despite Aperel's cunning, however, the chamber had been penetrated in antiquity (perhaps by the undertakers themselves) before being reclosed – the condition in which Zivie found it. What had the robbers left behind?

'The room contained the once-mummified bones and a part of the funerary equipment and "treasury" of three people: 'Aper-El himself … his wife, Tauret, and his son, Huy … Excavation of the artefacts was very difficult, because wooden objects had been either dismantled or broken up, and at one stage fire on the third level transformed the room into a furnace and the material suffered severe scorching …

Some of the objects discovered are quite exceptional because they are beautiful, or rare, or both. A short list from among the myriad objects is headed by coffins with masks full of life, the wood originally gilded and retaining wonderful glass inlays. There are canopic jars of the lady Tauret, [Taweret] or of 'Aper-El himself, whose lids are precious pieces of sculpture, alabaster vessels, ceramics imported from the Aegean world, jewels, amulets, cubits and so on. Despite the plundering there was a relatively large quantity of gold from the coffins or spread about the room …'

(above) Beautifully modelled wooden mask from the innermost coffin of Taweret, with eye-inlays of coloured glass.

(below left) The face of Taweret's second (middle coffin).

(below right) Alain Zivie in the tomb of Maia, Tutankhamun's wet-nurse, shortly after its discovery in 1997. The tomb owner, wearing a heavy wig and with her hands raised in adoration, may be seen in the partially cleared wall decoration.

(right) Three of the four limestone canopic jars prepared for Taweret, Aperel's wife.

Who was Aperel?

Aperel's principal title was that of vizier, an office he seemingly held during the reigns of Amenophis III and Akhenaten, and among his other titles he could number those of 'god's father' and 'child of the *kap*', or royal nursery. His name, however, is clearly a semitic one. A foreigner as prime minister of Egypt? Or a man merely of foreign lineage? Many problems relating to this mysterious tomb and its intriguing owner wait to be addressed.

Tutankhamun's wet-nurse

Further tombs have since been cleared by Zivie's mission among the cemetery of the Bubastieion cats. Most significant of all is the burial place of the previously unknown wet-nurse of Tutankhamun, Maia – 'the one who has fed the god's body' – with its unique and now famous depiction of the young king seated on the woman's knee. As Zivie rightly observes, 'Her tomb' – which is not yet fully excavated – 'may throw light on the still-obscure origins of this famous king and on events at the end of the Amarna period when the court returned to Memphis'.

223

Discovery/excavation
1987
by
Manfred Bietak

Site
Tell el-Daba

Period
Second Intermediate Period,
15th Dynasty
c. 1525 BC

'The Aegean connections of the early 18th Dynasty [at Tell el-Daba] remain a puzzle to us .... One conclusion can be drawn, however: that the site of Avaris, because of its excellent strategic situation at the north-eastern border, was important not only for the Hyksos but for the early 18th Dynasty also.'

MANFRED BIETAK

The Austrians, under the direction of Manfred Bietak, have been excavating at Tell el-Daba in the eastern Nile Delta – a site known for over a century but long ignored – since 1966. Thanks to Bietak's recent work here, our understanding of the history and topography of Egypt during the 2nd millennium BC has been completely transformed: for the Austrian excavations have proved beyond any reasonable doubt that Tell el-Daba is the city of Avaris, capital of the Hyksos rulers of the 15th Dynasty referred to in the Kamose texts (•p. 202). Avaris had previously, and erroneously, been located by Egyptologists at Tanis (•p. 189), in part due to Mariette's discovery there in 1863 of the 'Stela of 400 Years' and the so-called 'Hyksos sphinxes' (•p. 53).

In 1987 Manfred Bietak's brilliant work at Tell el-Daba revealed, at Ezbet Helmi, what many would previously have believed impossible: fragments of painted wall plaster decorated not with traditional Egyptian motifs but with scenes of 'bull-leaping' and other activities associated with the Minoans of Crete in the 2nd millennium BC, executed in pure Aegean style in fresco with details *al secco*. As excavations have continued, the total number of such fragments has increased to several thousands, some still *in situ* on walls of a monumental mud-brick structure at the site. As a result, Minoan fresco painting is now better represented in Egypt than in its Cretan homeland. Despite the Cretans' sea-going prowess, the explanation for the presence of such non-portable Aegean antiquities on Egyptian soil is still unclear; but Bietak suggests:

'As Minoan art is primarily ritual it is only logical to suppose that the representations in Avaris were also for ritual purposes and were not simply decorative art destined to adorn the palace of the ruler or high officials. The ritual significance of the wall paintings

MANFRED BIETAK (1940–)

- Born Vienna, 6 October 1940
- Studies Prehistory and Egyptology, University of Vienna; Ph.D 1964
- Participates and directs Austrian excavations at Sayala/Nubia, 1961–65
- Director of the excavations at Tell el-Daba, 1966–69 and 1975 to the present; and in Late Period necropolis, Western Thebes, 1969–78

(below) A reconstruction (from small though diagnostic fragments) by the Austrian Archaeological Institute of one of the scenes which formerly embellished the interior walls of a building at Tell el-Daba. The background maze pattern and representations of 'bull-leaping' are characteristically Minoan.

would point to the conclusion that Minoans lived in Avaris and in close contact with the ruling class there, and that they were able to pursue their own ritual life.'

Similar fragments, it may be noted, have been found at other sites outside Thera and Crete – at both Tell Kabri and Alalakh in Syria, attesting to the breadth and depth of international contact at this time. The Ezbet Helmi paintings were executed at the end of the 15th Dynasty and destroyed, the archaeologists tell us, at a date between Year 11 and Year 15 of Ahmose.

(below) Fragmentary detail of another section of decorated wall: a hunting dog is unleashed on two deer or gazelles, fleeing through a rocky landscape.

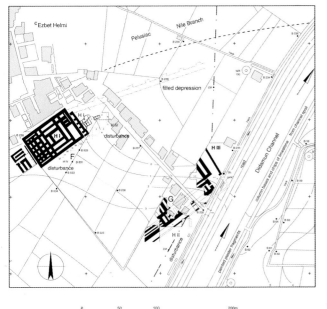

(left) Ezbet Helmi, findspot of the Minoan painting fragments – a plan showing the remains of structures so far excavated superimposed on the modern landscape.

1987
An Asiatic Dignitary

Tell el-Daba has been the scene of several important discoveries over recent years – none more problematic than the remains of this striking limestone statue, almost twice life size, which was uncovered in 1987.

A seated tomb figure, the subject is clearly an Asiatic dignitary of the early 2nd millennium BC, shown wrapped in a multi-coloured shawl, clutching a throwstick to his right shoulder. Intentionally destroyed and its features completely obliterated during a subsequent period of political turmoil, the fragments had been buried in a robbers' pit sunk into the floor of a tomb chapel of the late 12th Dynasty. Although fragmentary in the extreme, the original quality of the carving was excellent.

The Tell el-Daba image is without parallel in Egypt itself, though a very similar, if less accomplished, sculpture is known from 18th-century BC Ebla in Syria.

The el-Daba statue fragments – as much else at this site – are intriguing, and for at least one historian, David Rohl, of immense significance. According to him, they are nothing less than the remains 'of a cult statue of [the biblical] Joseph, awarded to him by Amenemhat [Ammenemes] III for the Hebrew vizier's outstanding services to the Egyptian nation during a time of great trials and tribulations'.

THE LUXOR STATUE CACHE

1989 The Dush Treasure

Discovery/excavation
1989
by
Mohammed el-Saghir

Site
Thebes (Luxor temple)

Period
New Kingdom–Late Period,
1479–750 BC

'President Mubarak visited Luxor to see the unearthing of the first five statues, which had been found 3ft beneath the surface during cleaning operations in January 1989, but no one expected a further 19 pieces of statuary to come from beneath the temple, each carefully buried under a layer of small stones ....'
EGYPTIAN ARCHAEOLOGY

One of the most dramatic finds of recent years was the unexpected discovery, beneath the solar court of Amenophis III at Luxor Temple, of a large group of statues of exceptionally high quality, a number in an excellent state of preservation. Buried at the time of the Roman conversion of the area into a military camp during the late 3rd century AD, they would remain hidden for the next millennium and a half – until uncovered during the course of routine maintenance by the Luxor antiquities inspectorate under the overall direction of Mohammed el-Saghir on 22 January 1989.

The first piece to be brought to light in the course of this work was a rectangular plinth of diorite lying north–south and recessed on its top surface for two statues. The following day, further digging revealed a magnificent image of the divine Amenophis III standing on a sled, carved in a beautiful, purple-red quartzite. A gentle brushing revealed it to be a sculpture without equal in any collection of Egyptian art anywhere in the world.

Following checks to establish that further digging would not destabilize the surrounding temple structure, work resumed on 9 February, establishing the original form of the pit – an oval measuring 3 by 3.8 m (10 by 12 ½ ft) – in which the statues had been deposited. Further digging uncovered more statues at a depth of 2.5 m (8 ft) below ground level – images of the pharaohs Amenophis III and Horemheb and of the deities Hathor, Iunyt and Atum. All were sculptures of the finest quality, and by a miracle preserved intact. And there were further revelations to come:

(above) The goddess Hathor – a life-sized sculpture from the reign of Amenophis III, carved in grey granite and perfectly preserved.

(far left) The statue-pit in Amenophis III's solar court at Luxor Temple. The columns of the king's colonnade are clearly visible in the background.

(left) Readying the newly found sculptures for removal from their ancient hiding place.

THE STATUES FROM THE LUXOR CACHE

DESCRIPTION	MATERIAL	DATE	SIZE
Tuthmosis III, kneeling, headless	black granite	Tuthmosis III	H 0.59 m
Tuthmosis III as sphinx	alabaster	Tuthmosis III	L 0.95 m
Queen Isis, seated, fragment, headless	black granite	Tuthmosis III	H 0.63 m
Amenophis III, standing	quartzite	Amenophis III	H 2.49 m
Amenophis III with Horus, seated	basalt	Amenophis III	H 0.46 m
Amenophis III as sphinx, headless	greywacke/sandstone	Amenophis III	L 0.51 m
the goddess Hathor, seated	diorite	Amenophis III	H 1.54 m
the goddess Iunyt, seated	grey granite	Amenophis III	H 1.45 m
falcon on papyrus capital	alabaster	Amenophis III	H 0.96 m
Tutankhamun as sphinx	alabaster	Tutankhamun	L 0.56 m
Horemheb kneeling before Atum	diorite	Tutankhamun?	H 1.91 m
Horemheb and Amun	diorite	Tutankhamun?	H 1.52 m
Horemheb, headless, and Amun	diorite	Tutankhamun?	H 1.41 m
Ramesses II, kneeling, headless	alabaster	Ramesses II	H 0.77 m
the god Amun and consort Mut, seated	alabaster	Ramesses II?	H 2.48 m
sphinx fragment, headless	limestone	New Kingdom or later	L 0.92 m
sphinx fragment, headless	sandstone	New Kingdom or later	L 0.43 m
lion, recumbent	limestone	New Kingdom or later	L 0.87 m
falcon statue	alabaster	New Kingdom or later	H 0.74 m
ba-bird statue	sandstone	New Kingdom or later	H 0.23 m
double crown	rose granite	New Kingdom or later	H 0.50 m
double feather headdress	sandstone	New Kingdom or later	H 0.65 m
the god's wife Amenirdis I	black granite	temp. Kashta	H 0.77 m
Amun-Re-Kamutef serpent	grey granite	temp. Taharqa	H 1.52 m
Amun-Re-Kamutef serpent	grey granite	temp. Taharqa?	H 1.00 m
the goddess Taweret	sandstone	temp. Taharqa?	H 0.61 m

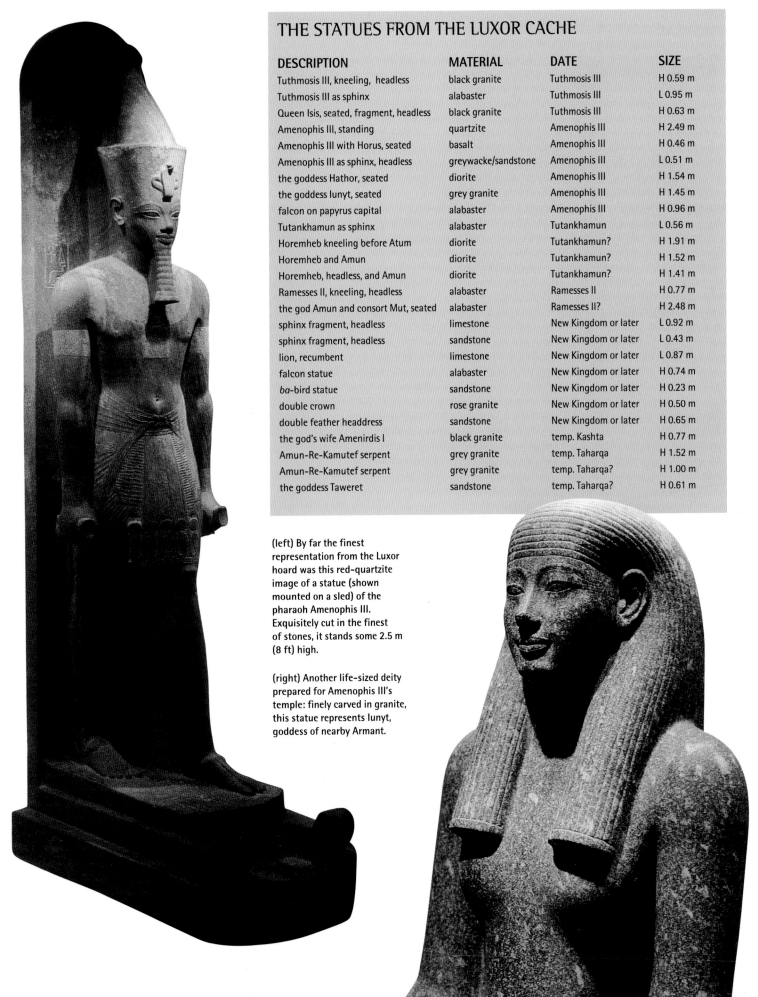

(left) By far the finest representation from the Luxor hoard was this red-quartzite image of a statue (shown mounted on a sled) of the pharaoh Amenophis III. Exquisitely cut in the finest of stones, it stands some 2.5 m (8 ft) high.

(right) Another life-sized deity prepared for Amenophis III's temple: finely carved in granite, this statue represents Iunyt, goddess of nearby Armant.

when the waterlogged lower levels of the pit were explored towards the end of February, yet more statues were uncovered, including an alabaster sphinx of Tutankhamun.

Other objects of interest have come to light at Luxor during the course of the recent conservation drive within the Amenophis III colonnaded court – including foundation deposits and 'twelve hieratic texts … inscribed on the temple's foundations, the preliminary translations of which indicate [that] these discuss the original planning and construction of the temple'. Further details are keenly awaited.

(left) Kneeling figure of Horemheb, from a composite image mounted on a separate tableau showing the king making offering to the god Amun.

(right) Though his features are not immediately recognizable, this alabaster sphinx (with separately carved double crown), still preserving substantial traces of its original paint, was carved in the reign of Tutankhamun.

1989
The Dush Treasure

The modern settlement of Dush marks the site of the Greco-Roman town of Kysis in Kharga Oasis, largest of the western oases situated in the Libyan Desert some 175 km (110 miles) west of Luxor. Dush is dominated today by the remains of a stone-built temple dedicated both to Osiris and to Sarapis and Isis, and an adjacent mud-brick 'fort', the walls of which still stand in places to a height of 12 m (30 ft). During the excavation of a small room in the western sector of this mud-brick magazine complex, in March 1989, a loose-lidded pottery jar of 4th–5th century date was unearthed which had originally been concealed in the masonry structure. Close by were a linen-wrapped, gilded lead statuette of Isis, a small bronze figure of Horus dressed as a Roman legionary, and a bronze Osiris.

When the lid of the jar was removed, the excavators were amazed to glimpse the characteristic matte-yellow

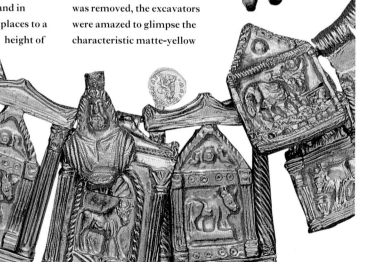

of ancient gold. Squashed into the container was a hoard of precious metal jewelry totalling well over 1 kg (2 lb) in weight. Cautiously, delicately the gleaming contents were prised out – to reveal an elaborate gold crown (*above*) and two gold bracelets, a gold pendant collar (*left*), and a whole collection of plaques and other items.

The assemblage comprises two distinct classes of material: higher quality, 1st–2nd century sacerdotal objects (the crown and bracelets) and cheap, repoussé ex-votos of somewhat later date. The items were already old when they were grabbed and hidden for safety in a time of imminent danger, presumably by a member of the temple priesthood.

THE TOMBS OF THE
PYRAMID BUILDERS AT GIZA

1993 Surprises of a Theban Tomb

Discovery/excavation
1990
by
Zahi Hawass

Site
Giza

Period
Old Kingdom, 4th–6th
Dynasties, 2575–2134 BC

(below) The field of modest
grave monuments erected for
the pyramid builders at Giza,
located beyond the 'Wall
of the Crow' and excavated
by Egyptian archaeologist
Zahi Hawass.

'The theories that the pyramids were built by people that came out of space, or the Jews or people from Atlantis have been disproved. The major discoveries that we made at Giza were the tombs of the pyramid builders which prove that the Egyptians built the pyramids and that they are the unique people who made this wonderful civilization.'

ZAHI HAWASS

Zahi Hawass, Undersecretary of State for Egypt's Giza Plateau, and his colleagues have many impressive discoveries to their credit, a success based as much on solid research as good fortune, as the following story illustrates.

In 1987, Hawass presented a dissertation to the University of Pennsylvania on the cults of Khufu, Khephren and Menkaure. In this study, he put forward the view that the tombs of the men actually responsible for building the pyramids – as opposed to the various high officials and royal family members whose greatest exertion in the enterprise was the pushing of reed pens – were probably to be located in the area south of the Great Sphinx. He based this theory on the existence of a huge limestone construction popularly known as Heit el-Shorab or 'the Wall of the Crow', which he believed had been built to separate the tombs and living quarters of the lower classes from the pyramids proper.

In 1990, working in co-operation with American archaeologist Mark Lehner, Hawass undertook a trial excavation at the site, bringing to light a few bones but otherwise

ZAHI HAWASS (1947–)

- Born Damietta, 28 May 1947
- B.A. Greek and Roman
  Archaeology, Alexandria,
  followed by Diploma in
  Egyptology, Cairo University,
  1980; M.A. University of
  Pennsylvania, 1983; Ph.D.
  University of Pennsylvania,
  1987
- Inspector of Antiquities
  Department, Egypt, since
  1969, working at many sites
  including Tuna el-Gebel and
  Mallawi, Edfu-Esna, Abydos,
  Alexandria, Giza, Abu Simbel,
  Bahariya Oasis; Chief
  Inspector of Giza Pyramids,
  1980; General-Director of
  Giza, Saqqara and Bahariya
  Oasis, 1987–98;
  Undersecretary of State for
  the Giza Monuments,
  1998–present, undertaking
  extensive excavation and
  conservation work and
  teaching and lecturing
  extensively both in Egypt
  and abroad

nothing of particular note. Work was therefore stopped. A short time later, however, the chief of the pyramid guards, Muhammad Abdel Razek, reported to Hawass that an American tourist had been thrown from her horse in this same area – the animal had stumbled (a means of discovery encountered elsewhere in this book) over a sanded-up and previously unnoticed mud-brick wall. Hawass decided to take another look.

The wall proved to belong to a tomb chapel with a long, vaulted chamber and two false-door stelae to enable the dead to commune with the outside world. Crude hieroglyphs scrawled on these stelae identified the owners as one Ptahshepsesu and his wife, who had been buried, probably with their son, at the back of the chambers in three vertical grave shafts. In front of the vaulted chapel

(below right) A general view of the pyramid-builders' cemetery, with its range of mud-brick superstructures.

was a square courtyard built with low walls of limestone, granite and basalt fragments – waste from the nearby pyramids building site.

The discovery was to prove an astonishing vindication of Hawass's theory: it was the cemetery of the pyramid builders, with further excavation revealing, clustered around Ptahshepsesu's tomb, several small shaft burials prepared by his subordinates. More have come to light, so that the graves of around 30 overseers and the burials of some 600 labourers are now known.

The workers' cemetery

The workers' tombs are modest in the extreme, and exhibit an interesting variety of forms. Some clearly followed the configuration of the giant pyramids, if in an extremely simplified form, with stepped domes, 'beehives', and gabled roofs, each standing between 0.6 and 1 m (2 and 6 ft) in height and covering a rectangular grave pit in which the deceased was interred, unmummified, laid out in a foetal position with his or her face to the east. One of the superstructures featured a miniature ramp leading up to and around its dome, perhaps representing the construction ramp of a royal pyramid. Others among the tombs resemble miniature mastabas with tiny courtyards and inscribed stone doors.

The bodies of the pyramid builders showed evidence not only of the strains and stresses of long-term and very hard physical labour – in particular, degenerative arthritis in the lumbar region and in the knees – but also of effective emergency medical treatment, including the setting of broken limbs (most commonly ulna, radius and fibula) and even two amputations (a left leg and a right arm). The average age of death of the men was 30–35, and that of the women lower still. Two females were dwarves no more than 1 m (3 ft) in height; one had died in childbirth.

As the excavation of what is now termed the lower cemetery continued, a ramp was discovered running up the slope towards the west to an upper level of burials.

1993
Surprises of a Theban Tomb

An integral part of the furniture of the New Kingdom tomb was a statue of the tomb owner, usually carved in stone and often shown seated beside his wife, to act as a focus for the prayers and offerings of family and friends.

Often these statues were sculpted directly into the living rock of the tomb-chapel interior, sometimes on a large scale, where, though battered, they may still be seen. More frequently, however, the statues were freestanding and portable, and as a result today, broken or intact, they have usually been carried off by persons unknown for reuse or for sale. On site, therefore, tomb statues are rare finds; good, well-preserved tomb sculptures are even more uncommon.

It therefore came as a welcome surprise when one such statue was brought to light by Nigel Strudwick of Cambridge University in 1993, during the excavation and documentation of much-destroyed Theban

tomb 99 in Sheikh Abd el-Qurna, Thebes. Carved in sandstone and preserving still extensive remains of its original paint, the piece turned up, headless, in a later, Third Intermediate Period shaft where it had been thrown by intruders; fortunately the head itself, thrown into another shaft nearby, turned up a short time later allowing the piece to be reconstructed.

Interestingly, the subject of this fine sculpture is not the mid-18th Dynasty tomb owner, Sennuferi, but his son-in-law, Amenhotep. Amenhotep's tomb appears to have been located in the 1880s, somewhat higher up the hill, though its precise location is now lost. A false door of the man (perhaps from here?) was found reused at Karnak in 1970.

goddess Neith and king's acquaintance', Intyshedu, showing the owner at different stages of his life. The burial of Intyshedu himself, with its modest pottery equipment, was still intact. Another tomb – that of Nefertjetjes, whom Hawass believes might have been supervisor of the bakery complex recently brought to light by Mark Lehner in the plain below – contains three limestone false-door stelae inscribed with the names of the owner, his two wives and their 18 children. The most interesting of all, however, is the tomb of the man Petety and his wife, with its oddly naive curse:

> *'Listen all of you! The priest of Hathor will beat twice any of you who enters this tomb or does harm to it. The gods will confront him because I am one honoured by his lord. The gods will not allow anything to happen to me. Anyone who does anything bad to my tomb, then the crocodile, the hippopotamus and the lion will eat him.'*

Sadly, it had not saved him: the mummy was long-gone.

The pyramid-workers' cemetery appears to have been in use from the reign of Khufu through until the end of the 5th Dynasty. Only 20 per cent of the site has so far been excavated; if, as Hawass believes, the cemetery 'extends across the escarpment where we have found production and storage facilities', the find represents nothing less than an Old Kingdom Deir el-Medina (•p. 174) – offering a unique and fascinating glimpse into the lives and deaths of the 20,000 and more ordinary men and women responsible for erecting perhaps the greatest monuments of ancient times – the Giza pyramids.

These elevated tombs, so far numbering 43, are larger and more elaborate than those of the lower cemetery, and the titles of their owners reflect their higher status – 'overseer of the side of the pyramid', 'director of the craftsmen', 'overseer of masonry', 'director of workers' and 'director of royal works' being among them. A number of statues of the owners and their family members were recovered from this upper cemetery, four of the best being those of an 'overseer of the boat of the

(above) The small, beehive-shaped, mud-brick superstructure of one of the workers' tombs.

(left) A detail of the limestone false-door of Nefertjetjes, showing the tomb-owner and his son and, below, two men making beer and pouring it into jars.

(right) The curse-inscription from the tomb of Petety and his wife, Nesisokar: 'Anyone who does anything bad to my tomb, then the crocodile, the hippopotamus and the lion will eat him'.

1994
EGYPTOLOGY UNDERWATER: ALEXANDRIA AD AEGYPTUM

1994 Jewels in the Sands and Other Dahshur Finds
1997 The New Vizier • 1995 Iufaa

Discovery/excavation
1994
by
Jean-Yves Empereur;
Frank Goddio

Site
Alexandria

Period
Ptolemaic Period
332–30 BC

The city of Alexandria, as its name indicates, was a foundation of the 4th century BC by the Macedonian conqueror Alexander the Great, who, by tradition, was buried here in the Soma, or royal mausoleum, beneath the mosque of Nebi Daniel. Lacking any substantial previous pharaonic presence, Alexandria developed as a virtually autonomous city along Hellenistic lines; as a result, it would be known to the Romans as *Alexandria ad Aegyptum* – 'Alexandria adjacent to Egypt'.

The city has naturally attracted excavators for many years, and much has been brought to light; what, until recently, was generally ignored, however, was the fact that a great deal of the ancient site now lies beneath the harbour waves. The first to consider the potential of this underwater museum was an Egyptian, Kamal Abu el-Saadat, who in 1961 persuaded the Egyptian navy to haul out from the harbour's murky depths a colossal statue of the goddess Isis which is now located in the gardens of the city's Maritime Museum. Not until 1994, however, with the arrival on the scene of the French archaeologist Jean-Yves Empereur and a team of 30 divers from the National Centre for Scientific Research (CNRS), did the work of exploration begin in earnest. A second underwater project in the area soon followed, led by another Frenchman, Frank Goddio of the European Institute of Underwater Archaeology.

Empereur's survey of the Qait Bey site has revealed more than 300 enormous blocks (some estimated at as much as 75 tonnes), which he believes (others dissent) represents the remains of the Pharos lighthouse – one of the Seven Wonders of the Ancient World – as well as architectural elements (including columns and obelisks) and statuary and 'some 40 particularly well-preserved Greek and Roman shipwrecks ... along a line of rocks parallel to the coast'. The first of the sculptures – the torso of a Ptolemaic queen – was raised

(above) Head (weighing more than 800 kg or 1,764 lb) from the colossal statue of a Ptolemaic king – one of the finds of the recent sea-bed survey.

(left) The underwater Egyptologist: a diver of Jean-Yves Empereur's team measures and draws a massive granite capital of Ptolemaic date from Alexandria's submerged ruins. The column itself would have had a diameter of some 1.4 m (4½ ft).

4000 BC

3000 BC

2000 BC

1000 BC

0

AD 700

1994
Jewels in the Sands and Other Dahshur Finds

'In early November [1994], the Egyptian Expedition of the Metropolitan Museum of Art discovered the Tomb of Queen Weret, a structure of the Twelfth Dynasty dating to ca. 1880 BC. The previously unexcavated tomb is located near the Pyramid of Senusret [Sesostris] III at Dahshur, fifteen miles southwest of Cairo ...'
ADELA OPPENHEIM

After a hiatus of many decades, during which the area was under tight military control, Dahshur is turning out to be one of the more richly productive areas of current Egyptological exploration. And the most stunning finds so far are those made by the Metropolitan Museum of Art, New York (see table).

This welcome addition to the corpus of jewelry previously discovered at Dahshur (•p. 88) was found sealed in a small niche in the passage of a tomb which had otherwise been ransacked in antiquity. Given the fact that the burial itself was represented by no more than a few bones and the usual sherds of broken pottery, it was a miraculous survival.

The owner of the tomb and this little treasure was Queen Weret, identified from a broken alabaster canopic jar. A lady previously known to history from a fragmentary Elephantine statue and from a passage in one of the Kahun papyri (•p. 80), she was the probable daughter of Ammenemes II, a queen of Sesostris II, and the mother of Sesostris III.

THE INTACT TOMB OF LADY SITWERUT
Located to the north of the pyramid complex of Sesostris III at Dahshur lies a field of mastaba-type tombs first explored in 1894 by Jacques de Morgan, Director of the Service des Antiquités (•p. 90), in 1894, and untouched until work was resumed at the site by Dieter Arnold and the Metropolitan Museum of Art a century later.

One of the principal discoveries to date has been the intact burial of the lady Sitwerut, wife of a vizier named Nebit (II), a probable contemporary of king Ammenemes III. The mastaba in which this burial was found (no. 31) was previously unknown to Egyptologists, but had been entered by thieves in antiquity. They had made a poor job of it. For, 'at the east side of the same shaft, adjoining the man's tomb, we discovered uncased chambers containing an intact burial belonging to a woman who was probably the wife of the tomb owner'. As the excavator continues:

'The floor of the antechamber was completely covered with pottery bottles, dishes, cups and several vats filled with meat, representing the complete Middle Kingdom funerary offering. The narrow, shallow rock-cut burial chamber was nearly filled by a huge limestone sarcophagus [above], which contained a rectangular, cedar wood coffin. Bands of blue hieroglyphic texts on the lid and end boards of the coffin revealed that the burial belonged to the Khekheret nisut ['royal adornment'] Sit-werut. Pieces of a badly decayed, wooden, inner anthropoid coffin were found, with remains of stucco and gilded decoration. Additional damage was caused by the ancient collapse of the heavy lid of the outer, wooden coffin, which crushed the head end of the burial. Remains of sticks, staves, faience beads and gilded wooden funerary jewellery were preserved, indicating a burial outfit typical for an upper-class lady of the later Twelfth Dynasty.

In the south wall of the burial chamber was a niche that contained a wooden canopic chest, also inscribed with religious formulae and the name of Sit-werut. Found in the decayed box was a set of uninscribed canopic jars with lids in the form of human heads. The serious expression of the faces, particularly noticeable in the downturned mouths, reflects the sombre mood characteristic of late Twelfth Dynasty sculpture.'

WERET'S JEWELRY: the principal items

QUANTITY	DESCRIPTION
2	amethyst scarabs of Ammenemes II
2	broad, beaded claw bracelets of gold, carnelian, lapis lazuli and turquoise
1	inlaid gold motto clasp
7	cowrie-form gold beads
2	gold lion amulets

(above) A large granite door-frame fragment is rescued from the murky depths in 1995. One of two found, suggesting a height in excess of 11 m (36 ft), it is thought to come from the legendary Pharos lighthouse, one of the Seven Wonders of the Ancient World.

(right) An Egyptian diver from Empereur's team sketches a black granite sphinx inscribed with the cartouches of Ramesses II. Unusually, its head, though worn, is still intact: most were knocked off to produce more regular blocks suitable for reuse.

on 4 October 1995, followed shortly after by the recovery of a colossal statue of a Ptolemaic king weighing 11.4 tonnes. More has since followed.

Goddio's work has focused ('in a painstaking series of 3,500 dives, augmented by satellite tracking') on the remains of a submerged palace with marble floors situated within the Eastern Harbour of Alexandria. 'A wide-ranging series of piers and fallen columns has been revealed, apparently in situ, and mapped .... Their place-ment echoes the description of Strabo, the Greek geographer who visited Alexandria's Library in 25 BC, just five years after the Battle of Actium. "It was a fantastic feeling diving on the remains of the city", Mr Goddio said. "To think when I touched a statue or a sphinx, that Cleopatra herself might have done the same …"'.

1997
The New Vizier

'The deceased and several of his wives appear frequently in the reliefs and paintings of the funerary chapel …. Two false-doors were found on the west wall of the room, and beautifully rendered scenes of daily life appear on its eastern and western walls. Relatively well preserved, these polychrome reliefs are extremely fragile and required immediate conservation.'

K. MYSLIWIEC

The brilliant colours with which Egypt's tombs and temples were originally painted are today, for the most part, wholly gone or, where preserved, of a relatively subdued hue which conveys but a poor impression of their once gaudy appearance. The work of the Polish Centre of Mediterranean Archaeology at Warsaw University, under the direction of Karol Mysliwiec, has restored to us much that had previously been lost, and not only at the Centre's principal site, the

temple of Hatshepsut at Deir el-Bahri (•p. 208). To the west of the Djoser Step Pyramid complex at Saqqara the Polish mission has recently located the tomb of a previously unknown, 6th-Dynasty vizier, Merefnebef, 'good name' Fefi, 'great name' Unasankh.

For reasons as yet obscure – but for which we should be extremely grateful – the tomb chapel had been sealed off before it had been fully completed, and as a result the colours and internal decoration of the reliefs and inscriptions are preserved in full (if fragile), brilliant panchromatic detail. The excavation of the tomb's burial apartments is ongoing.

1995 Iufaa

'Our most extraordinary day yet. The basalt sarcophagus lid is pulled to the side, revealing a wooden sarcophagus. It is broken into many pieces with a few glints of blue in the cracks. A silence falls as the wood shards are carefully removed, and little by little an intricate beadwork begins to appear. Finally, we can see the entire pattern of beadwork atop the mummy – completely intact! So rare!'
MARGARET BURNETTE

Intact tombs in Egypt are an increasingly scarce commodity, though discoveries do occasionally occur. The tomb of the lady Sitwerut by Dieter Arnold at Dahshur we have already encountered (•p. 233); while the winter of 1995–96 witnessed the discovery, at Elkab by Belgian Egyptologist Luc Limme, of 'an intact rock tomb of the beginning of the 18th Dynasty, with coffins, mummies, fine pottery and a bronze parade axe' – though little about this find has yet been disclosed.

One intact burial which has received rather more publicity is the late Saite-early

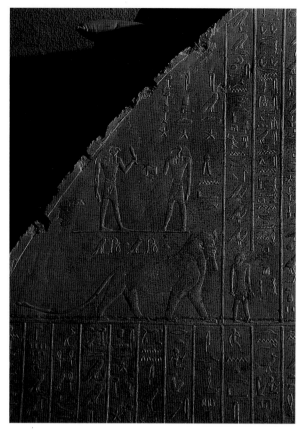

Persian period shaft tomb of a high official ('lector priest and controller of the palace') of Amasis and Psammetichus III named Iufaa, who probably died and was interred under Darius I. This tomb, which was brought to light at Abusir in 1995 by Ladislav Bares of the Czech Institute of Egyptology,

'has a panelled mud-brick enclosure wall, with a large central niche (originally with stelae) in each of its four sides. At the base of the [22-m/72-ft] deep main shaft is a limestone-built burial chamber with stone blocking still in situ. The massive, inscribed, stone sarcophagus was found within, with funerary furniture,

including a wooden box containing dozens of blue faience shabtis [below right; 408 in total].'

Other items of Iufaa's funerary equipment included a set of four canopic jars, a fifth, much larger jar of similar form, papyri, stone vessels, and a great deal of pottery (*above*), much of it non-Egyptian. The walls of the vaulted burial chamber itself are covered with finely carved hieroglyphic inscriptions (*left*) from the Pyramid Texts and the Book of the Dead, with vignettes.

The 'raising of the huge monolithic lid of the outer, box sarcophagus' (which was of limestone and inscribed both inside and out) took place in February 1998 and would reveal 'an inner anthropoid sarcophagus of [basalt; left], covered with hieroglyphic texts. This, in turn, contained a wooden anthropoid coffin which, like the mummy inside, was badly damaged by humidity, as the underground water level is very close to the bottom of the shaft …'.

The mummy itself, covered with a splendid network of faience beads, 'was unwrapped and investigated by an anthropologist [E. Strouhal]. In the course of unwrapping, some amulets …

were discovered. On the tips of fingers and toes of the mummy, thin golden foils were found. Preliminary examination seems to indicate that Iufaa died at the age of about 25–30 years'.

'The importance of this find cannot be [overestimated]. No precious items were present, but the most valuable aspect of the discovery is the information regarding burial practices and religious beliefs in the early Persian period of Egyptian history. This is something about which we so far know very little.'
MIROSLAV VERNER

VALLEY OF THE GOLDEN MUMMIES:
THE NECROPOLIS IN THE OASIS

Discovery
1996;
excavation since 1999
by
Zahi Hawass

Site
Bawit, Bahariya Oasis

Period
Greco-Roman Period
(330 BC–AD 400)

'An antiquities guard had been riding his donkey along the road leading to the town of Farafra, three and one-half miles south of Bawit, capital of Bahariya, when the animal tripped, its leg slipping into a tomb. When the guard peered inside he saw numerous mummies covered in gilt....'
ZAHI HAWASS

If the oases of Egypt's Western Desert were for years a relative backwater of Egyptian archaeology, they have today a distinct capacity to surprise – as with the excavation in the 1970s of a rich cemetery prepared for Balat's Old Kingdom governors, and the more recent discovery at Dakhla of virtually intact Roman houses buried in the wind-blown sand. In June 1999, the Western Desert was again in the news – this time with an announcement by the Egyptian Government that a cemetery estimated to contain upwards of 10,000 mummified dead had been found at Bawit in the Bahariya Oasis. The cemetery had first been located three years before, in May 1996, but its existence had been kept secret in order to deter plunderers. The Bahariya mummies so far recovered date from the 1st and 2nd centuries AD and before, when the remote oasis enjoyed a resurgence in its fortunes thanks to its success in the production of wine.

The temples of the oases, never completely obscured by the passage of time, are well known, the most famous being the oracle consulted by Alexander the Great at Siwa. But it is only recently that serious attention has been turned to the funerary remains of the

(below and right) Typical, plaster-modelled faces of the Bahariya dead. Crudely painted and displaying minimal restraint, such late creations were memorably described by Herbert Winlock (●p. 156) as 'atrocities of hideousness'.

area, with large numbers of provincial-style burials of Greco-Roman date having now been unearthed at Kharga (Baghawat and Dush) and Dakhla (Isman el-Kherab). If early reports prove correct, the cemetery at Bawit will prove to be the largest of them all – it appears to cover an area of over 5 sq. km (2 sq. miles).

The Bahariya tombs excavated so far are cut into the sandstone bedrock and are multi-chambered. The rooms are fitted with shelves to support the bodies of the mummified dead contained in a variety of cartonnage (glued and plastered linen, either gilded or painted) or terracotta coffins, or simply wrapped. Among the accompanying burial equipment are mourner-figures, pottery and, of course, precious jewelry of typical Greco-Roman style, as well as coins, including one of the legendary Cleopatra VII.

With the vast bulk of its tombs still unexcavated, the Bahariya find promises in due course to shed immeasurable light not only on the art and archaeology of the region, but also on the people themselves and their diet, state of health and life-expectancy – providing what Roger Bagnall of Columbia University has described as 'an invaluable database of statistically reliable information on Egyptian life at that time'.

'I began work on the first tomb, which, like the others, was filled with the mummies of men, women, and children. All of them appeared to be in good condition, mummified in a Roman-Egyptian manner known from sites such as Hawara in the Faiyum, 150 miles to the northeast. The mummies still smelled of the resin used to embalm them millennia ago. In one corner, I saw a

(right) Detail of one of the gilded mummy carapaces from Bahariya, with representations of the goddess Nut, her wings spread in a gesture of protection, and the four sons of Horus – genii responsible for safeguarding the viscera.

(above & right) Access to the lost catacombs was gained from above. Only a small number of the tombs have so far been excavated, in a vast cemetery, which, it has been estimated, might yield as many as 10,000 mummies.

(left) Dr Zahi Hawass, Director of excavations at the site, gently brushes away the dust and decay of 2,000 years.

(left) Interior of one of the Bahariya tombs, carved in the living rock and with an extensive (if formalized) range of funerary scenes still retaining their original, bright colours.

(far right) A painted detail: the embalmer god Anubis tends to the mummy while the spirit of the deceased – the *ba*, shown here as a human-headed bird – takes flight. The sister-goddesses Isis and Nephthys mourn at either end of the funerary couch.

touching scene – a woman lying beside her husband, her head turned affectionately towards him. My eyes were then drawn to the mummy of another woman, the sun glinting off her gilded mask. About five feet in height, she had a beautiful gilded plaster crown with four decorative rows of red curls ending in spirals that framed her forehead ….'
ZAHI HAWASS

This is a site with much in store, and not all of it Roman in date, as the latest reported find – the burial of a 26th-Dynasty governor of Bahariya Oasis – serves to underline.

'I still say all the time that you never know what the sand of Egypt might hold of secrets. And that's why I believe until today we have discovered only thirty percent of our monuments. Still seventy percent is buried underneath the ground.'
ZAHI HAWASS

Two hundred years after Napoleon first opened Egypt up to the west, digging solely to find objects is very much a thing of the past; of the material remains of ancient Egypt there is no shortage. What today's archaeologist seeks is answers to questions posed by the materials already to hand, with the best excavations closely targeted and having precise objectives and deliberate aims. As Egyptology knows to its cost, all digging is destruction, and cannot be done twice; ancient sites are a finite resource, and not to be squandered.

Yet for all the science, system, and technique of the modern excavator, the subject is driven still by excitement and a quickening of the pulse, and by the certainty that discoveries will continue to be made, and on a regular basis, to surprise, delight, inspire and occasionally confound professional and public alike. Every day the work goes on, in Alexandria, at Giza, Saqqara, Dahshur, and at Thebes and all points between and beyond. Without the slightest doubt, further caches of mummies, statues and buried treasure are in prospect, more 'lost' pyramids, solar boats, historical texts and ritual papyri – perhaps even other royal tombs to match the awesome splendour of Tutankhamun.

The rediscovery of ancient Egypt is a story still being told – and all we can conclude, so far, is that the unveiling of this miraculous land and its breathtaking civilization has barely begun.

(above & below) Extraordinary, Mesopotamian-style clay tablets incised in hieratic with a stylus. Rare, if not previously unknown in Egyptian archaeology, the tablets were the surprise finds of a French institute team, working at Ain Asil, Dakhla Oasis since 1974.

(opposite) This superb grandiorite statue of a god with the features of a 25th-Dynasty, Kushite king (probably Taharqa) is one of the finest sculptural representations of the period extant. Unrecognized in the basement of Southampton Museum for over a century, much of that time employed as a handy bike rack, its identification was recently confirmed by British Museum Egyptologist Vivian Davies. The find emphasizes that not all great discoveries are necessarily to be expected in Egypt (or the Sudan) itself.

(right & below) The work of The Amarna Royal Tombs Project takes up where Howard Carter left off, excavating anew in the Valley of the Kings, for the first time since 1922. Is there more still to be found in Eygpt's principal royal burial ground? Perhaps, but only time, and much painstaking work, will tell.

Glossary

Amduat
Funerary writings dealing with the journey of the sun-god through the twelve hours of darkness, found inscribed on the walls of royal tombs during the New Kingdom and later, for private use, on rolls of papyrus.

Apis bull
Physical manifestation of Ptah, the creator-god of Memphis.

ba-bird
The 'personality' of the deceased, represented as a human-headed bird.

Book of the Dead
Collection of funerary spells ('The Book of Coming Forth by Day') found inscribed upon papyri and amulets from the New Kingdom on.

broad collar
Deep, beaded necklace, commonly of faience, worn by both men and women throughout the dynastic period of Egyptian history.

canopic jars/chest
Jars/chest, the former generally of stone and with human or human- and animal-head stoppers, the latter of stone or wood, used as containers for the embalmed viscera of the deceased.

cartonnage
A material consisting of alternating layers of linen or papyrus and glue, stiffened with an application of gesso, commonly used for the manufacture of mummy masks and cases.

cartouche
Oval rope frame containing the hieroglyphs of the royal prenomen and nomen.

Coffin Texts
Edited versions of the Pyramid Texts for non-royal use, primarily found inscribed upon coffins of the First Intermediate Period and Middle Kingdom.

demotic
Cursive and primarily documentary script in use from the 26th Dynasty into the Roman period.

djed-pillar
The hieroglyphic sign for 'stability', purporting to represent the backbone of the god Osiris and commonly used as an amulet or decorative motif.

faience
Ceramic material with a body composed of crushed quartz sand and a soda-lime-silica glaze, usually blue or green, commonly used for jewelry, amulets and *shabti*-figures.

Four Sons of Horus
The genii charged with the protection of the internal organs of the deceased: Duamutef (human- and later jackal-headed, for the stomach); Hapy (human- and later ape-headed, for the lungs); Imsety (human-headed, for the liver); Qebhsenuef (human- and later falcon-headed, for the intestines).

heart scarab
Large scarab wrapped in with the bandages of the mummy, generally inscribed with Chapter 30 from the Book of the Dead to prevent the heart from testifying against its owner in the divine tribunal.

hieratic
Cursive form of the hieroglyphic script in use throughout the dynastic period.

Isis
The sister-wife of Osiris, lord of the underworld; mother of the god Horus – of whom the king was regarded as an earthly manifestation.

ka-statue
Repository for the 'life spirit' of the deceased, sometimes represented in human form with the upraised-arms hieroglyph upon the head.

khedive
Old Persian title meaning 'lord' or 'master', commonly associated with Ismail Pasha, who ruled Egypt between 1863 and 1879.

Maat
Personification of truth, justice and order, generally represented as a seated woman wearing a large feather on the head.

mamur
Arabic 'boss'.

mastaba
Tomb of the Early Dynastic Period or Old Kingdom with 'bench'-shaped superstructure.

Neith
Creator goddess whose cult-centre was Sais in the Delta; usually depicted wearing the red crown of Lower Egypt.

nemes-headdress
Kingly headdress consisting of a striped cloth wig cover with pigtail and lappets.

Nephthys
Divine sister of Isis and wife of Seth, lord of chaos, generally shown with the hieroglyphs of her name upon her head.

nome
District or province of ancient Egypt, governed by a nomarch; each had a symbol by which it was identified, thus 'hare' nome.

Osiris
Divine king of the Underworld, murdered and dismembered by his evil brother Seth and reconstituted by his sister-wife Isis.

palace façade
The recessed panelling of the royal palace, reproduced in stone and mud-brick and characteristic of Egypt's earliest funerary architecture.

prenomen/nomen
The cartouched throne- and birth-names of the Egyptian king.

Pyramid Texts
Funerary texts found written within various royal pyramids of the 5th-8th Dynasties.

red crown
Flat-topped crown, red in colour, symbolizing the king's rule over Lower Egypt.

sa-amulet
Hieroglyphic sign with the meaning 'protection', frequently used as an amulet or decorative motif.

sarcophagus
Stone container for the body, either rectangular or anthropoid in shape.

scarab
Amulet in the form of the scarab beetle, laying its eggs in dead matter from which new life was subsequently seen to emerge; earthly manifestation of the solar god Khepri.

sebakh/sebakhin
Arabic, applied to the decayed mud-brick from ancient settlement sites; those who dig it for use as fertilizer.

sed-festival/*heb-sed*
Ritual of kingly rejuvenation, generally held after 30 years to demonstrate the king's fitness to rule, and sporadically thereafter.

serdab
Arabic word for 'cellar', applied to the *ka*-statue room of a mastaba tomb.

serekh
Rectangular frame with palace façade, generally surmounted by a falcon and containing the first of a king's five name-forms, the 'Horus name'.

shabti
Mummiform statuette of stone, faience or wood, often inscribed with extracts from Chapter 6 of the Book of the Dead, summoning the figure, if called, to attend for work in the next world on the deceased's behalf.

shebyu-collar
Necklace composed of gold disc beads, presented by the king as rewards to his officials; during the late 18th Dynasty worn by the king himself and, by its metal, closely associated with the solar cult.

sistrum
Ritualistic rattle of wood and/or metal, associated particularly with Hathor, goddess of love and music.

stela
Rectangular or round-topped slab of stone or panel of wood, bearing images and texts usually votive or funerary in character.

touria
Modern Arabic agricultural hoe, the standard tool for archaeological clearance work.

uraeus
The cobra, earthly manifestation of the goddess Wadjyt, usually represented alongside the vulture goddess Nekhbet on pharaoh's brow as a symbol of kingly rule.

wadj-amulet
Amulet in the form of the hieroglyphic sign for 'green', 'fresh', symbolizing renewal of life.

wedjat-eye
Left eye of the falcon-god Horus, torn out by the god Seth and magically restored by the goddess Hathor, often used as an amulet or decorative motif.

white crown
Tall, elongated crown, white in colour, symbolizing the king's rule over Upper Egypt.

Further Reading

The sources on which this book draws are many and various, unpublished as well as published. The following (with an emphasis on works in English) is a selection of the most important published studies, with a few bibliographical pointers towards the rest. References to other books and articles of interest will be found in Sources of Quotations.

Reference materials
Much of the basic data of Egyptian archaeology is to be found in the pages of specialist Egyptological journals such as *Annales du Service des Antiquités de l'Égypte, Bulletin of the Metropolitan Museum of Art,* Part 2. *Egyptian Expedition, Bulletin de l'Institut français d'archéologie orientale, Journal of Egyptian Archaeology* and *Mitteilungen des Deutschen Archäologischen Instituts, Abteilung Kairo.*

Within these periodicals, articles may be located, with greater or lesser ease, by means of the principal Egyptological bibliographies, which are as follows:

C. Beinlich-Seeber, *Bibliographie Altägypten 1822–1946* (Wiesbaden, 1998)
I. Hilmy, *The Literature of Egypt and the Soudan* (London, 1886)
J. M. A. Janssen, et al., *Annual Egyptological Bibliography* (Leiden etc., 1948-)
B. Porter, R. Moss, E. Burney & J. Málek, *Topographical Bibliography of Ancient Egyptian Hieroglyphic Texts, Reliefs, and Paintings* (Oxford, 1934-) (P-M)
I. A. Pratt, *Ancient Egypt. Sources of Information in the New York Public Library* (New York, 1925) (with *Supplement,* New York, 1942)

Besides reports in the popular national and international press (the reliability of which varies), useful and sober summaries of current archaeological work appear in the journal *Orientalia,* as well as in more popular magazines such as *Egyptian Archaeology, KMT* and *Minerva* – to mention only those published in English. The internet, too, is an increasingly useful bulletin board for the announcement of new discoveries and work in progress – a convenient point of departure here being Nigel Strudwick's *Egyptology Resources* at http://www.newton.cam.ac.uk/egypt

Other basic sources of information include:

K. Baedeker, *Egypt and the Sûdân* (8th ed., Leipzig, 1929)
J. Baines & J. Málek, *Atlas of Ancient Egypt* (Oxford, 1980)
K. A. Bard (ed.), *Encyclopedia of the Archaeology of Ancient Egypt* (London, 1999)
J. von Beckerath, *Handbuch der*

ägyptischen Königsnamen (Mainz, 1999)
W. R. Dawson, E. P. Uphill & M. L. Bierbrier, Who Was Who in Egyptology (3rd ed., London, 1995)
W. Helck, E. Otto & W. Westendorff (eds), Lexikon der Ägyptologie (Wiesbaden, 1975–92)
B. J. Kemp, Ancient Egypt. Anatomy of a Civilization (London, 1989)
W. J. Murnane, The Penguin Guide to Ancient Egypt (London, 1983)
I. Shaw & P. Nicholson, British Museum Dictionary of Ancient Egypt (London & New York, 1995)

General works
The bibliography of archaeological exploration in Egypt is extensive. The following general histories, biographies and studies, popular and less so, are of particular interest or value:

C. Aldred, Jewels of the Pharaohs (London, 1971)
G. d'Athanasi, A Brief Account of Researches and Discoveries in Upper Egypt, made under the Direction of Henry Salt, Esq. (London, 1836)
G. B. Belzoni, Narrative of the Operations and Recent Discoveries within the Pyramids, Temples, Tombs, and Excavations, in Egypt and Nubia (London, 1820), and Plates
E. A. W. Budge, By Nile and Tigris (London, 1920)
J. F. Champollion, Monuments de l'Égypte et de la Nubie (Paris, 1835–47)
P. Clayton, The Rediscovery of Ancient Egypt (London & New York, 1984)
Commission des Monuments d'Égypte, Description de l'Égypte (Paris, 1809–28)
L. Cottrell, The Lost Pharaohs (London, 1950)
L. Cottrell, The Mountains of Pharaoh (London, 1956)
E. David, Mariette Pacha 1821–1881 (Paris, 1994)
C. Desroches-Noblecourt (ed.), Un siècle de fouilles françaises en Égypte 1880–1980 (Paris, 1981)
S. Donadoni, S. Curto & A.-M. Donadoni Roveri, Egypt from Myth to Egyptology (Milan, 1990)
M. S. Drower, Flinders Petrie. A Life in Archaeology (London, 1985)
A. B. Edwards, Pharaohs, Fellahs and Explorers (New York, 1891)
R. Engelbach, Introduction to Egyptian Archaeology (Cairo, 1946)
A. H. Gardiner, Egyptian Grammar (3rd ed., Oxford, 1957)
L. Greener, The Discovery of Egypt (London, 1966)
E. Iversen, The Myth of Egypt and its Hieroglyphs in European Tradition (Princeton, 1993)
T. G. H. James (ed.), Excavating in Egypt. The Egypt Exploration Society 1882–1982 (London, 1982)
T. G. H. James, Howard Carter. The Path to Tutankhamun (London, 1992)
G. Maspero, Egypt. Ancient Sites and Modern Scenes (London, 1910)
G. Maspero, Guide du visiteur au

Musée du Caire (4th ed., Cairo, 1915)
G. Maspero, New Light on Ancient Egypt (London, 1908)
H. W. Müller & E. Thiem, The Royal Gold of Ancient Egypt (London, 1999)
W. M. F. Petrie, Ten Years Digging in Egypt, 1881–1891 (London, 1892)
W. M. F. Petrie, Seventy Years in Archaeology (London, 1931)
K. R. Lepsius, Denkmäler aus Aegypten und Aethiopien (Berlin, 1848–59)
S. Mayes, The Great Belzoni (London, 1959)
R. T. Ridley, Napoleon's Proconsul in Egypt. The Life and Times of Bernardino Drovetti (London, 1998)
I. Rosellini, I Monumenti dell'Egitto e della Nubia (Pisa, 1832–44)
M. Saleh & H. Sourouzian, The Egyptian Museum, Cairo. Official Catalogue (Mainz, 1987)
A. Siliotti, Egypt Lost and Found. Explorers and Travellers on the Nile (London & New York, 1998)
J. L. Smith, Tombs, Temples and Ancient Art (Norman, 1956)
N. Thomas (ed.), The American Discovery of Ancient Egypt. Catalogue and Essays (Los Angeles, 1995)
F. Tiradritti (ed.), The Cairo Museum. Masterpieces of Egyptian Art (London & New York, 1999)
A. Wilkinson, Ancient Egyptian Jewellery (London, 1971)
J. A. Wilson, Signs and Wonders Upon Pharaoh (Chicago, 1964)

Specific topics
Space permits only selected references for the principal entries – wherever possible or appropriate to Porter, Moss, Burney & Málek, Topographical Bibliography (P-M; above, Reference Materials), to a contemporary account of the find, and to a recent commentary; for papyri and other texts, references to transcriptions and translations are also given. Interested readers will find further information on older individual finds in the pages of the Lexikon der Ägyptologie, and in the general works listed above. For more recent discoveries which have not yet found their way into the mainstream Egyptological literature, published accounts are few, generally popular and as a result archaeologically sketchy; this is reflected in the sometimes summary content of those entries here, and in the sources for further reading it is possible to suggest.

Finally, many of the greatest finds in Egyptian archaeology are now in the Cairo Museum, and a good proportion of those discovered during the 19th and early 20th centuries are illustrated in the plates of the Catalogue général du Musée du Caire. A listing of the published titles of this series may be found in the Lexikon der Ägyptologie, I, pp. xix–xx and in F. Tiradritti (ed.), The Cairo Museum. Masterpieces of Egyptian Art

(London & New York, 1999), pp. 413–15.

p. 14 1799 The Rosetta Stone: Cracking the Hieroglyphic Code
P-M IV, 1; Description de l'Égypte, Antiquités, Planches, V, 52–54, Texte, X, pp. 547–50; J. F. Champollion, Lettre à M. Dacier, relative à l'alphabet des hiéroglyphes phonétiques, employés par les Égyptiens (Paris, 1822); J. F. Champollion, Précis du système hiéroglyphique des anciens Égyptiens (Paris, 1824); S. Quirke & C. Andrews, The Rosetta Stone. Facsimile Drawing with an Introduction and Translations (London, 1988); R. Parkinson, Cracking Codes (London, 1999)

p. 16 1799 The Tomb of Amenophis III
P-M I/2 (2nd ed.), pp. 547–50; Description de l'Égypte, Antiquités, Planches, II, 80–88, Texte, III, p. 193; X, p. 218; N. Reeves & R. H. Wilkinson, The Complete Valley of the Kings (London & New York, 1996), pp. 110–15

p. 16 1799 Denon's Papyrus
V. Denon, Travels in Upper and Lower Egypt, II (London, 1803), pp. 217–18; M. Coenen, Journal of Egyptian Archaeology 81 (1995), pp. 237–41

p. 18 1816–18 The Adventure Begins: The Great Belzoni
(a) Valley of the Kings: P-M I/2 (2nd ed.), pp. 534–46; G. B. Belzoni, Narrative of the Operations and Recent Discoveries within the Pyramids, Temples, Tombs, and Excavations, in Egypt and Nubia (London, 1820), pp. 123f., 222–48; N. Reeves & R. H. Wilkinson, The Complete Valley of the Kings (London & New York, 1996), passim; (b) Giza pyramids: P-M III/1 (2nd ed.), pp. 25–26; G. B. Belzoni, Narrative of the Operations and Recent Discoveries within the Pyramids, Temples, Tombs, and Excavations, in Egypt and Nubia (London, 1820), pp. 255–75; M. Lehner, The Complete Pyramids (London & New York, 1997), pp. 49, 122–24

p. 19 After 1816 The Durham Servant Girl
P-M I/2 (2nd ed.), pp. 670–71; S. Smith, British Museum Quarterly 14 (1939–40), pp. 28–29; C. Aldred, Journal of Near Eastern Studies 18 (1959), p. 113; A. Kozloff, in A. Kozloff, B. M. Bryan & L. M. Berman (eds), Egypt's Dazzling Sun. Amenhotep III and his World (Cleveland, 1992), pp. 361–62

p. 20 1813–17 Abu Simbel
P-M VII, pp. 95–111; J. L. Burckhardt, Travels in Nubia (London, 1819), pp. 90–92; L. Christophe, Abou-Simbel et l'épopée de sa découverte (Brussels, 1965)

p. 24 After 1819 An Early Glimpse of Amarna Art
M. Etienne, in R. E. Freed,

Y. J. Markowitz & S. D'Auria (eds), Pharaohs of the Sun. Akhenaten, Nefertiti, Tutankhamen (Boston & London, 1999), p. 230

p. 24 After 1816 The Late Ramessid Letters
J. Cerny, Late Ramesside Letters (Brussels, 1939); E. F. Wente, Late Ramesside Letters (Chicago, 1967); E. F. Wente, Letters from Ancient Egypt (Atlanta, 1990), pp. 171–204; J. J. Janssen, Hieratic Papyri in the British Museum, VI. Late Ramesside Letters and Commentaries (London, 1991)

p. 25 Before and after 1816 Sekhmet and her Many Statues
P-M II (2nd ed.), pp. 262–68 and 451–52; A. M. Lythgoe, Bulletin of the Metropolitan Museum of Art, Part 2 (October 1919); J. Yoyotte, Bulletin de la Société française d'Égyptologie 87–88 (1980), pp. 46–75

p. 26 1820 Captain Caviglia and the Colossus of Ramesses II
P-M III/2 (2nd ed.), pp. 836–37; D. G. Jeffreys, J. Málek & H. S. Smith, Journal of Egyptian Archaeology 73 (1987), p. 20

p. 27 1822–25 Passalacqua and the Tombs of Two Mentuhoteps
(a) Queen Mentuhotep: P-M I/2 (2nd ed.), p. 604; E. Thomas, The Royal Necropoleis of Thebes (Princeton, 1966), p. 37; N. Reeves, Minerva 7/2 (March/April 1996), pp. 47–48; (b) the steward Mentuhotep: P-M I/2 (2nd ed.), pp. 622–23; J. Passalacqua, Catalogue raisonné et historique des antiquités découvertes en Égypte (Paris, 1826), pp. 117–38

p. 29 1820s Papyrus Treasures of Bernardino Drovetti
(a) Turin king-list: A. H. Gardiner, The Royal Canon of Turin (Oxford, 1959); (b) Plan of the tomb of Ramesses IV: A. H. Gardiner & H. Carter, Journal of Egyptian Archaeology 4 (1917), pp. 130–56; (c) Gold-mines papyrus: G. Goyon, Annales du Service des Antiquités de l'Égypte 49 (1949), pp. 337–92

p. 30 1824 The Tomb of an Egyptian Hero: General Djehuty
C. Lilyquist, Metropolitan Museum Journal 23 (1988), pp. 5–68; N. Reeves, Journal of Egyptian Archaeology 79 (1993), pp. 259–61

p. 32 1827 The First Intact Burial of an Egyptian King: Nubkheperre Intef
P-M I/2 (2nd ed.), pp. 602–03; H. E. Winlock, Journal of Egyptian Archaeology 10 (1924), pp. 226–33; E. Thomas, The Royal Necropoleis of Thebes (Princeton, 1966), pp. 37–38; M. Dewachter, Revue d'Égyptologie 36 (1985), pp. 43–66

p. 33 1828 The Metternich Stela
P-M IV, p. 5; V. S. Golenischeff, Die Metternichstele in der Originalgrösse (Leipzig, 1877);

N. E. Scott, Bulletin of the Metropolitan Museum of Art 9/8 (April, 1951), pp. 201–17; C. E. Sander-Hansen, Die Texte der Metternich Stele (Copenhagen, 1956)

p. 35 1834 The Gold of Meroe: Ferlini's Treasure
P-M VII, pp. 245–46; G. Ferlini, Cenno sugli scavi operati nella Nubia e Catalogo degli oggetti ritrovati (Bologna, 1837); K.-H. Priese, The Gold of Meroe (New York, 1993); Y. Markowitz & P. Lacovara, Journal of the American Research Center in Egypt 33 (1996), pp. 1–9

p. 36 1837 Blasting at Giza: Howard Vyse and the Pyramid of Menkaure
P-M III/1 (2nd ed.), pp. 33–34; H. Vyse, Operations Carried on at the Pyramids of Gizeh in 1837, II (London, 1840); M. Lehner, The Complete Pyramids (London & New York, 1997), pp. 50–53, 134–36

p. 40 1851 The Burial Place of the Apis Bulls: Mariette and the Serapeum
P-M III/2 (2nd ed.), esp. pp. 780–805; A. Mariette, Le Sérapéum de Memphis (Paris, 1857–82); A. Dodson, KMT 6/1 (spring 1995), pp. 18–32

p. 42 1850 The Louvre's Seated Scribe
P-M III/2 (2nd ed.), pp. 458–59; W. S. Smith, A History of Egyptian Sculpture and Painting in the Old Kingdom (Oxford, 1946), p. 47; C. Ziegler, Musée du Louvre, Département des Antiquités Égyptiennes: Les statues égyptiennes de l'Ancien Empire (Paris, 1997), pp. 204–08

p. 45 1855 The Harris Papyri: The Greatest Collection Ever Found
S. Birch, Facsimile of an Egyptian Hieratic Papyrus of the Reign of Rameses III (London, 1876); T. E. Peet, The Great Tomb-Robberies of the Twentieth Egyptian Dynasty (Oxford, 1930); P. Grandet, Le Papyrus Harris I (BM 9999), I (Cairo, 1994), pp. 3–10

p. 46 1860 Rhind's Tomb
P-M I/2 (2nd ed.), p. 671; A. H. Rhind, Thebes, its Tombs and their Tenants (London, 1862), pp. 87–113; S. Birch & A. H. Rhind, Facsimiles of Two Papyri Found in a Tomb at Thebes (London, 1863)

p. 47 1857 Prince Plonplon and the Burial of Kamose
P-M I/2 (2nd ed.), p. 600; H. E. Winlock, Journal of Egyptian Archaeology 10 (1924), pp. 259–65; E. Thomas, The Royal Necropoleis of Thebes (Princeton, 1966), pp. 39–40

p. 47 Before 1858 The Boston Pectoral
P. Lacovara & R. Newman, Journal of the Museum of Fine Arts, Boston 2 (1990), pp. 22–37; A. Jahnke, Boston (August, 1991), pp. 78–81, 117–22

p. 48 **After 1858 The Montu Priests**
P-M I/2 (2nd ed.), pp. 643–49; L. Vassalli, *I Monumenti istorici egizi, il Museo e gli scavi d'antichità eseguiti per ordine di S.A. Vicerè Ismail Pascia; notizia sommaria* (Rome, 1869); H. Gauthier, *Cercueils anthropoïdes des prêtres de Montou* (Cairo, 1913)

p. 49 **1858 The Queen of Punt**
P-M II (2nd ed.), pp. 344–47; A. Mariette, *Deir-el-Bahari* (Leipzig, 1877); M. Saleh & H. Sourouzian, *The Egyptian Museum, Cairo. Official Catalogue* (Mainz, 1987), no. 130; J. F. Nunn, *Ancient Egyptian Medicine* (London, 1996), p. 83

p. 50 **1859 An Egyptian Queen: The Coffin and Jewels of Ahhotep**
P-M I/2 (2nd ed.), pp. 600–02; W. von Bissing, *Ein thebanischer Grabfund aus dem Anfang des neuen Reiches* (Berlin, 1900); H. E. Winlock, *Journal of Egyptian Archaeology* 10 (1924), pp. 252–55; E. Thomas, *The Royal Necropoleis of Thebes* (Princeton, 1966), pp. 39–40; M. Saleh & H. Sourouzian, *The Egyptian Museum, Cairo. Official Catalogue* (Mainz, 1987), nos. 120–26

p. 52 **1859 Mariette's Abydos Burial**
P-M V, p. 44 (called Ramesses XII); A. Mariette, *Catalogue général des monuments d'Abydos* (Paris, 1880), pp. 527–29

p. 53 **1859 'Hyksos' Sculptures**
P-M IV, pp. 16–17; J. Capart, *Recherches d'art égyptien*, I. *Les monuments dits Hycsos* (Brussels, 1914); J. Vandier, *Manuel d'archéologie égyptienne*, III. *Les grandes époques. La statuaire* (Paris, 1958), esp. pp. 204–08; M. Saleh & H. Sourouzian, *The Egyptian Museum, Cairo. Official Catalogue* (Mainz, 1987), nos. 102–04

p. 53 **1860 The Sheikh el-Beled**
P-M III/2 (2nd ed.), pp. 459–60; A. Mariette, *Les mastabas de l'Ancien-Empire* (Paris, 1889), pp. 127–29; C. Vandersleyen, *Journal of Egyptian Archaeology* 69 (1983), pp. 61–65

p. 54 **1860 The Statue of Khephren**
P-M III/1 (2nd ed.), p. 21; A. Mariette, *Lettre de M. Auguste Mariette à M. le Vicomte de Rougé sur les résultats des fouilles entreprises par ordre du Vice-roi d'Égypte* (Paris, 1860), pp. 7–8; Metropolitan Museum of Art, *Egyptian Art in the Age of the Pyramids* (New York, 1999), p. 253

p. 55 **1860 Finding the Tomb of Hesyre, Chief Royal Scribe**
P-M III (2nd ed.), pp. 437–39; J. E. Quibell, *Excavations at Saqqara (1911–1912). The Tomb of Hesy* (Cairo, 1913); W. Wood, *Journal of the American Research Center in Egypt* 15 (1978), pp. 9–24

p. 56 **1863 Statues from the Tomb of Psamtek**
P-M III/2 (2nd ed.), pp. 670–71; A. Mariette, *Monuments divers recueillis en Égypte et en Nubie* (Paris, 1872), pl. 96; B. V. Bothmer, *Egyptian Sculpture of the Late Period, 700 BC–AD 100* (Brooklyn, 1960), p. 64; M. Saleh & H. Sourouzian, *The Egyptian Museum, Cairo. Official Catalogue* (Mainz, 1987), nos. 250–52

p. 57 **1864 The Tale of Setne-Khaemwaset**
A. Mariette, *Les papyrus du Musée de Boulaq*, I (Cairo, 1871), pls. 29–32; G. Maspero, *Popular Stories of Ancient Egypt* (London, 1915), pp. 115–17; M. Lichtheim, *Ancient Egyptian Literature*, III (Berkeley, 1980), pp. 125–51

p. 57 **Before 1862 The Edwin Smith Papyri**
J. H. Breasted, *The Edwin Smith Surgical Papyrus* (Chicago, 1930); J. F. Nunn, *Ancient Egyptian Medicine* (London, 1996), pp. 25–30

p. 57 **Before 1865 The Palermo Stone**
P-M III/2, pp. 873–74; H. Schäfer, *Ein Brüchstück altägyptischer Annalen* (Berlin, 1902); H. Gauthier, in G. Maspero (ed.), *Le Musée égyptien*, III (Cairo, 1919), pp. 29–53; W. M. F. Petrie, *Ancient Egypt* (1916), p. 119; C. N. Reeves, *Göttinger Miszellen* 32 (1979), pp. 47–51; T. Wilkinson, *Royal Annals of Ancient Egypt* (London, 2000)

p. 58 **1871 The Meidum Sculptures**
P-M IV, pp. 90–94; A. Daninos, *Receuil de Travaux relatifs à la philologie et à l'archéologie égyptienne et assyrienne* 8 (1886), pp. 69–73; W. M. F. Petrie, *Medum* (London, 1892); M. Saleh & H. Sourouzian, *The Egyptian Museum, Cairo. Official Catalogue* (Mainz, 1987), nos. 26–27

p. 58 **1871 The Tomb of Ti**
P-M III/2 (2nd ed.), pp. 468–78; G. Steindorff, *Das Grab des Ti* (Leipzig, 1913); L. Épron, F. Daumas & G. Goyon, *Le tombeau de Ti* (Cairo, 1939–66)

p. 59 **1874 The Karnak Taweret**
P-M II (2nd ed.), p. 299; A. Mariette, *Monuments divers recueillis en Égypte et en Nubie* (Paris, 1872), pls. 91–92; M. Saleh & H. Sourouzian, *The Egyptian Museum, Cairo. Official Catalogue* (Mainz, 1987), no. 248

p. 60 **1881 The Pyramid Texts: The World's Oldest Religious Literature**
P-M III/2 (2nd ed.), pp. 393ff.; G. Maspero, *Les inscriptions des pyramides de Saqqarah* (Paris, 1894); A. Piankoff, *The Pyramid of Unas* (Princeton, 1966)

p. 61 **1881 A Votive *Shabti* of Ptahmose, Mayor of Thebes**
P-M V, pp. 60–61; A. Mariette,

Catalogue général des monuments d'Abydos (Paris, 1880), pp. 61–63; J.-F. & L. Aubert, *Statuettes égyptiennes. Chaouabtis, ouchebtis* (Paris, 1974), pp. 49–50

p. 61 **1881 The Wilbour Plaque**
J. Capart (ed.), *Travels in Egypt (December 1880 to May 1891). Letters of Charles Edwin Wilbour* (Brooklyn, 1936), pp. 95–96; R. A. Fazzini, in R. E. Freed, Y. Markowitz & S. D'Auria (eds), *Pharaohs of the Sun. Akhenaten. Nefertiti. Tutankhamen* (Boston & London, 1999), p. 245

p. 64 **1881 Royal Mummies: the Deir el-Bahri Cache**
P-M I/2 (2nd ed.), pp. 658–67; G. Maspero, *Les momies royales de Déir el-Baharî* (Cairo, 1889); C. N. Reeves, *Valley of the Kings. The Decline of a Royal Necropolis* (London, 1990); G. B. Johnson, *KMT* 4/2 (1993), pp. 52–57

p. 65 **Before 1881 New Light on Egyptian Medical Science**
N. Reeves, in W. V. Davies (ed.), *Studies in Egyptian Antiquities. A Tribute to T. G. H. James* (London, 1999), pp. 73–77

p. 67 **1883 Greeks in Egypt: Naukratis**
P-M IV, 50; W. M. F. Petrie & E. Gardner, *Naukratis* (London, 1886–88); J. Boardman, *The Greeks Overseas* (new ed., London, 1980), pp. 111–40

p. 69 **1886 The Tomb of Sennudjem, Servant in the Place of Truth**
P-M I/1 (2nd ed.), pp. 1–5; G. Daressy, *Annales du Service des Antiquités de l'Égypte* 20 (1920), pp. 147–60; D. Valbelle, 'Les ouvriers de la tombe'. *Deir el-Médineh à l'époque ramesside* (Cairo, 1985), pp. 294–98

p. 72 **1887 Pharaoh's Diplomatic Archive: The Amarna Letters**
P-M IV, p. 199; E. A. W. Budge, *By Nile and Tigris*, I (London, 1920), pp. 128–29, 139–43; W. L. Moran, *The Amarna Letters* (Baltimore, 1992); S. Izre'el, *The Amarna Scholarly Tablets* (Groningen, 1997)

p. 74 **Before 1887 The Berlin Green Head**
B. V. Bothmer, *Egyptian Sculpture of the Late Period, 700 BC–AD 100* (Brooklyn, 1960), pp. 164–66; R. S. Bianchi (ed.), *Cleopatra's Egypt* (Brooklyn 1988), pp. 140–42

p. 74 **1888 The Statue of Hetepdief**
P-M III/2 (2nd ed.), p. 864; G. Maspero (ed.), *Le Musée égyptien*, I (Cairo, 1890–1900), pp. 12–13; E. L. B. Terrace & H. G. Fischer, *Treasures of the Cairo Museum* (London, 1970), pp. 25–28; M. Saleh & H. Sourouzian, *The Egyptian Museum, Cairo. Official Catalogue* (Mainz, 1987), no. 22

p. 74 **1887 Foreign Tribute**
W. Culican, *Levant* 4 (1972), pp. 147–48; S. Spurr, N. Reeves & S. Quirke, *Egyptian Art at Eton College* (New York, 1999), pp. 34–35

p. 75 **Before 1888 Wallis Budge and the Book of the Dead**
E. A. W. Budge, *By Nile and Tigris* I (London, 1920), pp. 136ff.; E. A. W. Budge, *Facsimile of the Papyrus of Ani in the British Museum* (2nd ed., London, 1894); E. A. W. Budge, *Facsimiles of the Papyri of Hunefer, Anhai, Karasher and Netchemet with supplementary texts from the Papyrus of Nu* (London, 1899); C. Andrews (ed.), R. O. Faulkner (trans.), *The Ancient Egyptian Book of the Dead* (London, 1985)

p. 76 **1888 Faces from the Past: The Faiyum Portraits**
P-M IV, p. 103; W. M. F. Petrie, *Hawara, Biahmu, and Arsinoe* (London, 1889), pp. 8ff.; W. M. F. Petrie, *Roman Portraits and Memphis IV* (London, 1911); K. Parlasca & H. Seeman (eds), *Augenblicke. Mumienporträts und ägyptische Grabkunst aus römischer Zeit* (Frankfurt, 1999)

p. 77 **1888 The Labyrinth**
P-M IV, pp. 100–01; W. M. F. Petrie, *Hawara, Biahmu, and Arsinoe* (London, 1889), pp. 4–8; W. M. F. Petrie, G. A. Wainwright & E. Mackay, *The Labyrinth, Gerzeh and Mazghuneh* (London, 1912), pp. 28ff.; E. Uphill, *Pharaoh's Gateway to Eternity* (London, 2000)

p. 77 **1888 A Colossal Head of Ammenemes III from Bubastis**
P-M IV, p. 28; É. Naville, *Bubastis (1887–1889)* (London, 1891), pp. 26ff.; H.-G. Evers, *Staat aus dem Stein*, I (Munich, 1929), pls. 113–16

p. 79 **1888 The Palace of Amenophis III**
P-M I/2 (2nd ed.), pp. 778–81; G. Daressy, *Annales du Service des Antiquités de l'Égypte* 4 (1903), pp. 165–70; P. Lacovara, *Amarna Letters* 3 (1994), pp. 6–21

p. 80 **1888 Artists' Sketches from the Valley of the Kings**
G. Daressy, *Annales du Service des Antiquités de l'Égypte* 18 (1919), pp. 270–74; G. Daressy, *Ostraca* (Cairo, 1901); W. H. Peck & J. G. Ross, *Egyptian Drawings* (New York, 1978)

p. 80 **1889 The Kahun Papyri**
P-M IV, pp. 111–12; F. Ll. Griffith, *The Petrie Papyri. Hieratic Papyri from Kahun and Gurob* (London, 1898); L. Borchardt, *Zeitschrift für ägyptische Sprache und Altertumskunde* 37 (1899), pp. 89–103; U. Luft, in S. Quirke, *Lahun Studies* (Reigate, 1999), pp. 1ff.

p. 81 **1891 Mummies of the Priests of Amun: Bab el-Gasus**

P-M I/2 (2nd ed.), pp. 630–42; G. Daressy, *Annales du Service des Antiquités de l'Égypte* 1 (1900), pp. 141–48; G. Daressy, *Annales du Service des Antiquités de l'Égypte* 8 (1907), pp. 3–38; A. Niwinski, *21st Dynasty Coffins from Thebes* (Mainz, 1988), pp. 25–27; J. Lipinska, *KMT* 4/4 (1993–94), pp. 48–58

p. 83 **1891–92 Paintings from Akhenaten's Palace at el-Amarna**
P-M IV, pp. 197–99; W. M. F. Petrie, *Tell el Amarna* (London, 1894); N. de G. Davies, *Journal of Egyptian Archaeology* 7 (1921), pp. 1–7; F. Weatherhead, *Journal of Egyptian Archaeology* 78 (1992), pp. 179–94, and subsequent volumes

p. 86 **1893 The Tombs of Kagemni and Mereruka**
P-M III/2 (2nd ed.), pp. 521–37; F. W. von Bissing, *Die Mastaba des Gem-ni-kai* (Berlin, 1905–11); C. Firth & B. Gunn, *Teti Pyramid Cemeteries*, I (Cairo, 1926), pp. 20–21; P. Duell, *The Mastaba of Mereruka* (Chicago, 1938)

p. 86 **1893 The Min Colossi**
P-M V, p. 130; W. M. F. Petrie, *Koptos* (London, 1896); J. C. Payne, *Catalogue of the Predynastic Egyptian Collection in the Ashmolean Museum* (Oxford, 1993), pp. 12–13

p. 87 **1893 or before The Soldiers of Mesehti**
P-M IV, p. 265; G. Maspero (ed.), *Le Musée égyptien*, I (Cairo, 1890–1900), pp. 31–34; E. Brovarski, in W. K. Simpson & W. Davis (eds), *Studies in Ancient Egypt, the Aegean, and the Sudan. Essays in Honor of Dows Dunham* (Boston, 1981), p. 24, n. 75

p. 87 **1893 The Abusir Papyri**
P-M III/1 (2nd ed.), pp. 339–40; P. Posener-Kriéger & J. L. de Cenival, *Hieratic Papyri in the British Museum*, 5th series. *Abu Sir Papyri* (London, 1968); P. Posener-Kriéger, *Les archives du Temple funéraire de Néferirkare-Kakai (les papyrus d'Abousir)* (Cairo, 1976)

p. 88 **1894–95 Jewels of Egyptian Princesses: de Morgan at Dahshur**
P-M III/2 (2nd ed.), pp. 883–89; J. de Morgan, *Fouilles à Dahchour* (Vienna, 1895–1903); R. L. Cron & G. B. Johnson, *KMT* 6/2 (1995), pp. 34–43; and *KMT* 6/4 (1995–96), pp. 48–62; A. Oppenheim, in F. Tiradritti (ed.), *The Cairo Museum. Masterpieces of Egyptian Art* (London & New York, 1999), pp. 136ff.

p. 91 **1894–95 A Cache of Statues of Sesostris I from el-Lisht**
P-M IV, pp. 82–83; J.-E. Gautier & G. Jéquier, *Mémoire sur les fouilles de Licht* (Cairo, 1902), pp. 30–38; M. Saleh & H. Sourouzian, *The Egyptian Museum, Cairo. Official Catalogue* (Mainz, 1987), no. 87

p. 92 **1895 The Finest Faience: The Tuna el-Gebel Find**
H. Wallis, *Egyptian Ceramic Art* (London, 1900), pp. xvi–xviii; G. A. D. Tait, *Journal of Egyptian Archaeology* 49 (1963), pp. 93–139

p. 94 **1895 Predynastic Graves at Naqada**
W. M. F. Petrie & J. E. Quibell, *Naqada and Ballas* (London, 1896); W. M. F. Petrie, *Diospolis Parva* (London, 1901), pp. 4–12; M. A. Hoffman, *Egypt Before the Pharaohs* (London, 1980), pp. 105–24

p. 95 **1896 The Israel Stela**
P-M II (2nd ed.), pp. 447–48; W. M. F. Petrie, *Six Temples at Thebes* (London, 1896), p. 13; A. J. Peden, *Egyptian Historical Inscriptions of the Nineteenth Dynasty* (Jonsered, 1997), pp. 173–87

p. 96 **1896 The Tomb of Hatiay**
P-M I/2 (2nd ed.), p. 672; G. Daressy, *Annales du Service des Antiquités de l'Égypte* 2 (1901), pp. 2–13; L. M. Berman, in A. P. Kozloff, B. M. Bryan & L. M. Berman (eds), *Egypt's Dazzling Sun. Amenophis III and his World* (Cleveland, 1992), pp. 312–17

p. 96 **1896 The Ramesseum Papyri**
(a) Papyri: P-M I/2 (2nd ed.), p. 679; J. E. Quibell, *The Ramesseum* (London, 1896), p. 3; A. H. Gardiner, *The Ramesseum Papyri* (Oxford, 1955); cf. *LÄ* IV, cols. 726–27; (b) Meryetamun statue: P-M II (2nd ed.), p. 431; W. M. F. Petrie, *Six Temples at Thebes* (London, 1897), pp. 6–7; M. Saleh & H. Sourouzian, *The Egyptian Museum, Cairo. Official Catalogue* (Mainz, 1987), no. 208

p. 97 **1897–99 Hierakonpolis: City of the Falcon-God**
P-M V, pp. 191–99; J. E. Quibell & F. W. Green, *Hierakonpolis* (London, 1900–02); B. Adams, *Ancient Nekhen. Garstang in the City of Hierakonpolis* (New Malden, 1990); D. Forbes, *KMT* 7/3 (1996), pp. 46–59, 68; F. Tiradritti & R. Pirelli, in F. Tiradritti (ed.), *The Cairo Museum. Masterpieces of Egyptian Art* (London & New York, 1999), pp. 88–89

p. 99 **Before 1897 The Wife of Nakhtmin**
G. Maspero (ed.), *Le Musée égyptien*, I (Cairo, 1890–1900), pp. 39–40; E. L. B. Terrace & H. G. Fischer, *Treasures of the Cairo Museum* (London, 1970), pp. 137–40

p. 100 **1897 The Tomb of Neithhotep**
P-M V, pp. 118–19; J. de Morgan, *Recherches sur les origines de l'Égypte*, II. *Ethnographie préhistorique et tombeau royal de Négadeh* (Paris, 1897), pp. 147–202; M. A. Hoffman, *Egypt Before the Pharaohs* (London, 1980), pp. 120, 280, 323

p. 101 **1898–99 Loret in the Valley of the Kings**
P-M I/2 (2nd ed.), pp. 551–59; G. Schweinfurth, *Sphinx* 3 (1900), pp. 103–07; V. Loret, *Bulletin de l'Institut égyptien* (3 sér.) 8 (1899), pp. 91–112; C. N. Reeves, *Valley of the Kings. The Decline of a Royal Necropolis* (London, 1990)

p. 105 **1890s and before Aramaic Papyri from Elephantine**
P-M V, pp. 226–27; B. Porten, et al., *The Elephantine Papyri in English* (Leiden, 1996)

p. 106 **1898 Bab el-Hosan: 'The Tomb of the Horse'**
P-M II (2nd ed.), p. 282–83; H. Carter, *Annales du Service des Antiquités de l'Égypte* 2 (1901), pp. 201–05; M. Saleh & H. Sourouzian, *The Egyptian Museum, Cairo. Official Catalogue* (Mainz, 1987), no. 67

p. 107 **1896–1906 The Oxyrhynchus Papyri: In Search of the Classics**
B. P. Grenfell & A. S. Hunt, *The Oxyrhynchus Papyri*, I (London, 1898), and subsequent volumes; E. Turner, in T. G. H. James (ed.), *Excavating in Egypt. The Egypt Exploration Society 1882–1982* (London, 1982), pp. 161–78

p. 109 **1899 Tombs of Egypt's Earliest Kings at Abydos**
P-M V, pp. 78–89; É. Amélineau, *Les nouvelles fouilles d'Abydos* (Paris, 1899–1905); W. M. F. Petrie, *The Royal Tombs of the Earliest Dynasties* (London, 1900–01); G. Dreyer, *Umm El-Qaab*, I. *Das prädynastische Königsgrab U-j und seine frühen Zeugnisse* (Mainz, 1999)

p. 111 **1900 Six 18th-Dynasty Ladies**
P-M IV, p. 115; É. Chassinat, *Bulletin de l'Institut français d'archéologie orientale* 1 (1901), pp. 225–34; C. N. Reeves, *Apollo* (November, 1987), p. 348

p. 111 **1899 The 'Persian' Tombs**
P-M III/2 (2nd ed.), pp. 648–49; A. Barsanti, *Annales du Service des Antiquités de l'Égypte* 1 (1900), pp. 161ff. and 230ff.; E. Bresciani, S. Pernigotti, M. P. Giangeri Silvis, *La tomba di Ciennehebu, capo della flotta del Re* (Pisa, 1977), and others in the series, forthcoming

p. 112 **1900 The Pyramidion of Ammenemes III**
P-M III/2 (2nd ed.), p. 888; G. Maspero, *Annales du Service des Antiquités de l'Égypte* 3 (1902), pp. 206–08

p. 113 **1902–14 Theodore Davis: 'A New Tomb Every Season'**
P-M I/2 (2nd ed.), pp. 546ff.; T. M. Davis, *The Tomb of Thoutmôsis IV* (London, 1904); T. M. Davis, *The Tomb of Hâtshopsîtû* (London, 1906); T. M. Davis, *The Tomb of Iouiya and Touiyou* (London, 1907, repr.

London, 2000); T. M. Davis, *The Tomb of Siphtah; the Monkey Tomb and the Gold Tomb* (London, 1908); T. M. Davis, *The Tomb of Queen Tîyi* (2nd ed., ed. N. Reeves, San Francisco, 1990); N. Reeves & R. H. Wilkinson, *The Complete Valley of the Kings* (London & New York, 1996)

p. 117 **1902–04 John Garstang at Beni Hasan**
P-M IV, pp. 141ff.; J. Garstang, *The Burial Customs of Ancient Egypt* (London, 1907); S. Orel, *KMT* 8/1 (1997), pp. 54–63

p. 118 **1903 The Karnak Cachette: The Largest Find of Statues Ever Made**
P-M II (2nd ed.), pp. 136–67; G. Maspero, *Egypt. Ancient Sites and Modern Scenes* (London, 1910), pp. 168–82; H. De Meulenaere, in F. Tiradritti (ed.), *The Cairo Museum. Masterpieces of Egyptian Art* (London & New York, 1999), pp. 334–41

p. 119 **1903 Glazed Tiles from Medinet Habu**
P-M II (2nd ed.), pp. 524–25; G. Daressy, *Annales du Service des Antiquités de l'Égypte* 11 (1911), pp. 49–63; M. Saleh & H. Sourouzian, *The Egyptian Museum, Cairo. Official Catalogue* (Mainz, 1987), no. 226

p. 120 **1903 The Face of Khufu**
P-M V, p. 46; W. M. F. Petrie, *Abydos*, II (London, 1903); Z. Hawass, in *Mélanges Gamal Eddin Mokhtar*, I (Cairo, 1985), pp. 379–94

p. 121 **1904 In 'the Place of Beauties': Nefertari and her Tomb**
P-M I/2 (2nd ed.), pp. 762–65; E. Schiaparelli, *Relazione sui Lavori della Missione Archeologica Italiana in Egitto*, I. *Esplorazione della "Valle delle Regine" nella Necropoli di Tebe* (Turin, 1923); C. Leblanc, *Ta Set Neferou. Une nécropole de Thèbes-ouest et son histoire* (Cairo, 1989–)

p. 123 **1904–05 Two Portraits of Queen Tiye**
(a) P-M VII, pp. 361–62; W. M. F. Petrie, *Researches in Sinai* (London, 1906), pp. 126–27; (b) P-M IV, p. 113; L. Borchardt, *Der Porträtkopf der Königin Teje* (Leipzig, 1911); D. Wildung, *Antike Welt* 26/4 (1995), pp. 245–49

p. 124 **1905 The 'Proto-Sinaitic' Script**
P-M VII, pp. 360–61; W. M. F. Petrie, *Researches in Sinai* (London, 1906), pp. 129–32; B. Sass, *The Genesis of the Alphabet and its Development in the Second Millennium BC* (Wiesbaden, 1988); B. Sass, *Studia Alphabetica. On the Origin and Early History of the North-west Semitic, South Semitic and Greek Alphabets* (Freiburg/Göttingen, 1991)

p. 124 **1904 The Gold Harsaphes from el-Ihnasya**
P-M IV, p. 119; W. M. F. Petrie, *Ehnasya 1904* (London, 1905), p. 18

p. 124 **1905 The Brussels Relief of Queen Tiye**
P-M I/1 (2nd ed.), p. 87; H. Carter, *Annales du Service des Antiquités de l'Égypte* 4 (1903), pp. 177–78; B. van de Walle, L. Limme & H. De Meulenaere, *La Collection égyptienne. Les étapes marquantes de son développement* (Brussels, 1980), pp. 18–20

p. 125 **1905 The Treasure of Tukh el-Qaramus**
P-M IV, p. 27; C. C. Edgar, *Annales du Service des Antiquités de l'Égypte* 7 (1906), pp. 205–12; C. C. Edgar, in G. Maspero (ed.), *Le Musée égyptien*, II (Cairo, 1907), pp. 57–62

p. 126 **1906 The Tomb of Kha, Architect of Pharaoh**
P-M I/1 (2nd ed.), pp. 16–18; E. Schiaparelli, *Relazione sui Lavori della Missione Archeologica Italiana in Egitto*, II. *La tomba intatta dell'architetto Cha nella necropoli di Tebe* (Turin, 1927); A. Weigall, *The Treasury of Ancient Egypt* (Edinburgh, 1911), pp. 177–82; S. Tyson-Smith, *Mitteilungen des Deutschen Archäologischen Instituts, Abteilung Kairo* 48 (1992), pp. 193–231

p. 128 **1906 Hathor at Deir el-Bahri**
P-M II (2nd ed.), pp. 380–81; H. R. Hall & E. R. Ayrton, *The XIth Dynasty Temple at Deir el-Bahari*, I (London, 1907), pp. 63–67; G. Maspero, *New Light on Ancient Egypt* (London, 1908), pp. 272–77; M. Saleh & H. Sourouzian, *The Egyptian Museum, Cairo. Official Catalogue* (Mainz, 1987), no. 138

p. 128 **1906 Nubian Snow**
P-M VII, p. 98; J. A. Wilson, *Signs and Wonders Upon Pharaoh* (Chicago, 1964), p. 135; A. J. Peden, *Egyptian Historical Inscriptions of the Nineteenth Dynasty* (Jonsered, 1997), pp. 117–43

p. 129 **1906 Two Treasures from Tell Basta**
P-M IV, pp. 34–35; C. C. Edgar, in G. Maspero (ed.), *Le Musée égyptien*, II (Cairo, 1907), pp. 93–108; W. K. Simpson, *Bulletin of the Metropolitan Museum of Art* 8 (1949), pp. 61–65

p. 130 **1907–11 Five Years' Explorations at Thebes**
P-M I/2 (2nd ed.), pp. 615–20; The Earl of Carnarvon & Howard Carter, *Five Years' Explorations at Thebes* (Oxford, 1912); N. Reeves & J. H. Taylor, *Howard Carter: Before Tutankhamun* (London, 1992), pp. 85–103

p. 131 **1907 The Tomb of Two Brothers**
P-M V, p. 3; M. A. Murray, *The Tomb of Two Brothers* (Manchester, 1910); A. R. David (ed.), *Manchester Museum Mummy Project* (Manchester, 1979), *passim*

p. 132 **1908–10 Statues of Menkaure: Reisner at Giza**
P-M III/1 (2nd ed.), pp. 27ff.; G. A. Reisner, *Mycerinus. The Temple of the Third Pyramid at Giza* (Cambridge, Ma., 1931); W. Wood, *Journal of Egyptian Archaeology* 60 (1974), pp. 82–93

p. 133 **1908 Petrie's Qurna Burial**
P-M I/2 (2nd ed.), p. 606; W. M. F. Petrie, *Qurneh* (London, 1909); S. Tyson-Smith, *Mitteilungen des Deutschen Archäologischen Instituts, Abteilung Kairo* 48 (1992), pp. 193–231

p. 134 **1912 Nefertiti, Icon of Ancient Egypt: The Workshop of the Sculptor Thutmose**
P-M IV, pp. 202–03; G. Roeder, *Jahrbuch der preussischen Kunstsammlungen* 62/4 (1941), pp. 145–70; J. Phillips, *Amarna Letters* 1 (1991), pp. 31–40; Do. Arnold, *The Royal Women of Amarna* (New York, 1996), pp. 41–83

p. 136 **1913 The Tomb of Impy**
P-M III/1 (2nd ed.), pp. 91–92; W. S. Smith, *Ancient Egypt as Represented in the Museum of Fine Arts* (6th ed., Boston, 1961), pp. 66, 68–69

p. 137 **Before 1914 The Gebel el-Araq Knife**
P-M V, p. 107; G. Bénédite, *Monuments Piot* 22 (1916), pp. 1–34; É. Delange, forthcoming

p. 137 **1913 Statues of Amenhotep Son of Hapu and Paramessu from Karnak**
P-M II (2nd ed.), p. 188; G. Legrain, *Annales du Service des Antiquités de l'Égypte* 14 (1914), pp. 13–38; E. L. B. Terrace & H. G. Fischer, *Treasures of the Cairo Museum* (London, 1970), pp. 117–20

p. 138 **1914 The Hidden Treasure of Sithathoriunet**
P-M IV, pp. 109–10; G. Brunton, *Lahun*, I (London, 1920); H. E. Winlock, *The Treasure of el Lahun* (New York, 1934); A. Dodson, *KMT* 11/1 (2000), pp. 39–49

p. 141 **1914 Middle Kingdom Wooden Sculptures from el-Lisht**
P-M IV, p. 84; A. Lythgoe, *Bulletin of the Metropolitan Museum of Art*, Part 2. *Egyptian Expedition* (February, 1915), pp. 6–20; S. B. Johnson, *Journal of the American Research Center in Egypt* 17 (1980), pp. 11–20

p. 144 **1915 The Tomb of Djehutynakht at Deir el-Bersha**
P-M IV, pp. 177–79; S. D'Auria, P. Lacovara & C. H. Roehrig, *Mummies and Magic. The Funerary Arts of Ancient Egypt* (Boston, 1988), pp. 109–17

p. 145 **1915 Ptolemaic Egypt and the Zenon Archive**
C. Préaux, *Les Grecs en Égypte d'après les archives de Zenon* (Brussels, 1947); E. G. Turner, *Greek Papyri* (Oxford, 1968), *passim*

p. 146 **1915 The Jewels of Tell el-Muqdam**
P-M IV, p. 39; H. Gauthier, *Annales du Service des Antiquités de l'Égypte* 21 (1921), pp. 21–27

p. 147 **1916–20 Nubian Tombs of the 25th Dynasty: Nuri and el-Kurru**
P-M VII, pp. 195–98, 223–33; D. Dunham, *The Royal Cemeteries of Kush*, I. *El-Kurru* (Boston, 1950); II. *Nuri* (Boston, 1955); T. Kendall, *Kush. Lost Kingdoms of the Nile* (Brockton, 1981)

p. 149 **1916 The Carnarvon Gold Amun**
C. Aldred, *Journal of Egyptian Archaeology* 42 (1956), pp. 3–7

p. 150 **1916 'The Treasure of Three Egyptian Princesses'**
P-M I/2 (2nd ed.), pp. 591–92; H. E. Winlock, *The Treasure of Three Egyptian Princesses* (New York, 1948); C. Lilyquist, in C. J. Eyre (ed.), *Proceedings of the Seventh International Congress of Egyptologists, Cambridge, 3–9 September 1995* (Leuven, 1998), pp. 677–81

p. 152 **1919 The Tomb of Petosiris at Tuna el-Gebel**
P-M IV, pp. 169–74; E. Lefebvre, *Le tombeau de Petosiris* (Cairo, 1923–24); B. Menu, *Bulletin de l'Institut français d'archéologie orientale* 94 (1994), pp. 311–27, and subsequent volumes

p. 153 **1920 The Burial of Ashayet and 'Little Mayet'**
P-M II (2nd ed.), pp. 386–88; H. E. Winlock, *Excavations at Deir el Bahari, 1911–1931* (New York, 1942), pp. 35–46

p. 154 **1920 Letters from a Hectoring Father: The Heqanakht Papers**
P-M I/2 (2nd ed.), p. 651; H. E. Winlock, *Excavations at Deir el Bahari, 1911–1931* (New York, 1942), pp. 58–67; T. G. H. James, *The Hekanakhte Papers and Other Early Middle Kingdom Documents* (New York, 1962); Do. Arnold, *Metropolitan Museum Journal* 26 (1991), pp. 5–48; J. P. Allen, forthcoming

p. 154 **Before 1921 The Yellow Jasper Face from the Carnarvon Collection**
Do. Arnold (ed.), *The Royal Women of Amarna* (New York, 1996), pp. 35–39

p. 155 **1922 or before Flesh of the Gods: A Silver Cult Image of Horus the Elder**
N. Reeves & J. H. Taylor, *Howard Carter: Before Tutankhamun*

(London, 1992), pp. 170, 172; C. Roehrig, in Metropolitan Museum of Art, *Ancient Art from the Shumei Family Collection* (New York, 1996), pp. 4–7

p. 156 **1920 The Models of Meketre: Ancient Egypt in Miniature**
P-M I/1 (2nd ed.), pp. 359–64; H. E. Winlock, *Excavations at Deir el Bahari, 1911–1931* (New York, 1942), pp. 19–30; H. E. Winlock, *Models of Daily Life in Ancient Egypt* (Cambridge, Ma., 1955); Do. Arnold, *Metropolitan Museum Journal* 26 (1991), pp. 5–48; D. Forbes, *KMT* 6/3 (1995), pp. 24–37

p. 157 **1920 The Golden Uraeus of Sesostris II from el-Lahun**
P-M IV, p. 109; W. M. F. Petrie, G. Brunton & M. A. Murray, *Lahun*, II (London, 1923), pp. 12–13; M. Saleh & H. Sourouzian, *The Egyptian Museum, Cairo. Official Catalogue* (Mainz, 1987), no. 108

p. 158 **1920 Unwrapping the Mummy of Wah**
P-M I/2 (2nd ed.), p. 667; H. E. Winlock, *Excavations at Deir el Bahari, 1911–1931* (New York, 1942), pp. 29–30, 222–28

p. 159 **1920 Statues of Meryrehashtef**
P-M IV, p. 115; W. M. F. Petrie & G. Brunton, *Sedment*, I (London, 1924), pp. 2–5

p. 160 **1922 The Tomb of Tutankhamun**
P-M I/2 (2nd ed.), pp. 569–86; H. Carter & A. C. Mace, *The Tomb of Tut.ankh.Amen* (London, 1923–33); H. Carter, *Tut.ankh.amen. The Politics of Discovery* (ed. N. Reeves, London, 1998); N. Reeves, *The Complete Tutankhamun* (London & New York, 1990)

p. 167 **1923 The Slain Soldiers of an Egyptian King**
P-M I/2 (2nd ed.), pp. 650–51; H. E. Winlock, *The Slain Soldiers of Neb-hepet-Re' Mentu-hotpe* (New York, 1945); Do. Arnold, *Metropolitan Museum Journal* 26 (1991), pp. 5–48

p. 168 **1925 The Mystery Tomb of Queen Hetepheres**
P-M III/1 (2nd ed.), pp. 179–82; G. A. Reisner, *The Tomb of Hetepheres, the Mother of Cheops* (Harvard, 1955); M. Lehner, *The Pyramid Tomb of Hetep-heres and the Satellite Pyramid of Khufu* (Mainz, 1985)

p. 169 **1924–33 Statues and Tiles at the Step Pyramid of Djoser**
P-M III/2 (2nd ed.), pp. 399ff.; C. M. Firth, J. E. Quibell & J.-P. Lauer, *The Step Pyramid* (Cairo, 1935); R. Pirelli, in F. Tiradritti (ed.), *The Cairo Museum. Masterpieces of Egyptian Art* (London & New York, 1999), pp. 46–47

p. 172 **1925 An Amarna King and his Queen: The Karnak Colossi**
P-M II (2nd ed.), pp. 253–54; H. Chévrier, *Annales du Service des Antiquités de l'Égypte* 26 (1926), pp. 121–27, and subsequent volumes; D. Forbes, *Amarna Letters* 3 (1994), pp. 46–55

p. 173 **1926 Scarabs from Deir el-Bahri**
H. E. Winlock, *Excavations at Deir el Bahari, 1911–1931* (New York, 1942), pp. 132–33

p. 174 **1928 The Library of Kenherkhepshef, Scribe and Scholar**
A. H. Gardiner, *The Library of A. Chester Beatty. The Chester Beatty Papyri, No. 1* (London, 1931); A. H. Gardiner, *Hieratic Papyri in the British Museum. Third Series. Chester Beatty Gift* (London, 1935); J. Cerny, *Papyrus de Deir el-Médineh*, I (Cairo, 1978); Y. Koenig, *Bulletin de l'Institut français d'archéologie orientale* 81 (1981), pp. 41–43

p. 176 **1929 The Tomb of Queen Meryetamun**
P-M I/2 (2nd ed.), pp. 629–30; H. E. Winlock, *The Tomb of Queen Meryet-Amun at Thebes* (New York, 1932); H. E. Winlock, *Excavations at Deir el Bahari, 1911–1931* (New York, 1942), pp. 174–200

p. 177 **1930 A Crock of Gold from el-Amarna**
H. Frankfort & J. D. S. Pendlebury, *The City of Akhenaten*, II (London, 1933), pp. 59–61; M. Chubb, *Nefertiti Lived Here* (London, 1998), pp. 132–36

p. 178 **1929–30 Mersuankh and his Statues**
P-M III/1 (2nd ed.), pp. 269–70; S. Hassan, *Excavations at Giza*, I (Cairo, 1932), pp. 104–17; C. N. Reeves, *Göttinger Miszellen* 35 (1979), pp. 47–49

p. 179 **1931–34 Emery at Ballana and Qustul: Tombs of the X-Group**
P-M VII, p. 123; W. B. Emery & L. P. Kirwan, *The Royal Tombs of Ballana and Qustul* (Cairo, 1938); W. B. Emery, *Nubian Treasure* (London, 1948)

p. 179 **1931 Tutankhamun's Colossi**
P-M II (2nd ed.), pp. 458–59; U. Hölscher, *The Excavation of Medinet Habu*, II (Chicago, 1939), pp. 102–05; M. Saleh & H. Sourouzian, *The Egyptian Museum, Cairo. Official Catalogue* (Mainz, 1987), no. 173; D. Forbes, *KMT* 9/3 (1998), pp. 30–33

p. 181 **1932 The Statues of Heqaib**
P-M V, p. 233; L. Habachi, *Elephantine IV. The Sanctuary of Heqaib* (Mainz, 1985)

p. 182 **1935–39 Great Tombs of Early Egypt: Emery at Saqqara**
P-M III/2 (2nd ed.), pp. 440–47;

W. B. Emery, *Great Tombs of the First Dynasty* (Cairo/London, 1949–58); W. B. Emery, *Archaic Egypt* (Harmondsworth, 1961); B. J. Kemp, *Antiquity* 41 (1967), pp. 22–32

p. 183 **1930s The Jewelry of the High Priest Herihor**
H. W. Müller, *Pantheon* 38 (1979), pp. 237–46; M. Seidel, in A. Eggebrecht (ed.), *Pelizaeus-Museum, Hildesheim. Die ägyptische Sammlung* (Mainz, 1993), p. 76

p. 184 **1936 The Tomb of the Parents of Senenmut, Hatshepsut's Favourite**
P-M I/2 (2nd ed.), pp. 669–70; A. Lansing & W. C. Hayes, *Bulletin of the Metropolitan Museum of Art, Part 2. Egyptian Expedition* (January, 1937), pp. 5–39; S. Tyson-Smith, *Mitteilungen des Deutschen Archäologischen Instituts, Abteilung Kairo* 48 (1992), pp. 193–231; P. Dorman, forthcoming

p. 186 **1936 The Tod Treasure: Tribute from East and West**
P-M V, p. 167; F. Bisson de la Roque, *Trésor de Tôd* (Cairo, 1950); and *Le Trésor de Tôd* (Cairo, 1953); B. J. Kemp & R. Merrilees, *Minoan Pottery in Second Millennium Egypt* (Mainz, 1980), pp. 290–96

p. 187 **1937 The Unas Causeway: a Gallery of Egyptian Art**
P-M III/2 (2nd ed.), pp. 418–20; S. Hassan, *Annales du Service des Antiquités de l'Égypte* 38 (1938), pp. 519–20

p. 189 **1939–46 Royal Tombs at Tanis: Treasures of the Third Intermediate Period**
P. Montet, *La nécropole royale de Tanis* (Paris, 1947–60); J. Yoyotte et al., *Tanis. L'or des pharaons* (Paris, 1987); G. Goyon, *La découverte des trésors de Tanis* (Paris, 1987); J. Yoyotte, in F. Tiradritti (ed.), *The Cairo Museum. Masterpieces of Egyptian Art* (London & New York, 1999), pp. 302–09

p. 194 **1939 Amarna Reliefs from Hermopolis**
G. Roeder, *Amarna-Reliefs aus Hermopolis* (Hildesheim, 1969); J. D. Cooney, *Amarna Reliefs from Hermopolis in American Collections* (Brooklyn, 1965); R. Hanke, *Amarna-Reliefs aus Hermopolis* (Hildesheim, 1978)

p. 194 **1942 The Tomb of Prince Shoshenq**
P-M III/2 (2nd ed.), p. 846; A. Badawi, *Annales du Service des Antiquités de l'Égypte* 54 (1957), pp. 157–77; S. Schoske (ed.), *Nofret die Schöne* (Mainz, 1984), pp. 164–65

p. 195 **1944 Ptahshepses' Belt**
P-M III/2 (2nd ed.), p. 645; G. Brunton, *Annales du Service des Antiquités de l'Égypte* 47 (1947), pp. 125–33; A. Y. Moustafa, *Annales du Service des Antiquités de l'Égypte* 54 (1957), pp. 149–51; M. Vilimkova,

Egyptian Jewellery (London, 1969), no. 8

p. 195 **1945 The Nag Hammadi Codices**
Department of Antiquities of the Arab Republic of Egypt/ UNESCO, *The Facsimile Edition of the Nag Hammadi Codices. Introduction* (Leiden, 1984); J. M. Robinson (ed.), *The Nag Hammadi Codices in English* (Leiden, 1996)

p. 198 **1947 The Tell el-Maskhuta Treasure**
J. D. Cooney, *Five Years of Collecting Egyptian Art 1951–1956* (Brooklyn, 1956), pp. 43–44

p. 199 **1950 The Treasure of Queen Takhut**
J. Leclant, *Orientalia* 19 (1950), pp. 495–96

p. 200 **1952 The Lost Pyramid of Sekhemkhet**
P-M III/2 (2nd ed.), pp. 415–17; Z. Goneim, *Horus Sekhem-khet. The Unfinished Step Pyramid at Saqqara*, I (Cairo, 1957); Z. Goneim, *The Buried Pyramid* (London, 1956); J.-P. Lauer, *Saqqara. The Royal Cemetery of Memphis* (London, 1976), pp. 137–40

p. 202 **1954 The Stela of Kamose**
P-M II (2nd ed.), p. 37; L. Habachi, *The Second Stela of Kamose* (Glückstadt, 1972); H. S. Smith & A. Smith, *Zeitschrift für ägyptische Sprache und Altertumskunde* 103 (1976), pp. 48–76

p. 203 **1954 Khufu's Boats at the Great Pyramid**
P-M III/1 (2nd ed.), p. 15; M. Z. Nour et al., *The Cheops Boats*, I (Cairo, 1960); N. Jenkins, *The Boat Beneath the Pyramid* (London & New York, 1980); P. Lipke, *The Royal Ship of Cheops* (Oxford, 1984)

p. 204 **1956 Nefruptah**
N. Farag & Z. Iskander, *The Discovery of Neferwptah* (Cairo, 1971); M. Saleh & H. Sourouzian, *The Egyptian Museum, Cairo. Official Catalogue* (Mainz, 1987), nos. 114–16

p. 205 **1957 A Head of King Userkaf**
P-M III/1 (2nd ed.), p. 325; H. Ricke, *Annales du Service des Antiquités de l'Égypte* 55 (1958), pp. 73–77; E. L. B. Terrace & H. G. Fischer, *Treasures of the Cairo Museum* (London, 1970), pp. 53–56

p. 206 **1964–71 The Sacred Animal Necropolis, Saqqara**
P-M III/2 (2nd ed.), pp. 820–27; W. B. Emery, *Journal of Egyptian Archaeology* 51 (1965), pp. 3–8, and subsequent volumes; H. S. Smith, *A Visit to Ancient Egypt* (Warminster, 1974)

p. 208 **1964–65 A Statue Finds its Face**
J. Lipinska, *Deir el-Bahari*, II. *The Temple of Thutmosis III: The Architecture* (Warsaw, 1977), p. 11;

and *Deir el-Bahari*, IV. *The Temple of Thutmosis III: Statuary and Votive Monuments* (Warsaw, 1984), p. 16; Roemer- und Pelizaeus-Museum, Hildesheim, *Ägyptens Aufstieg zur Weltmacht* (Mainz, 1987), pp. 184–87

p. 209 **1965 The Akhenaten Temple Project: Rebuilding by Computer**
R. W. Smith, *National Geographic Magazine* 138 (1970), pp. 634–55; R. W. Smith, D. B. Redford, et al., *The Akhenaten Temple Project* (Warminster, etc., 1976–)

p. 211 **1967 Amenophis III and Sebek: a Statue from Damansha**
H. S. K. Bakry, *Mitteilungen des Deutschen Archäologischen Instituts, Abteilung Kairo* 27 (1971), pp. 131–46; B. V. Bothmer (ed.), *The Luxor Museum of Ancient Egyptian Art. Catalogue* (Cairo, 1979), pp. 82–84 and 94–95

p. 211 **1960s A Hoard of Middle Kingdom Bronzes from the Faiyum**
G. Ortiz, *In Pursuit of the Absolute. Art of the Ancient World from the George Ortiz Collection* (London, 1994), nos. 33–37

p. 212 **1974 The Unfinished Pyramid: Secrets of Raneferef**
P-M III/2 (2nd ed.), p. 340;

M. Verner, *Forgotten Pharaohs, Lost Pyramids. Abusir* (Prague, 1994)

p. 213 **1978 The Verses of Cornelius Gallus**
R. D. Anderson, P. J. Parsons & R. G. M. Nisbet, *Journal of Roman Studies* 69 (1979), pp. 125–55

p. 215 **1975 New Kingdom Tombs at Saqqara**
P-M III/2 (2nd ed.), pp. 655ff.; G. T. Martin, *Journal of Egyptian Archaeology* 62 (1976), pp. 5–13, and subsequent volumes; G. T. Martin, *The Hidden Tombs of Memphis* (London, 1991)

p. 217 **1978 A Treasure of Ramesses XI**
[J. Romer], *Theban Royal Tomb Project. Introduction* (Brooklyn, 1979), p. 16; M. Ciccarello & J. Romer, *A Preliminary Report of the Recent Work in the Tombs of Ramesses X and XI in the Valley of the Kings* (Brooklyn, 1979), pp. 4–7

p. 219 **1982 The Face of Most Ancient Egypt**
J. Eiwanger, *Mitteilungen des Deutschen Archäologischen Instituts, Abteilung Kairo* 38 (1982), pp. 67–82; F. Tiradritti, in F. Tiradritti (ed.), *The Cairo Museum. Masterpieces of Egyptian Art* (London & New York, 1999), p. 34

p. 219 **1981 The Colossal Statue of Meryetamun**
Y. S. S. Al-Masri, *Annales du Service des Antiquités de l'Égypte* 69 (1983), pp. 7–13

p. 220 **1987 A Tomb for the Sons of Ramesses II**
K. R. Weeks, *The Lost Tomb* (New York, 1998); K. R. Weeks (ed.), *KV5. A Preliminary Report* (Cairo, 2000)

p. 222 **1987–97 Akhenaten's Prime-Minister, Aperel**
(a) Aperel: P-M III/2 (2nd ed.), p. 562; A. Zivie, *Découverte à Saqqarah. Le vizier oublié* (Paris, 1990); (b) Maia: A. Zivie, *Egyptian Archaeology* 13 (1998), pp. 7–8

p. 224 **1987 Avaris and the Aegean: Minoan Frescoes in Egypt**
M. Bietak & N. Marinatos, *Ägypten und Levante* 5 (1994), pp. 50–71; M. Bietak, *Avaris. The Capital of the Hyksos* (London, 1996); M. Bietak, in E. D. Oren (ed.), *The Hyksos: New Historical and Archaeological Perspectives* (Philadelphia, 1997), pp. 117–24

p. 225 **1987 An Asiatic Dignitary**
M. Bietak, *Ägypten und Levante* 2 (1991), pp. 47–75; M. Bietak, in E. D. Oren (ed.), *The Hyksos: New Historical and Archaeological*

Perspectives (Philadelphia, 1997), pp. 100–01; D. M. Rohl, *A Test of Time*, I (London, 1996), p. 36

p. 226 **1989 The Luxor statue Cache**
M. el-Saghir, *Das Statuenversteck im Luxortempel* (Mainz, 1992); W. R. Johnson, *Amarna Letters* 3 (1994), pp. 129–49

p. 228 **1989 The Dush Treasure**
M. Reddé, *Douch*, IV. *Le trésor* (Cairo, 1992); A. Leone, in F. Tiradritti (ed.), *The Cairo Museum. Masterpieces of Egyptian Art* (London & New York, 1999), pp. 398–99

p. 229 **1990 The Tombs of the Pyramid Builders at Giza**
Z. Hawass, in M. Bietak (ed.), *Haus und Palast im Alten Ägypten* (Vienna, 1996), pp. 53–67; Z. Hawass *Archaeology* 50/1 (1997), pp. 39–43

p. 230 **1993 Surprises of a Theban Tomb**
www.newton.cam.ac.uk/egypt/tt9/index.html

p. 232 **1994 Egyptology Underwater: Alexandria ad Aegyptum**
J.-Y. Empereur, *Alexandria Rediscovered* (London, 1998), pp. 62–80; F. Goddio (ed.),

Alexandria: The Submerged Royal Quarters. Surveys and Excavations 1992–97 (London, 1998)

p. 233 **1994 Jewels in the Sands and Other Dahshur Finds**
A. Oppenheim, in F. Tiradritti (ed.), *The Cairo Museum. Masterpieces of Egyptian art* (London & New York, 1999), pp. 146–47; Di. Arnold, *Egyptian Archaeology* 9 (1996), p. 24

p. 235 **1997 The New Vizier**
K. Mysliwiec, in *Egyptian Archaeology* 13 (1998), pp. 37–39

p. 236 **1995 Iufaa**
K. Bares & K. Smolarikova, *Göttinger Miszellen* 156 (1997), pp. 9–26; Z. Hawass, *National Geographic Magazine* 194 (1998), pp. 102–13; M. Verner, *KMT* 10/1 (1999), pp. 18–27

p. 237 **1999 Valley of the Golden Mummies: The Necropolis in the Oasis**
Z. Hawass, *Archaeology* 52/5 (1999), pp. 38–43; Z. Hawass, *Valley of the Golden Mummies* (New York & London, 2000)

Sources of Quotations

Abbreviations

ASAE Annales du Service des Antiquités de l'Égypte
BIE Bulletin de l'Institut d'Égypte, Cairo
BMMA Bulletin of the Metropolitan Museum of Art, New York
BSFE Bulletin de la Société française d'Égyptologie
CRAIBL Compte-Rendus de l'Academie des Inscriptions et Belles-Lettres
EEFAR Egypt Exploration Fund Archaeological Report
JEA Journal of Egyptian Archaeology
JRS Journal of Roman Studies
MDAIK Mitteilungen des Deutschen Archäologischen Instituts, Abteilung Kairo
RdT Recueil de travaux relatifs à la philologie et à l'archéologie égyptiennes et assyriennes
ZÄS Zeitschrift für ägyptische Sprache und Altertumskunde

p. 10 '[Abou Abd Allah ... year [AH] 511' H. Vyse, *Operations carried on at the Pyramids of Gizeh in 1837* (London, 1840), II, p. 334. **p. 11** 'fable ... to beget wonder' George Sandys, quoted in L. Cottrell, *The Mountains of Pharaoh* (London, 1956), p. 84. **p. 11** 'theories ... their imaginative folly' A. H. Gardiner, *Egyptian Grammar* (3rd ed., Oxford 1957), p. 11. **p. 12**

'Soldiers, ... down upon you' quoted by J. C. Herold, *Bonaparte in Egypt* (London, 1962), p. 95. **p. 14** 'They shall write ... living forever' translation after S. Quirke & C. Andrews, *The Rosetta Stone. Facsimile Drawing with an Introduction and Translations* (London, 1988), p. 22. **p. 15** 'however Mr. Champollion ... and extending it' T. Young, *An Account of Some Recent Discoveries in Hieroglyphical Literature, and Egyptian Antiquities* (London, 1823), p. 46. **p. 16** 'When [the corpse] ... the known world' V. Denon, *Travels in Upper and Lower Egypt*, III (London, 1803), pp. 217–18. **p. 17** 'You want it ... you please' quoted by J. C. Herold, *Bonaparte in Egypt* (London, 1962), p. 387. **p. 17** 'I have just ... not prevent them' ibid., pp. 387–88. **p. 18** 'we embarked for Egypt ... primitive nation' G. B. Belzoni, *Narrative of the Operations and Recent Discoveries within the Pyramids, Temples, Tombs, and Excavations, in Egypt and Nubia* (London, 1820), p. viii. **p. 20** '"But pray", ... perhaps, thank God!"' ibid., p. 119. **p. 20** 'I cannot boast ... on the walls' ibid., p. 124. **p. 21** 'I perceived immediately ... the Hall of Pillars' ibid., pp. 232–34. **p. 23** 'My torch, ... with the floor' ibid., p. 271. **p. 24** 'The Master Mohammed ... the closing up' ibid., p. 272. **p. 24** 'To the fan-

bearer ... which we know' British Museum EA 10375, after E. F. Wente, *Late Ramesside Letters* (Chicago, 1967), pp. 59–61, no. 28. **p. 25** 'Mr. Belzoni has ... remains unexplored' R. Richardson, *Travels Along the Mediterranean and Parts Adjacent; in the Company with the Earl of Belmore During the Years 1816, 1817-18* (London, 1822), II, p. 78. **p. 25** 'a monumental litany ... the dangerous goddess' J. Yoyotte, *BSFE* 87–88 (1980), p. 46. **p. 26** 'Very many years ... any important gift ...' F. W. Fairholt, *Up the Nile, and Home Again* (London, 1862), p. 92. **p. 26** 'tied up in ... out the money' H. Vyse, *Operations Carried on at the Pyramids of Gizeh in 1837* (London, 1840), II, p. 157. **p. 26** '[Since] its removal ... abandon all claim' E. A. W. Budge, *By Nile and Tigris*, I, pp. 82 and 103. **p. 28** 'Dec. 4 [1823] ... carrying flambeaux' J. Madox, *Excursions in the Holy Land, Egypt, Nubia, Syria, &c.* (London, 1834), II, pp. 392–93. **p. 28** 'The chamber was ... place for interment' ibid., p. 393. **p. 28** 'Passalacqua's men got ... to the other.' ibid., pp. 393–94. **p. 28** 'a dispute ... up in arms' ibid., pp. 394–95. **p. 30** 'And he caused ... bonds straightaway' after E. F. Wente, in W. K. Simpson (ed.), *The Literature of Ancient Egypt* (New Haven & London, 1973), p. 83. **p. 31** 'In the winter ... the Leyden Museum ...' J. Bonomi

Transactions of the Royal Society of Literature (2nd series) 1 (1843), pp. 108–12. **p. 32** 'during the researches ... attached to it.' G. d'Athanasi, *A Brief Account of the Researches and Discoveries in Upper Egypt, made under the direction of Henry Salt, Esq.* (London, 1836), pp. xi-xii. **p. 33** 'One day in ... ...and the Pharaoh ...' N. E. Scott, *BMMA* 9/8 (April, 1951), p. 201. **p. 33** 'to seal the mouth ... to glorify Re' ibid., p. 212. **p. 33** 'Flow out, poison ... Back, poison!' ibid., p. 205. **p. 34** 'Into this Egypt ... admirable monuments' E. Prisse d'Avennes, quoted by E. David, *Mariette Pacha 1821-1881* (Paris, 1994), pp. 59-60. **p. 35** 'The discovery of Ferlini ... find treasures there ...' R. Lepsius, *Letters from Egypt, Ethiopia, and the Peninsula of Sinai* (London, 1853), p. 197. **p. 37** 'The exposed opening ... from the Arabs ...' G. Ferlini, *Cenno sugli scavi operati nella Nubia e Catalogo degli oggetti ritrovati* (Bologna, 1837), translated in K.-H. Priese, *The Gold of Meroe* (New York, 1993), p. 13. **p. 37** 'soul filled with joy ... museums of Europe ...' ibid., p. 14. **p. 37** 'so much expenditure ... returns were expected' A. H. Rhind, *Thebes: its Tombs and their Tenants* (London, 1862), pp. 265-66. **p. 38** 'The interest of ... blind cupidity' J. F. Champollion, *Lettres écrites d'Égypte et de la Nubie* (Paris,

1833), pp. 460-61. **p. 40** 'M. Mariette proposes ... of his researches' quoted in E. Davis, *Mariette Pacha 1821-1881* (Paris, 1994), p. 35. **p. 40** 'One day, walking ... was therefore found' A. Mariette, *Le Sérapeum de Memphis* (Paris, 1882), pp. 5–6. **p. 42** '... nothing can ... plague of Egypt' quoted in E. David, *Mariette Pacha 1821-1881* (Paris, 1994), p. 88. **p. 43** 'Although 3700 years ... its original condition ...' quoted in K. Baedeker, *Egypt*, I. *Lower Egypt* (Leipzig, 1878), p. 374. **p. 46** 'when opened, was ... together with mortar' A. A. Eisenlohr, quoted by P. Grandet, *Le Papyrus Harris I (BM 9999)*, I (Cairo, 1994), p. 7. **p. 47** 'Few excavations have ... published afterwards' H. E. Winlock *The Rise and Fall of the Middle Kingdom in Thebes* (New York, 1947), p. 113. **p. 47** 'Said Pâshâ wanted ... the proposed itinerary' H. E. Winlock, *JEA* 10 (1924), p. 259. **p. 49** 'You will ensure ... inside a temple' A. Mariette, *CRAIBL* 3 (1862), quoted by R. T. Ridley, *Abr-Nahraim* 22 (1983–84), p. 121. **p. 49** 'a whirlwind which ... to destroy Egypt' E. David, *Mariette Pacha 1821-1881* (Paris, 1994), p. 103. **p. 50** 'I have pleasure ... serpent is missing' quoted in G. Maspero, *RdT* 12 (1892), p. 214. **pp. 50–51** 'We had just ... against a receipt ...' quoted in H. E. Winlock,

JEA 10 (1924), p. 253. **p. 52** 'A large wooden ... turned to dust ...' A. Mariette, *Catalogue général des monuments d'Abydos* (Paris, 1880), p. 528. **p. 52** '[Mariette] only visited ... as was prudent ...' W. M. F. Petrie, *Seventy Years in Archaeology* (London, 1931), pp. 49-50. **p. 53** 'You see, Monsieur, ... not better supervised' quoted in E. David, *Mariette Pacha 1821-1881* (Paris, 1994), p. 131. **p. 54** '[The statues] are ... sculptor only yesterday' A. Mariette, *Lettre de M. Auguste Mariette à M. le Vicomte de Rougé sur les résultats des fouilles entreprises par ordre du Vice-roi d'Égypte* (Paris, 1860), p. 7. **p. 54** 'A few hundred ... Musée du Louvre' A. Mariette, *Le Sérapéum de Memphis*, I (Paris, 1882), p. 93. **p. 55** 'The tomb of Hosi ... precious panels ...' A. Mariette, *Album du Musée de Boulaq* (Cairo, 1871), opp. pl. 12. **p. 55** 'There were no ... in a gallery' J. E. Quibell, *Excavations at Saqqara (1911-12). The Tomb of Hesy* (Cairo, 1913), p. 2. **p. 57** 'Up to that ... repelled them' G. Maspero, *Popular Stories of Ancient Egypt* (London, 1915), pp. x-xi. **p. 58** 'He had found ... back at him' A. Daninos, *RdT* 8 (1886), p. 71. **pp. 58–59** 'I have sometimes ... done to it' A. A. Quibell, *A Wayfarer in Egypt* (London, 1925), p. 113. **p. 60** 'O ye who ... terrible faces!' trans. after A. Piankoff, *The Pyramid of Unas* (Princeton, 1968), p. 29. **p. 61** 'The pyramids ... and decorated' G. Maspero, *Egyptian Archaeology* (2nd ed. London, 1889), pp. 135–36. **p. 61** 'at the expense ... E. Brugsch Bey' E. A. W. Budge, *The Mummy* (2nd ed., Cambridge, 1925), p. 37. **p. 61** 'one of the ... of Egyptian decipherment' ibid., p. 226. **p. 62** 'He will go far' E. David, *Mariette Pacha 1821–1881* (Paris, 1994), p. 176. **p. 64** 'For the last ... suspicion became certainty ...' A. B. Edwards, *Illustrated London News*, 4 February 1882. **p. 65** 'cases of porcelain ... to stagger me' É. Brugsch, quoted in E. L. Wilson, *Century Magazine* 34/1 (May, 1887), p. 6. **p. 65** 'Collecting my senses ... my own ancestors' É. Brugsch, ibid. **p. 66** 'Year 15, 3rd month ... priest of Pinudjem' after C. N. Reeves, *Valley of the Kings* (London, 1990), p. 235. **p. 67** '[Here at el-Nebira] ... Greek pottery ...' W. M. F. Petrie, *Ten Years' Digging in Egypt, 1881-1891* (London, 1892), pp. 36–7. **p. 67** 'smashings ... vase-rooms' W. M. F. Petrie, *Seventy Years in Archaeology* (London, 1931), p. 38. **p. 68** 'determined to understand its history' W. M. F. Petrie, *Ten Years' Digging in Egypt, 1881–1891* (London, 1892), p. 38. **p. 68** 'The only place ... had a name ...' ibid., p. 38. **p. 68** 'All that day ... and well found' ibid, p. 38. **p. 68** 'as a commercial ... altars and temples' Herodotus II, 178, trans. by A. de Sélincourt, *Herodotus. The Histories* (Harmondsworth, 1954), p. 200. **p. 69** 'At five in ... the last body ...' E. Toda y Güell, *ASAE* 20 (1920), p. 147. **p. 69** 'It was clear ... and the Arabs' ibid., p. 150. **p. 69** 'The ground was ... were first made' ibid, p. 151. **p. 71** 'appointment was unfortunate ... local Egyptians' W. R. Dawson, E. P. Uphill & M. L. Bierbrier, *Who Was Who in Egyptology* (3rd ed., London, 1995), p. 176. **p. 71** 'out of all reason' W. M. F. Petrie, *Seventy Years in Archaeology* (London, 1931), p. 135. **p. 71** 'all those who ... regretted the appointment' E. A. W. Budge, *By Nile and Tigris*, I (London, 1920), p. 133. **p. 72** 'Whilst the official ... *i.e.* cuneiform' ibid., pp. 128–29. **p. 72** 'May my brother ... plentiful as dirt' EA19, after W. L. Moran, *The Amarna Letters* (Baltimore, 1992), p. 44. **p. 73** 'On the largest ... historical importance' ibid, pp. 140–41. **p. 73** 'shewn to Prof. Sayce ... tablets were found' W. M. F. Petrie, *Tell el-Amarna* (London, 1894), p. 23. **p. 73** 'in a chamber ... two rubbish pits' ibid. **p. 73** 'It has been ... entirely disappeared' J. D. S. Pendlebury, *The City of Akhenaten*, III (London, 1951), p. 114. **p. 73** 'To the king ... Apiru destroy us' EA299, after W. L. Moran, *The Amarna Letters* (Baltimore, 1992), p. 340–41. **p. 75** 'Send me much ... taken to you' EA9, ibid., p. 18. **p. 77** 'A short work ... from the ground' W. M. F. Petrie, *Ten Years Digging in Egypt, 1881–1891* (London, 1892), pp. 83–84. **p. 77** 'an area about ... 800 feet broad' W. M. F. Petrie, *Hawara, Biahmu, and Arsinoe* (London, 1889), p. 5. **p. 77** 'could be erected ... on the west' ibid. **p. 78** 'So soon as ... they were painted' W. M. F. Petrie, *Ten Years Digging in Egypt, 1881–1891* (London, 1892), p. 97. **p. 78** 'kept above ground ... with the house' ibid., p. 99. **p. 80** 'This is a ... to run away' trans. after E. F. Wente, *Letters from Ancient Egypt* (Atlanta, 1990), p. 86. **p. 80** 'As only five ... to our sources' W. M. F. Petrie, *Ten Years' Digging in Egypt, 1881–1891* (London, 1892), pp. 120. **p. 81** 'At Luxor they ... mummy tomb' J. Capart (ed.), *Travels in Egypt (December 1880 to May 1891). Letters of Charles Edwin Wilbour* (Brooklyn, 1936), p. 590, 25 February 1891. **p. 82** 'A day or two ... French could find' W. M. F. Petrie, *Seventy Years in Archaeology* (London,1931), pp. 136–37. **p. 82** 'great satisfaction was ... expressed by everyone' E. A. W. Budge, *By Nile and Tigris*, II (London, 1920), p. 328. **p. 84** 'surely one of ... bequeathed to us' N. de G. Davies, *JEA* 7 (1921), p. 1. **p. 84** 'a couple of ... the season's work' ibid., p. 1. **p. 85** 'the department ... pick up the pieces' W. M. F. Petrie, *Seventy Years in Archaeology* (London, 1931), p. 138. **p. 85** 'Those who trod ... his beneficent rays; M. Saleh & H. Sourouzian, *The Egyptian Museum, Cairo. Official Catalogue* (Mainz, 1987), no. 170. **p. 88** 'During the winter ... justified his decision ...' *Illustrated London News* 7 March 1896: quoted in E. Bacon (ed.), *The Great Archaeologists* (London, 1976), p. 114. **p. 89** 'Like Princess Ita's ... were very resplendent' J. De Morgan, *Fouilles à Dahchour en 1894–1895* (Vienna, 1903), pp. 55–56 (trans. after R. L. Cron). **p. 90** 'a heap of jewels ... without any arrangement' ibid., p. 5 (trans. after R. L. Cron). **p. 91** '... soon we found ... 4500 years ago' J. de Morgan, *Fouilles à Dahchour, mars–juin, 1894* (Vienna, 1895), p. 108 (trans. after R. L. Cron). **p. 91** 'Beware of subjects... day of woe!' trans. after M. Lichtheim, *Ancient Egyptian Literature*, I (Berkeley, 1973), p. 136. **p. 92** 'Among the important ... known as Tunah ...' H. Wallis, *Egyptian Ceramic Art* (London, 1900), p. xvi. **p. 92** 'vessels of all ... the Roman conquest' ibid., p. xvii. **p. 93** 'The sum total ... taking first honours' ibid., p. xvii. **p. 94** 'Nearly 2,000 ... wholly by hand ...' *The Times*, 5 July 1895. **p. 94** 'female figure ... on the body' W. M. F. Petrie & J. E. Quibell, *Naqada and Ballas, 1895* (London, 1896), p. 45. **p. 95** 'The prehistoric pottery ... blackened this pottery' W. M. F. Petrie, *The Arts and Crafts of Ancient Egypt* (London, 1909), p. 130. **p. 95** 'I had the ... was his reply' W. M. F. Petrie, *Seventy Years in Archaeology* (London, 1931), p. 160. **p. 96** 'about one-third ... of small objects' J. E. Quibell, *The Ramesseum* (London, 1898), p. 3. **p. 97** 'The distinctive merit ... a recordless antiquity' *The Times*, 9 July 1898. **p. 97** 'Quibell ... man to exasperation' M. A. Murray, *My First Hundred Years* (London, 1963), p. 109. **pp. 97–98** 'there came into ... plumes of gold' J. E. Quibell & F. W. Green, *Hierakonpolis*, II (London, 1902), p. 27. **p. 98** 'The two legs ... of Pepy I' ibid., pp. 27-28. **p. 101** '[Émile] Brugsch said ... is twenty devils' W. M. F. Petrie, *Seventy Years in Archaeology* (London, 1931), p. 168. **p. 101** 'gain his respectful ... his official arrogance' ibid., p. 168. **p. 101** 'Soon after [Loret's] ... And it never did' A. H. Sayce, *Reminiscences* (London, 1923), p. 306. **p. 103** 'The find is ... kings are intact ...' *The Times*, 13 April 1898. **pp. 103–04** 'The coffins and ... everywhere cartouches!' V. Loret, *BIE* 9 (3 sér.) (1898), pp. 108-09. **p. 105** 'Loret was now ... else was available ...' W. M. F. Petrie, *Seventy Years in Archaeology* (London, 1931), p. 173. **p. 106** 'We must get ... Lyons' A. H. Sayce, *Reminiscences* (London, 1923), p. 306. **p. 106** 'Maspero had one ... part in them' ibid. **p. 106** 'the last representative ... Egyptology' É. Naville, *JEA* 3 (1916), p. 234. **p. 106** 'when riding home... of stone work' H. Carter, *ASAE* 2 (1901), p. 201. **p. 107** '[A] workman, angry ... a large premium' H. I. Bell, *Egypt, from Alexander the Great to the Arab Conquest* (Oxford, 1948), p. 17. **p. 108** 'The site ... way to England ...' *The Times*, 29 May 1897. **p. 108** 'shortly before sunset ... been thrown away' *EEFAR* 1905-06, pp. 8–9. **p. 109** 'The Egypt Exploration Fund ... brilliantly justified him' *The Times*, 24 April 1900. **p. 109** 'a vault built ... a granite cenotaph' *The Standard*, 3 March 1898. **p. 110** 'The pottery jars ... in the rubbish' W. M. F. Petrie, *The Royal Tombs of the Earliest Dynasties*, II (London, 1901), p. 2. **p. 110** 'Brugsch ... a dangerous place' W. M. F. Petrie, *Seventy Years in Archaeology* (London, 1931), p. 174. **p. 112** 'Dreyer contends ... tomb into another' L. P. Brock, *KMT* 2/4 (1991–92), p. 8. **p. 112** 'for export to ... trade relations' G. Dreyer, *Egyptian Archaeology* 3 (1993), p. 12. **p. 112** 'Labels ... four hieroglyphic signs' L. P. Brock, *KMT* 2/4 (1991–92), p. 8. **p. 112** 'May the face ... eternity and indestructible' trans. after I. E. S. Edwards, *The Pyramids of Egypt* (Harmondsworth, 1985), p. 263. **p. 113** 'His interest in ... quick to go' J. L. Smith, *Tombs, Temples, and Ancient Art* (Norman, 1956), p. 189. **p. 115** 'You lived on ... ate the tin' M. A. Murray, *My First Hundred Years* (London, 1963), p. 112. **p. 115** 'Imagine entering ... just been disturbed ...' A. Weigall, *The Treasury of Ancient Egypt* (Edinburgh & London, 1910), pp. 174–75. **p. 117** 'Number inscriptions... Wire reply' quoted S. Orel, *KMT* 8/1 (1997), p. 58. **p. 118** 'For a year ... at the end ...' G. Maspero, *Egypt. Ancient Sites and Modern Scenes* (London, 1910), p. 168. **p. 118** 'never to abandon ... were brought out' ibid., p. 169. **p. 118** 'This energetic and ... Egyptian government ...' J. L. Smith, *Tombs, Temples and Ancient Art* (Norman, 1956), p. 23. **p. 119** 'They seemed to ... picked them out' G. Maspero, *Egypt. Ancient Sites and Modern Scenes* (London, 1910), p. 171. **p. 119** 'numerous wooden statuettes, impossible to preserve' G. Legrain, *EEFAR* 1904–5, p. 23. **p. 120** 'Unhappily the head ... by the digger' W. M. F. Petrie, *Seventy Years in Archaeology* (London, 1931), p. 182. **p. 120** 'Petrie set the... he did not' M. S. Drower, *Flinders Petrie. A Life in Archaeology* (London, 1985), p. 266. **p. 120** 'After three weeks ... head was recovered' W. M. F. Petrie, *Seventy Years in Archaeology* (London, 1931), p. 182. **p. 120** 'the tip of ... a life-size statue' ibid., p. 182. **p. 121** 'A great, learned ... Such was Schiaparelli' *JEA* 14 (1928), p. 181. **p. 124** 'During the course ... in the ground ...' W. M. F. Petrie, *Ehnasya 1904* (London, 1905), p. 18. **p. 125** 'About the beginning ... and silver coins' C. C. Edgar, *ASAE* 7 (1906), p.206. **p. 125** 'some 117 ozs.' H. Carter, in *EEFAR 1904–5*, p. 29. **p. 125** 'no one will ... the whole history' C. C. Edgar, in G. Maspero (ed.), *Le Musée égyptien*, II (Cairo, 1907), p. 93. **p. 126** 'The mouth of ... ever seen before' A. Weigall, *The Treasury of Ancient Egypt* (Edinburgh & London, 1911), p. 178. **p. 126** 'The wood retained ... it is, sir'" ibid., p. 178. **p. 127** 'One asked ... was yet unaccomplished' A. Weigall, *The Treasury of Ancient Egypt* (Edinburgh & London, 1911), pp. 180–81. **p. 128** 'a cow's head ... through the opening' G. Maspero, *New Light on Ancient Egypt* (London, 1908), p. 272. **p. 128** 'On Washington's birthday... the first time' J. A. Wilson, *Signs and Wonders Upon Pharaoh* (Chicago, 1964), p. 135. **p. 129** 'One man turned ... to a dealer ...' G. Maspero, *New Light on Ancient Egypt* (London, 1908), p. 285. **p. 129** 'As soon as ... with some difficulty' C. C. Edgar, *Le Musée égyptien*, II (Cairo, 1907), p. 95. **p. 129** 'It lay in ... nothing was lost' ibid., p. 95. **p. 130** 'part of the stock ... a small town ...' G. Maspero, *New Light on Ancient Egypt* (London, 1908), p. 287. **p. 131** 'The whole of ... of this period ...' W. M. F. Petrie, *Gizeh and Rifeh* (London, 1907), p. 12. **p. 132** 'Reisner's excavations ... hardly contain himself ...' J. L. Smith, *Tombs, Temples and Ancient Art* (Norman, 1956), p. 122. **p. 132** 'the finder ... and Concreta!' quoted by T. Hoving, *Tutankhamun, the Untold Story* (New York, 1978), p. 51. **p. 133** 'Previous to the ... great creative period ...' G. A. Reisner, *Mycerinus. The Temples of the Third Pyramid at Giza* (Cambridge, Ma., 1931), p. 108. **p. 134** 'cocky little Ludwig Borchardt' J. A. Wilson, *Thousands of Years* (New York, 1972), p. 58. **p. 134** 'one whom ... himself instructed' Biri Fay, *Egyptian Museum Berlin* (Berlin, 1985), p. 78. **p. 136** 'What the Germans ... they keep!' Lecture, H. G. Güterbock, University of Chicago, February 1987. **p. 137** 'of all the ... Gebel el Araq knife' M. Hoffman, *Egypt Before the Pharaohs* (New York, 1980), p. 340. **p. 138** 'No one but ... jewellery to London' W. M. F. Petrie, *Seventy Years in Archaeology* (London, 1931), p. 233. **p. 140** 'For a week... then photographed it' ibid., p. 233. **p. 140** 'I named in ... had found'; 'The answer from ... closed that door' ibid., pp. 233–34. **p. 141** 'with a lovely ... on her head' J. L. Smith, *Tombs, Temples and Ancient Art* (Norman, 1956), p. 163. **p. 141** 'the eyes, ears ... far larger statues' W. C. Hayes, *The Scepter of Egypt, I* (New York, 1953), p. 194. **p. 142** 'Maspero saw the ... announced a change ...' J. L. Smith, *Tombs, Temples and Ancient Art* (Norman, 1956), p. 139. **p. 144** 'The outstanding object ... coffin ever found' D. Dunham, *The Egyptian Department and its Excavations* (Boston, 1958), p. 67. **p. 145** 'Above all ... gives them coherence' C. C. Edgar, *Zenon Papyri in the University of Michigan Collection* (Ann Arbor, 1931), p. 3. **p. 145** 'the largest and ... documents in history' E. G. Turner, *Greek Papyri. An Introduction* (Oxford, 1966), p. 35. **p. 145** 'In one letter ... of Ptolemy Philadelphus' S. R. K.

Glanville (ed.), *The Legacy of Egypt* (Oxford, 1942), p. 272. **p. 146** 'The north chamber … and remove it' C. C. Edgar, quoted by H. Gauthier, *ASAE* 21 (1921), pp. 22–23. **p. 147** 'Of the many … thirty-two inches' D. Dunham, *The Egyptian Department and its Excavations* (Boston, 1958), p. 111. **pp. 148–49** 'A few miles … the [Boston] Museum' ibid., p. 102. **p. 150** 'When we saw … some palace conspiracy' H. E. Winlock, *The Treasure of Three Egyptian Princesses* (New York, 1948), pp. 5–6. **p. 150** 'Before the middle … had been found' ibid., p. 8. **p. 151** 'The names of … for foreign words'; 'since such names … of Syrian chieftains' ibid., p. 3. **p. 151** 'It is clear … somewhere near by' ibid., p. 7. **p. 152** 'The love of … to lose it' T. G. Wakeling *Forged Egyptian Antiquities* (London, 1912), pp. 8–9. **p. 152** '… a much-travelled … funerary monument' C. Aldred, *Egyptian Art in the Days of the Pharaohs, 3100–320* BC (London, 1980), p. 236. **p. 152** 'a complete town … or three days' A. H. Zayed, *The Antiquities of El Minia* (Cairo, 1960), p. 101. **p. 153** 'tipped on edge … "Ashayet"' H. E. Winlock, *Excavations at Deir el Bahri, 1911–1931* (New York, 1942), pp. 38–39. **p. 153** 'her statuette … by white suspenders' ibid., p. 44. **p. 153** 'a little white … "the Cat"' ibid., p. 39. **p. 153** 'must … to our imaginations' ibid., p. 43. **p. 154** '… the private letters … days of Abraham' H. E. Winlock, *BMMA*, Part 2, *Egyptian Expedition 1921–22* (1922), p. 38. **p. 154** '… you must turn … my new (?) wife' P. Heqanakht I, trans. E. F. Wente, *Letters from Ancient Egypt* (Atlanta, 1990), p. 60. **p. 154** 'From a … Nofretete [Nefertiti]' Burlington Fine Arts Club, *Catalogue of an Exhibition of Ancient Egyptian Art* (London, 1921), p. 80, no. 40. **p. 155** '[Heqanakht] relished … or his brother"' H. E. Winlock, *Excavations at Deir el Bahri, 1911–1931* (New York, 1942), p. 67. **p. 155** 'It is a son … in the work …!' P. Heqanakht II, trans. E. F. Wente, *Letters from Ancient Egypt* (Atlanta, 1990), pp. 60–61. **p. 155** 'Solid silver … exposed good …' Howard Carter's 'rough diary', 6 April 1922, quoted in N. Reeves & J. H. Taylor, *Howard Carter: Before Tutankhamun* (London, 1992), p. 170. **p. 156** 'The site is … of the courtiers …' H. E. Winlock, *Excavations at Deir el Bahri, 1911–1931* (New York, 1942), p. 18. **p. 156** 'to re-clear the … on this occasion' ibid., pp. 18–19. **p. 156** 'There was … before us' ibid., p. 21. **pp. 156–57** 'The beam … reach my ears' H. E. Winlock, *Models of Daily Life in Ancient Egypt* (New York, 1955), p. 3. **p. 156** 'Extraordinarily articulate, … and jealous colleague' T. Hoving, *Tutankhamun, the Untold Story* (New York, 1978), p. 51. **p. 157** '[The Qufti worker … a new site' Z. Goneim, *The Buried Pyramid* (London, 1956), p. 49. **p. 157** 'There had been … an Egyptian king' W. M. F. Petrie, G. Brunton & M. A. Murray, *Lahun*, II (London, 1923), pp. 12–13. **p. 158** 'The supposedly … man, named Wah' H. E. Winlock, *Excavations at Deir el Bahri, 1911–1931* (New York, 1942), p. 29. **p. 158** 'During the week … dried crust' ibid., pp. 29–30. **p. 159** 'neck, his chest… about 2000 B.C.' ibid., p. 222. **p. 159** '… we were at … the Old Kingdom' W. M. F. Petrie, *Seventy Years in Archaeology* (London, 1931), pp. 242–43. **p. 160** 'We are working … something good …' Letter, Howard Carter to Lord Carnarvon, 27 December 1920, quoted by N. Reeves & J. H. Taylor, *Howard Carter: Before Tutankhamun* (London, 1992), p. 138. **p. 160** 'At last have … your arrival; congratulations' Telegram, Howard Carter to Lord Carnarvon, quoted by H. Carter & A. C. Mace, *The Tomb of Tut.ankh.Amen*, I (London, 1923), p. 90. **p. 162** 'At first I … glint of gold' ibid., pp. 95–96. **p. 164** 'A reed which … his own hand' N. Reeves, The *Complete Tutankhamun* (London & New York, 1990), p. 178. **p. 165** 'In April, 1923 … will be exhumed' R. Engelbach, *Air Force News*, 17 February 1945, p. 12. **p. 165** 'was not unusual … the same way' S. Donadoni, S. Curto & A. M. Donadoni Roveri, *Egypt from Myth to Egyptology* (Milan, 1990), p. 177. **p. 166** '… M. Lacau, in … you given us?' quoted by J. A. Wilson, *Signs and Wonders Upon Pharaoh* (Chicago, 1964), pp. 192–93. **p. 167** '… the place had … anything for us …' H. E. Winlock, *Excavations at Deir el Bahri, 1911–1931* (New York, 1942), p. 122. **p. 167** 'In the hot sun… the bandages' ibid., p. 123. **p. 167** 'to be … soldiers from Assiut' ibid., p.124. **p. 167** 'We … of its chest' ibid., p. 123. **p. 168** 'This intact tomb … gold-cased furniture' G. A. Reisner, *Illustrated London News*, 12 March 1927, p. 436. **p. 169** 'as though … rising in it' E. Drioton & J.-P. Lauer, *Sakkarah, les monuments de Zoser* (Cairo, 1939), p. 22. **p. 169** 'From 1924 to … hard stone vases' ibid., p. 7. **p. 170** 'I remember once, … by the noise' D. Dunham, *Recollections of an Egyptologist* (Boston, 1972), p. 33. **p. 170** 'a miracle of patience' R. Engelbach, *Introduction to Egyptian Archaeology* (Cairo, 1946), p. 85. **p. 171** 'On March 3, … of the box …' D. Dunham, *Recollections of an Egyptologist* (Boston, 1972), p. 33. **p. 171** 'When it was … at the camp"' J. L. Smith, *Tombs, Temples and Ancient Art* (Norman, 1956), p. 148. **p. 173** 'which, on the … authors' particular bent' J. R. Harris, *Acta Orientalia* 38 (1977), p. 5. **p. 174** 'My heart … do not flutter' after M. Lichtheim, *Ancient Egyptian Literature*, II (Berkeley, 1976), pp. 183–84. **p. 175** 'Now as for … my (great-grand)father' after P. W. Pestman, in R. J. Demarée & J. J. Janssen (eds), *Gleanings from Deir el-Medîna* (Leiden, 1982), p. 157. **p. 176** 'By the middle … under their feet' H. E. Winlock, *Excavations at Deir el Bahri, 1911–1931* (New York, 1942), pp. 173–74. **p. 176** 'The silence, the dark, … in digging' ibid., p. 180. **pp. 176–77** 'festooned with … of their flowers' ibid., p. 180. **p. 177** 'Year 19, 3rd month … king's wife Meryetamun' C. N. Reeves, *Valley of the Kings* (London, 1990), p. 236, no. 25 (with correction). **p. 177** 'The vase was … inconvenient to print' H. Frankfort & J.D.S. Pendlebury, *City of Akhenaten*, II (London, 1933), p. 61, n. 1. **p. 177** 'With a certain… a gold cap' ibid., p. 59. **p. 177** 'part of a thief's loot' ibid., p. 61. **p. 177** 'gave us £200 … following season' M. Chubb, *Nefertiti Lived Here* (London, 1998), p. 175. **p. 179** 'In 1931 members … in the Sudan' R. Engelbach, *Introduction to Egyptian Archaeology* (Cairo, 1946), pp. 103–04. **p. 180** '… one royal burial … made at Ballana …' *Illustrated London News*, 10 March 1934, p. 351. **p. 184** 'it is not … favorite mount' A. Lansing & W. C. Hayes, *BMMA* Part 2. *Egyptian Expedition 1935–36* (1937), p.10. **p. 185** 'The removal of … space remained' ibid., p. 14. **p. 185** 'the eye was … baskets, and jars' ibid., p. 14. **p. 185** 'by raising … "Ra'-mose"' ibid., p. 15. **p. 187** 'some of these … and artistic merit' S. Hassan, *ZÄS* 80 (1955), p. 136. **p. 187** '… one of the … in the extreme' ibid., p. 139. **p. 187** 'These figures … unhappy creatures' ibid., p. 139. **p. 189** 'We removed … an important moment …' P. Montet, letter to his wife dated 27 February 1939, quoted in H. Coutts (ed.), *Gold of the Pharaohs* (Edinburgh, 1988), p. 19. **p. 189** '"Do you see … out at last …' G. Goyon, *La découverte des trésors de Tanis* (Paris, 1987), p. 90. **p. 190** 'Montet, seeing his … paralysed by emotion' ibid., p. 90. **p. 191** 'I had the … quickly as possible …' P. Montet, letter to his wife dated 27 February 1939, quoted in H. Coutts (ed.), *Gold of the Pharaohs* (Edinburgh, 1988), p. 19. **p. 191** 'a day of marvels … and one nights' ibid., p. 20. **p. 194** 'In the season … been found there' J. D. Cooney, *Amarna Reliefs from Hermopolis* (Brooklyn, 1965), pp. 1–2. **p. 194** 'fragments of papyri … on Coptic textiles' S. Donadoni, S. Curto & A. M. Donadoni Roveri, *Egypt from Myth to Egyptology* (Milan, 1990), p. 262. **p. 194** 'Dr Reuder … over a mud brick …' quoted by T. G. H. James, *Egyptian Archaeology* 7 (1995), p. 37. **p. 195** 'gold belt … at each side' G. Brunton, *ASAE* 47 (1947), p. 125. **p. 196** 'It is … a secondary consideration' A. H. Gardiner & A. E. P. Weigall, *A Topographical Catalogue of the Private Tombs of Thebes* (London, 1913), p. 8. **p. 198** 'In 1947 the … now in Brooklyn …' J. D. Cooney, *Five Years of Collecting Egyptian Art 1951–1956* (Brooklyn, 1956), p. 43. **p. 198** 'seem to have … foreign goddess Alat' ibid., p. 43. **p. 200** '"Where's the pyramid?" … was looking for' Z. Goneim, *The Buried Pyramid* (London, 1956), p. 44. **p. 200** 'a series of … *of the walls*' ibid., p. 50. **p. 200** 'a long, open … supporting walls' ibid., p. 77. **p. 200** 'Most of the … good humour' L. Cottrell in ibid., p. viii. **p. 201** 'When we had … "Is it intact?"' ibid., p. 99. **p. 202** 'I went down … was empty' ibid., p. 123. **p. 202** 'I was strangely … still within it' ibid., pp. 87–88. **p. 202** 'No Egyptological discovery … among scholars …' A. H. Gardiner, *Egypt of the Pharaohs* (London, 1961), p. 165. **p. 202** 'found among the … Deir el Bahari valley' A. H. Gardiner, *JEA* 3 (1917), p. 95. **p. 202** 'one of the … Temple of Karnak' L. Habachi, *The Second Stela of Kamose* (Glückstadt, 1972), p. 20. **p. 202** 'narrate a hitherto … Hyksos rule' ibid., preface. **p. 203** 'Like a cat … boat was there' Kamal el-Mallakh in N. Jenkins, *The Boat Beneath the Pyramid* (London & New York, 1980), p. 53. **p. 206** 'Since December 1964 … Imhotep's tomb …' *Illustrated London News*, 29 July 1967, p. 23. **p. 207** 'At a conservative … million …' H. S. Smith, *A Visit to Ancient Egypt* (Warminster, 1974), p. 27. **p. 207** '…the most notable … from the shrines.' W. B. Emery, *JEA* 56 (1970), p. 6. **p. 208** '… the waste-paper basket of a troubled man' J. D. Ray, *The Archive of Hor* (London, 1976), p. xiv. **p. 209** 'Through photography … thousands of years …' R. W. Smith, *National Geographic Magazine*, 138/5 (Nov. 1970), pp. 634–35. **p. 209** 'None of us … heart is pleased"' ibid., p. 638. **p. 210** 'We've been … of the temple' D. B. Redford, *KMT* 2/2 (1991), p. 26. **p. 211** 'The monument … lead and bronze …' H. S. K. Bakry, *MDAIK* 27 (1971), p. 139. **p. 211** 'By means of … open the basin' ibid., p. 139. **p. 212** 'The Czech excavations … place of Raneferef …' M. Verner, *Egyptian Archaeology* 7 (1995), p. 19. **p. 213** 'forgetful of the … in despair' J. Lemprière, *A Classical Dictionary* (ed. F. R. Sowerby, London, n.d.), p. 279. **p. 213** 'exclude the pleasant … he installed' R. D. Anderson, P. J. Parsons & R. G. M. Nisbet, *JRS* 69 (1979), p. 127, n. 19. **p. 215** 'A visitor to … tomb courtyards' G. T. Martin, *Egyptian Archaeology* 1 (1991), p. 24. **p. 215** 'Shortly after the … of Tutankhamun' G. T. Martin, in T. G. H. James (ed.), *Excavating in Egypt* (London, 1982), p. 119. **p. 217** 'One evening, … in three millennia …' J. Romer, *TV Times*, 29 September–5 October 1984. **p. 218** 'My God, it's Maya!' quoted by G. T. Martin, *The Hidden Tombs of Memphis* (London & New York, 1991), p. 177. **p. 219** 'At the beginning … golden yellow!' ibid., pp. 149–52. **p. 220** '"Kent! … in the valley!"' K. R. Weeks, *The Lost Tomb* (London, 1998), pp. 126–27. **p. 220** 'an octopus, with … by tentacles' K. R. Weeks, quoted in *Time*, 29 May 1995, p. 52. **p. 221** 'the tomb … we have today …' K. R. Weeks, *The Lost Tomb* (London, 1998), pp. 297–98. **p. 222** 'After 10 years … coming to light …' *Sunday Express*, 12 November 1989. **p. 223** 'The room contained … about the room …' A. Zivie, *Egyptian Archaeology* 1 (1991), p. 27. **p. 223** 'the one who … to Memphis' A. Zivie, *Egyptian Archaeology* 13 (1998), p. 7. **p. 224** 'The Aegean … 18th Dynasty also' M. Bietak, in *Seventh International Congress of Egyptologists, Cambridge, 3–9 September 1995. Abstracts of Papers*, p. 21. **pp. 224–25** 'As Minoan art … own ritual life' M. Bietak, *Egyptian Archaeology* 2 (1992), p. 28. **p. 225** 'of a cult statue … and tribulations' D. M. Rohl *A Test of Time* (London, 1995) p. 366. **p. 226** 'President Mubarak … of small stones …' *Egyptian Archaeology* 2 (1992), p. 9. **p. 228** 'twelve hieratic texts … the temple' S. Ikram, *KMT* 8/1 (1997), p. 69. **p. 229** 'The theories … wonderful civilization' Z. Hawass, *Horus* (July–September 1997), p. 11. **p. 231** 'Listen all of you! … will eat him' ibid., p. 18. **p. 231** 'extends across … storage facilities' ibid., p. 18. **p. 232** 'some 40 … to the coast' *Egyptian Archaeology* 10 (1997), p. 27. **p. 233** 'In early November … of Cairo …' A. Oppenheim, *KMT* 6/1 (1995), p. 10. **p. 233** 'at the east … the tomb owner' Di. Arnold, *Egyptian Archaeology* 9 (1996), p. 24. **p. 233** 'The floor of … Dynasty sculpture' ibid., pp. 24–25. **p. 234** 'in a painstaking … by satellite tracking' *Egypitan Archaeology* 10 (1997), p. 15. **p. 234** 'A wide-ranging series … done the same"' ibid., p. 15. **p. 235** 'The deceased … immediate conservation' K. Mysliwiec, *Egyptian Archaeology* 13 (1998) pp. 38–39. **p. 236** 'Our most … So rare!' M. Burnette, www.national geographic.com/media/tv/onlocation/abusir. **p. 236** 'an intact … parade axe' *Egyptian Archaeology* 9 (1996), p. 28. **p. 236** 'has a panelled … [408 in total]' *Egyptian Archaeology* 9 (1996), p. 27. **p. 236** 'raising of the … box sarcophagus' *Egyptian Archaeology* 13 (1998), p. 14. **p. 236** 'an inner anthropoid… of the shaft…' ibid., p. 14. **p. 236** 'was unwrapped and … 25–30 years' www.ff.cuni.cz/~krejci/ Iufaaeng. html.CP1250. **p. 236** 'The importance … very little' ibid. **p. 237** 'An antiquities … covered in gilt …' Z. Hawass *Archaeology* 52/5 (1999), pp. 39–40. **p. 237** 'atrocities of hideousness; H. E. Winlock *Excavations at Deir el Bahri, 1911–1931* (New York, 1942), p. 99. **pp. 238–39** 'I began work … gilded plaster crown …' Z. Hawass *Archaeology* 52/5 (1999), p. 41. **p. 240** 'I still say … underneath the ground' Z. Hawass, BBC/The Learning Channel 'Nefertiti, Egypt's Mysterious Queen', 1999.

Illustration Credits

The publishers would like to thank the following for their help and advice in the preparation of the illustrations for this book: Miroslav Barta, Manfred Bietak, Lyla Pinch Brock, Patrick Chapuis, Peter Clayton, Vassil Dobrev, Aidan Dodson, Yvonne Harpur, George Johnson, Jurgen Liepe, Yvonne Marzoni, Bernhard Rasch, Maarten Raven, John Rutter, John G. Ross, Paulo Scremin, Patricia Spencer, Henri Stierlin, Nigel Strudwick, Alain Zivie.

t=top; a=above; l=left; r=right; c=centre; b=bottom.

AKG London/photos: Erich Lessing 31tl, 127t, 189l
Akhenaten Temple Project 209tr
Cyril Aldred 83
Staatliche Museen zu Berlin – Aegyptisches Museum und Papyrussammlung © bpk 27br, 35ac, 49r, 74t, 123r, 134r & 135l photos: Margarete Büsing 135c, 135r
Birmingham Library Services 113r
Courtesy, Museum of Fine Arts, Boston. Reproduced with permission. © 1999 Museum of Fine Arts, Boston. All Rights Reserved 47b, 105l, 124cr, 136, 145bl, 148c, 148b, Photo © Egyptian Photographic Archive 132t, 132b, 133br, 144l, 144r, 147, 148t, 149bl, 168b, 170
Musée Municipal, Boulogne-sur-Mer 40r
Brussels:
Bibliothèque Royale 47r
© IRPA-KIK Brussels 124b
Cairo:
Courtesy archives of the Austrian Archaeological Institute, all rights reserved 224tr, 225al, 225b; M. Bietak, N. Marinatos and C. Palyvou 224b, 225ar
Courtesy Director of Antiquities Service 180t
DAI 110br, 112t, 125
Egyptian Museum 49l, 53t, 106tr, 120tl, 120al, 120ar, 133tl, 137r, 182al, 189r, 218ac
Lehnert & Landrock 26l
Fitzwilliam Museum, Cambridge 20b
Patrick Chapuis 219b, 226r
Oriental Institute of the University of Chicago 128b
Peter Clayton 14ar, 15br, 16al, 19al, 24cl, 43al, 72–73, 94al, 138r, 139t, 139bl, 151t, 151b, 152tl, 152al, 174, 188t, 188b, 206l, 208b, 217r, 226l, 226ar, 227l, 227r, 228tl, 228tr
Stéphane Compoint/Sygma 197, 232t, 232b, 234r, 234b
Aidan Dodson 60bl, 91br, 153t, 191l
Lucinda Douglas-Menzies, courtesy of Euphrosyne Doxiades 78l, 79l, 79r
Trinity College, Dublin 108a
Durham University Oriental Museum, Co. Durham 19b
Trustees of the National Museums of Scotland, Edinburgh 133bl
Myers Museum, Eton College, Eton 74br, 92t, 92b, 93al, 93cl,

93bl, 93r
Philippe Plailly/99 Eurelios 237l, 238b, 238c, 238t, 239tl, 239bl, 239br
Werner Forman Archive 112b, 1901 & 192t; Collection of George Ortiz, Vandoeuvres 211
Ray Gardner 183bl
Photos: Heidi Grassley/©Thames & Hudson Ltd. London 30bl, 50l, 54bl, 54ar, 168tr, 169tr, 172r, 173b, 201tr, 211t, 215l, 215r, 216t, 217tl
Photos: Hirmer 55, 69, 91l, 120c, 120cr, 217bl
© IFAO/photo: A. Lecler 240tl, photo: J.-Fr. Gout 240bl
George Johnson 24t, 36br, 70t, 114tr, 141r, 145c, 145tr, 149br, 153br, 191r, 193tr, 195tr, 204c, 208r, 233l, 233bc
A.F. Kersting 61c
Photos: Keystone 190tl, 190tr
Kodansha Ltd, Tokyo 103b, 164l
Miho Museum, Shigaraki, Kyoto 155
P. Lacau 118t, 118b
J.-P. Lauer 41r, 42cr, 43br, 60br, 183tl, 187c, 187b, 200bl, 200br, 201br
Brita LeVa 231t, 231bl, 231br
Rijksmuseum van Oudheden, Leiden 30c, 30bl, 31b, 32l, 218tr, 219l
Jürgen Liepe, Berlin 53ar, 53br, 55l, 56l, 56r, 58tl, 58bl, 59br, 61tr, 63, 66cr, 70b, 74c, 85c, 85b, 87l, 87r, 96bl, 96br, 98tl, 98bl, 99r, 106br, 119t, 133c, 138l, 152tr, 152b, 156b, 157tr, 169br, 171b, 176l, 178l, 178r, 184, 194br, 195al, 195cl, 195bl, 210tl, 219r
London:
© British Museum 15a, 17a, 17b, 19cr, 21cl, 21tr, 23br, 24br, 26b, 31b, 32r, 33tl, 33cl, 45b, 46t, 65tr, 67b, 68b, 72t, 72bl, 73t, 74bl, 75t, 75b, 76l, 77b, 78r, 82br, 102c, 109l, 110tr, 124tl, 159b, 175, 198
Egypt Exploration Society 84b, 85t, 107bl, 108b, 109b, 110tl, 110bl, 128t, 177t, 177b, 182tr, 206r, 207tr, 207b, 208tl; EES and Rijksmuseum van Oudheden, Leiden expedition 218bl, 218br
Courtesy of the Petrie Museum of Egyptian Archaeology, University College London 6, 67t, 68t, 68c, 80tr, 80br
Courtesy of the Getty Conservation Institute, Los Angeles, California, © 1992 J. Paul Getty Trust/Photos: Guillermo Aldana 122r, 122–23
Manchester Museum, University of Manchester 131l, 131r
Bildarchiv Foto-Marburg 76l, 76r
University of Michigan Papyrus Collection 145cl
Staatliche Sammlung Ägyptischer Kunst, Munich 35bl, 35br
New York:
Brooklyn Museum of Art, Charles Edwin Wilbour Fund 10br, 14c, 61b, Gift of Miss Theodora Wilbour from the Estate of her father, Charles Edwin Wilbour 47.218.89 105r
Wilbour Library, Brooklyn 101b
Metropolitan Museum of Art 79b, 78cr, 103ar, 111tr, 116c, 140, 149tr, 150tr, 150al, 153l, 154tr,

154b, 156al, 156tr, 157b, 159t, 159c, Egyptian Expedition 167l, 167r, 185bl, 185r, Fletcher Fund, 1950 (50.85) 33cr, Purchased with Funds given by Henry Walters and Edward S. Harkness, 1926 150bl, Museum Excavations, 1919–20; Rogers Fund, supplemented by contribution of Edward S. Harkness (20.3.203) 158l, 158tr, 158cr,158br
New York Academy of Medicine 57tr
David O'Connor 97b
Oxford:
Ashmolean Museum, University of Oxford 84t, 86br, 94bl, 94r, 98tr, 100b
Bodleian Library, University of Oxford – MS Wilkinson dep. A. 17, fols. 21v–22r 28t MS Gr, th. E. 7 (P) 107r
Griffith Institute, Ashmolean Museum 4–5, 160b, 161t, 162bl, 162br, 163bl, 163t, 163br, 166tl, 166br
Paris:
Bibliothèque Nationale, Paris 64tr
© Hypogées (MAFB) – Photo: P. Chapuis, 222b, 223bl, 223br Drawing: M.-G. Froidevaux 222t Photos: Alain Zivie 223c, 223tr
Musée du Louvre – 42b, 137l, ©Photo: RMN Chuzeville 21tl, 39, 44, 186, ©Photo: RMN Hervé Lewandowski 48t
Soprintendenza alle Antichità, Palermo 7, 57br
Popperfoto/Reuters 237r
Robert Partridge:The Ancient Egypt Picture Library 213c
Courtesy of the Archive of the Czech Institute of Egyptology, Prague 212b, 212t, 213br, 214cl, 214tr, 214b, 214bl, 236bl, 236tl, 236tr, 236br
Private Collection 27l
Nicholas Reeves 33tr, 42cl, 57bl, 65tl, 65b, 66r, 66l, 102tr, 104t, 104c, 104r, 104b, 111bl, 113l, 115tr, 116tl, 116b, 117t, 118tr, 129b, 130bl, 164tr, 165tr, 179r, 194bl, 229b, 229t, 230br
Nicholas Reeves/The Amarna Royal Tombs Project 241
John G. Ross 25, 80bl, 80tl, 95l, 98br, 114r, 115cr, 123l, 165b, 195br, 202l, 203l, 203r, 204br, 205tl, 205bl, 205br, 210tr, 215tr
Miss A. M. Rowlatt 45t
Washington University Gallery of Art, St. Louis, gift of Charles Parsons, 1896 96al
St. Peter's Abbey, Salzburg/Photo: O. Anrather 18b
Albert Shoucair 50r, 51t, 51b, 52t, 58tr, 58–59, 59t, 59c, 86cl, 89t, 89c, 89b, 130tl, 130al, 130ar, 164b, 164cr, 187t, 190br, 191t, 191b, 192b
Alberto Siliotti/Geodia, Archivio Image Service 2, 22br, 102b
Archaeological Collections, Southampton City Council 240
Henri Stierlin 146, 157tl
Nigel Strudwick 230l
John Taylor 48bl
Frank Teichmann 21b, 71b, 103al, 114bl
E. Thiem – Lotos Film,

Kaufbeuren 52b, 183tr, 183cr
John Topham Picture Library 200tl
Soprintendenza per le Antichità Egizie, Museo Egizio, Turin 29t,29c, 29b, 121t, 121b, 126l, 126c, 126r, 127l, 127r
Eileen Tweedy 183br
David Wallace/BBC 220bl, 221t, 221b
Polish Centre of Mediterranean Archaeology, Warsaw University 235l, 235t, 235r
Emory Kristoff/National Geographic Image Collection, Washington D.C. 209bl
Archivio Whitestar/Photos: Araldo da Luca 53bl, 99, 119l, 119b, 139r, 141l, 161l, 165al, 169bl, 171t, 182bl, 193bl, 193br, 201al, 204tl, 228bl, 228ar, Photo: Giulio Veggi 120b
Roger Wood 179l, 180l, 180r

Other sources of illustrations:
C. Aldred *Akhenaten, King of Egypt* (London & New York, 1991) 210l
R. D. Anderson, P. Parsons & R. G. M. Nisbet, *Journal of Roman Studies*, 69 (1979) 213t
Giuseppe Angelelli *The Franco-Tuscan Expedition*, Museo Archeologico, Firenze/Scala 34
Annales du Service des Antiquités de l'Égypte,1901 106bl, 1947 101t
E. Bacon *Vanished Civilisations*, (London & New York, 1963) 181br
After *Bulletin of the Metropolitan Museum of Art*, Part 2, *Egyptian Expedition 1928–29* 176c
G. B. Belzoni *Narrative of the Operations and Recent Discoveries within the Temples, Tombs, and Excavations, in Egypt and Nubia*, Plates (London, 1820) 22t, 22bl,
F. Cailliaud *Voyage à Meroe* (Paris, 1823–27), pl. XLI 37b
J. F. Champollion *Grammaire Égyptien* (Paris, 1836–41) 16
La Description de l'Égypte (Paris, 1809) 11ar, 14b, 16ar, 16br,
Documentation photographique, Paris 182br
European Magazine, London1822 18t
D. Forbes *Tombs, Treasures and Mummies* (Santa Fe, 1998) 60tr
L. N. P. A. de Forbin, *Voyage dans le Levant* (Paris, 1819) 1
H. Frankfort & J. D. S. Pendlebury *The City of Akhenaten* II (London, 1933) 134l
G. Frey from *Das Haus Lepsius*, Berlin 1933, courtesy of Mrs Susanne Lepsius/Photo: Eileen Tweedy 37t
O. Guerville *La Nouvelle Égypte* (Paris, 1905) 97t
G. Denning *after Landström* 1970 in N. Jenkins *The Boat Beneath the Pyramid* (London & New York, 1980)
A.H. Gardiner, *The Ramesseum Papyri* (Oxford, 1955) 96tr
Illustrated London News 1882 13, 23l, 64bl, 1896 88b, 90
B. J. Kemp *Ancient Egypt. Anatomy of a Civilization* (London, 1989) 86bl
A. Kircher *Oedipus Aegyptiacus* Vol

III (Rome, 1652–54) 11bl
E. W. Lane *The Thousand and One Nights* (London, 1861) 10al
J.-P. Lauer *Saqqara. The Royal Cemetery of Memphis* (London & New York, 1976) 207c
K. R. Lepsius *Denkmäler aus Aegypten und Aethiopien* (Berlin, 1849–58) 36t, 77t
L. M. A. Linant de Bellefonds *Excavation of the Great Temple of Ramesses II at Abu Simbel*, 1819, courtesy of Philip Barker, London 20a
Revd S. Manning *The Land of the Pharaohs* (London, 1887; after original photograph by Émile Brugsch) 64br
A. Mariette *Choix des monuments* (Paris, 1854) 40l, 41l
G. Maspero *La Trouvaille de Deir-el-Bahari* (Cairo, 1881) 65br, 65cr
J. de Morgan *Fouilles à Dahchour, mars–juin 1894* (Vienna, 1895) 88f
J. de Morgan *Les Recherches sur les origines de l'Égypte. L'âge de la pierre et les métaux.* II: *Ethnographie préhistorique et tombeau royale de Négadah* (Paris, 1897) 100tl, 100tr
Orientalia 19 (1950), 199cr, 199br
G. Passalacqua *Catalogue raisonné et historique des antiquités découvertes en Égypte* (Paris, 1824), by permission of the British Library (1044.c.25) 28br
W. M. F. Flinders Petrie *The Labyrinth, Gerzeh and Mazguneh* (London, 1912) 77cl, 77cr
W. M. F. Flinders Petrie *The Arts and Crafts of Ancient Egypt* (London, 1909) 95r
P. Philippoteaux, *Unwrapping the Mummy of Ta-uza-ra*. Collection of Mr & Mrs Taghert, Chicago. Photo courtesy of MFA, Boston
J. E. Quibell, *Excavations at Saqqara (1911–1912). The Tomb of Hesy* (Cairo, 1913) 56t
N. Reeves *The Complete Tutankhamun* (London & New York, 1990) 120l
A. H. Rhind *Thebes: its Tombs and their Tenants* (London, 1862), by permission of the British Library (7702.c.22) 46b
A. Rhoné *L'Égypte à petites journées* (Paris, 1910) 42t
B. G. Trigger *Egypt under the Pharaohs* (London & New York, 1976) pl. 42 202r
H. Vyse , *Operations carried on at the Pyramids of Gizeh in 1837* (London, 1840) 36bl
R. H. Wilkinson *The Complete Temples of Ancient Egypt* (London & New York, 2000) 212bl
H. E. Winlock *Excavations at Deir el Bahri,1911–1931* (New York, 1942) 173c
Philip Winton 8–9, 135t *after Barry Girsch*, 162t, 176r *after an unpublished drawing by H. Parkinson, now in the Griffith Institute, Oxford; copyright H. and R. B. Parkinson*, 185t *after Egyptian Expedition, Metropolitan Museum of Art,* 193tl, 212bl, 220br

Index

Page numbers in *italics* refer to illustrations; for individual tomb numbers (KV1 etc.) see under 'tombs' DB = Deir el-Bahri; KV = Valley of the Kings; QV = Valley of the Queens

Abadiya 94
Abbas Pasha 41
Abbott, Henry 46
Abbot Papyrus 48
Abu Ghurab 136
Abu Rawash 189
Abu Simbel 18, 19, 20, *20*, 229; temple of Ramesses II 19, 20, *20*
Abu'l-Hol (colossus of Ramesses II) 26, *26*
Abuqir Bay 12
Abusir 58, 61, 111, 136, 205, 212, *212*, 236; lake of 207
Abusir Papyri 83, 87, 212
Abydos 40, 47, 50, 52, 61, 67, 94, 100, *109*, 109–12, *110*, 115, 182, 203, 229; temple of Khentimentiu 120
Achaemenid empire 105
Actium, Battle of 234
Adam, Shehata 199
Aeschylus 108
Afghanistan 188
Africa 35
agate 146, 198
Ahhotep, Queen 48, 50, 51, 52, 176, 184
Ahmose 48, 50, 51, *51*, *64*, 125, 225
Ahmose-Nofretiri, Queen 176
Ain Asil 240
Akerblad, Johan David 15
Akhenaten (Amenophis IV) 14, 16, 24, 61, 73, 75, 83, 83, 84, 85, 95, 96, 115, 116, 117, 134, *135*, 136, *142*, 154, 164, 172–73, *172*, 179, 194, *195*, 202, 209–10, 222
Akhenaten Temple Project 209–10
Akhetaten 83, *83*
Akhethotep 59
Akhmim 96, 219
Al Mamoon 10
alabaster *12*, 23, 28, 33, 43, 50, 51, 65, 91, *119*, 127, 132, *133*, 146, *164*, 168, 169, 195, 201, *201*, *211*, 227, 228, *228*, 233
Alalakh 225
Alashiya (Cyprus) 75
Alat 198
Albert IV, Abbot 18
Alcaeus 108
Aldred, Cyril 149, 152
Alexander the Etesian 145
Alexander the Great 42, 107, 152, 231
Alexandria 11, 33, 40, 45, 62, 68, 108, 145, 196, 229, 232, 234, 237; Library 234; mosque of Nebi Daniel 231; Treaty of 14
Ali, Muhammad 18, *18*, 19, 26, 29, 33, 37
Altenmüller, Hartwig 166
Amanishakheto 26, 35
Amarna *see* el-Amarna
Amarna archive 72–75, 83, 144
Amarna art 18, 24, *24*, 61
Amarna Royal Tombs Project 241, *241*
Amarna style 172, 194
Amasis 41, 44, 56, 68, 236
Amélineau, Émile 100, 109, 110, 112, 182
Amenemheb 130
Amenemope 192, 193
Amenemopet 117
Amenherkhepshef 125, 166
Amenhotep 184
Amenhotep (artist) 80
Amenhotep son of Hapu *118*, 134, 136, 137, *137*
Amenkha 47
Amenmose 17

Amennekhu 71
Amenophis I 65, 118, 175
Amenophis II 102, 103, 104, 120, *120*, 127, 128
Amenophis II mummy cache 113, 117
Amenophis III 19, *23*, 25, 43, 44, 61, 72, 73, 75, 79, 95, 103, 111, 114, 115, 119, 120, 124, 126, 128, 134, 136, 137, 154, 202, 209, 211, *211*, 223, 226, 227, *227*, 228; palace of 7, 79; shrine of *14*
Amenophis IV–Akhenaten *see* Akhenaten
Amer, Mustafa 199
amethyst 188, 199
Amherst of Hackney, Lord 15, 74
Ammenemes I 91, 154, 156, 157, 158, 159, 167
Ammenemes II 88, 90, 186, 233
Ammenemes III 53, 76, 77, *77*, 78, 88, 89, 91, 109, 112, 120, 138, 139, 140, 141, 204, 211, 233
Ammennakht 175
Amr ibn el-As 107
amulets 35, 37, 43, 44, 48, 67, 90, 93, 111, 116, 127, 132, *138*, 145, 146, 148, 150, 151, 161, 173, 177, 195, 199, 204, 223, 236
Amun 19, 24, 35, 45, *51*, 53, 65, 75, 81, 82, 119, 149, 172, 227, *228*
Ananiah *see* Elephantine, Jewish Archives
Anastasi, Giovanni 45
Anedjib (Adjib) 111
Angelelli, Giuseppe *34*
Anhai 75
Aniba 35
animal burials 40–44, 184, 206–08, 222
Ankhefenmut 192, 193
Ankhesenpepy II 202
Antinoe 108
Antiochus IV Epiphanes 208
Antiphon 108
Anubieion temple 222
Anubis (god of embalming) 43, *70*, 207
Any 75
Apa Jeremias, monastery of 216
Aperel (Aperia) 222–23
Aphrodite 67
Apis bulls 195, 207; burials 40–44
Apollonius 145
Apries 11, 44
Archaeological Survey of Nubia 179, 182
Aristotle 107
Arkeoloji Müzeleri, Istanbul 74
Armant (Hermonthis) 182, 186, 227
Arnold, Dieter 233, 236
Arnold, Dorothea 154–55
Artemidorus *79*
Arzawa 75
Asasif 27
Ashayet 153, *153*
Ashmolean Museum, Oxford 74, 84, 86, 99,
Asklepios 206
Assyria 75, 127
Astemkheb *66*
Aswan 72, 106, 118, 179, 181, 187, 200
Asyut 62, 87, 121, 167
Aten 85, 172, 194, *210*
Athanasi, Giovanni d' (Yanni Athanasiou) 19, 24, 28, 32, 33, 45
ATP *see* Akhenaten Temple Project
Atum 33, 226
Atumemtaneb 129
Augustus 36, 213
Auibre Hor *see* Hor
Austrian Archaeological Institute 224
Avaris 189, 224–25
Avennes, Émile Prisse d' *34*
Ay 20, 61, 99, 123, 136, 179, 216
Ayrton, Edward Russell *113*, 115, 116, 117

Bab el-Gasus 82; cache of mummies 81
Bab el-Hosan 101, 106
baboons 206–07
Babylonia 75
Bacchias 107
Bacchylides 107
Badawi, Ahmad M. 195
Bagnold, Major A. H. *26*
Bahariya Oasis 229, 237–39
Baines, John 7
Baketaten 134, *134*
Bakr, Abdel-Moneim Abu 178
Bakr, Mohammed Ibrahim 199
Ballana 179–81, 182
Ballas 94
Ballerini, Francesco 165
Bankes, W. J. 15
Baraize, Émile 174
Bares, Ladislav 236
Baring, Sir Evelyn 26, 62
Barker, John 32
Barsanti, Alexandre 85, 111
basalt 15, 17, 36, 60, 100, 213, 227, 230, 236
baskets 71, 82, 126, 127, 133, 161, 165, 177, 185
Bastet 129, 222
Bawit 237–39
Bayoumi, Abbas 199
beads *see* jewelry
Bek 134
Bell, Harold Idris 107
Bellefonds, Linant de *20*
Belmore, Earl of 21
Belzoni, Giovanni Battista 12, 15, 18–25, 34, 36, 40, 45, 101, 102, 105
Belzoni, Sarah 19
Bénédite, Georges 106
Beni Hasan 113, 117
Beni Suef 52
Benson, Margaret 25
Berlin Green Head 72, 74, *74*
Berlin Museum 27, 28, 29, 35, 37, 49, 70, 73, 80, 87, 96, 123, 129, 130, 134, 194
Bes 33, 181, 199, 207
Biahmu 77
Biban el-Harim *see* Valley of the Queens
Bibliothèque Royale, Brussels 48
Bibliothèque Nationale, Paris 40
Bietak, Manfred 182
Bintanat, Princess 218
Birâbi 202
Bissing, Baron Friedrich Wilhelm von 86, 106
Bisson de la Roque, Fernand 186
boats 28, 51, 106, 109, 117, 131, 132, 145, 157, 161, 213, 237; Khufu's 203–05, *203*, *204*, *205*
Bocchoris 44
Bodleian Library, Oxford 27, 28
Bodmer Papyri 195
Bologna 31
Bonaparte, Napoleon 11, 12, 15, 17, 19, 109, 237; *see also* Expeditions
bone 112
Bonomi, Joseph 30
Book of the Dead 16, 27, 29, 30, 61, 74, *74*, 127, 146, 152, 191, 236
Book of the Night 191
Book of the Underworld 102
Borchardt, Ludwig 80, 87, 106, 134, 136, 166, 212
Boston Museum of Fine Arts 105, 124, 125, 132, 133, 144, 148, 149
Boston Pectoral 47, *47*
Bouchard, Lieutenant Pierre 14
Bouriant, Urbain 69, 87
bowls *see* vessels 109
boxes/caskets 48, 71, 82, 89, 96, 105, 111, 113, 127, 133, 139, *140*, 145, 146, 161, 164, *171*, 185, *186*, 201, 213, 236

breccia 100
Breccia, Evaristo 194
Brine, Charles 144
British Museum, London 14, 23, 26, 30, 31, 32, 33, 36, 45, 46, 57, 64, 65, 73, 74, 75, 77, 82, 87, 96, 102, 107, 115, 140, 175, 194, 198
British School of Archaeology 131, 142, 166
Brock, Lyla Pinch 112
bronze 31, 37, 48, 51, 64, 90, 119, 125, 126, 127, 146, 149, 175, 180, 181, 186, 188, *206*, 207, 208, *208*, 209, 211, 228, 236
Brooklyn Museum 15, 61, 120, 195, 198
Brugsch, Émile Charles Adalbert 60, 61, 64, *64*, 65, 101, 102, 110, 125
Brugsch, Heinrich 60, 61
Brunton, Guy 138, 140
Bruyère, Bernard 174
Bubastieion cats, cemetery of 223
Bubastis (Tell Basta) 75, 77, 129
Bucheum 182
Budge, Ernest Alfred Thompson Wallis 60, 62, 64, 71, 72, 73, 74, 107
Buhen 215
Bulaq 49
Bulaq Museum 40, 54, 60, 64, 65, *65*, 71, 73, 79, 87, 106
bull-leaping *224*
bulls 206, 207; Apis bull burials 41–44
Burckhardt, Johann Ludwig 19, 20
Burlington Fine Arts Club 154
Burnette, Margaret 236
Burra-Buriyas, King of Babylon 75
Burton, Harry 117, 119, 156, 165
Burton, James 34, 56, 220
Butehamun 24, 151, 175
Byblos 189

Cailliaud, Frédéric *37*
Cairo 10, 11, 17, 19, 38, 40, 50, 52, 68, 70, 72, 75, 102, 107, 137, 149, 155, 177, 182, 194, 195, 198, 233
Cairo Museum 40, 56, 57, 58, 59, 60, 69, 70, 74, 85, 86, 87, 95, 97, 98, 99, 106, 116, 119, 125, 128, 130, 132, 141, 152, 157, 166, 169, 178, 188, 190, 192, 194, 195, 199, 200
calcite 31, 139, 145, 151
Callender, 'Pecky' *166*
Callimachus 108
Cambyses 41, 44
canopic jars/chests 27, 28, 31, 43, 65, 71, 82, 89, 91, 105, 131, 132, 139, 145, 149, 150, 151, 161, 163, *164*, 171, 185, 192, 195, 220, 223, 233, 236
Capart, Jean 86, 124
Capture of Joppa, The 30
Carnarvon, George Herbert, Fifth Earl of 62, 117, 129, 130, 149, 150, 151, 154, 160, *160*, 162, 164, 165, 166, 170, 179, 202
Carnarvon Gold Amun 147, 149, *149*
carnelian 51, 89, 116, 138, 150, 151, 157, 159, *171*, 181, 188, 201, 204
Cartagena 36
Carter, Howard 16, 50, 62, 83, 97, 105, 106, 113, 114, 117, 119, 124, 129, 130, 142, 144, 149, 150, 151, 154, 155, 160, *160*, 163, 164, 166, *166*, 170, 179, 191, 220, 241
cartouches 11, 15, 16, 31, 42, 44, 48, 64, 102, 104, 111, 115, *119*, 123, 129, 160, 179, 186, 189, 191, 199, 203, 212
caskets *see* boxes
CAT-scanning 123, 131, 144
Caton-Thompson, Gertrude 219
Caunus (Asia Minor) 145
causeways, Abusir 187; Pepy II

(Saqqara) 187; Sahure 187; Unas 186, 187, *187*, 200
Caviglia, Giovanni Battista 19, 26
Cecil, Lady William 105
Cemetery of the Apes *see* Qabbanet el-Qurud
cenotaphs 109, 111, 182
censer *180*
Cercidas 108
Chaillan, Louis 49
chalcedony 199
chalices 92, *92*, *183*
Champollion, Jean François 12, 14, 15–16, 23, 34, *34*, 37, 38, 40, 121, 128
Champollion-Figeac, Jacques Joseph 16
chapels 128, 131, 148, 156, 174, 230, 235
Charles University, Prague 212
Charles X of France 29
Charles Felix, King of Sardinia 29
Chassinat, Émile 87, 111
Cheops *see* Khufu
Chephren *see* Khephren
Chester Beatty, Sir Alfred 174
Chester, Greville 105
chests *126* , 127, 161, 186
Chevrier, Henri 172, 202, 209
Chicago Natural History Museum 105
Chois, Auguste 118
Christie, Agatha 154
Cilicia 75
clay 72, 94, 126, 134, 158; clay tablets 240
Cleopatra III 15
Cleopatra VII 207
Clot, Antoine 40
coffins 27, 28, *32*, 36, 42, 43, 47, 48, *48*, 50, *50*, 51, 52, 57, 64, *64*, 65, *65*, 66, *66*, 69, *70*, 71, 82, 89, 90, 91, *91*, 96, *96*, 103, 104, *104*, 106, 111, 115, *115*, 116, 117, 123, 127, 131, 133, 136, 139, 144, 145, *145*, 148, 150, 152, 153, 154, 156, 158, 161, 162, 163, 164, *165*, 176, *176*, 184, 185, *191*, 192, 193, 199, 202, 204, 217, 220, 223, 233, 236; *rishi* (feather-decorated) coffins *32*, 48, 133
Coffin Texts 61, 156
coins 125, 198
Collège de France, Paris 62, 64
colossi 77, 86; Horemheb 137; Karnak 172–73, *172*, *173*, 210; Memnon, Thebes 134, 137; Meryetamun 219, *219*; Ramesses II 195; Tutankhamun's 179, *179*
computer technology 209–10
Cook, John 61
Cooney, John D. 194, 195, 198
copper 33, 42, 56, 96, 97, 98, 99, 100, 124, 127, 136, 139, *140*, 153, 159, 164, 182, 186, 192, 201; copper-gold alloy 211
Cornelius Gallus 212, 213
cosmetics/cosmetic vessels 71, 117, 127, 28, 27, *140*, 140, 151, 161, 164, *201*
Crete 80, 224, 225
Cromer, Lord 106
crowns *see* jewelry
crystal 58
cups 67, 68, *68*, 115, 116, 129, 130, 160
Currelly, Charles Trick 198
Curto, Silvio 165
Curzon, Lord 40
Czech Institute of Egyptology 212, 236

Dahshur 82, 88–91, 118, 139, 140, 202, 203, 233, 236, 237
Dakhla Oasis 237, 238, 240

251

Damansha (ancient Sumenu) 209, 211
Daninos, Albert 58
Daressy, Georges 48, 79, 80, 81, 82, 84, 95, 144, 156
Darius I 44, 236
Darius II 198
Darnell, John and Deborah 24
Daud Pasha 65
David, Rosalie 131
Davies, Vivian 241
Davis, Theodore Monroe 62, 64, 105, 113–17, *113*, 114, 115, 116, 117, 119, 160, 166, 216
Defterdar, Mohammed 31
Deir el-Bahri 21, 48, 49, 56, 60, 69, 81, 106, 114, 115, 128, 153, *153*, 154, 156, 167, 172, 173, 176, 184, 202, 208; cache of royal mummies 64–66, *65*, 81, 102, 104, 117, 176; temple of Hatshepsut *65*, 173, 176, 235
Deir el-Ballas 132, 133
Deir el-Bersha 133, 144
Deir el-Gebrawi 58
Deir el-Medina 24, 29, 49, 57, 68, 70, 80, 121, 126, 174, *174*, 175, 231; Great Pit 174; papyri 175
della Valle, Pietro 76
demotic script 14
Den *109*, 111, *110*, 111, 182, 83
Denon, Vivant 16, 29
Denon's Papyrus 14, 16, *16*, 29
dentistry 55
Der 72
Derry, Douglas 165, *166*
Description de l'Égypte, La 11, 12, 14, 17, 18
Deutsche Orient-Gesellschaft 87, 134, 177
Devéria, Théodule 49, 50
Diodorus 77
diorite 213, 226
Dishna Papers 195
Djedefre 203
Djedhor (priest) 16
Djedkare 87, 214
Djehuty, General 30
Djehuty (King) 27
Djehutymose 151, 175
Djehutynakht 144, *144*, 145, *145*
Djer 110, 111, 182, 183
Djesertyankh 201
Djet 111, 112
Djoser 155, 68, 169, 187, 200
DNA analysis 131
dockets 65, *126*, 162, 167, *176*, 218
Donati, Vitaliano 25
Dorman, Peter F. 150
Dra Abu'l-Naga 27, 32, 47, 48, 50, 130, 133
Dreyer, Günter 112
Drioton, Étienne 169, 199
Drovetti, Bernardino 19, 25, 27, 29, 30, 31, 34, 38, 67, 70, 128
Drower, Margaret S. 67
Duell, Prentice 86
Duhi, Salam Abu 69, 70
Dunham, Dows 144, 147, 149, 169, 170, *170*, 171
Durham Servant Girl 18, 19, *19*
Durham University Oriental Museum 19
Dush 238; Treasure 226, 228

Ebers, Professor George 57
Ebers medical papyrus 57
Ebla 225
Edfu 52, 101, 200, 229
Edgar, Campbell Cowan 125, 129, 145
Edinburgh 133
Edward, Prince of Wales (King Edward VII) 47
Edwards, Amelia B. 64, 77
Egypt Exploration Fund 67, 68, 88, 96, 107, 108, 109, 128, 144, 153, 198, 208
Egypt Exploration Society 73, 85, 34, 142, 166, 177, 182, 209, 213, 216, 218, 222

Egyptian Antiquities Organization 196
Egyptian Antiquities Service *see* Service des Antiquités
Egyptian Research Account 96, 97, 198
Eisenlohr, A. A. 46
el-Ahaiwa 133
el-Amarna 24, 61, 72–75, 16, 118, 119, 134, 136, 154, 176, 177, 182, 194; Great Palace 83, 84, *84*; Great Pavement 84–85, *85*; Great Temple 83; King's House 83, *83*, 84, 85; Records Office 72, *73*, 83; royal wadi 215; Small Temple of the Aten *83*, 84
el-Ashmunein (Hermopolis Magna) 121, 152, 166, 194; Sphinx Gate 194, 195
el-Bahnasa (Oxyrhynchus) 107
el-Din, Mohammed Abdel Halim Nur 199
el-Gieif 68
el-Hammamania 121
el-Hamzawi, Usama *214*
el-Hawawish 58
el-Hiba 107
el-Ihnasya 121, 124
el-Kurru 36, 147–49
el-Lahun 67, 38, 80, 138, 140, 156, 157
el-Lisht 88, 91, 138, 141, 155, 156
el-Mallakh, Kamal 203, *203*
el-Malwata 79
el-Mamun 11
el-Marna 74
el-Minya 52, 57
el-Nebira 67–68
el-Niqrash 58
el-Oraby, Fuad 199
el-Qasr (ancient Chenoboskion) 195
el-Rashid, Caliph Harun 11, 14
el-Rassul family 64–65, *64*, 66, 81
el-Rubaiyat 76
El-Saadat, Kamal Abu 232
el-Saghir, Mohammed 226
el-Tod (Djerty) 186, 188, *188*
electrum 116, 129, 133, 211
Elephantine Island 14, 40, 47, 101, 105, 181, 233; Jewish Archives 105
Elkab 236
emeralds 89
Emery, Walter Bryan 111, 179, 182–83, 206, 207
Empereur, Jean-Yves 196, 232, 234
enamel 35, 50
encaustic technique 76
Engelbach, Rex 165, 179
English Society for the Preservation of the Monuments of Ancient Egypt 84
engraving 27, *27*
Erfai 131
Erman, Adolf 128, 132, 136, 194
Eros *181*
Esna 52, 97, 101, 229
Ethiopia 49
Eton College 74, 87
Eugénie, Empress 52
Euphrates 30
Euripides 107, 108
European Institute of Underwater Archaeology 23
Expeditions, Franco-Tuscan 32, 34, *34*, 37; Harvard-Boston Egyptian Expedition 132, 133, 138, 168; Metropolitan Museum of Art Egyptian Expedition 154, 156, 184, 233; Napoleon's 11, 14, 16, 18, 25, 34, 41; Oxford 59; Phoebe Apperson Hearst 132; Prussian 35, 36, 37, *37*, 121
Ezbet Helmi 224–25

Fadil Pasha 50
faience 28, 31, 32, 35, 43, 61, *65*, 75, 79, 92–93, *93*, 99, 100, 105, 115, *115*, 116, 119, 127, 136, 138, 145, 146, 151, 159, *159*, 160, 184, 201, 213, *213*, 233, 236
Fairholt, Frederick William 26

Faiyum 76, 78, 91, 111, 141, 145, 209, 211, 219; bronzes 211; portraits 76–80
Farouk, King 192
felspar 51, 139, 151, *193*, 204
Ferlini, Giuseppe 35–37
figures/figurines 94, 100, 111, 116, 119, 152, 161, 162, 177, 186, 191, 194, 222
Firka 179
Firth, Cecil M. 86, 97, 169, 182, 194, 206
Firth, Diana 194
Fitzwilliam Museum, Cambridge 20
Floris, Matteo 49
food 71, 110, 127, 139, 145, 148, 158, 161, 165, 233
forgery 151–52
Fougerousse, J.-L. 191
Fouquet, Daniel Marie *81*
Frankfort, Henri 177
French Archaeological Institute, Cairo 60, 62, 71, 87, 91, 111, 118
French Surrender List 17
frescoes 224
Freud, Sigmund 76
Frey, Georg *37*
Friedrich Wilhelm IV 37
furniture *18*, 28, 69, 70, 71, 82, 110, 115, 124, 126, 127, 131, 133, 145, 161, 163, 164, 168, 177, *185*, 208, 222, 236

Gaballa, Ali Gaballa 199
Gabet, Charles Edmond 49, 53
Gabra, Sami 152, 207
Galioubia 52
Gammai 179
Gardiner, Alan H. 124, 174, 196, 202
Garis Davies, Norman de 134, 184
Garstang, John 100, 113, 117
Gauthier, Henri 106
Gebel Abu Mena 195
Gebel Barkal 30, 36, 72, 147, 148, 149
Gebel el-Araq 137
Gebel el-Araq Knife 134, 137, *137*
Gebel el-Silsila 118
Gebel el-Tarif 195
Gebelein, cemetery of 128
George II, King 17
German Archaeological Institute, Cairo 112, 219
gesso 53, 91, 96, 115
Getty Conservation Institute 122, 125
Gharbia 52
gilt 128, *158*, 159
Girga 52
Giza 11, 23, 26, 36, 40, 47, 52, 54, 55, 60, 61, 67, 112, 120, 121, 132, 133, 136, 147, 166, 168, 169, 170, 171, 178, 203, 229–31, 237; Great Pyramid 11; Great Sphinx 26, 54, 120, 229; Second Pyramid 18, 24
Giza boat museum 203, 205
Giza Museum 71, 82, 87, 99, 106, 108, 110
Glanville, Stephen 145
glass 35, 37, 43, 47, *65*, 79, 105, 127, 150, 151, 152, *165*, 177, *193*, 207, 223
gneiss 100
Goddio, Frank 232, 234
Goedicke, Hans 154
gold 11, 30, 31, 32, 33, 35, 37, 38, 43, 44, 47, 48, 50, 51, 52, 65, 88, 89, 98, 110, 115, *115*, 116, 123, 125, 125, 129, 130, 133, 136, 138, 140, *140*, 146, 148, 149, 150, 151, 153, 155, 157, 159, *159*, 161, 162, 163, 164, 168, *171*, 176, 177, 183, 186, 188, *190*, 190, 192, *193*, 195, 199, 201, 204, 211, 223, 228, 236; sheet gold 151, *151*, *192*; gold foil 51, 91, 110, 115, 129, 161, *161*, 177; gold leaf 43, 50, 66, 115, 129, *161*, 177; gold wire 110, 141

Golden Uraeus of King Sesostris II 156, 157, *157*
goldmines map 29, *29*
Goneim, Zakaria 157, 200, 201–02
Gourlay, Janet 25
Gourna 50
Goyon, Georges 189, *190*, 191
Graf, Theodor 76
Grammaire égyptien (Champollion) 16
grandiorite 241
granite 21, 41, 53, 74, 77, 95, 99, 100, 109, 123, 139, 178, *184*, 191, 192, 204, 211, *226*, 227, *227*, 230, 234
Great Harris Papyrus 45, *45*, 46, *46*
Great Sphinx 26, 229
Grébaut, Eugène 71, 81, 82, 86, 101, 106, 142, 144
Greece 127; Greek 181, 198; Greeks 67–68
Green Head (Berlin) 72, 74, *74*
Green, Frederick William 97, 100
Grenfell, Bernard P. 107–08, *108*
Grenoble 14, 16
greywacke 33, 56, 99, *120*, 205, 227
Griffith, Francis Llewellyn 68
Gunn, Battiscombe 154, 202

Habachi, Labib 181, 202
Hadrian 10, 78
haematite 94, 100
Hall, H.R. 115
Hamilton, Gavin 10
Hanke, Rainer 195
Hapimen 17, 102, *102*
Harpokrates 207
Harpur, Yvonne 59
Harris Papyri 45–46, 174
Harris, Anthony Charles 29, 44–45, 48
Harris, J. R. 173
Harris, Selima 45, 46
Harsaphes (Herishef) 124, *124*
Harvard University 132, 133, 156
Harvey, William 10
Hassan, Ali 199
Hassan, Selim 166, 178, 187, 200
Hathor 71, *103*, *114*, 116, 126, 128, *146*, 199, 207, 226, *226*, 227, 231
Hatiay 96
Hatnufer 184–85
Hatshepsut 48, 49, 81, 82, 95, 114, 117, 151, 173, 176, 184, 185, 217
Hauron *189*, 190
Hawara 76, 78, 107, 204, 211
Hawass, Zahi 112, 178, 202, 229–30, 231, 237
Hay, Robert 34
Hayes, William C. 184, 185
Hearst Medical Papyrus 132
Hearst, Phoebe Apperson 132
Hearst, William Randolph 15, 132
heb-sed ceremonies 202; *see also sed* festival
Heh 1116
Heit el-Shorab 229
Hekekyan, Joseph 26
Heliodorus 68
Heliopolis 33, 121
Heliopolitan gods 46
Hellenion, the 68
Hemaka 182, 183
Hemiunu 120
Henutwedjebu 95
Heqaib 179, 181
Heqakheperre Shoshenq II 191, 192, 193
Heqanakht 154–55
Heqanakht Papers 154–55, *154*
Hera, temple of (Samos) 67, 68
Herakleopolis 124
Herbert, Lady Evelyn *160*, 162
Herihor 183
Hermopolis 144, 152, 194–95
Herodas 107
Herodotus 68, 77, 129
Herunufer 155

Hesyre 55–56, 97
Hetepdief 74, *74*
Hetepet 155
Hetepheres, Queen 136, 168, 170–71
Hetepsekhemwy 74
Hetepu 71
Hety 155
Hierakonpolis (Kom el-Ahmar) 97–100, *97*, 111, 211; 'Main Deposit' 99
Hierakonpolis falcon 98, *98*
hieroglyphs 10, *11*, 14, 15, 16, 21, 28, 56, 60, *60*, *61*, 87, 89, 100, *103*, *150*, 159, 188, 193, 207, 219, 236, 240
Highclere Castle 162
Hildesheim 120
Hilmy, Abd el-Fattah 199
Hilmy, Prince Ibrahim 75
Hitler, Adolf 136
Hittites, the 75
Hoffman, Michael 137
Hogarth, D. G. 68, 107
Holladay, J. S. Jr 198
Homer 107
Hor of Sebennytos 208
Hor (Auibre) 88, 90–91, *91*
Hor-Aha 100, 111, 112
Horakhty 112
Horapollo 11
Horemakhet *119*
Horemheb 44, 117, 137, 179, 209, 215, 216, *217*, 218, 219, *219*, 226, 227, *228*; colossus of 137
Horemkhauef, stela of 98
Hori 175
Hormose 184
Hornakht 191, 192
Horsheri 175
Horus 33, 35, 54, 14, 92, *93*, 155, *155*, 175, 181, *191*, 195, 207, *207*, 227, 228
Hoving, Thomas 156
Hu 94
Hunt, Arthur S. 107–08, *108*
Husein, Abdel Salam N. 195
Huy 223
Hyksos, the 48, 50, 130, 184, 189, 224
'Hyksos' sculptures 50, 53, *53*
'Hyksos sphinxes' 224

ibises 206, 207, *207*, 208
IBM 209
Ibn Tulun, mosque of 102
Ibrahim, Hosni 157
Ibscher, Hugo 96
idols 37
Imhotep 125, 169, 200, 206, *206*, 207, 208
Impy 136, 168
Ineni 114
Inhapy, Queen 21, 66
Ini 128
inlay 31, 33, 74, 88, 90, *91*, *93*, *104*, 105, *115*, 116, 119, *134*, 136, *138*, 140, 146, 150, 151, *151*, 152, 164, *165*, 168, 169, 176, 177, *182*, 188, 193, *193*, 207, 223
Insinger, Jan Herman 69
Institut d'Égypte 14
Institut français d'archéologie orientale (IFAO), Cairo 174, 189
Intyshedu 231
Ipi 154, 155
Ipuit, Queen 61
Iseum 207
Isiospolis 208
Isirar 95
Isis (goddess) 56, *56*, *70*, 71, 82, *103*, *133*, *148*, 175, 181, 207, *207*, 227, 228, 232
Iskander, Dr Zaki 204
Ismail 48, 52, 62
Isocrates 108
Israel Stela 94, 95, *95*
It, Princess 88, 89, 90
Itet 58
Itjawy, cemetery of 91, 155
Itweret, Princess 88, 90

Ity 49
Iufaa 111, 232, 236
Iunyt (goddess) 226, 227, *227*
Iuty 134, *134,*
Iuroy 32
ivory 94, 99, 100, *109*, 110, 111, 112, 120, 134, 137, *137*, 140, 181, *182*, 201
Iyneferti *69*, 71, *71*

jadeite 199
Jaffa 30
James, T. G. H. 154
Jaritz, Horst 95
jasper 74, 154
Jedaniah *see* Elephantine, Jewish Archives
Jéquier, Gustave 61
jewelry 37, 43, 44, 50, *51*, 66, 103, 111, 115, 116, 125, 129, 138–40, 141, 145, 146, 150–52, 159, 162, 164, 177, 181, 183, 199, 220, 222, 223, 228, 232, 233, *233*; anklets 90, 140, 159, 181, 204; armlets *50*, 51, *51*, 140, 201; Ashburnham ring *31*; bangles 133, 151; beads 35, 51, *51*, 67, 89, 90, 94, 111, 116, 123, 125, 129, 133, 138, 139, 140, 151, *152*, 159, 161, 188, 195, 201, 233, 236; bracelets 25, 31, *31*, *35*, 48, *48*, 89, 90, 94, 110, *110*, 116, 130, *130*, *138*, *145*, 146, 150, 151, *151*, 153, 159, *171*, 188, *190*, *191*, 204, 228; chains *30*, 31, 37, 188; circlets 90, 116, 141, 146; clasps *89*, 90; collars *35*, 51, 89, *89*, 90, 127, 133, 136, *136*, *145*, 150, 151, *151*, *152*, 159, 204, 228; crowns 27, *90*, 155, 157, 181, 219, 227, 228; Dahshur caches 88–91, *89*; diadems 27, *27*, 28, 32, *32*, 90, 123, 140, 150, 199; ear-pendants 116, 188, *218*; earrings 52, 116, *116*, 123, 127, 133, 150, 151, 177, 181; el-Lahun 67; finger-rings 31, *35*, 89, 90, 93, 116, 127, 140, 150, 151, 177, 188, *191*; finger-stalls 150, 151, 195, 199; girdle 90, 133, *138*; necklaces 50, 51, 125, 129, 140, *150*, 153, 159, *159*, 181; pectorals *43*, 44, *44*, 47, *47*, 51, *51*, 71, 89, *89*, 90, *139*, 140, 146, *146*, *164*, *193*; pendants 51, 89, 90, 116, 188, 218; pendant streamers *27*; penis-stalls 195; precious stones 10, 47, 110; semiprecious stones 43, 50, 125, *151*, 159, *159*, *165*; spacers 93, *93*, 116, 201; toe rings 181; toe-stalls 150, 151, 195, 199; uraei 27, 28, 146, 156, 157, *157*; wristlets 51, 90, 140
Johnson, John 108
Jollois, Prosper 16
Jones, Ernest Harold 100, 117
Josephine, Empress 15
Judicial Papyrus 29
Julius Caesar 107
Junker, Hermann 166, 178, 219

ka-figures 90, 91, *91*
Kaaper 53, *53*
Kafr Ghattati 133
Kagemni 59, 82, 83, 86
Kahun Papyri 76, 87, 80, *80*, 233
Kama, Queen 146
Kamal, Ahmed 144, 166
Kamal, Moharram 199
Kamose 47, 48, 50, 51, 130, 200, 202, 224
Kar 24
Karnak 25, 52, 59, 69, 95, 106, 128, 134, 137, 142, 172, *173*, 202, 209–10; cachette 118–20, 172, 184; colossi 172–73, *172*, *173*; Gem-pa-aten temple complex 210, *210*; Great Temple of Amun 118, *118*, 149, 172, 202; Taweret 55, 59, *59*; Temple of Osiris 209
Kashta 149, 227
Kay 42
Kemp, Barry 111, 177, 188

Kemsit 153
Kenherkhepshef 174–75; library of 174–75, *175*
Kerma 148
Kha 71, 126, *126*, 127, 128, 174
Khababash 42, *42*, 44
Khabekhenet 71
Khaemwaset, Prince *26*, 42, 43, 44, 125
Kharga Oasis 156, 228
Khartoum 35, 36
Khasekhem(wy) *98*, 99, 111
Khedebneitirtbint 56
Khedive Abbas II Hilmy 82
Khedive's School of Egyptology, Cairo 60
Khentimentiu 120
Khentkaus, Queen 212
Khephren 36, 40, 50, 54, *54*, 168, 229
Kheruef 200
Khnemet, Queen 88, 90
Khnum 75, 105, *146*, 207
Khnumaa 131
Khnumibremen 17
Khnumet 89
Khnumnakht 131
Khonsu *70*, 71, 118, 119
Khufu 11, 36, 118, 120, *120*, 168, 170, 171, 203, 229, 231
Khuwit 202
Kingston Lacy, Dorset 15
Kircher, Athanasius 11, 16
Kirwan, L. P. 179
Kiya 135, 154
Kom Aushim (Karanis) 107
Kom el-Ahmar 97–100
Kom el-Asl (Bacchias) 107
Kom el-Fakri 195
Kom el-Heitan 23, 25, 95
Kom Medinet Ghurab 107, 111, 123
Kom Ombo 118
Koptos (Qift) 86, 97, 133
Kumma 148
Kurneh 150
Kush (Nubia) 24, 35, 36, 148
Kysis 228

L'Hôte, Nestor 34, 40
labels *109*, 110, 111, 161, *182*
Labrousse, Audran 202
Lacau, Pierre 142, 166, 199
Lacovara, Peter 37
Lafayette College, Mass. 47
lamp *179*, *180*, *181*
Lane, Edward William 10
Lansing, Ambrose 184, 185
lapis lazuli 51, 89, *100*, 116, 129, 130, 140, 146, 155, 157, 159, *171*, 186, 188, *193*
Late Ramessid Letters 18, 24, 175
Lauer, Jean-Philippe 169, 202
Lawrence, T. E. 67
lead 211, 228
leather 75, 105, *105*, 128, 181, 189
Leblanc, Christian 121
Lefebvre, Gustave 152
Legrain, Georges 106, 118, 119, 137, 172
Lehner, Mark 171, 229, 231
Leiden 27, 31, 213
Leipzig 57
Lenormant, Charles 40
Lepsius, Karl Richard 23, 29, 35, 35, 36, 37, 61, 82, 83, 121, 215
Lesseps, Ferdinand de 47
Lézine, Alexandre 192, 193
libation stand *149*
Lilyquist, Christine 150
limestone 24, 26, 49, 52, 58, 59, 71, 81, 91, 95, 96, 99, 100, 112, 136, 139, 153, 162, 168, 169, 174, 178, 185, 191, 194, 202, 203, 208, 212, 213, *214*, 223, 225, 227, 229, 230, 231, 233, 236
Limme, Luc 236
Linant de Bellefonds, Louis 40
linen 37, 61, 68, 71, 106, 110, 141, *144*, 145, 153, 158, 159, 162, 167, 201, 228

Lipinska, Jadwiga 208
'Little Mayet' 153
Liverpool 46
Logia Iesou (Oxyrhynchus papyri) *107*, 108
Loret, Victor 86, 101–06, 113, 142, 189
Louvre, Paris 14, 20, 24, 27, 29, 31, 40, 42, 44, 47, 48, 49, 54, 64, 73, 74, 83, 128, 137, 188, 211
Lucas, Alfred 165
Ludwig I of Bavaria, King 37
Luxor 16, 20, 34, 50, 57, 64, 74, 81, 97, 118, 150, 182, 209, 210, 211, 228; cache 226–28; Temple 226, *226*
Luxor Museum 217
Lycoris 213
Lyons, Henry George 106
Lythgoe, Albert M. 125, 141

Maat *146*
Macedonia 145
Macgregor, William 87
Mackay, Ernest 131
Madja 174
Madox, John 28
Madrid 17
Mahdi, Mohammed 199
Maia 111
Maia (wet-nurse of Tutankhamun) 223
Maiherpri 104, *104*, 105, 113
malachite 100
Málek, Jaromír 7
Mallawi 229
Malmaison, Château de 15
Malqata 80; Palace of 84, 158
Malta 36
Manchester Museum 131
Manshiyet Ramla 52
Mansura, cemetery of 76
Marcus Aurelius 17
Mariette, François Auguste Ferdinand 25, 32, 38, 40–43, 45, 46, 47, 48–49, 50, 51, 52, 53, 54, 55, 56, 58, 58, 59, 60–61, 62, 64, 65, 77, 102, 106, 109, 207, 224
Markowitz, Yvonne 37
Martin, Geoffrey Thorndike 215, 218, 219
Maspero, Gaston Camille Charles 57, 60–61, *60*, 62, 64, *64*, 65, 66, 69, 70, 71, 77, 79, *81*, 91, 105, 106, 113, 118, 121, 129, 130, 136, 140, 142, 166
mastaba *see* tomb
Maunier, Galli 50
Maximilian of Austria, Archduke 52
Maya 215, 218–19, *219*
maze 224
Mecca 20
Medamud 209
medicine 55, 65
Medina 20
Medinet Habu 29, 45, 52, 118, 119
Meidum 58
Meidum Sculptures 55, 58, *58*
Meir 58, 107
Meketre 156–57, 158, 159
Meketre models 156–57, *156*, *157*, 158
Memnon, Colossi of 134, 137
Memphis 26, 30, 41, 52, 57, 74, 84, 129, 182, 195, 216, 223; necropolis 215; temple of Ptah 26
Men 134
Mena 110
Mendes 107, 209
Menes 100
Menhet 150, 151
Menkaure 36, 132, *132*, *133*, 205, 229; temples of 132–33
Menkheperenre 173
Menkheperre 66
Menou, General 17
'Mensa Isaiaca' *11*

Mentuherkhepshef, Prince 21, 166
Mentuhotep the Steward 27
Mentuhotep V (Merankhre) 120
Mentuhotep, Queen 27, 28
Menwi 150, 151
Merefnebef 235
Merenptah 103, 174, 192, 194, 218
Merenre 61
Mereruka 59, 82, 83, 86
Meret 88, 90
Meritites 202
Merneith 111
Meroe 35, 36, 72, 147, 148
Merrillees, Robert 188
Mersuankh 176, 178
Merti 150, 151
Merton, Arthur 165
Merydjehuty 74
Meryet 126, 127, 219
Meryetamun 96, 176–77, 219
Meryintef 80
Meryptah 19
Meryrehashtef 158, 159, *159*
Mesaid 133
Meseh 154
Mesehti 87; Soldiers of *63*, 87
Mesheikh 133
metal 65, 71, 155, 119, 125, 150, 182, 201, 228
Metropolitan Museum of Art, New York 33, 47, 70, 74, 79, 98, 125, 129, 130, 140, 141, 142, 149, 150, 154, 156, 157, 159, 166, 167, 173, 184, 195, 208
Metternich Stela 32, 33, *33*
Metternich-Winneberg, Prince Clemens 33
Mi 111
Mibtahiah *see* Elephantine, Jewish Archives
Miho Museum, Shigaraki, Japan 155
Milner, Lord 82
Min (god of fertility) 86, 183, 207
Min Colossi 83, 86, *86*
Minoan frescoes 224–25
Minoan pottery 188
Minutoli, Baron von 29
Mirgissa 148
mirrors 48, 51, 16, *140*, 117, *139*, 140, 150, 151, 159
Mission archéologique française du Bubastieion 222
Mit Faris 52
Mitanni *72*, 75
Mnevis bulls 33
models *62*, 117, 144, 152, 156–57, 161; Meketre 156–57, *156*, *157*
Mohammed, Mohammed Abd el-Qader 199
Möller, Georg 174
Mond, Robert 105, 124, 156, 182, 201, 228
Monneret de Villard, Ugo 179
Montet, Pierre 189, *190*, 191, 192, 195
Montu 28, 48, 52, 155, 186
Montu Priests 47, 48, *48*, 52
Morgan, Henri de 101
Morgan, Jacques de 55, 59, 82, 86, 88–91, *90*, 94, 100, 101, 106, 139, 140, 182, 203, 233
mosaic work 32
Mose 71
Moustafa, Hag Ahmed Youssef 195, 204, *204*, 205
Mubarak, President 226
Mukhtar, Gamal 199
mummies 11, 16, 24, 27, 28, 31, 32, 33, 43, 46, 47, 48, 50, 51, 52, 64, 65, 66, 70, 71, 78, 81–82, 89, 90, *90*, 92, 94, 102, 103, 103, 104, 105, 111, 115, 117, 127, 131, *144*, 152, 153, 158–59, *158*, 160, 161, 162, 163, 164, *166*, 167, *176*, 177, *190*, 191, 192, 193, 199, 202, 231, 236; animal 206–08, *207*, 208
Munich 35, 37, 211
Murray, Margaret 97, 131
Musée de l'Homme, Paris 48

Musée du Cinquantenaire, Brussels 74
Museum of Fine Arts, Boston 47
musical instruments 117, 161, 164, 184
Mut 25, 35, 119, 207, 227
Mutnodjmet 192, 216, 218
Mycerinus *see* Menkaure
Myers, William Joseph 74, 87, 92, *92*
Mysliwiec, Karol 235

Nag Hammadi 137
Nag Hammadi Codices 194, 195, *195*
Naga el-Deir 132, 133
Naga el-Hai 133
Nakht 55
Nakhtankh 131
Nakhtmin 99
Nany 176
Napata region 36, 147
Napoleon I, Emperor *see* Bonaparte, Napoleon
Napoleon III, Emperor 47, 48, 52
Napoleon, Prince (Plonplon) 47, 48
Naqada 82, 94, 95, 100, 111, 182
Narmer 110, 111
Narmer Palette 99–100
National Centre for Scientific Research (CNRS) 232
Naukratis 67–68, 69
Naville, Édouard 56, 67, 71, 77, 87, 106, 107, 124, 125, 128, 153, 198
Nebetia 111
Nebhepetre Mentuhotep 106, 144, 153, 154, 157, 159, 173; soldiers of 167, *167*; temple of 128
Nebiry 125
Nebit II 233
Nebnufer 80, 211
Nebtu 75
Necho II 44
Nectanebo II 17, 33; obelisks of 17, *17*
Nedji 56
Neferhotep II (Mersekhemre) 120
Nefeirkare, King 58, 212
Neferkare Peftjawybastet, King 124
Nefermaat 58
Nefertari 96, 121–23
Nefertiti 61, 83, 84, 85, 134–36, *134*, *135*, 154, 166, *172*, 173, 194, *210*
Nefertjetjes 231
Nefertum (god) *208*
Neferure *184*
Nefruptah, Princess 203, 204
Neith (goddess) 231
Neith, Queen 61
Neithhotep 100, 182
Nekhbet *44*, 50
Nekhen *21*, 97
Nekheny 97
Nenit 188
Nepherites I 44
Nephthys *70*, 82, *114*
Nesatum 33
Netjerykhet-Djoser 56; *see also* Djoser
Newberry, Percy 73, 117, 144, 182
Nile 11, 19, 36, 50, 57, 62, 64, 67, 72, 77, 88, 105, 112, 119, 155, 175, 179, 186, 189, 196, 200, 219, 224
Ninenetjer 74
Nineveh 72
Niuserre (Isi) 58, 120, 212
Nofret 58
Nu 75
Nubheteptikhered 88, 90, 91
Nubia 20, 24, 35, 72, 106, 179, 182, 194
Nubkheperre Intef 27, 32
Nueir, Rashid 199
Nuri 36, 147–49
Nut *92*
Nytankhsekhmet 159

obelisks *16*, 17, *17*, 119
obsidian 33, 98, 139, 140, 140, 188
O'Connor, David 203
Onuris 207
openwork technique *93*
Oppenheim, Adela 233
Oppert, Jules 73, 74

Oriental Institute, University of Chicago 74, 128, 179
Ortiz, George 211
Osiris 11, 43, 56, 61, 65, 75, 82, 105, 109, *114*, 127, 186, 207, *221*, 228
Osiris-Apis 41, 43
Osorkon I 191
Osorkon II 144, 189, 191, 192, 195
Osorkon III 146
ostraca 71, 80; 'dream ostraca' 208
Othman, Master 24
Oxyrhynchus 107–08, *108*
Oxyrhynchus Papyri 107–08, 213

Pabasa (high priest) 59
Pachomius, St 195
Padienaset 111
Padua 19
Pahernefer 42
Paiankh 24
Palanque, Charles 87
Palermo Stone 57, *57*
Palestine 30, 67, 75, 142, 166
palettes 31, 94, 99–100; Narmer Palette 99–100
Pami 44
Panehsy 24, 175
papyri 20, 24, 27, 29, 30, 33, 47, 48, 57, 64, 66, 68, 75, 82, 105, 116, 127, *127*, 128, 137, 145, 165, 174, 182, 194, 195, 208, 213, *214*, 236, 237; Abusir Papyri 83, 87, 212; Aramaic 101, 105; Bodmer Papyri (Dishna Papers) 195; Chester Beatty 175, *175*; Deir el-Medina 175; Denon's 14, 16, 29; Ebers medical papyrus 57; Edwin Smith 57, *57*; Great Harris Papyrus 45, *45*, 46, *46*; Harris Papyri 45–46, 174; Harris Magical Papyrus 45; Hearst Medical Papyrus 132; Heqanakht Papers 154–55, *154*; Judicial Papyrus 76, 80, *80*, 87, 233; Kahun papyri 76, 80, 80–02, 204; Logia Iesou *107*; mathematical leather roll (BM) 57; Naunakht 175; Oxyrhynchus 107–08, 107, *108*, 213; Papyrus Abbott 32, 46, 48; Papyrus Ambras 46; Papyrus Amherst VI 46; Papyrus de Burgh 46; Papyrus Geneva 175; Papyrus Leopold II 46; Papyrus Mayer A 46; Papyrus Mayer B 46; Ramesseum papyri 174, 96, *96*; Rhind mathematical papyrus 57; Ritual of Amenophis I 175; Tale of Setne-Khaemwaset 57, *57*
Paraemnekhu 71
Parahetep 71
Parahu 49
Paramessu (Ramesses I) 137
Paser 218
Passalacqua, Giuseppe 27–29
Pe *21*
Pediaset 208
Peet, Thomas Eric 182
Pelizaeus, Wilhelm 120
Pelizaeus-Museum, Hildesheim 194
Pendlebury, J. D. S. 73, 177
Pepi I 61, 98, *98*, 211
Pepy II 61, 187, 214
Percy, Lord Algernon 19
Peribsen 111
Perring, John Shae 36
Persia 42, 68, 101
Petosiris 150
Petrie Museum, University College London 57, 67, 87, 98
Petrie, William Matthew Flinders 24, 52, 59, 61, 62, 67, 68, 71, 73, 76, 77, 78, 80, 82, 83, 84, 85, 87, 88, 94, 95, 96, 100, 105, 107, 109, 110, *110*, 111, 112, 115, 120, 123, 124, 131, 132, 133, 134, 138, 140, 142, 166, 177, 182, 198
Phanes of Halicarnassus 68
Pharos lighthouse 232, 234
Philadelphia (Darb el-Gerza) 145

Philae 15
Philoppoteaux, Paul *81*
Piazzi Smyth, Charles 67
Pierpont Morgan Library, New York 46
Pierret, Paul 118
Pillet, Maurice 209
Pindar 108
Pinudjem I 25, 65, 176, 177
Pinudjem II 66
Pithom 198
Piye (Piankhi) 149
plaster *135*, 136, 220
Plato 107, 108
Pliny 77
Plonplon *see* Napoleon, Prince
Polish Centre of Mediterranean Archaeology, Warsaw University 235
porphyry 17, 100
Posener-Kriéger, Paule *214*
pottery 67, 69, 79, 82, 91, 93, 94, 95, 98, 99, 100, 105, 110, *110*, 112, *112*, 123, 125, *126*, 131, 136, 139, 148, 182, 202, 207, *207*, 208, 220, 228, 231, 233, 236; Greek 67–68; Kamares 80
'proto-Sinaitic' script 124
Prussia 136
Psammetichus I 41, 44, 68, 199, 208
Psammetichus II 199
Psammetichus III 236
Psammuthis 207
Psusennes I 190, *190*, 191, 192, 193
Psusennes II 182, 192
Ptah 31, 41, 57, 207
Ptahhotep 59
Ptahmose, Mayor of Thebes 60, 61, *61*
Ptahshepses 194, 195, 212
Ptahshepsesu 212
Ptolemy II Philadelphus 107, 145
Ptolemy V 14
Ptolemy VI Philometor 44, 208
Ptolemy VIII Euergetes II 6, 44, 115
Ptolemy IX 213
Punt, Queen of 47, 49, *49*
Pushkin Museum, Moscow 70, 74
Pypu 146
pyramid builders 229–31
Pyramid Texts 60, 60–61, 61, 64, 156, 236
pyramidion, Ammenemes III 109, 112, *112*
pyramids 10, 35, 36, 58, 67, 77, 78, 80, 89, 90, 112, 128, 138, 147, 148, 149, 157, 170, 187, 200–02, 204, 229–31; Abusir 212–14, *212*; Ammenemes III 112, 211; Begarawiya North 6 (Amanishakheto) 35, *36*; Dahshur 88–91; el-Kurru 147–49; GI-a 171; GI-b 171; GI-x 171; Great Pyramid (Khufu) 36, 37, *37*, 67, 120, 168, *168*, 203; Khephren 18, 23, 36, *168*; 'lost pyramids' 200–02, 237; Menkaure 35, 36, 132; Neferirkare *214*; Nuri 147–49; Amanishakheto 37, *37*; Ankhesenpepy II 202; Meritites 202; Raneferef 212–14, *212*; 'Red Pyramid' (Snefru) 192; Sekhemkhet 200–01, *200*, *201*; Sesostris I 141; Sesostris II 138, 233; Sesostris III 202, 233; Step Pyramid (Djoser) 37, 56, 97, 168, 169, 200, 202, 206, 216, 235; Teti 86; Unas 60, *61*, 111

Qaa 111, 183
Qabbanat el-Qurud 150
Qait Bey 232
Qantir 84, 119
Qasr el-Nil 106
Qasr Ibrim (ancient Primis) 213
Qau el-Kebir 121
Qena 50, 52, 65, 160
Qerdan 52
quartz 42, 90, 100, 163, 188

quartzite 15, 102, *102*, *119*, 134, *135*, 162, 163, 179, 199, 213, 226, 227, *227*
Qubbet el-Hawa 181
Queen of Punt 47, 49, *49*
Quibell, James Edward 55, 56, 96, 97, 100, 114, 117, 169, 206
Qurna 52, 150
Qustul 182

Rahotep 58
Raia 218
Ramesses I 19, 20, 21, 21, *21*, 25, 26, 43, 44, 57, 64, 65, 66, 116, 121, 128, 129, 130, 137, 166, 175, 189, 190, 202, 209, 211, 218, 219, Ramesses II (the Great) 21, 65, 66, *66*, 96, 194, *194*, 220, 227, 234; colossus of (Abu'l-Hol) 26, *26*
Ramesses III 29, 45, *46*, 65, 115, 119, 131, 166, 221
Ramesses IV 103, 104, *113*
Ramesses V 103, 175
Ramesses VI 44, 103, 166
Ramesses IX 32, 44, 46, 65, 115, 116
Ramesses XI 46, 52, 217, *217*
Ramesseum 94, 96, 97
Ramesseum Papyri 96, *96*, 174
Ramose 71, 184–85, 219
'Ramses' 189
Raneb 74
Raneferef 212, *214*
Rawer 178
Ray, John 208
Razek, Mohamed Abdel 230
Re 33, *46*, *51*, 60, 169, 175, 183, *193*
Red Sea 86
Redford, Donald B. 209, 210
Reeves, Nicholas 215
Reil, Dr 58
Reinach, Adolphe 86
Reisner, George Andrew 37, 132–33, 136, 144, 147, 148, 149, 168, 170, 171, 178, 179, 206
Rekhmire 128
reliefs 49, *49*, 56, 66, 86, 95, 121, 123, 124, *124*, 194–95, 216, 218, 219, 220
repoussé decoration *31*, *129*, *130*, 228
resin 43, 115, 123, 158, 159, *161*
Revillout, Eugène 118
Revolution, Egyptian 65
Rhind mathematical papyrus 57
Rhind, Alexander Henry 37, 46
Rhoikos 67, 68
Ricci, Alessandro 34, 54
Richardson, Robert 25
Ricke, Herbert 205
Rijksmuseum van Oudheden, Leiden 32, 216, 218
robbers/robberies 24, 45, 66, 82, 89, 102, 148, 152, 156, 162, *162*, 163, 171, 177, 202, 214, 219, 221, 223, 225, 233
Rochester 46
rock crystal 42, 90, 100, 110, *134*, 155
Rockefeller, John D. Jr 86, 128, 166
Roeder, Günther 166, 194–95
Roemer-Pelizaeus Museum, Hildesheim 183
Rohl, David 225
Roman period 78
Rome 10, 127
Romer, John 183, 217
Rosellini, Gaetano *34*
Rosellini, Ippolito 14, 23, 34, *34*, 37, 40
Rosetta Stone 14, *15*, 17, 18
Rossi, Francesco 21
Rowe, Alan 168
Rubensöhn, Otto 194

sacrifice, human 94, 112, 181; animal 181
Sacy, Baron Antoine Isaac Sylvestre de 14
Sahure 120, 187, 212
Sai, island of 179
Said Pasha 48, 49, 50, 52
St Athanasius, mosque of (Cairo) 17
Sais 14, 52

Saite kings 68
Salt, Henry 18, 19, 20, 23, 24, 25, 26, 27, 28, 29, 32, 32, 34, 38, 45, 76
Salzburg, St Peter's Abbey 18
Samos 67
Sân 53
sandals 17, 71, 82, 116, 123, 150, 151, *192*, 199
sandstone 17, 41, 43, 77, 106, 163, 172, 209, *210*, 211, 227, 230
Sappho 108
Saqqara 11, 30, 31, 37, 40–44, 47, 52, 53, 55, 56, 58, 60, 82, 86, 87, 97, 111, 182–83, 200, 202, 212, 215–19, 222, 235, 237; Necropolis 200, 215; Unas causeway 56; Sacred Animal Necropolis 206–07, *206*, *207*; Serapeum 38, 40–44, *41*, *42*, 407
Sarapis 228
sarcophagus *12*, 15, 17, *17*, 20, *23*, 28, 32, 36, 41, 42, *42*, 50, 52, *60*, 91, 102, *102*, 103, *103*, *114*, *122*, 123, 139, 147, 153, *153*, 161, 162, 163, 164, 166, 168, 169, 191, 192, 195, 199, 201–02, *201*, 204, 220, 233, 235, 236
Sati 61
Savoy, King of 25
Sawahel Armant Canal 211
Sayce, Revd Professor Archibald Henry 73, 74, 101, 105, 106
scabbards 51
scarabs *30*, 31, 32, *33*, 35, 43, 47, 48, 51, 89, 90, *92*, 99, 100, 127, 140, 146, 148, 151, 152, 172, 173, *173*, 195, 199, 140, 147, 159, *159*
Schaden, Otto 21
Schiaparelli, Ernesto 105, 121, 123, 125, 126, 127, 128, 165, 174, 194
Schimmel, Norbert 195
schist 31, 100, 195
Schliemann, Heinrich 68
Schweinfurth, Georg 219
'Scorpion' 111, 112
Scott, Nora 33
sculpture 15, 17, 20, 25, 26, 53, *53*, 54, 56, 58, *58*, 59, 61, 97, 119, *119*, 123, 128, 132, 134, 141, 154, 169, 173, 178, 181, 208, 211, 212, 213, 226, *226*, 223, 230, 232
seals/sealings 56, 109, 112, 154, 160, *160*, 161, 186, 188, 201
Seated Scribe 42, *42*, 44
Sebek 209, 211, *211*
Sebekemsaf I (Sekhemrewadjkhau) 120
Sebekemsaf 32, 33
Sebekhotep I 27, 91
Sebekhotep VI (Merhetepre) 120
sed-festival (jubilee) 25; *see also* heb-sed ceremonies
Sehel rock inscription 187
Sekhemhra 42
Sekhemkhet 200, 201
Sekhmet 17, 18, 25, 207; statues 18, 25, *25*
Selkis *163*
Semerkhet (Mersekha) 111
Semna 72, 148
Seneb 178
Senebhenaef 27
Senebtisi 141
Senedjemib family 136
Senen 154
Senenmut 184–85, *184*
Sennudjem 64, *69*, *71*, 69–71, 174
Sennufer 174
Sennuferi 230
Senwosret-senebefni *14*
Septimius Severus 17
sepulchre 69, 104, 157, 190
Serabit el-Khadim 123
Serapeum 38, 40–44, *41*, *42*, 207
serdab (statue room) 59, 157, 169, 178
Service des Antiquités 65, 69, 81, 82, 94, 101, 102, 106, 118, 126, 140,

142, 166, 181, 182, 194, 196, 198, 199, 203, 204, 109, 222, 233
Service for the Conservation of Antiquities 38
Sesostris I 88, 91, *91*, 118, 141, 154, 186
Sesostris II 80, 88, 90, 140, 156, 157, 188, 233
Sesostris III 80, 88, 89, 90, 120, 202, 233
Sesostris (IV) (Sneferibre I) 120
Seth 175
Sethe, Kurt 132
Sethherkhepshef 125
Sethnakht 103, *104*
Sethos I *12*, 21, 34, 37, 40, 44, 52, 65, 66, 69, 71, 109, 119
Sethos II 103, 116, 117, 175, 194
Setne I 57
Setne-Khaemwaset, Tale of 57, *57*
Severus Alexander 213
Shabaka 119
shabtis 43, 44, 60, 61, *61*, 64, 65, 71, 82, 111, *111*, 119, 123, 125, 146, 147, *148*, 149, 161, *165*, 192, 195, 199, 220, 236
Shalfak 148
Sheikh Abd el-Qurna 46, 65, 96, 184
Sheikh el-Beled statue 50, 53, *53*
Sheikh Farag 133
Shelley, P.B. 96
shells 116
Shepenwepet 199
Shepseskare 212
Shoshenq 119
Shoshenq I 25, 66
Shoshenq II *see* Heqakheperre Shoshenq II
Shoshenq III 44, 47, 190, 191, 192
Shoshenq V 44
Shoshenq, Prince 195
Shoucri, Asmahan 209
Shoukry, Mohammed Anwar 199
shrines 59, 104, 112, 115, 141, 161, 162, 163, 164, 181, 210
Shu 173
Shunet el-Zebib 111
Shuroy 32
Siamun 192
Sicily 57
silver 27, 28, 31, 32, 47, 51, 68, 89, 111, 116, 123, 125, 129, 130, 140, *140*, 146, *150*, 151, 155, 159, *159*, 164, 177, 181, 186, 188, *188*, *191*, 192, 193, 198
Simon, Dr James 136
Simonides, Constantine 5
Simpson, William Kelly 130
Sinai 123, 124
Siptah 103, 115, 117
Sithathor 88, 89, 90, 139
Sithathoriunet 88, 138–40
Sitnebsekhtu 155
Sitwerut 233, 236
Smendes 191
Smith, Edwin 57
Smith, Joseph Lindon 118, 132, 142, 171
Smith, Ray Winfield 209
Snefru 58, 112, 120, 170
Soane, Sir John *12*, 23
Sohag 52
Soldiers of Mesehti 63, 83, 87, *87*
Sophocles 108
Sotheby's, London 19, 32
Southampton Museum 241
Spencer, Jeffrey 194
Sphinx (Great Sphinx, Giza) 26, 54, 120, 229
sphinxes 10, 41, 41, *41*, 51, *119*, 120, 218, 227, 228, *228*, 234; 'Hyksos sphinxes' 224
Spiegelberg, Wilhelm 95, 105
statue room *see serdab*
statues/statuettes 10, 19, *21*, 24, 25, 26, *26*, *30*, 43, 50, 53, *53*, *54*, 56, *56*, 57, 59, 66, 67, 68, *74*, 77, 82, 83, 86, 87, 91, 96, 98, 99, 99, 100, 106, 111, 118–20, *119*, *119*, 120,

120,*126,* 130, 131, 132, *132,* 133, *133,* 141, *142,* 149, 153, *153,* 154, 158, 159, *161,* 162, 167, *166,* 168, 169, *169,* 171, 172, *172,* 176, 178, 179, 179, 181, *181,* *184,* *189,* 190, 202, 207, *208,* 209, 211, *214,* 219, *219,* 225, *227,* 228, 230, 233, 234, *240*
steatite 100, 123, 146, *159,* 173, *182*
Stefani, Antonio 35, 36, 37
stelae 14, 41, 56, 57, 80, 82, 109, 111, 119, 128, 134, 148, 181, 207, 230; Israel Stela 94, 95, *95;* Marriage Stela (Abu Simbel) 128; Metternich Stela 32; stela of Horemkhauef 98; Stela of Kamose 200, 202, *202,* 'Stela of 400 Years' 224
stone *10,* 33, 35, 43, 54, 68, 91, 94, 99, 105, 110, 119, 147, 148, 150, 169, 169, 182, *182,* 207, 208, 217, 219, 230, 236
Story, H. Lyman 144, 145
Strabo 40, 41, 77, 213, 134
Strouhal, E. 236
Strudwick, Nigel 230
stucco 79, 91, 233
Sudan 35, 36, 49, 132, 142, 148, 179, 215
Suez Canal 47, 196
Supreme Council of Antiquities 196
Susa 101
Swiss Institute of Archaeology, Cairo 95
Syria 175, 208, 225

Taahuty *82*
Taharqa 44, 147, 148, 149, 227, 241
Takelot II 191, 192
Takelothis II 44
Takhut 198, 199
talatat 209, 210, *210*
Tameket 71
Tanis 52, 66, 77, 189–93, *189*
Tano, Nicolas 155
Tantamani 149
Tashesen 71
Tattam, Henry 40
Tauret 223
Tawer 75
Taweret 59, *59,* 227, *227*
Tawfik, Sayed 199
Tawosret 116, 117, 129
Tebtunis 107
Tefenet 173
Tell Atrib (Athribis) 199
Tell Basta (Bubastis) treasures 129–30, *129,* *130*
Tell el-Daba 224–25
Tell el-Hesi 74, 75
Tell el-Maskhuta 198–99
Tell el-Muqdam 146
Tell el-Yahudiya 52, 119
Tell Kabri 225
Tell Timai treasure 125
tempera 76, 84
temple 10, 19, 25, 41, 46, 49, 52, 54, 77, 95, 96, 97, 100, 123, 128, 129, 132, 137, 149, 156, 172, 173, 174, 179, 186, 187, 188, 189, 190, 194, *194,* 200, 205, 207, 209, 210, 213, 219, 222, 226, 228, 235; Amun (Tanis) 53; Hatshepsut 81, 82; Koptos 86; Medinet Habu 45; Neferirkare (Abusir) 58; Niuserre (Abusir) 58; Raneferef (Abusir) 58; Sahure (Abusir) 58; Sesostris

II 80; Sethos I 109; Valley Temple of Khephren 40
Terrage, Édouard de Villiers du 16
Teti 61, 86
Theban Mapping Project 166
Theban Tomb Survey 209
Thebes 18, 19, 23, 25, 27, 28, 29, 30, 32, 40, 45, 46, 47, 48, 50, 60, 61, 64, 65, 68, 76, 77, 79, 81, 95, 101, 113, 118, 119, 121, 124, 126, 128, 129, 130, 133, 150, 153, 156, 159, 160; 167, 172, 174, 176, 184, 196, 209, 213, 219, 220, 226, 230, 237; necropolis 202, 215; Ramesseum 19
Thera 225
Thomas, Elizabeth 166
Thoth 152, 194, 206, 207, 208
Thucydides 108
Thutmose 134, 135, 136
Ti 58
Tia, Princess 218
Tiaa 118, 120
tiles 119, *119,* 168, 169, *169,* *213*
Timai (ancient Thmuis) 125
Tiy 111
Tiye, Queen 103, 114, 115, 116, 117, 121, 123, *123,* 124, *124,* 134, 154, 165
Tjuyu 105, 114, 115, 117
Toda y Güell, Eduardo 69
tombs 19, 24, 46, 48, 50, 54, 56, 57, 59, 70, 86, 96, 102, 138, 156, 166, 178, 235, 237; 99 (Sheikh Abd el-Qurna) 230; 507 (Deir el-Bahri) 167; 1165 (Deir el-Medina) 174; 3610 (Saqqara) 207; Abydos 52, 67, 100, 109–12, 109, *182,* 183; Amarna royal tomb 116; Amenemope 191, 192, 193; Amenkha 47; Amennakht 175; Amenophis II tomb 116; Amenophis III 14; Ammenemes III 204; Anedjib (Adjib) (X) 111; Aperel 222–23; Apis bull burials 40–44; Ashayet 153; Aspelta 148; Ay 20, 21, *21;* Bab el-Gasus 81–82; Butehamun 175; Carnarvon tomb no. 9 130; DB320 64, *64,* 65, DB320 66, *66;* DB320 (Pinudjem II) 82; DB358 (Meryetamun) 176–77; Den (tomb T, Abydos) 109, *110,* 111; Djehutynakht (tomb 10a, Wadi Deir el-Nakhla) 144, *144;* Djer (tomb O, Abydos) 110, 111, 112; Djet (Wadj) (tomb Z, Abydos) 111; 'Elder Lady' 116; G7000X (Hetepheres) 168, *168,* 170–71; General Djehuty 30, 31, *31;* Hatiay 96; Hemaka 183; Herihor 183; Hesyre 55–56, *55, 56,* 97; Hetepheres 136; Hor-Aha (tomb B-19, Abydos) 111, 112; Horemheb and Meryet 215–16, *216,* 218, 219; Hornakht 192; Huya 134, *134;* Imhotep 138, 141, 206, 208; Impy 134, 136, 168; Inhapy 21, 66; Ini 128; Ipi (tomb TT315, Deir el-Bahri) 154; Ipuit 61; Iuroy 32; Kagemni 59, 82, 83, 86; Kama 146; Kamose 47; Kashta 149; Kha 71; Khaemwaset 41–42; Khasekhem(wy) (tomb V, Abydos) 111; Khuwit 202; KV3 115; KV4 (Ramesses XI) 217; KV5 (sons of Ramesses II) 166, 201, 220–21,

220; KV6 (Ramesses IX) 80, 115; KV9 (Ramesses VI) 80, 160; KV12 115; KV13 (Bay) 166; KV16 (Ramesses I) 21, *21;* KV17 (Sethos I) 21, *22, 23,* 66; KV19 21; KV20 113, 114; KV21 21; KV26 105; KV27 105; KV28 105; KV29 105; KV30 21, 105; KV31 105; KV32 105; KV34 (Tuthmosis III) 102, *102,* 103, 104, 105; KV35 (Amenophis II) 103, *103,* 104, *104,* 105; KV36 (Maiherpri) 104–05, 113; KV37 105; KV 38 (Tuthmosis I) 104, 105; KV39 105; KV40 105; KV41 105; KV43 (Tuthmosis IV) 113, 114, 117; KV45 (Userhet) 113, 117; KV46 (Yuya and Tjuyu) 114, 115, *115,* 117; KV47 (Siptah) 115, 117; KV48 (Amenemopet) 117; KV49 117; KV50–52 ('animal tombs') 115, 117; KV53 117; KV 54 116, 117; KV55 (Akhenaten?) 116, *116,* 117; KV56 ('Gold Tomb') 116, 117; KV57 (Horemheb) 117, *117,* 216; KV58 116, 117; KV60 113, 117; KV 61 113, 117; KV62 (Tutankhamun) 160–66, *161, 162* ; KV L 105; KV M 105; lady Madja 174; lady Sitwerut 233, 236; 'Little Mayet' 153, *153,* Maia (wet-nurse of Tutankhamun) 223; Maiherpri 104–05, 113; mastaba tombs 42, 53, 55, *55, 56,* 58, 85, 100, 149, 190, 202, 206, 213, 233; mastaba 'Giza V' 182; mastaba 3500 *183;* mastaba 3035 182; mastaba 3504 *182,* *183;* mastaba 3506 *183;* mastaba C8 (Saqqara) 53; mastaba G 4000 (Giza) 120; mastaba 3471 182; Maya 218–19; Mentuherkhepshef (Prince) 21; Mentuhotep (Queen) 27; Mentuhotep the Steward 27, 28, *28;* Merenptah 192; Merenre 61; Mereruka 59, 82, 83, 86; Merneith (Queen) (tomb Y, Abydos) 111; Meseh 154; Narmer (B-10) 111; Nefermaat and Itet 58; Nefertjetjes 231; Neith (Queen) 61; Neithhotep (Queen) 100, 182; New Kingdom tombs (Saqqara) 215–19; Nubkheperre Intef 32; Nuri and el-Kurru cemeteries (Nubia) 147–49; Osorkon II 189, 191, 192; Padienaset 111; parents of Senenmut 184; Pepi I 61; Peribsen (tomb P, Abydos) 111; 'Persian' 109, 111, 191; Petosiris 150, 152; Petrie tomb no. 8 (Sithathoriunet) 138, 139; Piye (Piankhi) 149; Predynastic 94–95; Psamtek 55, 56; Psusennes I 190, 191, 192; Ptahhotep and Akhethotep (D 64) 59; Ptahmose 61; Ptahshepsesu 230; pyramid builders 229–31; Qaa (Q) 111; QV30 (Nebiry) 125; QV36 125; QV43 (Sethherkhepshef) 125; QV44 (Khaemwaset) 125; QV46 (Imhotep) 125; QV47 (Ahmose) 125; QV55 (Amenherkhepshef) 125; QV66 (Nefertari) 121, *122,* 125; QV 87 125; QV88 (Ahmose) 125; QV 89 125; QV90 125; QV91 125; Rahotep and Nofret 58; Ramesses II 121; Ramesses III 20,

21; Ramesses IV 29, *113;* Ramose and Hatnufer 184–85; Rekhmire 128; Rhind's 45; 'Scorpion' (tomb U-j, Abydos) 111, 112, *112;* Semerkhet (tomb U, Abydos) 111; Sennufer 174; Sennuferi 230; Sennudjem 64, 69–71, 174; Sethos I 12, 34, 37, 40, Sethos I 66; Shoshenq (Prince) 194, 195; Shoshenq III 192; Shuroy 32; sons of Ramesses II 220; Taharqa 147, 148, 149; Takelot II 192; Takhut (Queen) 199; Tanis royal tombs 66, 189–93, *189, 193,* 195; Tantamani 149; 'Three Princesses' 150–51; Ti (tomb D 22, Saqqara) 58–59, *58;* Tiyi 115; Tjanenhebu 111; Tomb of Two Brothers 129, 131, *131;* 'Tomb of the Horse' 101, 106, *106;* 'Tomb of the Unknown' 128; TT1 (Sennudjem) 69, *69;* TT8 (Kha and Meryet) 126–27, *127;* TT47 (Userhet) 124; TT71 (Senenmut) 184; TT95 65; TT192 (Kheruef) 200; TT280 156, 158; TT311 (Chancellor Khety) 167; TT353 (Senenmut) 173, 184; Tutankhamun 21, 117, 142, 155, 170; Tuthmosis IV 105; Wah 158; Wedjebten 61; Wedjebauendjedet 192, 193; Weret 233; WV23; WV25 21; X-group 179; Yuya and Tjuyu 105
Trajan 76
Troy 68
Tukh el-Qaramus 94; treasure 121, 198
Tuna el-Gebel 52, 92–93, 150, 152
turbinella 74
Turin, Egyptian Museum 116, 29, 31, 21, 123, 128, 152, 174
Turin Royal Canon 29, *29*
turquoise 51, 124, 150, 157, *171,* 183
Tushratta 72
Tutankhamun 16, 20, 44, 61, 72, 74, 75, 83, 99, 106, 115, 116, 117, 118, 120, *120,* 160–66, *164, 165,* 179, 183, 191, 195, 215, 216, *217,* 218, 227, 228, 237; colossi 195
Tuthmosis I 65, 114, 120
Tuthmosis II 64, 65
Tuthmosis III 30, *30,* 65, 95, 102, 104, 119, 120, 128, 149, 150, 151, 173, 208, , 217, 227
Tuthmosis IV 95, 103, 114, *114,* 117, 118, 120, 128
Tuty 111

Umm el-Baragat (Tebtunis) 107
Umm el-Qaab 109, 110, 111, 182
Unas 60, 61, 187, 195; Causeway 186
UNESCO 196
University of Cairo 152
University of California, Berkeley 133
University of Hamburg 166
Urlin, Amy *110*
Uronarti 148
Userhet 117, 124
Userkaf 203, 205, *205,* 212

Valley of the Kings 16, 18, 20, 23, 24, 29, 34, 70, 76, 80, *80,* 83, 101, *101,* *102,* 113–17, *113,* 160, 163, 164, 165, 166, 174, 192, 201, 215, 216, 217, 220, 221, 241

Valley of the Queens 70, 121–25, *121,* 165, 174
van Dijk, Jacobus 218
vases 37, 50, 69, 94, 110, 129, 145, 146, 169, 177, 198
Vassalli, Luigi 49
vellum 75
Verner, Miroslav 212, 236
vessels/bowls 19, 28, 31, *31,* 54, 64, 65, 68, 71, 82, 91, 92, 94, 100, 109, 110, *110,* 112, *112,* 125, 129, *129,* 130, *130,* 136, 144, 148, 150, 151, 161, *171,* 177, 181, 182, 186, *186,* 188, *188,* 192, 193, 195, 198, 198, 201, 213, 236
Vorderasiatisches Museum, Berlin 74
Vyse, Colonel Richard William Howard 10, 26, 35, 36

Wadi Halfa 20, 179
Wadi Natrun 40
Wadj 183
Wadjyt *44*
Wah 80, 158–59, *158,* 159
Wakeling, T.G. 152
'Wall of the Crow' *see* Heit el-Shorab
Wallis, Henry 75, 92, 93
Waseda University, Tokyo 16, 79, 205
Wawi 179
weaponry 32, 51, 74, 90, 94, 109, 110, 117, 145, 161, 164, 181; axes 51; bows and arrows 32; daggers 31, *47,* 48, 51; Gebel el-Araq Knife 137, *137*
Webensenu 113
Wedjebten 61
Weeks, Kent R. 166, 220, *221*
Weidenbach, Ernst *36*
Weigall, Arthur 86, *113,* 115, 118, 124, 126, 165, 179
Weigall, Corinna *113*
Wendjebauendjedet 192, 193
Weret 233
Wife of Nakhtmin 99, *99*
Wilbour, Charles Edwin 61, 81, 83, 101, 105
Wilbour Plaque 60, 61, *61*
Wilkinson, John Gardner 21, 27, *28,* 34, 83, 121
Winlock, Herbert Eustis 32, 47, 132, 140, 150, 151, 153, 154, 155, 156–57, 158, 167, 173, 176, 177, 184
wood 28, 36, 42, 50, 51, 52, 53, 56, 65, 69, 82, 89, 90, 91, 96, 98, 102, 104, 110, 111, 115, 117, 119, 123, 126, 127, 131, 133, 139, 140, 141, 144, 145, 152, 153, 155, 158, 159, *161,* 163, *165,* 169, 170, *171,* 181, 184, 186, 199, 201, 202, 203, 204, 207, 212, 213, 217, 233, 236; acacia 203, 204; cedar 203, 204, 233; ebony 42, 110, 139, 140; gilded 43; sidder 203, 204; sycamore 48, 69; yew 123

X-group people 179–81

Yellow Jasper Face (Carnarvon Collection) 154, *154*
Young, Thomas 15, *15,* 16
'Young Memnon' statue *19*
Yuya 105, 114, 115, 117

Zagazig 129
Zawiyet el-Aryan 133, 201
Zenon Archive 144, 145, *145*
Zivie, Alain-Pierre 222–23
Zizinia, Count Stephan 40

255

Acknowledgments

A note on dates:

Establishing the precise date of a discovery has occasionally proved difficult: either no direct indication of it is given in the sources, or else more than one date is recorded. Readers should note that the date or date-range employed here is that which appears likely, rather than definitively correct.

This book owes much to the encouragement, practical assistance and musings of several friends and colleagues, in particular Morris Bierbrier, Manfred Bietak, Vivian Davies, Aidan Dodson, Carla Gallorini, John Harris, George Hart, Zahi Hawass, Peter Lacovara, Stephen Quirke, Jeffrey Spencer, Nigel Strudwick, John Taylor, Yumiko Ueno, Miroslav Verner, and Alain Zivie. Basic research on a number of topics was entrusted to Jackie Pegg. For her exceptionally hard work, I am indebted to Thames & Hudson editor Sarah Vernon-Hunt; picture-research was carried out by Elizabeth Mitchell. The index was compiled by Anna Bennett.

This book is for the members of The Amarna Royal Tombs Project, the Project's generous supporters and, above all, for my Egyptian friends, colleagues and co-workers.

Half-title: Bernardino Drovetti and his assistants (•p. 29)
Title-page: The tomb of Nefertari (•p. 121)
Contents pages: The Antechamber of the tomb of Tutankhamun (•p. 160)

Design concept by Ivan Dodd Designers

First published in hardcover in the United States of America in 2000 by Thames & Hudson Inc., 500 Fifth Avenue, New York, New York 10110

Library of Congress Catalog Card Number 99-69519
ISBN 0-500-05105-4

Printed and bound in Hong Kong by Toppan